Women
———

Filmmakers
———

in Mexico
———

Women Filmmakers in Mexico

The Country of Which We Dream

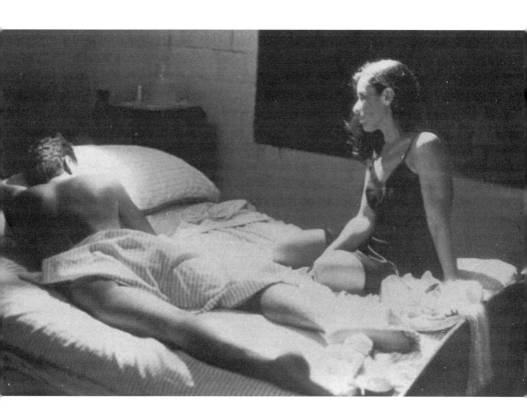

Elissa J. Rashkin

UNIVERSITY OF TEXAS PRESS, AUSTIN

Requests for permission to reproduce material from this work should be sent to
Permissions, University of Texas Press, P.O. Box 7819, Austin, TX 78713-7819.

♾ The paper used in this book meets the minimum requirements of ANSI/NISO
Z39.48-1992 (R1997) (Permanence of Paper).

LIBRARY OF CONGRESS CATALOGING-IN-PUBLICATION DATA

Rashkin, Elissa.

Women filmmakers in Mexico : the country of which we dream / Elissa J. Rashkin.

p.   cm.

Includes bibliographical references and index.

ISBN 0-292-77108-8 (alk. paper) — ISBN 0-292-77109-6 (pbk. : alk. paper)

1. Motion pictures—Mexico—History.   2. Women motion picture producers
and directors—Mexico.   I. Title.

PN1993.5.M4 R33   2001

791.43′082′0972—dc21   00-041772

To the women "without face or name" whose struggle for justice, democracy, and liberty is the light that illuminates these pages.

Contents

Acknowledgments

This book exists thanks to the encouragement of many individuals over many years, beginning with professors Ed Norris, Kate Miller, Allston James, Rosalind Petchesky, Louise Spence, Tonglin Lu, and Maria Duarte. Its first incarnation as a dissertation at the University of Iowa was partially funded by a Foreign Language and Area Studies Fellowship from the Center for International and Comparative Studies in 1994, and especially benefited from the guidance of Kathleen Newman and Charles A. Hale, as well as Rick Altman, Joy Hayes, and Corey Creekmur. A version of chapter seven appeared in *Spectator*'s "Street Smarts" issue, whose editor Karen Voss offered many helpful suggestions. Participants at the Cine-Lit III and Cine-Siglo conferences provided useful feedback on versions of chapter five and the conclusion.

In Mexico City, research was facilitated by Moisés Jiménez at IMCINE, Celia Barrientos, Salvador Plancarte and Antonia Rojas at the Filmoteca de la UNAM, Claudia Prado at the Centro de Capacitación Cinematográfica, and Leticia Medina at the Cineteca Nacional. In Mexico and the United States, Patricia de la Peña, Patricia Torres San Martín, Joanne Hershfield, Susan Dever, Alejandra Novoa at Telemanita, Karen Ranucci at the Latin American Video Archives, Nancy Deffebach, B. Ruby Rich, and Bob Dickson generously shared information and materials.

Others who provided invaluable support include: Stephanie Savage, Diana McKenzie, Heather von Rohr, Randy Russell, Anne Gill, Claire Fox, Sergio de la Mora, Joan Clinefelter, Jim Clinefelter, Ian Phillips, Peggy Zebroski, Pedro González, Mark Farrier, Jena Camp, the members of Chiapas Urgent Call, Juan Mendoza, the Islas Hernández family, Ian Rashkin, Laura Rashkin, Beverly Jarvis, Ed Jarvis, Alan Burns, Hattie Catania, Camille Carter, Peter Rashkin, and José Islas.

Women
——
Filmmakers
——
in Mexico
——

My intention and my defense for making films was to make "the other cinema." To make the other world. Women are half of humanity, but almost everything is explored and explained through men. Women explained through men. At that time I thought that the cinema that I made, and I still think today, that the cinema that I make is from the woman's point of view. Not that of the romantic and subjugated woman, but on the contrary, of woman as thinker.

Matilde Landeta[1]

Introduction

An "Other Cinema"

When veteran director Matilde Landeta explained her notion of a feminist *otro cine* or "other cinema" to interviewer Patricia Martínez de Velasco in 1988, only Landeta and a handful of other women in Mexico had directed feature films. Moreover, those women's work, although spanning the near-century of the cinema's existence, had been irregular, fragmentary, and often compromised by external obstacles; many early films had been lost due to critical and curatorial neglect, while later directors had seen their work shelved and forgotten. The status of women's filmmaking was aptly expressed in the title of Martínez de Velasco's 1991 book, *Directoras de cine: Proyección de un mundo obscuro,* as "a dark world."

In the late 1980s and the 1990s, however, this situation dramatically changed. Following two decades of sporadic short films, independent and institutional documentaries, and student efforts, women at last began to emerge as professional feature film directors. In 1988, two debut features, Busi Cortés's *El secreto de Romelia* and Marisa Sistach's *Los pasos de Ana,* marked the beginning of what would soon become the widely recognized phenomenon labeled *cine de mujer* or women's cinema.[2] These were followed by María Novaro's *Lola* and Dana Rotberg's *Intimidad* in 1989, a second feature from Cortés, *Serpientes y escaleras,* in 1991, and Guita Schyfter's *Novia que te vea* in

1992. Novaro's second feature, *Danzón*, went to Cannes in 1991, as did Rotberg's *Angel de fuego* in 1992. Marcela Fernández Violante, an active director since the 1960s, began production on *Golpe de suerte* in 1991, and even Matilde Landeta, by then in her late seventies, returned to directing that year with *Nocturno a Rosario*. Landeta's films from the 1940s were rediscovered, exhibited, and restored, as were those of Adela Sequeyro from the 1930s; festivals and special programs highlighted these discoveries, linking them to the work of the new generation of women filmmakers. For the first time, the possibility of an *otro cine* had become an historical reality.

The emergence of a "women's cinema" meant more than the addition of female names to the film credits of the era; in fact, it posed a formidable challenge to a long-standing cinematic tradition of female objectification, erasure, and displacement. For although the foregrounding of female *characters* had been a consistent distinguishing feature of the Mexican cinema (from *Santa,* one of the first Mexican sound films, in 1931, to *Enamorada* and *María Candelaria* in the Golden Age a few years later, to the action-heroine subgenre exemplified by the *Lola la trailera* series of the 1980s), the industry had always been better at what actress Diana Bracho has called "pimping" (an ironic reference to the abundance of prostitutes on the Mexican screen) than allowing women to tell their own stories (Bracho 413). Feminist theorist Teresa de Lauretis's well-known distinction between Woman as "the representation of an essence inherent in all women" (*Technologies of Gender* 9) and women as historical beings was amply supported by the Mexican cinema: its particular formulae, such as the veneration of the suffering mother and the vilification of the treacherous *mala mujer* (bad woman), functioned to displace women as historical subjects and replace them with symbolic figures whose repetitive trajectories were depicted as essential to the reproduction of the social order within the context of a clearly patriarchal nation-state.[3]

Given the history of women's erasure from the field of representation and their replacement by the iconic, passive image of Woman, the presence of women directors in the 1990s represented a qualitative breakthrough that went well beyond the question of quantitative equity. This breakthrough took place on many levels, both within and outside of the film texts themselves, for the work of these directors embodied what film scholar Patricia Torres San Martín has described as a "symbiosis" between filmic creation and social praxis ("La investigación sobre el cine de mujeres en México" 44). Several of the filmmakers considered themselves feminists, some came from the women's movement, and all dedicated themselves to telling women's stories and directly or indirectly to revising the image of women on the Mexican screen. Referring to these developments, Torres pointed to "a new female identity" in the cinema, an identity which had been forged by "sujetos activos que han partipado en la sociedad de una manera específica pese al dominio de ideologías y estructuras patriarcales" [active subjects who have participated in society in a specific manner in spite of the domination of patriarchal ideologies and structures] ("La investigación" 41–42).

As Torres's comment suggests, neither the origins nor the political implications of women's filmmaking were confined to the cinematic realm. Rather, they took place within and reflected the changing cultural geography of Mexico in the 1990s, a complex and highly ambivalent landscape marked by a number of important social, political, economic, and even psychological factors. These included a changing intellectual sector, characterized by the emergence of new media, new forms of participation, and new participants; a deep crisis in the unifying mythos of national identity, resulting in a proliferation of critical analysis and debate and the emergence of new social actors; a film industry also deeply in crisis and in need of rejuvenation; increased participation by women in formal education and professional employment, albeit in a social climate of complexity and contradiction; and finally, a presidential administration acutely sensitive to the ideological functions of culture and willing to lend its support to the production of film images in the interests of self-promotion and social control. While not entirely separate from one another or from the broad social and economic changes of the era—namely, the globalization and privatization of production and consumption, cultural and otherwise—it is worth examining each of these areas in detail in order to locate the significance of the *cine de mujer,* not simply as a subgenre of Mexican cinema but as an historical phenomenon.

The Shifting Intellectual Sector

The emergence of a body of films made by women and centered around gender issues and women's experiences reflected a long history of feminist struggle. Women filmmakers of the 1990s, whether or not they identified themselves or their work as feminist, were on the front lines of the battle for a form of representation which would take into account the point of view of women, not, as Landeta puts it, romanticized or submissive, but "woman as thinker" (Martínez de Velasco 64). In this sense, they reflected a convergence of two subtle but important long-term reconfigurations of the traditional intellectual sector in Mexico: the increased participation of women and the broad shift in that sector away from an exclusive emphasis on literate/print culture and toward an embrace of the audiovisual communications media of the era, changes that are themselves indicative of larger real and potential transformations in historically constituted fields of power and knowledge.

In *The Lettered City,* a provocative study of literate culture, urbanism, and state power in Latin America, Angel Rama shows how since the colonial era, state power has both depended on and produced groups of literate men *(letrados)* charged with managing the expanding bureaucracy of the colony (later the nation-state) and with creating ideological visions of its past, present, and future. In Mexico, asserts Rama, the basic arrangement by which a small group of urban elites imposed their ideal maps of nationhood onto an unruly and heterogeneous territory continued almost unabated from viceregal times on, with Independence and Revolution doing little more than shifting players (if that much) and vocabularies. Moreover, in spite of late-nineteenth-century economic modernization and corresponding professional specialization, culture in the limited sense of arts and letters continued to be inseparable from politics (Rama 86 – 87).

Written accounts of the Mexican Revolution speak to this phenomenon. In numerous novels and testimonies (notably Mariano Azuela's 1915 *Los de abajo,* from which much of Rama's argument is drawn), the actual fighting is characterized as emerging out of a massive, inchoate sense of rage and injustice on the part of Mexican *campesinos,* yet this almost primal force is shown to be quickly co-opted by the educated men who would renovate legal systems and write constitutions that paid homage to the desires of the populace while in fact reinstating their own class privileges. Being themselves emissaries from the lettered city, the narrators of these texts can do little but chronicle this co-optation with irony and bitterness.

The extent to which power has been linked to the written word in a largely illiterate context can scarcely be overstated. Rama writes that the "exclusive place of writing in Latin American societies made it so revered as to take on an aura of sacredness." Like the sacred in general, this place was somewhat distinct from the realm of everyday life: "Written documents seemed not to spring from social life but rather to be imposed upon it and to force it into a mold not at all made to measure" (30). While many Mexicans may therefore have a deep and well-founded cynicism toward the lettered city, they have rarely escaped its coercive authority. Rama concludes his book with an allusion to "two forms of power, that which rests on the sword, and the other, which flows from the pen" (125).

With the rise of broadcast media in the twentieth century, however, come important changes. In an essay titled "What's Left of the Intelligentsia?: The Uncertain Future of the Printed Word," Jean Franco notes:

> The new technologies of communication have created a class of tech-
> nocrats and new audiences for whom print culture has lost its luster and
> now competes with—and is often superseded by—visual and aural cul-
> ture. . . . Music and the television image, rather than the printed word,
> have become the privileged vehicles for the exploration of Latin Ameri-
> can identity and the nature of modernity. (17)

These shifts are not inevitable results of the technologies themselves but rather resonate with social and political developments both particular to Mexico and consistent with the evolution of capitalism worldwide. The need to incorporate more and more of the populace into the postrevolutionary national project implies the development of media which circumvent requirements of literacy and elite education, for instance, while at the same time the expansion of consumer culture requires the creation of consumers on a massive scale. But in any case, the growing importance of radio, television, film, the music industry, and hybrid print-visual media such as comics and *fotonovelas* has required adaptation on the part of the traditional intellectual sector, whose lettered city has in many ways been engulfed by a multinational, electronic megalopolis.

This phenomenon has been chronicled by Néstor García Canclini in his book *Culturas híbridas: Estrategias para entrar y salir de la modernidad,* in which he outlines the increasing links between traditional elite culture (formerly the province of state patronage) and private enterprise as well as the ways that traditional Latin American intellectuals have adapted to the mass media. Franco, in *La cultura moderna en América Latina,* similarly describes how writers of the 1960s were forced to confront a growing mass culture whose conservative generic forms—gothic romance, melodrama, detective story—replicated themselves as if impervious to modernist avant-garde challenges.[4] Many novels of that period took up mass culture as a theme, often by means of parody (*La cultura* 324). Moreover, writers like Octavio Paz, Jorge Luis Borges, Gabriel García Márquez, and Carlos Fuentes became media icons, their texts and ideas sold through the same marketing channels as the consumer products of industry. García Canclini recounts a meeting between Paz and Borges that could not be filmed because of the authors' obligations to rival television stations (García Canclini, *Culturas híbridas* 101); the humorous anecdote is emblematic of the configuration Franco sums up in her chapter title, "Narrador, autor, superestrella" (Franco, *La cultura* 311). At the same time, social and political concerns are taken up—if only, more often than not, to be contained and defused—in the texts of mass media, while individuals coming out of pop culture, such as rock stars, actors, and athletes, compete with more traditional figures as the icons and spokespersons of their epoch.

These developments, it should be emphasized, are politically ambiguous, although not neutral; while the mass media in Mexico overwhelmingly reinforce a conservative understanding of the status quo, the challenge to traditional elitism that they symbolize rather than embody may also provide space for the expression of oppositional values. As Franco suggests, that the increasing power of the corporate media in Latin America (and throughout the world) has displaced and engulfed the traditional intellectual sector is not a particularly progressive development ("What's Left" 20); moreover, hybrid formations that appear "postmodern" may simply be the lettered city's attempt to map itself onto yet another configuration of political and economic power. Yet if much of what constitutes contemporary culture can be seen as linked to the expansionist project of neoliberal capitalism, new kinds of intellectuals have emerged to respond to and challenge this monopolistic regime of power and knowledge. Such is the case within the field with which we are presently concerned, that is, the cinema.

Whereas the "classic" cinema in Mexico, as in Hollywood, was characterized by a star system which rendered off-screen production almost invisible, the director as auteur has since come to the fore. Since the 1960s, filmmakers have sought and won recognition not only as purveyors of entertainment but as artists, cultural workers, and thinkers. As we will see, the film industry remains split between a "cinema of quality" that retains much of the elitist aura of the traditional fine arts and a commercial cinema that manufactures generic products as if from an assembly line; yet many filmmakers elude both of these categories, participating instead in the cross-pollination and hybridization of cultural strains and the blurring of lines among elite, mass, and popular cultural domains that García Canclini described. These individuals are among the best positioned to fulfill the role of intellectual in a "postliterate" era, creating images and representations that reflect—and shape—the concerns, experiences, values, and beliefs of broad audiences.

Even as the intellectual sector has seen itself transformed by historical shifts in communication and economic structures—what Franco summarizes as "the growing privatization of culture" ("What's Left" 17)—resulting in increased interface with film, television, and other mass media, it has also been affected by the demands of disenfranchised sectors for greater participation in the life of the nation. Roderic Camp's 1985 study *Intellectuals and the State in Twentieth-Century Mexico* depicts an intellectual establishment based primarily on old-boy networks formed at exclusive educational institutions and names only one woman (Elena Poniatowska) among its list of recognized figures; yet an enormous increase in female participation in education has begun to change this scenario. While, for example, women made up 18.5 percent of students enrolled in higher education in 1969, they comprised 30 percent in 1980; in 1994, women made up 44.6 percent of the collegiate population, concentrated in health sciences, education, and humanities. Because overall numbers of students rose dramatically during those twenty-five years, the gains in women's education have been far greater than the percentages reflect.[5] These educated women have gone on to achieve visible (if not proportional) representation in the professions and among the intelligentsia.

If we take film studies as a case in point, we find that while only a handful of women studied film when the discipline emerged in the 1960s, their representation in the nation's film schools was equal to that of men by the late 1980s. This had important ramifications for their subsequent access to what in the case of film can be described as the means of production; for while the film industry's professional guilds have long resisted admitting women, the majority of women directors in the 1990s came from the universities rather than working their way through the ranks of the industry. Moreover, immersed in the university milieu, they not only learned the techniques of their trade but also were exposed to and often participated in the debates and struggles of their epoch, as a result becoming outspoken critical thinkers as well as skilled professionals.

Social and political activism per se has also brought women to the forefront of intellectual debate, as in the case of Rosario Ibarra de Piedra, the founder of an organization of parents of "disappeared" political victims who became an opposition congresswoman in the 1990s, or that of *Debate feminista* magazine founder Marta Lamas and others associated with feminist organizing and publishing. In fact, many contemporary filmmakers first approached film as a way to communicate feminist and progressive ideas to broad audiences. Their work is thus closely linked to the larger project of creating what Franco terms a "feminist public sphere" (*Plotting Women: Gender and Representation in Mexico* 184). Clearly, few if any of these women have achieved the cultural status and prestige of an Octavio Paz, José Vasconcelos, or Carlos Fuentes (to name three widely recognized figures cited by Camp), yet the transformation of the intellectual sector that they represent renders the comparison somewhat irrelevant. In fact, in a society characterized by overwhelming cynicism and distrust of the official establishment, it is those voices, both male and female, which seem to speak from outside the lettered city that have begun to gain substantial credibility and appeal. In any case, the partial democratization of the intellectual sphere as well as the increasing power and influence of the communications media are crucial factors in making film a terrain of intellectual activity in which women as well as men have become protagonists.

Mexicanidad in Crisis

The transformation of the traditional intellectual sector as the result of global pressures and local demands parallels another phenomenon which, although impossible to measure in quantitative terms, was perceptible on almost every level of cultural and social activity toward the end of the twentieth century: the breakdown of nationalist ideologies to a degree that put into question the existence of the nation itself as a meaningful entity. Charles Ramírez Berg analyzes this breakdown in detail in his 1992 book, *Cinema of Solitude: A Critical Study of Mexican Film, 1967–1983.* Although his study concludes before the period in question here, his observations regarding film as a scenario of collective identity formation help us to understand the conditions under which feminism and other oppositional (re)visions were able to flourish in the cinema.

For Ramírez Berg as for other observers, the ideology of Mexican cinema hinges on the concept of *mexicanidad,* or "Mexican-ness." This elusive notion, he asserts, "has been the key concept in Mexican intellectual, political, and artistic thought for most of this century" (*Cinema of Solitude* 2); it encompasses identity, culture, national sovereignty, and authenticity and is often set against a perceived encroachment by an alien (European or U.S.) value system and especially the embrace of such a system by a complicit intelligentsia. While *mexicanidad* is presumed to exist as a complex of recognizable traits, it is in fact always in process. Like all American nationalisms, *mexicanidad* originated as an anticolonial position, as both a line of defense and a process of collective self-discovery, over time growing in strength as what

Jesús Martín Barbero summarizes as "a popular revolution against creoles, private corporations, and foreign threats" ("Modernity, Nationalism, and Communication in Latin America" 136). Yet in the absence of true national unity—that is, in a large and populous country marked by ethnic, regional, and class divisions, among others—the discourse of *mexicanidad* seeks to homogenize and fix what in fact is heterogeneous and mobile. It creates strategic points of convergence that are then asserted as cultural essence, particularly within the seamless genealogies of *historia patria,* the master narrative par excellence. Like the cultural construct of the nation defined by Homi Bhabha as "a form of social and textual affiliation," *mexicanidad* in fact becomes a kind of metaphor for its own absence—the search itself, rather than an objective entity (Bhabha 140).

"The history of Mexican film," Ramírez Berg writes, "might be viewed as a quest for a filmmaking form, a cinematic aesthetic that would appropriately express the Mexican experience" (*Cinema of Solitude* 3). The Revolution of 1910–1920, roughly coinciding as it did with the development of narrative cinema, provided early filmmakers with subject matter that necessarily had the nation at its core. Carmen Toscano's 1950 compilation of footage shot by her father, the pioneering filmmaker and exhibitor Salvador Toscano, and by other documentarians of the period suggests the era's preoccupations: beginning with images of Porfirio Díaz's lavish celebration of the first century of Mexican independence, Toscano and his colleagues went on to chronicle the struggle against the Díaz regime and the subsequent years of conflict in which factions and regional armies battled for power in the country. Footage of such significant events as the Zapatista army entering Mexico City is breathtaking in its feeling of historical "authenticity"; such images would provide the material for spectacular re-creations in dramatic films of subsequent decades. Carmen Toscano's title for the edited compilation, *Memorias de un mexicano,* is oddly apt, for the cinema, in its lasting fusion of documentary realism and patriotic melodrama, posed individual history and memory as synonymous with that of that nation.

From the mid-1930s to the 1950s, known as the "classical" period or "Golden Age" of Mexican cinema, the Mexicanist aesthetic coalesced around particular genres (the family melodrama, the *ranchera* musical comedy, the urban *cabaretera* cycle, and so forth), landscapes (the maguey-dotted expanses captured by the lens of cinematographer Gabriel Figueroa), and thematic figures or stereotypes (strong, virile, macho men, juxtaposed with women as suffering mothers, virgins, and whores, whose value to the project of nation-building was almost always in direct proportion to the depth of their self-sacrifice). The product of the Golden Age was "an idealized, romanticized, and imaginary Mexico that illuminated the movie screens of Latin America" (*Cinema of Solitude* 15) but that could hardly be sustained given the contradictions inherent in the industry itself and the modernizing project to which it belonged. In fact, postrevolutionary novelists and essayists, writing for the lettered elite rather than the mass audience of the cinema, tended to view the national psyche as an edifice of denial constructed on the ruins of Revolutionary idealism, whose blustery nationalism and machismo was no more than a mask hiding failure and solitude.[6]

The late 1950s and the 1960s were years of turmoil in Mexico. The postwar economic policy of import substitution industrialization, whose statistical appearance of success led to its being labeled "the Mexican miracle," had not addressed the needs of the country's rural sector and in fact had brought about an increasingly uneven distribution of national income (Peter H. Smith 324–327). On the one hand, an expanding middle class found itself largely estranged from the populist mechanisms of the traditional corporatist state and began to demand greater freedom. At the same time, displaced *campesinos* filled the cities, and unemployed and unsatisfied workers increasingly took to the streets in protest. Financed by a debt that would soon lay bare its stranglehold over the economy, the "miracle" collapsed and with it the fiction of national cultural and political unity whose bankruptcy was definitively exposed on 2 October 1968 in the massacre of student protesters by the army at the Plaza de las Tres Culturas in the Tlatelolco neighborhood of Mexico City. The formation of an independent and radical film sector at this time, influenced by the theories and practices of New Latin American Cinema, was symptomatic of the need for alternative representations as well as alternative political formations. When events of the 1960s plunged the Mexican state into crisis, "national self-image" and its cinematic analog broke down, initiating what in subsequent decades would become a kind of return of the repressed: the appearance on the screen of the dark side of a nation (that is, a national construct, or in Benedict Anderson's famous phrase, "imagined community") founded on patriarchy and masculinist ideology.

As Ramírez Berg details, the archetypes and stereotypes of the Golden Age were grotesquely inverted in the films of the 1970s. Suffering mothers became vampires; swaggering machos were shown as impotent, alienated prisoners of their own defensive posturing; "fallen women" went from being *víctimas del pecado* to *víctimas del machismo* (victims of sin to victims of machismo), with insanity depicted as the inevitable outcome for women trying to balance the contradictions of patriarchy (*Cinema of Solitude* 77). In the cinema, as in life, the "taken-for-granted pillars of the old order, patriarchy and machismo, were rocked to their foundations" (4). During the 1970s and 1980s, the cinematic leitmotif that predominated, from the most commercial films to the most experimental, was radical alienation; if few filmmakers went so far as to imagine what a nonpatriarchal society might look like, all seemed to agree on the bankruptcy of past "solutions."

The decline of the old order, to be sure, did not automatically bring about progressive change. As economic crisis led to increasing civil unrest among many sectors of the population, part of the government's response in the 1970s was to bolster the by-then stagnant film industry. As Alberto Ruy Sánchez in *Mitología de un cine en crisis* and Jaime Tello in "Notas sobre la política del 'nuevo cine' mexicano" have convincingly argued, the supposed *apertura* (opening) of Luis Echeverría's government (1970–1976), which permitted the critical images discussed in *Cinema of Solitude,* served to co-opt dissent and fortify state control while creating an appearance of democracy. From a feminist standpoint, the results were certainly mixed; for example, relaxation of censorship codes during the 1970s meant that the national cinema became not only more "political" but also more blatantly sexist in its depiction of women as sexual objects. Nevertheless, the crisis in the dominant ideology ultimately provided an opening for what Martín Barbero has called the "formation of new subjects—ethnic, regional, religious, sexual, generational" manifesting "new forms of rebellion and resistance" ("Communication from Culture: The Crisis of the National and the Emergence of the Popular" 453). In this sense, the women filmmakers of the 1990s, confronted with the radical breakdown of old notions of *mexicanidad,* became part of a societywide movement toward the imagination of alternatives.

Mexican Cinema in the 1990s: Rising from the Ruins

The most obvious factor influencing the emergence of women as directors was the film industry itself, which at the end of the 1980s was clearly in disarray. In a scathing essay in which he referred to national cinema as a "dead corpse," *Dicine* editor Nelson Carro outlined the situation: even though the Mexican cinema had been proclaimed to be in crisis since at least the end of World War II, several factors made the 1980s especially difficult. The worldwide expansion of Hollywood cinema during the second half of the 1970s had put domestic film producers on the defensive in Mexico as around the world. Mexican films all but disappeared from South and Central American screens; meanwhile, the 1982 *peso* devaluation disproportionately affected film producers, whose costs often were accounted in dollars, and the emergence of home video (likewise foreign-dominated) reduced film attendance at theaters (Carro, "Cine mexicano de los ochenta: Ante el cadáver de un difunto" 2).

Although the number of films made suggested a healthy industry, Carro wrote, their quality left much to be desired; the bulk of films were either sex comedies or *aventuras norteñas,* action films often based on popular songs and aimed at audiences close to the northern border. The most successful films of the decade, *El mil usos* (1981) and La India María's *Ni de aquí, ni de allá* (1987), were distributed by Videocine, whose access to promotional resources was unmatched. And although directors such as Felipe Cazals and Arturo Ripstein continued to produce "quality" films at the margins of the industry, their output was negligible compared to that of the likes of formula directors Víctor "El Güero" Castro and Alfredo Crevenna (Carro, "Cine mexicano de los ochenta" 5).

In the pages of *Dicine,* the Colectivo Alejandro Galindo published "El cine mexicano y su crisis," a three-part critique of Mexican cinema that concluded with a set of recommendations more developed than but ultimately not all that different from the demands that film activists had made in the 1960s: infrastructure, promotion, and support for film production personnel as workers. Meanwhile, critics like Carro and Rafael Medina de la Serna bemoaned their fate as spectators, with Medina writing in 1988:

> Ir al cine en México es sin duda la actividad que menos satisfacciones produce a quienes la pratican y por ello cada vez menos personas se toman la molestia de praticarla. Pero si ir al cine en este país es tan poco gratificante, ser cinéfilo es poco menos que una perversión masoquista.
> [To go to the movies in Mexico is without a doubt the activity that produces the least satisfaction for those who practice it, and for that reason fewer people all the time are bothering to practice it. But if going to the movies in this country is ungratifying, to be a cinephile is little short of a masochistic perversion.] (6)

These texts reflect a number of biases, full discussion of which is beyond the scope of this chapter; apart from the obvious elitism, for example, Carro's dismissal of films with a northern focus ignores the concrete historical reasons that the cinema's attention shifted to the north and that stories of narcotraffic, migration, and border banditry have come to replace those set in the demi-monde of Mexico City or on bucolic haciendas. Moreover, these critics' negative prognoses often verge on becoming self-fulfilling prophecies. In contrast, director Busi Cortés has offered strong arguments against the critical establishment's habitual pessimism, accusing critics of assuming an "intellectual pose" that amounts to a double standard for Mexican films (Torralba in *El Sol de México*).

Nevertheless, it is true that during the 1980s, innovative, accomplished films like Paul Leduc's *Frida* (1984), Cazals's *Los motivos de Luz* (1985), and Ripstein's *El imperio de la fortuna* (1986), to name three of *Dicine*'s top ten of the decade, were the exception rather than the rule. Javier González Rubio's review of Cortés's *El secreto de Romelia* in *Dicine* indicates the general attitude toward national cinema at the end of the decade:

> Si tomamos en cuenta que en general los distintivos del cine mexicano son: a) guiones incongruentes, b) personajes inverosímiles y estereotipados al máximo, c) diálogos absurdos e increíbles, d) malas actuaciones y e) excusas de algunos directores de por qué la película no salió tan bien, entonces podemos considerar a *El secreto de Romelia* como una excelente película mexicana.
>
> [If we take into account that in general the characteristics of Mexican cinema are: a) incongruent scripts, b) unrealistic and supremely stereotyped characters, c) absurd and unbelievable dialogue, d) bad acting, and e) excuses from some directors for why the film came out so poorly, then we can consider *El secreto de Romelia* to be an excellent Mexican film.] (González Rubio 18)

The release of *El secreto de Romelia* in September 1989, under the auspices of four federal and two regional institutions, in some ways heralded a new era for the cinema. On the one hand, the Salinas administration had adopted a proactive policy toward filmmaking (and toward other media and cultural sectors) that contributed greatly to the "cinematic renaissance" of the *sexenio* (six-year presidential term). On the other hand, however, in keeping with the administration's shift toward neoliberalism, its policy was not so much outright sponsorship as brokering of partnerships between a range of private investors and governmental entities (Pérez Turrent, "Crises and Renovations" 112). While each of the films discussed in Chapters 3 through 7 received some funding from the federal government, none was entirely state-supported. The inter-institutional collaboration behind productions like *El secreto de Romelia* thus met the needs of the filmmakers (enabling newer directors with less institutional clout to find funding from a range of sources) and of the government, which sought to minimize its investment while enjoying the cultural cachet associated with a thriving national cinema.

Salinas's National Development Plan for the period 1989–1994 contained a number of provisions mandating support for the arts, which continued to bear the label "cultural patrimony" (Esteinou Madrid 16n). As in the previous decade, the administration of the government's relationship to cinema was in the hands of the Instituto Mexicano de Cinematografía (IMCINE), whose director under Salinas was Ignacio Durán. As David Maciel explains, Durán's appointment took place at a critical moment in which Salinas's party, the Partido Revolucionario Institucional (PRI), was struggling to maintain its credibility in the face of widespread accusations of fraud and corruption. Durán's mission was to streamline and decentralize the state cinema apparatus and, in keeping with Salinas's neoliberal ambitions, to encourage collaboration with the private sector and with foreign coproducers (Maciel 34).[7]

From its peak of state involvement during the Echeverría administration, the Mexican cinema, like other state enterprises, was increasingly privatized. As a result, foreign involvement increased, and so did the monopolistic practices by which film production was absorbed and reduced to a function of vertically and horizontally integrated media corporations. In 1990, for example, the state-owned theater chain COTSA was to be sold; symptomatic of the state of affairs were speculations that its new owner would be either a Japanese company or the powerful media conglomerate Televisa.[8]

However, the state continued to produce and distribute films, mainly through IMCINE and the Fondo de Fomento a la Calidad Cinematográfica (FFCC). During the Salinas *sexenio,* the state financed fifty-seven feature films and thirty-one shorts, a marked increase over the low of previous years yet still a small proportion of total national production ("El estado financió 57 filmes en 6 años" in *Esto*). What emerged as a result was a two-tiered system, dividing the "national" cinema into, on the one hand, a commercial industry infamous for its low-quality genre films characterized by sex and violence and, on the other, a state sector devoted to more "serious" subject matter but extremely limited in terms of distribution and exhibition. While state-sponsored films were more likely than commercial films to go to national and international festivals and to win prizes, most were unlikely to be seen by large numbers of Mexicans. If Alfonso Arau's 1991 *Como agua para chocolate* was a stunning exception, the commercial feature *Juana la cubana* (1994), starring Rosa Gloria Chagoyán and directed by Raúl Fernández Jr., was more representative of the rule: dismissed by critics, it nevertheless remained for weeks in

Mexico City theaters in the fall of 1994, during which time seven of the state's most promising new features premiered collectively during a single week, one per day at only one theater, in the annual program titled Hoy en el Cine Mexicano.

This situation was exacerbated by the general decline of moviegoing as a practice, the closure of hundreds of movie theaters, and the rise of home video. While it is perhaps too unexamined a reaction on the part of film scholars to see these developments as inherently negative, the results were concretely detrimental in the Mexican case, due mainly to the fact that the only producer able to respond effectively to the advent of the video age was Televisa, the broadcasting corporation formed in 1972 as a competitor of state-owned television and which quickly surpassed the latter in size and importance. The rise of video allowed the media giant to further consolidate its empire, cheaply producing films for video as well as movie-theater distribution and using its privileged access to television to promote its products, which in many cases were themselves little more than promotional vehicles for its musical and television stars.

During the 1980s, the government, apparently in an effort to avert film piracy, awarded a concession to Televisa to open video rental outlets which would contract with foreign and national producers to distribute their films. As Rodrigo Azuela reported in *El Universal* in October 1994, this caused many existing video rental outlets to close, creating a monopoly which resulted in a lack of choice for viewers as well as a potent threat to traditional exhibitors. In 1992, Televisa's Videovisión was operating 772 video stores throughout the country, renting and selling almost exclusively U.S.-made products (García Canclini, "¿Habrá cine latinoamericano en el año 2000?: La cultura visual en la época del postnacionalismo" 28). That same year, the state-run COTSA theater chain began a painful process of liquidation that left many union workers unemployed and many theaters sold and converted to other uses; of the 99 Mexico City theaters operated by COTSA in 1990 (more than a third of which had been dedicated to exhibiting Mexican films), 33 had been sold by July 1992, as had 164 more throughout the country.[9] By 1994, the theaters that remained operational, now in private hands, suffered from notorious mismanagement and neglect.

Of the exhibition spaces that remained, the majority were given over to Hollywood blockbusters or to pornography, with only a few devoting screen time to Mexican genre films, most often action-adventure or features starring popular musical artists. With the modification of the Ley de Cinematografía, the requirement that Mexican films be given 50 percent of screen time was abolished (although this had in effect already taken place with the liquidation of the COTSA theaters, the sole exhibition outlet for Mexican cinema in the 1980s). Thus, although the Cineteca Nacional and a few small *cine-clubes* continued to screen new and classic Mexican films, and although pirate copies of films such as Novaro's *Danzón* (1990), Jaime Humberto Hermosillo's *La tarea* (1991), and Jorge Fons's *Rojo amanecer* (1990) could sometimes be found alongside porno and martial arts videos in street vendors' stalls, "quality" films were almost completely absent from the big and small screens. The most frequent complaint made by Mexican filmmakers was that their films, once completed, never reached national audiences.

In short, the conditions under which Cortés, Novaro, Rotberg, and others entered film production were fraught with contradiction. Although it would be, in Meaghan Morris's sardonic phrase, "too paranoid for words" (Morris 38) to suggest a link between the apparently declining fortunes of the film medium and its rising accessibility to women (as Morris implies about the emergence of *l'écriture féminin* in Europe at a point when the status of the writer as intellectual was in decline), it is important to note that while women's involvement in film production quantitatively increased during the Salinas era, the increase took place overwhelmingly within the state sector and not the commercial film industry. While stars such as Chagoyán and Gloria Trevi undoubtedly enjoyed a certain level of influence over the films in which they appeared, the only woman to direct more than one commercial film (apart from the university-based Fernández Violante) was María Elena Velasco, a comic actress better known as La India María. Velasco's box-office record as a star gave her the power to produce and direct her own films, yet unlike the directors in this study, her clout derived from her acting success and not from her ambitions or abilities as a director per se. The majority of women filmmakers worked with state support, under the rubric of culture rather than commerce.

Given its confinement to a semi-marginal sector of film production, it is tempting to see the growth of women's involvement in filmmaking as a kind of tokenism not unlike that which was apparent in the electoral politics of the era, with the high visibility of a few masking the exclusion of many. Yet while this cynical analysis contains a great deal of truth, it also denies the real gains made by women during the past two decades, not only within the film industry but within society as a whole. In fact, somewhere between the idealistic view in which the high number of female directors represents progress and equality and the pessimistic view that sees their presence as window dressing covering an essentially unchanged situation lie the complex realities that women in contemporary Mexico face.

Representation of and by Women

While gender roles in Mexican society were never as static and one-dimensional as outside observers have often believed, by the late 1980s, they were perhaps more complex than ever. As traditional views of women's roles encountered modern, imported media images, and as uneven economic development meant that barefoot "India Marías" existed side by side with high-heeled businesswomen and bottle-blonde starlets (or at least their photographically reproduced images) on the streets of Latin America's gigantic metropoli, women's status became increasingly hard to define and evaluate.

Women now had greater access to education and professional employment than ever before, as the case of the cinema indicates; Martínez de Velasco writes, referring to the fact that the government-run Centro de Capacitación Cinematográfica (CCC) admitted more women than men in 1987:

[E]sto nos sugiere básicamente dos cosas: que hay un mayor número de mujeres interesadas en participar activamente en la realización cinematográfica y que, por otro lado, han desaparecido considerablemente los tabués que la consideraban con una capacidad menor a la del hombre.

[This suggests to us basically two things: that there is a greater number of women interested in participating actively in film directing, and that, on the other hand, the taboos that considered (women) to be less capable than men have considerably disappeared.] (99)

Yet if the number of women earning professional degrees has risen considerably in recent decades, so has the number of women whose way of life has been dramatically disrupted by national and global economic transformations. Most women who have entered the work force since the 1970s have not done so out of personal ambition but rather out of necessity; for example, with the increasing dependence of the Mexican economy on male migration to the United States, many women have been forced to sustain their families by entering the unstable informal sector or working in low-wage border industries. Thus the notion of women's increased economic mobility must be taken with caution, understanding that the increased privileges enjoyed by a few women are paralleled by a far more widespread social and economic instability whose effect on the majority of women has been ambivalent at best.

Beyond the question of economic opportunity, other issues that touch women's lives are equally fraught with ambivalence. As the cinema itself demonstrates through its relentless reproduction of stereotypes, dominant ideas about women's roles and in particular women's sexuality still are governed by patriarchal ideology; for even if the increased display of women's bodies and sexual behavior in the media is often interpreted as a challenge to conservative morality, the discursive framing of female sexuality negates any kind of protofeminist agency. To take just one example, Gloria Trevi, an outspoken advocate of single mothers, prostitutes, and independent women, was as well known in the early 1990s for her presidential ambitions as for her singing and her unusual "look" featuring wild hair and ripped stockings. Her refreshing candor earned Trevi the public admiration of Carlos Monsiváis and *fem* magazine; however, her calendars featuring nude photos were as much a part of her star apparatus as her records, and her politics, framed as an endearing eccentricity, were overshadowed in the fan press by commentary on her physical appearance. Another popular singer-actress, the Spaniard Marta Sánchez, was quoted often in the Mexican press complaining about being treated as a "sex symbol," yet her success was clearly dependent on this very treatment.

Among ordinary women as well as media superstars, sexuality has become, perhaps more than ever, a gray zone that is still dangerous despite its more liberal surface. Whereas young urban women learn via television, movies, and magazines that to be attractive is to be brazenly sexual, actual sexual activity is still condemned, in accordance with a double standard that winks at *mujeriegos* (promiscuous men) but has no equivalent term for women that is not synonymous with "whore." Although the November 1994 issue of *Nexos* featured an article in which middle-class women talked frankly about their sexual experiences, desires, and fantasies ("Tres mujeres conversan" 64–71), the juxtaposition of their discussion with male writers' reports on prostitution and pornography (which, among other things, pointed to a disproportionate number of young rural migrants working as prostitutes in urban areas, women whose voices were not included in the magazine's panorama of viewpoints) suggested that sexual freedom had more to do with class and gender than with any supposed progressiveness of the period.[10]

Furthermore, Mexican feminists have continued to struggle against the influence of the Vatican, particularly with respect to abortion; although hundreds of women die every year from illegal abortions, the practice has not been legalized, and few public figures have had the courage to advocate reform.[11] Traditional conservatism in this area is compounded by the increasing power of the right-wing Partido de Acción Nacional (PAN), which has manifested itself in reactionary legislation in many parts of the country, including curfews, laws criminalizing homosexuality, and even a ban on miniskirts for state employees in Guadalajara. Rape, domestic abuse, and sexual harassment also continue to be threats that many women face on a daily basis, threats that are sometimes intertwined with other forms of violence (such as the rape of indigenous women by military personnel in Chiapas as a technique of social control). Lack of health care and other basic services further curtails many women's freedom, especially in rural areas; and lesbians, in addition to whatever other circumstances they may endure, are almost totally marginalized.

Yet even given these deeply rooted social problems, the gains of the past thirty years should not be minimized; they are crucial to the kinds of representations that women have produced in the cinema. Before the advent of feminism, women's voices were seldom heard outside the boundaries of the domestic sphere, within whose walls as well such everyday oppressions as spousal abuse and rape, unwanted pregnancy, and the stifling of one's own desires and ambitions were also supposed to be accepted in silence. Poor women bore the crushing burdens of ethnic and economic inequality, while wealthier ones were constrained by models of femininity that required them to be passive objects of desire. As one of Poniatowska's informants in *Massacre in Mexico* put it, women's lives were lived "on the sly" (17), their self-knowledge and expression relegated to the discursive level of secrets and intimacy.

Such confinement, of course, was productive—in the Foucauldian sense of producing concrete effects rather than simply repressing other potential outcomes—as well as negative. In *Plotting Women,* Franco writes that "women have long recognized the imaginary nature of the master narrative. Without the power to change the story or to enter into dialogue, they have resorted to subterfuge, digression, disguise, or deathly interruption." Franco's book, the assumptions and methodology of which inform the present project, focuses on situations she describes as "pre-feminist insofar as feminism presupposes that women are already participants in the public sphere of debate" (xxiii). From the mystic nuns of the colonial era to twentieth-century writers and artists confronting dominant ideology in relative isolation, to poor and working-class women interviewed by academic researchers, she shows how women have waged "struggles for interpretive power" in arenas far more conducive to their silence. In her final chapter, she notes that with the emergence of feminism in the context of the social upheavals of the 1960s, women do begin to become participants in that public sphere—if not always on equal terms with men, at least in numbers sufficient to exceed and nullify the aberrant categorization historically imposed on women intellectuals.

The earliest women filmmakers, some of whose experiences I discuss in Chapter 1, improvised audacious strategies to fund and produce their work, strategies which succeeded in the short term but which ultimately sustained neither a single individual career nor a substantial female presence in the film industry. The filmmakers of the 1960s and 1970s, allied with feminism and/or with social movements connected to the university and to organized labor, took advantage of technologies that allowed for production outside the film industry and created film as part of a larger political project—leaving the film industry itself both male-dominated and patriarchal in its themes and modes of address (see Chapter 2). It is only during the late 1980s and the 1990s that feminism begins to make a limited but significant impact on feature film production and corollary institutions such as festivals, awards, and film criticism.

It is perhaps ironic that this change would occur during a period that already, with only a few years' hindsight, may be considered one of the most devastating in Mexico's modern history: the *sexenio* of Carlos Salinas de Gortari. As will become apparent in later chapters, the Salinas government occupies an ambivalent place in relation to the cinema in question. On the one hand, its policies undoubtedly encouraged and even enabled a surge in production, as I have noted. On the other, its perceived illegitimacy and its dismantling of protectionist economic structures in place since the Revolution (culminating in the signing of the North American Free Trade Agreement in 1993) fostered a culture of opposition, one component of which was feminism and in which, to greater or lesser degrees, the young directors of the period participated.

The Salinas Years: Culture of (Il)Legitimacy

Historically, twentieth-century Mexican presidents have been hand-picked by their outgoing predecessors (a ritual called the *dedazo*), ratified by the party, and voted into office with little meaningful opposition. But 1988, the year in which *Los pasos de Ana* and *El secreto de Romelia* were filmed, was different. The presidential election of that year was preceded by the strongest opposition movement the country had seen in decades, led by Cuauhtémoc Cárdenas, the former PRI governor of Michoacan and son of Mexico's most popular twentieth-century president, Lázaro Cárdenas (1934–1940). Unlike the trajectory in any previous election, Cuauhtémoc Cárdenas's dissident campaign picked up such steam that he came to be seen as a serious challenger to Salinas, the hand-picked PRI candidate. The election itself was hotly contested, and when the results were announced, many Mexicans believed that Salinas only won through blatant fraud. Although Salinas would soon recover and even achieve astounding popularity on the international political scene, the dubious origins of his presidential authority would not be forgotten in Mexico.

Just as the 1970s cultural policies of Luis Echeverría (discussed in Chapter 2) were an obvious attempt to regain the legitimacy among intellectuals and the middle class that the government had forfeited at Tlatelolco, so too did Salinas set out to affirm his own legitimacy and that of his program of neoliberal reform by means of a concerted appeal to and via the cultural sector. I have mentioned the Salinas government's overhaul of IMCINE and privatization of many of the state film organisms created under Echeverría; examples from other fields also could be cited, such as the prestigious *Mexico: Splendors of Thirty Centuries* exhibit at the Metropolitan Museum in New York in 1990 or the U.S.-Mexico Fund for Culture launched in September 1991 as a joint effort of Bancomer, the Rockefeller Foundation, and the Fondo Nacional para la Cultura y las Artes. Although his strategies were in some ways the opposite of those used in the 1970s, it seems clear that Salinas's effort to rejuvenate state-owned cultural institutions through partial or total privatization was rooted in a political motivation similar to that which had sparked Echeverría's interventionist policies. The external debt that had begun to spiral out of control during the Echeverría years remained a determinant factor in economic policy, preventing any real attention to cultural development as a sociopolitical strategy; yet the regime that took power in the 1980s was no less dependent than its predecessors on ideological apparatuses, namely the mass media, to legitimize its reformist policies.

As Philip Russell makes clear in *Mexico Under Salinas,* the key word of the era was "modernization." The vision offered by Salinas was that of Mexico leaving behind its turbulent past and emerging, modern, capitalist, and democratic, into the First World. This vision, which incorporated the PRONASOL and PROCAMPO social welfare programs as a way of appeasing the large contingent of Mexicans excluded from modernization and alienated by modernity, was aimed not only at the nation but also at foreign investors, whose capital would be the key to its success. For this reason, although privatization as a strategy may go against the notion of a centralized corporate state, the government had no choice but to invest in its cultural sector, for the image of Mexico in the world community had taken on a determining political importance.

Trivial as it may initially seem, the presence of Mexican films at international festivals served the interest of the state in an important way. Although superseded more and more by television and video, film is still a "modern" medium, and film festivals are symbolic "modern" events in which elite art culture openly encounters and celebrates commercial technology. Also, exotic images (namely so-called magical realism) offered help via a standardized medium to smooth over cultural differences, remaking underdevelopment as a salable commodity. Whereas Brazilian Cinema Novo director Glauber Rocha wrote his 1965 manifesto "An Esthetic of Hunger" denouncing a "formal exoticism that vulgarizes social problems" in order to appeal to the European consumer's "nostalgia for primitivism" (69), Alfonso Arau's comments to *La Opinion* in 1993 reflected the considerably more conciliatory vision of the 1990s: "El realismo mágico es una visión del mundo que no tiene ninguna otra cultura y que bien puede ser exportada por el cine mexicano hacia otros países" [Magic realism is a vision of the world that no other culture has and can readily be exported by Mexican cinema to other countries] (Rodríguez in *La Opinion*).

Mexico's film exports to the United States and Europe could enhance its First World image while simultaneously capitalizing on its "otherness" and denying its condition of dependence. Thus the fact that the Mexican government funded films which were rarely shown in Mexico was not as anomalous as it may seem, despite filmmakers' complaints; while the control of information, an obvious priority within the country, was served by the obstacles to distribution and by state-sanctioned media monopolies, the circulation of creative and diverse films outside national borders was equally useful to the neoliberal program.

The key component of the government struggle for image control was the notion of democracy. Whereas in earlier eras the PRI had presided without serious opposition over a kind of populist dictatorship, the emergence of opposition parties and the general rise of dissent dating back to the crisis of 1968 pressured the government to commit itself, at least superficially, to a policy of pluralism and inclusion. Simultaneously, the Mexican government's desire for free trade and foreign investment made it the prisoner of the U.S.-defined "New World Order" in which economic concessions were tied to compliance with U.S. standards of human rights, defined almost entirely in terms of multiparty elections. (The human rights standards defined by organizations like Amnesty International that focus on issues such as torture, prison conditions, and censorship have been routinely ignored.) In 1988, the elections that brought Salinas to power were widely denounced as fraudulent, with many voters believing that only a convenient computer failure at the Federal Electoral Institute kept Cárdenas from claiming victory. Yet Salinas's forceful response, continually attacking Cárdenas as a radical troublemaker whose goal was to destabilize the country, succeeded in defusing the crisis at least temporarily.

While the strength of both Cárdenas's center-left Partido de la Revolución Democrática (PRD) and the right-wing PAN could be seen as evidence of popular dissatisfaction with the PRI regime, the ruling party wisely utilized this growing opposition as proof of its own tolerance and co-opted dissent wherever possible while still maintaining a firm hold on power. Although such strategies were transparent to Mexican observers, they seemed to accomplish their purpose of satisfying foreign critics, who in 1994 made the national elections into a litmus test of Mexico's readiness for NAFTA and entrance into the First World community. Yet the persistence of opposition voices, culminating in the 1 January 1994 uprising in Chiapas, consistently undermined the *salinista* vision. Because Mexico had not, in fact, resolved its most pressing internal problems, the construction of "democracy," represented paradoxically as the systemic containment of dissent, was the ruling party's continuing ideological project.

Among the demands that appeared to have influenced government strategies were those made by women, as members of feminist and popular social movements, for greater political involvement, access to resources, and control over their own lives. By the time of the 1994 elections, it was a well-publicized fact that more than half of the eligible voters were women. The campaigns of all three major presidential candidates addressed women to some degree, with the PRI's main campaign slogan being "bienestar para su familia" (well-being for your family). Moreover, women ran as presidential candidates for the Partido Popular Socialista and the Partido del Trabajo, and for senate and deputy seats in many regions of the country.

Yet this emphasis on women's participation would appear to have been largely cosmetic; not only was female illiteracy among the electorate a problem noted by foreign and national election observers, but women's political participation also remained minimal. From 1991 to 1994, for example, only 3 percent of senators and 8 percent of congressional deputies were women (Esperanza Tuñón 52); following the 1994 election, Mexico City assembly-woman Amalia García reported on the television program "60 Minutos" that out of the congressional deputies representing the three major parties, only 12 percent from the PRD, 7 percent from the PAN, and 5 percent from the PRI were women. Moreover, few of the issues usually considered to be of special concern to women, such as abortion, rape, and domestic violence, were addressed in the 1994 campaigns, even by prominent female candidates (as Elvira Hernández Carballido complained in the feminist magazine *fem*).[12]

In this context, the sudden visibility of women filmmakers camouflaged women's persistent exclusion from the political life of the nation as a whole. Was the new Mexican cinema, as its critics suggested, out of touch with national reality? In fact, many films of the period demonstrated a cosmopolitan outlook that had few parallels in other arenas of discourse. From Jaime Humberto Hermosillo's quirky, comic meditations on sexual intimacy in *La tarea* and other films to the post-1960s angst of Gabriel Retes's *El bulto* (1991) and Juan Carlos de Llaca's *En el aire* (1993), and from the new age mysticism of Nicolás Echeverría's *Cabeza de Vaca* (1990) to Guillermo del Toro's vampire fantasy *Cronos* (1993), the content of many critically acclaimed films of the 1990s seemed to move away from the quest for *mexicanidad,* replacing cultural specificity with a certain generational universality. Yet cinema's continued direct and indirect dependence on the state was sharply revealed at the end of 1994, when the collapse of the *peso* brought the film "renaissance" to a grinding halt and, in doing so, exposed the actual fragility of the situation.

The virtual cessation of state-supported film production in 1995 laid bare what should have been clear all along: that the "new Mexican cinema," with its cadre of women directors at the forefront, was intimately linked to and dependent on the neoliberal economic project instigated by the government of Miguel de la Madrid (1980–1988) and accelerated under that of Salinas. Although Salinas's support for the film sector was not the only factor enabling women's emergence as directors, the end of his *sexenio* and the economic crisis that followed effectively put an end to this optimistic period, plunging the cinema—along with the rest of the country—into a state of uncertainty that at the time of writing shows no signs of coming to an end.

In *Bienvenido/Welcome* (1994), veteran actor/director Gabriel Retes parodies the situation facing filmmakers in the 1990s. His movie depicts a group of Mexican filmmakers working on an independent feature about AIDS—made entirely in English for the export market. With its nonexistent budget and relentless bad luck, however, the film-within-the-film is hardly competitive, its good intentions derailed by its quixotic post-NAFTA ambitions. While the new Mexican cinema—much like the new Mexican democracy—undeniably introduced themes and topics formerly excluded from the national screen, it was a long way from being what commentators such as García Canclini called for: a cultural catalyst capable of meeting the challenge of economic and cultural transnationalization ("¿Habrá cine latinoamericano?" 28).

Toward an Otro Cine/Otro Mundo

In his 1993 essay "¿Habrá cine latinoamericano?"[13] García Canclini pointed out that if national identity had always been a construct, its foundation in material reality had become much more precarious in the 1990s,

> un tiempo de globalización e interculturalidad, de coproduciones multinacionales y Cadenas de las Américas, de acuerdos de libre comercio e integraciones regionales, donde los mensajes, los artistas y los capitales atraviesan constantemente las fronteras.
>
> [a time of globalization and interculturalism, of multinational coproductions and Cadenas de las Américas (a satellite television network), of free trade agreements and regional integrations, where messages, artists, and capital constantly cross borders.] (28)

For women, who had long been marginalized from constructs of national identity and the institutions in which they were concretized, these developments may have been even more ambivalent, bringing new dilemmas but also hopeful apertures. As I have sought to indicate in these introductory pages, the present text is not intended as a celebration of national or women's cinema; rather, it seeks to address the contributions that women have made through the cinema to projects and processes of cultural reconversion and democratization in a complex historical moment.

Such contributions, I will argue, have been made from an explicitly gendered perspective; however, rather than try to isolate the nebulous and endlessly debatable traces of women's "difference," I have followed de Lauretis's suggestion to feminist theorists that "the emphasis must be shifted . . . toward the wider public sphere of cinema as a social technology: we must develop our understanding of cinema's implication in other modes of cultural representation and its possibilities of both production and counterproduction of social vision" (*Technologies of Gender* 134). What I hope to demonstrate are the ways in which women filmmakers have attempted to "construct other objects and subjects of vision, and to formulate the conditions of representability of another social subject" (135).

It should be noted that the films analyzed in this book are only a few of the films made by women during the late 1980s and the 1990s. In order to encompass multiple areas of investigation, such as production history, content, and reception, as comprehensively as possible, I have limited my analyses to a small number of feature films which received relatively wide attention due to their presence in competitions and festivals, in most cases generating broad coverage in both the mainstream and the specialized press. The choice to focus exclusively on narrative feature films meant that many relevant and interesting texts, such as the experimental video work of Ximena Cuevas and the documentary production of Maricarmen de Lara, Gloria Ribé, and Alejandra Islas, among others, had to be excluded. Yet I believe that the examples chosen not only show the range of women's production (across genres, formal approaches, and points of view) but also successfully address the issue of gendered national and/or "postnational" identity. As Franco might argue, they represent "diverse configurations of the struggle for interpretive power" in contemporary Mexico—a nation wrestling with the contradictions of a postnational or transnational age (*Plotting Women* xii). Their films illuminate forgotten or obscure aspects of Mexican history, analyze the crises of their times with humor and insight, and begin to postulate and explore new and liberating identities—even as they confront the limits and contradictions of their particular mode of production.

At a time when the culture industry was rapidly expanding and the images and sounds of film and television began to surpass the printed word in impact and influence, the work of these filmmakers raised serious and provocative questions about gender, commercial and popular culture, collective identity, and particularly the role of the woman artist in a time of globalization and national transformation. By transforming the central myths and narratives of national cinema, they attacked the patriarchal and exclusionary ideologies which that cinema once upheld. Their visible interventions in public discourse began to provide Mexico with a critical vision of its present and with what García Canclini described as necessary for its future: "una iconología electrónica que corresponda a la redefinición actual de la identidad" [an electronic iconology that would correspond to the current redefinition of identity] ("¿Habrá cine latinoamericano?" 33). The films they produced were not answers or manifestos but perhaps guideposts, pointing audiences toward what Matilde Landeta called not only an "other cinema," but an "other world."

PART ONE | Histories

How did they succeed in introducing their contraband through such jealously guarded borders? But above all, what was it that impelled them so irresistibly to risk being smugglers? Because what is certain is that the majority of women are quite tranquil in their houses and in their limits without organizing gangs to mock the law. They accept the law, observe it, respect it. They consider it adequate.

Rosario Castellanos[1]

CHAPTER 1

Trespassers

Women Directors before 1960

In spite of a sustained surge of interest during the past twenty years, the presence of women in the Mexican cinema before the 1960s is a phenomenon still somewhat shrouded in mystery. Thanks to the work of numerous film scholars, we now have a litany of names: Mimi Derba, Adriana and Dolores Ehlers, Candida Beltrán, La Duquesa Olga, Alice Rahon, Adela Sequeyro, and finally, Matilde Landeta, who unlike her predecessors reemerges to become the mentor and *grande dame* of an entirely new generation of women directors. But in spite of the growing body of research, these names remain little more than ephemeral sparks in an otherwise unrelenting darkness. For these filmmakers' work, like so much of early Mexican cinema, is mostly lost; the silent period in particular scarcely exists outside of memory and extratextual documentation, excavation of which has only just begun.

Moreover, what we know of these women's lives does not help us to formulate a unitary notion of "women's cinema." Their works are separated in time and disparate in content and approach. Unlike the feminist collectives and student "generations" who would follow, they seem to have worked in isolation from other women, although they often participated in the vanguard political and/or artistic movements of their times. Existing testimony indicates that their desires to make films were overwhelmingly personal struggles, not intentional feminist acts. And even though they nearly always worked within supportive artistic communities, their cinematic efforts were rarely sustained. Candida Beltrán, for instance, made only one film, *El secreto de la abuela* (1928), based on her own experiences as an orphan and advocating responsible paternity; the Chilean-born Eva Limiñana, also known as La Duquesa Olga, collaborated on many films with her husband José Bohr but retired from cinema after a film she codirected, *Mi lupe y mi caballo* (1942), was suspended in mid-production for lack of resources, then completed but shelved. French expatriate Alice Rahon's experimental film *The Magician* (c.1947), made in collaboration with her husband Edward FitzGerald, a set designer for Buñuel, was similarly derailed by funding problems and never exhibited.[2]

Given this lack of continuity, it would be far too simplistic to group disparate films together by virtue of the directors' sex and proclaim them "women's cinema." Yet simply to append them to the larger chronology of Mexican film history would be to ignore the very real battles women fought to be able to make films within a male-dominated industry as well as the markedly idiosyncratic sensibilities that surviving film texts reveal, sensibilities quite distinct from the prevailing cinematic models of their respective eras. Their struggles and innovations paved the way for the entrance of women into Mexican cinema many years later—although the relation should not be seen as a teleological progression. My intention in this chapter is not to create a false lineage or to pay homage to the achievements of a few exceptional women. Rather, understanding the ways in which filmmaking has been conditioned by social, national, and industrial formations and the ways in which these have been affected by changing constructs of gender in different eras will help put into clearer historical perspective the gains, losses, struggles, and achievements of the 1990s.

To this end, I have taken as a point of departure the question posed by Rosario Castellanos in "Sobre cultura femenina," her master's thesis in philosophy written at the National Autonomous University of Mexico (UNAM) in 1950: Given the overwhelming odds against them, how and why did women choose to trespass on the domain of male-dominated culture and to become producers themselves of women-centered cultural "contraband"? Although Castellanos did not specifically address the role of women in her country's then-flourishing industrial cinema, her thesis and subsequent writing posed a formidable challenge to dominant views regarding women's creative agency. For example, in his influential essay collection *The Labyrinth of Solitude,* also published in 1950, Octavio Paz characterized women's role in culture as essentially passive; descendants of La Malinche, whose participation as the translator and mistress of the conquistador Hernán Cortés was instrumental in effecting and consolidating Spanish rule in Mesoamerica, Mexican women were transmitters of values in which they themselves did not necessarily believe (Paz 35). Their role in perpetuating constructs of national identity was crucial, yet they themselves were excluded from that identity. Although for Paz this exclusion had its origins in the Conquest, he implicitly attributed it as well to the female condition or "taint" that "resides in her sex" (85).

Castellanos, in what would prove to be a prescient counterpoint to Paz's stifling analysis, agreed that women were for the most part complicit in maintaining a patriarchal regime. What bothered her, however, was that if the law of women's exclusion was total, how was it that some women eluded its mechanisms of control? That is, if culture was "una especie de enfermedad que, como la hemofilia, las mujeres no padecen pero transmiten" [a type of illness that, like hemophilia, women do not suffer from, but transmit] ("Sobre cultura femenina" 19), how had women like Sappho, Virginia Woolf, and Gabriela Mistral engaged in literary or cultural activity at all? How and, most importantly, *why* had they dared to become *contrabandistas,* trespassers in a realm defined and governed by men?

While Castellanos focused on literary production, the same question can be put to the cinema. To date, much writing about women in Mexican film has dwelt on their systematic exclusion; feminist scholars have pointed out that through a Manichean system in which women have been represented only as whores or as mothers, the complex experiences of Mexican women have been reduced to iconic, impossible models of Womanhood that uphold national and patriarchal ideologies at the expense of female agency and autonomy. The small number of women filmmakers—Marcela Fernández Violante, writing in 1987, could name only nine in sixty years, although subsequent research has recovered several more—is deplored and the recent augmentation of this figure seen as welcome and overdue. But the implications of their infiltration, their smuggling and border crossing, have yet to be explored in detail. While we are surely no longer satisfied with the biological determinist hypothesis Castellanos offered in "Sobre cultura femenina" (which she herself would revise substantially in her later work), an investigation of the circumstances surrounding their often short-lived and conflict-ridden careers can help us to address her provocative question and thus to begin to develop an historical understanding of the sources of and the limitations on women's creative agency in Mexican cinema.

In the pages that follow, I briefly examine three cases of film production by women during the first half of the century: the Ehlers sisters in the 1910s and 1920s, Adela Sequeyro in the 1930s, and Matilde Landeta in the late 1940s. Differing from one another in important ways, these cases are especially instructive because of the unique configurations each inhabited with respect to the film industry and to the ideology of the nation-state. While the films of Dolores and Adriana Ehlers are lost to us, their multifaceted careers and especially their relationship to the government of Venustiano Carranza provide a fascinating example of the possibilities and the constraints that existed in cinema's entrepreneurial period. In the films of Adela "Perlita" Sequeyro, on the other hand, the nation-state is a structuring absence; her films instead reflect a fascination with the European cinema and with modes of storytelling reminiscent of the silent screen, infused with an explicitly feminine sensibility. Finally, Matilde Landeta's work is directly and centrally about the construct of national identity and about women's contradictory place—or at least, the place of certain exceptional women—within that construct.

The very specificity and singularity of these cases, as opposed to an ideal or archetypal notion of women's cinema, is what makes them useful for the present study; for it is not their particular textual strategies or modes of production but rather their constant engagement with constructs of gender, nation, and identity that would be inherited by the women filmmakers of the 1990s. Despite their differences, each of these filmmakers can be seen as a trespasser in a labyrinth not of her own making, battling the unique professional solitude faced by women whose insistence on creative expression flies in the face of entire systems of gender and power, systems which seek to exclude women from the public sphere and count on their passivity and complicity.

The Ehlers Sisters: Entrepreneurship and State Patronage

The cinema in Mexico was born at the turn of the century during the period of dictatorship and development known as the Porfiriato: a symbol of modernity and progress, much like the railroads that had begun to connect disparate regions into an almost cohesive nation-state. More uniquely, the medium grew to maturity during the Revolution of 1910–1920, whose events it would document and whose epic themes it would obsessively revisit up to the present day. As in the rest of the world, filmmaking at its inception was an essentially artisanal enterprise; as John King points out, Pathé did not build studios in Mexico as it did elsewhere, leaving the field open for Mexicans whose passions and/or entrepreneurial impulses were roused by the magical-seeming French technology (King, *Magical Reels* 15).

Among those who answered the call was Salvador Toscano, whose footage of the Revolution would be compiled in 1950 into a full-length documentary, *Memorias de un mexicano,* by his daughter, Carmen Toscano. In the early 1900s, Toscano's movie house, featuring Lumière equipment and films, and Enrique Rosas's Pathé-equipped salon competed for audiences in Mexico City; both men also made films, which they exhibited alongside the European imports (Mora, *Mexican Cinema* 7–8). In the wake of their success, many other small-scale film producers emerged; among them were the sisters Adriana and Dolores Ehlers, who not only were among the first women filmmakers in Mexico but also were key in implementing the system of state patronage of cinema that is still in place today.

Historical data on the Ehlers sisters is scant, although Patricia Martínez's research on Dolores in the mid-1980s, included in *Directoras de cine,* adds a more detailed perspective to the account given by Gabriel Ramírez in his 1989 *Crónica del cine mudo mexicano.* Ramírez based his account on several revealing newspaper articles, the same sources subsequently utilized by Patricia Torres in her 1995 conference paper "Las primeras realizadoras en México" and in other articles. Martínez's account is more anecdotal, due to the fact that she had access to Dolores Ehlers's memoirs, which, at the time of writing, remain unpublished. A brief unsigned article published in *Cuadernos de la Cineteca Nacional,* attributed by Torres to Eugenia Meyer, includes the Ehlerses' filmography. The following section is based on these accounts.

As related by these historians, the very biographies of the Ehlers sisters exceed the boundaries of conventional representations of women's roles in the Revolution, for far from being women in service to men in service to a cause, they appear to have participated in political activity on their own account. As Martínez explains, they grew up in Veracruz in the house of their widowed mother and a godmother that before the fall of Porfirio Díaz was the site of clandestine meetings aimed at freeing political prisoners. Along with politics, Adriana and Dolores appear to have been introduced early on to the cinema and screened movies in their home for neighborhood children. Both sisters worked outside the home to aid their mother; Adriana got a job in a photo studio, where she began to learn what would become her lifelong trade. Later, the sisters opened a studio in their home.

As enterprising young photographers, the sisters attended an official ceremony in 1915 at which they photographed Venustiano Carranza. Ramírez speculates about this encounter:

> En un ámbito esencialmente masculino, tuvo que causar una enorme impresión la audacia de esas jóvenes lidiando con sus incómodas vestimentas y su insistencia en plantar esos pesados cajones ante el presidente para fotografiarlo.
>
> [In an essentially masculine context, the audacity of those young women battling with their uncomfortable outfits and their insistence in planting those heavy boxes in front of the president to photograph him must have made an enormous impression.] (110)

Whatever the public's reaction to the Ehlerses' "trespassing" might have been, Carranza was apparently impressed and awarded them a grant to study in the United States. In Boston, Washington D.C., and New York, the sisters studied photography and cinematography. During World War I, they worked for the U.S. government filming subjects related to soldiers' health. The fluidity of the boundaries between production and exhibition, between film itself as a product and the technology required to profit from it, and the openness of the field as a nascent industry all apparently worked in their favor; not only could they cross borders of gender and geography that would be much more rigid only a few years later, but they also could successfully combine their technical training with business acumen and political connections. In 1919, they returned to Mexico as the exclusive representatives of the Nicholas Power Company, a projector manufacturer, and were entrusted with government money for purchase of equipment for Mexican film labs. Shortly thereafter, Adriana was named head of the federal Film Censorship Department and Dolores head of the Film Department, major positions in what was to become the labyrinthine bureaucracy of the government film sector.

The Ehlerses' tenure coincided with the heyday of the U.S. film industry's "greaser" films, whose racist content had been given political overtones during the Revolution in accordance with U.S. foreign policy and with an ongoing debate regarding the wisdom or folly of U.S. intervention in Mexico (Orellana 4–6). As Carranza's centralized government coalesced out of the decade's fragmentation and chaos, it determined to improve Mexico's cinematic image at home and abroad. In July 1919, Adriana Ehlers announced the production of a series of films that would show the "best and most interesting" aspects of the country, in contrast to the work of producers who, in her view, had more often elected to show the most extreme examples of poverty and misery (Ramírez 111). The web of governmental regulation and censorship grew; exhibitors were now required to pay fees and solicit official approval of material shown, while producers had to obtain authorization before filming in the capital. The brunt of reaction fell on the Ehlerses, who were accused of exercising arbitrary judgment and of lacking artistic training and sensitivity (111).

Besides working with the Carranza regime as bureaucrats, the Ehlerses were part of the group which founded the first film industry union, the Unión de Empleados Confederados del Cinematógrafo, affiliated with the Confederación Revolucionaria Obrera Mexicana (CROM); they also produced films for the union. Although the extent of their involvement with the union remains to be investigated, the affiliation of cinema workers with CROM has important implications not only for our understanding of the Ehlers sisters but also for the development of the film industry as a whole. As urban historian Diane E. Davis relates, the Carranza years were difficult and crucial ones for the Mexican labor movement. Workers in Mexico City had originally organized under the umbrella of the Casa del Obrero Mundial, which became increasingly divided between a conservative-moderate sector, generally corresponding to the artisanal or white-collar occupations, and a more radical wing generally associated with industrial workers. Whereas the latter group tended to focus on workplace issues, favor radical tactics such as strikes, and be internationalist and often Communist in ideology, the former was strongly connected to Mexico City, organized around urban services such as transport and housing, sided with Carranza against Zapata and Villa, and was disposed to negotiation and compromise. As these divisions widened, the Casa split into two new organizations: the moderate wing became the CROM in 1918 and, due to its collaboration with the government, quickly rose to power. In 1921, the leftist wing founded the Confederación General de Trabajadores (CGT), an openly Communist organization that, unlike the CROM, suffered severe repression throughout the period (Davis 45–59).

The film industry's affiliation with the CROM is hardly surprising, for the industry of the 1910s shared many of the characteristics that Davis describes as common among CROM-affiliated professions. As the industry was still largely artisanal and entrepreneurial, filmmakers such as the Ehlerses were independent businesspeople for whom proletariat struggles were remote. Socially and economically they were mainly members of the urban petit-bourgeoisie with little relation to or sympathy for the *campesino* movements in the countryside, which (in contrast) many radical urban workers supported. Finally, their ability and willingness to work with the government propelled them into positions of power within the federal bureaucracy such that they played a small yet significant role in determining the direction of the postrevolutionary nation, through media regulation, censorship, and production of propaganda. The strong relationship between the government and the industry, particularly its unions, which would later come to be seen as obstacles to rather than promoters of creativity and innovation in the cinema, almost certainly has its roots in this period.

The Ehlerses were key figures in the foundation of the modern state-cinema edifice. But with the consolidation of government control (however incomplete it probably was in practice) over the cinema, the tradition began by which the offices overseeing film production, distribution, and exhibition, like all governmental bodies, were linked to the administration of a particular president. Although full-blown *presidencialismo* had not yet developed in the still-fragile postrevolutionary environment, a political conflict between the Ehlerses and Alvaro Obregón (rooted in their friendship with an Obregón rival) cost them their jobs when the latter took power in 1920. Undaunted, they opened their own lab with their mother as partner, founded a production company, Revistas Ehlers, which produced and sold newsreel footage between 1922 and 1929, and established a shop that repaired and sold projectors which went on to last fifty years.

The nature of the Ehlerses' film output can be ascertained from their titles: films such as *La industria del petróleo, Las aguas potables de la ciudad de México,* and *Real España vs. Real Madrid* were clearly films made under contract rather than products of personal inspiration. Having lost Carranza's financial backing upon his death, they almost went bankrupt but were able to recuperate their losses by contracting with the Modelo brewery to film a major soccer match at which, according to Dolores, their presence on the field attracted more attention than the game itself (Martínez de Velasco 37). Although Dolores eventually quit working due to illness, Adriana stayed involved in film until her death in 1972.

To what extent did being women affect the Ehlerses' careers? One can really only speculate, for apart from anecdotes such as that about the soccer game culled by Martínez from Dolores's unpublished memoirs, gender is not a theme overtly addressed in existing documentation of their lives. Growing up in a female-headed household, within which they were given economic responsibility and exposure to political activism at an early age, may well have fostered the independent spirit that enabled them to study and work abroad, run businesses, and move about in tense wartime situations and in high political circles. The history of their family's opposition to the Díaz regime, coupled with the fact that their biggest opportunity had been given to them by Carranza, helps account for their concern for the nation and its image in national and foreign cinema. But nothing in their biographies fully explains the anomaly of their acceptance and even prominence in a field that would soon be all but closed to women.

In January 1920, a government official interviewed in the newspaper *El Universal* inadvertently revealed the kind of biases the Ehlers sisters must have routinely encountered. Defending a censorship body called the Consejo de Censura, the official, Aguirre Berlanga, pointed out that

> no está integrado por señoritas, sino por respetables caballeros de ilustración bastante para que puedan juzgar en materia artística y moral. Uno de ellos es ingeniero de bien probada cultura; otro profesor de larga experiencia; el tercero es persona respetable. Todos tienen más de treinta años y son padres de familia.
>
> [it is not made up of señoritas, but rather of respectable gentlemen enlightened enough to be able to pass judgment on artistic and moral matters. One of them is an engineer of proven culture; another a professor of considerable experience; the third is a respectable person. All of them are over thirty years old and are heads of families.] (quoted in Ramírez 112)

The fact that none of the committee members apparently had links to the cinema did not matter: what counted for this official was their respectability, their class status, and above all, their gender. Yet it is difficult to understand why a government unwilling to trust "señoritas" with making judgments about film content would have placed the departments of film and of censorship in female hands—and why an employee of one of those departments was seemingly unaware of or unwilling to mention this fact.

Aguirre Berlanga was not the last to overlook the Ehlerses' contribution. On the basis of published testimony, it appears that they were not even known until recently; for instance, neither Marcela Fernández Violante, in her 1987 essay "Las directoras de la industria cinematográfica nacional," nor Landeta, in a 1980 interview in which she cited as predecessors Alice Guy, Germaine Dulac, Dorothy Arzner, and Ida Lupino, appeared to have been aware of their existence.[3] As Torres comments, "Un caso por demás lamentable sería el de éstas hermanas, perdidas en la burocracia gubermental y desaparecidas del ámbito cinematográfico repentinamente" [A too-regrettable case is that of these sisters, lost in governmental bureaucracy and disappeared abruptly from the cinema field] ("Las primeras realizadoras" 6).

Better known than the Ehlerses is Mimi Derba, the stage actress who cofounded Azteca Films with Enrique Rosas and who was involved in the production of five features during 1917, including *La tigresa*, which she directed.[4] Derba's role is undoubtedly crucial, both in the development of Mexican cinema as a whole and as the precursor of feature film directors such as Sequeyro and Landeta. Yet what is interesting about the Ehlers sisters is that unlike Derba, they did not come to the cinema through acting (an established occupation for women) but rather as photographers and cinematographers. They were trained artisans and entrepreneurs who influenced Mexican cinema through their numerous business ventures and institutionally as officials in the Carranza government. In spite of being makers of newsreels rather than fiction, they as much as Derba were the precursors of today's university-trained women directors. The Ehlers sisters' rise from provincial photographers to high-ranking bureaucrats and prolific producers raises questions about the fluidity of gender roles during and after the Revolution; although their lives are still cloaked in obscurity, their "trespassing" was an important step whose full implications remain to be investigated.

Adela "Perlita" Sequeyro: Beyond *el Rancho Grande*

In 1936, one film changed the history of Mexican cinema forever. Fernando de Fuentes's *Allá en el Rancho Grande*, starring Tito Guizar, initiated a new genre, the *comedia ranchera*, and with it, a new cinematic construct of *mexicanidad*. The *ranchera* films paid tribute to the *charro*, a specifically Mexican figure characterized by his costume and his aggressive masculinity, or machismo. The genre also elevated the *mariachi* style, originally the regional music of Jalisco, to the level of national "tradition." The valorization of such folkloric symbolism, as Carl Mora points out, served a concrete political function:

> The charro or *ranchero* was generally not trying to initiate social change but rather to maintain the status quo. He came to represent the traditional and Catholic values in defiance of the leftist, modernizing tendencies emanating from the cities.
>
> *Allá en el Rancho Grande* brought to life just such a traditional society but tellingly placed it in contemporary Mexico at a time when the Cár-

denas government was making it very clear that its objective was to extirpate all traces of prerevolutionary institutions and create a "classless" society. (*Mexican Cinema* 47)

The popularity of the *ranchera* films suggests that the moviegoing public, weary from decades of conflict and uncertainty and frightened by the rapid pace of change, perhaps welcomed the affirmation of traditional gender and class roles and the symbolic replacement of political and geographic fragmentation with a unifying "national" folklore. As Emilio García Riera wrote in his analysis of the moment "Cuando el cine mexicano se hizo industria":

Mientras la expropiación petrolera o el apoyo a la República española situaba a México en la vanguardia política del mundo, *Allá en el Rancho Grande* lo definía a ojos de millares y millares de espectadores de cine como un territorio ajeno a otras inquietudes que no fueran las del corazón sentimental o las de la guitarra.

[While the oil expropriation or the support for the Spanish Republic put Mexico in the political vanguard of the world, *Allá en el Rancho Grande* defined it in the eyes of thousands and thousands of spectators as a territory to which were foreign any disturbances other than those of the sentimental heart or the guitar.] (13)

Three years earlier, the young journalist-turned-actress Adela Sequeyro played what Fernández Violante has called her most important acting role, in a film by de Fuentes, *El prisionero número trece*.[5] Born, like Adriana and Dolores Ehlers, to a liberal family in Veracruz, Sequeyro, or "Perlita" as she was later known, began acting in 1923. In 1935, she decided to go into production, writing and producing *Más allá de la muerte*. She made her directing debut in 1937 with *La mujer de nadie*. Her three films have only recently been discovered and restored, and the third, *Diablillos del arrabal* (1938), is irretrievably incomplete; in 1943, bankrupt and lacking support within the industry, she retired from film production. Yet her work, particularly the wonderfully anachronistic *La mujer de nadie*, stands as a highly singular and unique challenge to the conservative, antimodernist regime of *mexicanidad* that dominated the era.

La mujer de nadie, which Sequeyro wrote, produced, and starred in as well as directed, begins in a locale typical of films of the period: on a hacienda, where a young girl (Sequeyro) is being beaten by her tyrannical stepfather. But this film is neither family melodrama nor even rural, for within its first few minutes, Ana María flees the oppressive *rancho* and literally falls into a life of bohemian modernity. Although the time is the nineteenth century and the country is imaginary and vaguely European, the seemingly casual integration of rural-to-urban flight and rejection of the conventional family into the film's opening episode can be read as a bold challenge to dominant cinema's romanticization of rural family values. The very title reinforces this challenge, for as many commentators have pointed out, women in the classic Mexican cinema always belonged to someone, whether as mother, daughter, wife, or whore. In this context, "nobody's woman" is a daring anomaly.

Interestingly, the formal mechanism by which Sequeyro effects her assault is that of a return to the past, specifically to the techniques of silent cinema. Her previous film, *Más allá de la muerte,* displayed an almost fetishistic fascination with visual detail, dwelling on such sensuous images as a drop of blood on a white rose, a glass falling out of the limp hand of a lover overwhelmed by passion, and a similar glass crushed in the clenched fist of a cuckolded husband. In *La mujer de nadie,* her directorial debut, she abandons dialogue almost completely, emphasizing instead the close-ups, suggestive glances, and provocative camera angles common on the silent screen, particularly the European art and horror films that she reportedly loved. Flamboyant images, such as a point-of-view shot from inside the fireplace or another framed by the man's elbow behind which Ana María is hiding, draw attention to the filmic apparatus, marking Perlita's auteurist intentions. However, as Torres suggests, it is the film's defiance of gender stereotypes (in its representations of both women and men) that is its most audacious aspect ("Adela Sequeyro" 5).

After fleeing from her stepfather's ranch, Ana María faints in the road and is picked up by three bohemians: a painter, a poet, and a musician, who live together, support one another, and have vowed never to bring a woman into their home. But once "temporarily" sheltered in the artists' abode, Ana María easily overturns their masculine domestic order by means of two spectacular actions. First, she disrobes behind a sheet, creating a beguiling silhouette that draws the men's stares. Then, when the men are still vacillating about letting her stay, she purposefully displays the wounds inflicted by her stepfather, transforming the marks of her victimization into a tool of power (Fig. 1.1). While these acts make her the object of a male gaze, they are less about her objectification per se than about her power over men: while she manipulates and solicits their gaze in order to gain a place in their home, they in turn become the objects of her gaze, which—far from being erotic—is tender and maternal and seems always on the verge of laughter. Her sensual undressing behind the sheet, for instance, is immediately contrasted with the bohemians' hapless fumbling under their bed covers and their disheveled appearances when they wake up in the morning. The order she brings to their household is less fulfillment of feminine duty than a kind of assertion of mastery (Fig. 1.2).

La mujer de nadie is not a flattering portrait of masculinity; as Torres writes, "el arquetipo macho es de alguna manera ridiculizado" [the male archetype is in a way ridiculed] ("Adela Sequeyro" 5). Yet its humor is gentle, for in spite of their clownish rivalry and dandyism, the bohemians are kind, tolerant, and generous, a stark contrast to the authoritarian stepfather. Ana María manipulates them, but without malice. She even parodies her own intentionality in a scene where she recounts, femme fatale-like, her "conquest" of someone listening off-screen; her auditor and ostensible object of pursuit turns out to be a cat. She provokes the men's erotic attention at every turn but does not wish to belong to any of them and is saddened by their feuds and rivalries over her affection. In the end, she decides to leave, ostensibly so that they may be brothers again. The title, however, suggests that it is her own freedom, as much as the men's domestic harmony, that is at stake. The ambiguous ending has been read by some viewers as implying her death; if this was the intended reading, then the price of women's freedom, as depicted by Sequeyro, was a high one indeed.

Torres's research suggests that Sequeyro's vision of life beyond conventional family structures and stereotypes was influenced by a cultural milieu that included the progressive movements and intellectuals of the period.[6] Her associates included Adolfo Best Maugard, whose 1937 film *La mancha de sangre* was censored for its amorally realist portrayal of prostitution; she was also peripherally associated with the avant-garde *estridentista* movement, a group of writers and artists who sought to keep alive the ideals of the Revolution and who fought against the co-optation of the intellectual sector by the new political establishment.[7] Yet in spite of her network of connections, her work as a filmmaker was largely unrewarded. According to García Riera, Sequeyro was charged double to rent a theater for the premiere of *La mujer de nadie;* the film was then rejected by exhibitors, chiefly for not conforming to the generic, i.e., nationalist models of the time. One impresario reportedly characterized the film as "made for Europe, not for the stupid public of Mexico," while another complained that lacking *charros,* it would never sell ("Perlita" 19). Although the exhibitors seem to have placed the blame on the supposedly unsophisticated Mexican spectators rather than the filmmaker, their rejection clearly bolstered the hegemony of the *Allá en el Rancho Grande* model.

Perlita's next film, *Diablillos del arrabal,* was to use fewer resources and cut

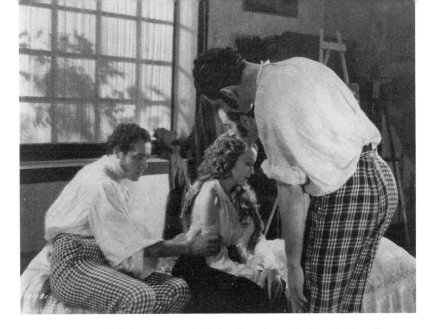

FIG. 1.1. Adela Sequeyro manipulating the male gaze in *La mujer de nadie.*

Courtesy Filmoteca de la UNAM.

costs; its story of male juvenile delinquents who band together to thwart adult criminals is also far more conventional. Yet it was not a box office success, and Sequeyro, bankrupt, unable to pay her crew, and abandoned by the union, was forced to sell the rights to the film in an agreement that left her powerless. Subsequent attempts to direct films were fruitless. She turned down what she regarded as condescending offers to work as an assistant director, arguing defiantly:

> Si demostré que puedo con el paquete de dirigir una película y de sacarle bien, no tengo por qué ponerme a las órdenes de otro señor para que me mande.
>
> [If I've (already) demonstrated that I can manage to direct a film and have it come out well, then I have no reason to place myself at the command of another man so that he can tell me what to do.] (Quoted in Fernández Violante, "Las directoras" 142)

In 1943, Sequeyro left filmmaking for good, returned to journalism until 1953, and was all but forgotten as a director until Fernández Violante interviewed her in 1986 (Torres and de la Vega 63). Her films were found and eventually re-

F I G. 1.2. Bohemian domesticity in *La mujer de nadie*.
Courtesy Filmoteca de la UNAM.

stored after the interview was published and have been widely exhibited since Sequeyro's death in 1992.

The case of Perlita supports the hypothesis that what had been an open playing field in the 1910s had considerably narrowed by the 1930s, especially with the entrenchment of postrevolutionary nationalist ideology as the privileged content of the national cinema. Yet Sequeyro's relative independence should not be overlooked. Rather than working her way through the ranks of the industry, she created a context in which she could make her own films. After more than a decade as an actress, she helped found the filmmaking cooperative that produced *Más allá de la muerte* with support from the Banco de Crédito Popular. When personal conflicts forced her to leave the group, she founded another cooperative, Producciones Carola.

Although the increasingly domineering union, the lack of equitable distribution, and the disproportionate power of exhibitors were formidable obstacles that ultimately curtailed her career, she did not face the kind of bureaucratic tyranny described, for example, by Irma Serrano ("La Tigresa"), whose efforts to produce an adaptation of Zola's *Naná* in 1975 were cut short under the administration of Rodolfo Echeverría, the president's brother and ultimate arbiter of cinematic content from 1970 to 1976. In her 1978 autobiography, *A calzón amarrado,* Serrano reproduced in full the letter she received from the governmental board from which she had solicited not credit but simply permission to film. The board criticized the quality of Serrano's script and attacked the subject matter, which it saw as irrelevant in the national context and incompatible with the administration's Third Worldist populism. What, asked the board, do the aristocrats and prostitutes of nineteenth-century France have to do with "el México de 1975, que busca por todos los caminos llegar a su verdadera idiosincracia?" [the Mexico of 1975, which is seeking by every route to arrive at its own true character?] (194).

The letter even suggests that Serrano's script, which might have been passable in the 1930s, "the worst era of our cinema," would in the 1970s be a betrayal of the nation itself. Like Perlita before her, La Tigresa had clearly trespassed too far into the jealously guarded domains of *mexicanidad.* Their twin exiles from the cinematic realm, during two intensely nationalist and ostensibly progressive periods of Mexican history, speak to the exclusion of women's stories and of women themselves from the master narratives of national identity. Serrano, however, would return to the cinema and gradually channel her indignation into genuine political activity, becoming the PRD (although soon independent) senator representing Chiapas in the 1990s. Perlita, on the other hand, although rediscovered as a pioneer and innovator and honored at the end of her life, was nearly doomed to disappear in the labyrinth.

Matilde Landeta: National History and Self-Invention

Of all of the early women directors, Matilde Landeta is certainly the most celebrated. Rediscovered in 1975 in the course of cinematic commemorations of the United Nations-declared International Year of the Woman, she quickly became the subject of homages, articles, interviews, and retrospectives. Her three early features, *Lola Casanova* (1948), *La negra Angustias* (1949), and *Trotacalles* (1951), appeared in festivals around the world, and her 1991 "comeback" film, *Nocturno a Rosario,* circulated alongside works by directors many years her junior. Together with her friend Fernández Violante, she was a vital force in the promotion of women's cinema; despite her years of professional exile, Landeta was a vigorous advocate for the Mexican cinema as a whole. Even in her eighties, up to her death in early 1999, she continued to be a strong presence in the Mexican cultural scene.

Yet in spite of Landeta's strong personal presence during the 1980s and

1990s, close study of published information about her career and life experience reveals many contradictions and certain disturbing silences. Documents that rightfully celebrate her early achievements glide over the difficulties of her later career: the years that passed between her rediscovery and her actual return to directing, the anomaly, in the context not only of her expressed convictions but also of nearly two decades of hopeful preparation of scripts and ideas, that is *Nocturno a Rosario*. It is as if the singularity of her status, as well as her personal charisma, precluded serious analysis; although Ayala Blanco included an intelligent and balanced evaluation of Landeta's work in his *La condición del cine mexicano* (444), few attempts have been made to position her in relation to the interplay of institutions and ideologies which make up the history of Mexican cinema.

Writing about Dorothy Arzner, a U.S. director whose career in some ways paralleled that of Landeta, Claire Johnston pointed out that "to understand the real achievement of her work, it is necessary to locate it within the constraints imposed by the Hollywood studio system and in relation to the patriarchal ideology of Hollywood cinema" (38). In Landeta's case, the constraints of the Mexican studio system do make up an important part of her public biography. Her battles within the industry are legendary and are encapsulated in interviews in several poignant anecdotes: a story she tells about adopting the habit of wearing pants on the set after catching the crew ogling her legs (Martínez de Velasco 52); the time, during her fight to become an assistant director, when she put on a sombrero and false mustache and stormed into an executives' meeting shouting "Silence!" (Moira Soto 72); and in contrast, a display of meekness during a union meeting that she claims provoked the protective instinct of the "macho" filmworkers and won their support (Gaxiola 13). Her betrayal by the Banco Cinematográfico, which purchased her screenplay for *Tribunal de menores* only to assign it to an inexperienced male director—the event which precipitated her exit from the Mexican cinema for thirty-five years—speaks for itself as an instance of repressive constraint.[8] But what, other than the loss of what might have been a much larger body of work, were the material consequences of such repression? That is, apart from her actual silencing and later triumphant return, how did Landeta's singular vision address, confront, adopt, and adapt to the patriarchal ideology of the classic Mexican cinema?

Although Landeta claimed to have wanted from the start to create an "other" cinema (*otro cine*) that would tell the untold stories of women, she did so within accepted generic boundaries. Her first two films, *Lola Casanova* and

La negra Angustias, are based on novels by Francisco Rojas González and deal with canonical national themes (respectively, *indigenismo* and the Revolution). *Trotacalles,* on the other hand, treats a topic which was extremely popular in the cinema of the time, that of prostitution; in fact, she claimed to have been talked into doing the film by writer Luis Spota on the basis of its assured commercial appeal (Gaxiola 15). In all three cases, the films' interest lies in her revision of typical themes; yet such revision does not fully replace or erase the ideology of the original. In fact, from the standpoint of the films' production, a dialectic emerges between constraint and intentionality, and it is this dialectic, I would argue, rather than one or the other of the forces, that finally shapes the films.

Each of the Rojas González films attempts to merge two basic themes: the development and trajectory of an exceptional woman (the title character) and the wholesale oppression of a given sector of Mexican society (indigenous communities, *campesinos*). Both are set in the past, and both depict unjust social conditions as specific to the time periods represented, with the implicit or explicit thesis that things have since changed for the better. This presumed change is linked to the actions of the protagonists but also transcends them and ultimately flows from the unidirectional progression of Mexican history. In short, Landeta attempts to incorporate women of valor into the master narrative of the nation, or *historia patria,* using the two novels as a point of departure. But given the fundamentally patriarchal nature of that narrative, her revisionist efforts produce mixed results.

Lola Casanova draws on the concept of Mexico as a mestizo nation, a concept which asserts the historical necessity of indigenous assimilation even as it postulates a myth of origin, the birth of the nation out of the sexual union of Cortés and Malinche, Europe and America. The importance of this myth in shaping national ideology is well documented; while Paz emphasized its essential ambivalence in *The Labyrinth of Solitude,* feminists have shown how the figure of Malinche is used to silence women, and they have tried to reconstruct the history of the European conquest in less grandiose/archetypal terms.[9] Yet from Independence to the present day, many thinkers and policymakers have used this Mexican genesis myth as their point of departure in approaching "the Indian question" and have assumed that assimilation of indigenous peoples into the national project was not only desirable but an inevitable fulfillment of national destiny.

In the factually based *Lola Casanova,* Rojas and Landeta substitute a white *conquistadora* with benign intentions for the alternately vilified and victim-

FIG. 1.3. Legitimate mother of the mestizo race:
Meche Barba in *Lola Casanova.*

Courtesy Cineteca Nacional.

ized Malinche. Lola (Meche Barba), the daughter of a prestigious Sonora family, is a willful, independent woman who rejects the marriage her father attempts to negotiate for her and who adopts an indigenous boy whose parents
have been killed by whites. In an act of revenge against the white community,
a group of Seri Indians attacks her coach and takes her prisoner. Although
they hope to exchange her for a high ransom, Lola soon demonstrates her
value as a healer (her European medicine is contrasted to the "backward"
tribal practices) and ingratiates herself into the tribe. Before long, she is be-
trothed to the tribe's young leader, who has killed her white "fiancé" in order
to win her devotion.

Lola's relation to the tribe is thus actualized through a sexual relationship to
a male leader, but in contrast to Malinche's stigma of illegitimacy, she is presented as the legitimate mother of the mestizo race (Fig. 1.3). Landeta herself
characterizes Lola as "una mujer que a través del amor logra hacer un grupo
étnico nuevo" [a woman who, by means of love, succeeds in creating a new
ethnic group] (Bustos, "Matilde Landeta" 31). After proving her ability to
function within traditional culture, she is able to persuade the tribespeople

that their only hope for salvation lies in abandoning that very culture and interacting with white society on its own terms. To this end, she provides the women with European-style dresses and finally, in defiance of the tribe's staunchest separatists (who are portrayed as vicious and treacherous, i.e., "primitive" in the most pejorative sense), re-enters the white community with her husband at her side.

From the optic of the present, *Lola Casanova* appears fundamentally patronizing and racist. Its "authentic" ritual sequences, for instance, are clearly artificial adaptations rooted in modern dance; moreover, Lola's relation to the indigenous people is consistently condescending, one of a mother and children rather than of equals. But perhaps most disturbing about the film is not so much what it shows as what it leaves out: the persistence of what anthropologist Guillermo Bonfil Batalla called *México profundo,* or indigenous identity and material being, within the myth of *mestizaje* that Lola exemplifies.

In *México profundo,* Bonfil advanced the thesis of two Mexicos divided by class, culture, ethnicity, and historical experience. For 500 years, he argued, Mexican society has been split between, on the one hand, participants in the "Occidental project," creators of an "imaginary Mexico" based on a colonial model of civilization, and, on the other, the indigenous peoples on the bottom of the social pyramid who constitute "deep Mexico":

> La coincidencia de poder y civilización occidental, en un polo, y sujeción y civilización mesoamericana en el otro, no es una coincidencia fortuita, sino el resultado necesario de una historia colonial que hasta ahora no ha sido cancelada en el interior de la sociedad mexicana.
> [The coincidence of power and Occidental civilization, at one end, and subjection and Mesoamerican civilization at the other, is not a fortuitous coincidence but rather the necessary result of a colonial history that even today has not been nullified in the interior of Mexican society.] (11)

Although essentially European and colonial in ideology, *México imaginario* (imaginary Mexico) strategically deploys notions of fusion, *mestizaje,* and assimilation to obscure the reality of a society in conflict. This has not, however, always been its intention. For the nineteenth-century intellectuals such as Justo Sierra who were instrumental in its formation, *mestizaje* provided a means of defining independent Mexico against its colonial past; advocates of what José Vasconcelos would later name the "cosmic race" certainly viewed their project as progressive and egalitarian, in contrast to the racially stratified society of New Spain. From the 1920s on, the postrevolutionary government sustained this project through its policies and directed its efforts toward incorporating indigenous society into a mestizo nation self-defined as universal (Bonfil 170). To this end, rural education programs were instituted in the 1920s, President Cárdenas created the Autonomous Department of Indian Affairs in 1936, and in 1948, the year *Lola Casanova* was released, the National Indigenist Institute was founded.

Yet in the wave of *indigenista* literature that emerged at that time, *mestizaje* was viewed with fatalistic ambivalence. As Braulio Muñoz points out, writers of the period did not have faith in the redeeming power of education to uplift Mexico's poorest sectors, but neither did they look toward indigenous cultures themselves as a site of resistance; rather, they could "only foresee the slow disintegration of the Indian's culture through *mestizaje*" (225). They tended to ignore the complexity of the changes taking place in indigenous communities and to see Indians as passive victims of a cruel present and uncertain future (226). *Lola Casanova* falls to some degree within this paradigm, as it portrays the Seris' "choice" as one between violence and assimilation, but it also attempts a utopian resolution, implying that the indigenous group's alliance with the whites will ultimately mean survival and redemption.

By Landeta's own account, when she set out to make the film, she hoped to film it in a neorealist style, using the actual Sonora locations where Lola's story had unfolded in the novel. Yet not only was location shooting too costly and difficult given her meager resources, but her preliminary research revealed a shocking reality:

Además encontré en tal estado de miseria a los seris, que consideré injusto presentar esa imagen de ellos. Era gente que vivía desgarrada, hecha pedazos, en un estado primitivo. Sin embargo, utilicé la música auténtica, los trajes, y los objectos de ellos.

[Furthermore, I found the Seris in such a state of misery that I considered it unjust to present that image of them. They were people who were living torn up, in pieces, in a primitive state. However, I used their authentic music, clothing, and objects.] (In Martínez de Velasco 55)

In other words, the actual, historical Seris were less adequate for *Lola Casanova*'s thesis of salvation through *mestizaje* than their re-creation in Churubusco Studios, which would use authentic ethnic accouterments but not authentic experience. What better illustration of Bonfil's thesis of *México imaginario*, a colonizing project which makes of the country's majority indigenous population a "civilización negada" (civilization denied)?

To be sure, the present-day scholar who has observed the resurgence of indigenous identity politics following the 1992 quincentennial commemoration of the so-called discovery of America, as well as the profound rejection of *México imaginario* initiated by the EZLN guerrillas in January 1994, cannot help but be distanced from the sentiments expressed in a well-intentioned indigenist melodrama of 1948 and must read Landeta's "However . . ." with skepticism and sadness. My point is not to diminish her work but to show how her chosen emphasis on exceptional women kept her from questioning key tenets of national ideology and muted potential aspects of her social critique—those based on class and caste—in the service of a basically individualist feminism.

This tendency becomes more pronounced in *La negra Angustias,* whose ending offers the clearest and most often-cited mark of Landeta's authorial intervention. Unsatisfied with the bleak conclusion of Rojas's novel, the director changed it so that instead of being betrayed and domesticated by her one-sided romance with the teacher Manuel, the protagonist Angustias remains independent and continues the Revolutionary struggle. Landeta explains that for her, the pessimistic ending of the novel did not do justice to Angustias's exceptional drive and ambition, as manifest in her determination to learn to read and write (Bustos 31). However, her recuperation of Angustias substitutes an individualist-heroic vision of female potentiality for Rojas's devastating critique of the Revolution, which his novel portrays as a complete inversion and betrayal of its most noble ideals. In the book, the triply marginalized Angustias, whose rebellion is perverted into the most grotesque form of servile oppression, is a powerful figure for the marginalization of Mexico's poor and for the distance between the Revolution's rhetoric and its actual accomplishments. While Landeta's attraction to the feisty, ambitious peasant woman—whose use of masquerade in some ways suggests Landeta's own—is understandable, her film actually softens the novel's social critique, insofar as it allows for the possibility of individual heroism that Rojas pessimistically mocked. In this sense, the film's feminism becomes its most important element, yet the marginalization of poor women throughout and after the Revolutionary period is paradoxically downplayed, compared to the original text.

La negra Angustias is thus typical of Revolutionary melodramas of the period, which generally advanced the argument that the Revolution was successful, that the current government was the proper heir to its ideals, and the events and social inequities depicted belong to the distant past. Its written preface—a title that opens the film—makes this claim openly:

Este episodio es un grito de rebelión de la clase más oprimida y pertenece al México de ayer. Es sólo un hecho de la Gran Revolución ese sacudimiento que dió lugar a la reintegración de una nacionalidad respetable y respetada que hoy en día levanta su estructura definitiva sobre bases de justicia y de equidad.

[This episode is a cry of rebellion from the most oppressed class and belongs to the Mexico of yesterday. It is just one event of the Great Revolution, that jolt that made way for the reintegration of a respectable and respected nationality that today builds its definitive structure on bases of justice and equity.]

The film's ending reinforces this thesis, as Angustias (María Elena Marqués) rides off bearing the national flag and shouting "¡Viva la Revolución! ¡Viva México!" Rojas, in contrast, ends his novel on a far more bitter note. On its final pages, Manuel, visiting the humble Mexico City home in which he now maintains Angustias as his mistress, explains to his companion:

Yo reconozco que mi cultura, mi origen y mi situación social chocan con tal estado de cosas; pero in realidad esto no es más que la casa chica.

[I recognize that my culture, my origin and my social situation conflict with this state of things; but in reality this is nothing more than the *casa chica* (mistress).] (219)

Meanwhile, Angustias herself is outside washing clothes and singing, just as at the beginning of the novel. Only now,

lavaba ropa propia; pero cantaba canciones ajenas: las de los vaqueros apasionados, las de las zagalas alegres de amores . . . Dentro de una cunita, un pequeño de piel morena y ojos verdes escuchaba embelesado el dulce canto materno, que se trenzaba con los gorjeos del mirlo prisionero.

[she washed her own clothes; but she sang the songs of others: those of impassioned cowboys, those of young maidens happy with love . . . In a cradle, a little one with dark skin and green eyes listened enraptured to the sweet maternal song that mingled with the gurgles of the imprisoned blackbird.] (220)

Having been the stepping-stone for Manuel's rise in the postrevolutionary power structure, Angustias's imprisoned status is a powerful indictment of that nascent power structure's manipulation and betrayal of *los de abajo* (Mexico's underdogs): *campesinos,* indigenous people, Blacks, women, the poor. In fact, more than the story of a particular woman, Rojas's novel is one of many literary works written in the wake of the Revolution that, unlike their cinematic counterparts, bitterly criticized the Revolutionary factions' contradictions, failures, and hypocrisy. Yet that critique would soon be displaced by the heroic, if amorphous, notion of the Revolutionary "legacy." Historians Héctor Aguilar Camín and Lorenzo Meyer argue that in the 1940s, "the Mexican Revolution and the constitution of 1917 gradually lost their condition of historical facts to become, as all the history of the country had become, a 'legacy,' that is, an accumulation of wisdom and achievements that guaranteed the revolutionary rightness of the present" (159). Film, like other forms of public discourse, invoked the Revolution in order to lend legitimacy to the current state of affairs and, ultimately, to the regime in power. Rojas's novel calls this legacy into question, while Landeta's version effaces Rojas's pessimism, inserting the story of Angustias into the master narrative of the patria.

Nevertheless, Landeta's *Angustias* may ultimately be the more powerful, to the extent that its feminism transcends its nationalist dogma. Its concluding sequence, in which Angustias is shown overcoming her personal difficulties and leading her troops into battle, is almost a direct reversal of another important Revolutionary melodrama, Emilio Fernández's 1946 *Enamorada*. In that film, the upper-class María Félix character succumbs to her love for the Zapata-like revolutionary played by Pedro Armendáriz; its final image is that of Félix on foot, one of many *soldaderas,* following her man into battle. The clear message is that women must submerge their own identities into that of their male lovers and masters for the greater good of the nation; Angustias, on the other hand, rejects the temptation of romantic love (and the identity loss it implies), is faithful to her incendiary ideals, and remains fiercely independent (Fig. 1.4).

It is hard not to sympathize with the fiery, heroic peasant leader that Landeta creates out of the material of the novel; Angustias's feeble attempts at coquetry and her doomed desire for the unattainable Manuel, which poignantly reveal her vulnerability as a woman, humanize but do not trivialize her. In some ways, *La negra Angustias* parallels Landeta's own life and career in the male-dominated film industry. Like Angustias, Landeta adopted masculine dress to carry out her work and adapted to pre-existing models (of filmmaking rather than revolution) while retaining a strong sense of self and of her identity as a woman. She was politically active, particularly in the labor movement; she defined herself as a socialist and defended the rights of the poor and oppressed, with whom she had sympathized since childhood (Camacho, in *La Jornada*). Also like Angustias, she relied on a network of male allies (her

F I G . 1 . 4 . María Elena Marqués as the feminist heroine of *La negra Angustias.*
Courtesy Cineteca Nacional.

brother Eduardo, who introduced her to the cinema and produced her films;
Roberto Gavaldón, the experienced filmmaker who stood up for her right to
direct; Luis Spota; and so forth) without playing the conventional roles of wife
and mother. (Landeta's only child died within days of birth, and her marriage
to a military colonel ended in divorce.) Although she did not set out to reject
family life, her work, like Angustias's struggle, always came first.

By the 1980s, Landeta had developed an articulate feminist analysis of
her own practice, as cited in the previous chapter and in her comments to
Patricia Camacho:

> Yo buscaba hacer en el cine lo que no había hecho ningún hombre: his-
> torias de mujeres bajo mi punto de vista femenino. No quería la resig-
> nada, la esposa de Jorge Negrete que lloraba en su rincón, los papeles de

Sara García, de Libertad Lamarque. En fin, todas tan lloronas, tan sufridas, tan resignadas, tan mensas.

[I sought to do in the cinema what no man had done: stories of women from my feminine point of view. I didn't want the resigned woman, the wife of Jorge Negrete crying in her corner, the roles of Sara García, of Libertad Lamarque. In the end, all of them so weepy, so suffering, so resigned, so dumb.] (6)

Unfortunately, the achievements represented by *La negra Angustias* and Landeta's third film, the powerful urban melodrama *Trotacalles* (1951), would not be sustained.[10] Prevented from filming her own scripts, Landeta worked making Howdy Doody shorts in the United States and later found employment supervising the production of foreign films in Mexico—all the while, she would claim, dreaming of her return to directing. Interviews of the 1970s and 1980s would find her planning numerous scripts, many of them returning to such themes as the urban poor or involving collaborations with other women, such as a trio of erotic films she hoped to make with Nancy Cárdenas and Fernández Violante (Torres, "Matilde Landeta" 30). In 1990, she told the press, "Cambiaría todos los homenajes por media película" [I would trade all the homages for half a film] (Gallegos in *Excélsior,* "Cambiaría"). In 1991, she finally directed another feature, the historical melodrama *Nocturno a Rosario.*

Landeta's comeback was generally received in the press as more of a noble failure than the question mark it might be, given its extreme difference from what she had been announcing for a decade as her future projects. Characteristically, Landeta displayed a fierce commitment to her new film, defending it as an alternative to the sexually exploitative and violent commercial cinema that had come to predominate during her long absence. Yet one wonders why this tepid period piece, which features a woman with a mysterious past as the muse of the male protagonist, was able to be made, while her more socially conscious or radical scripts were not. Perhaps the very emergence of women as directors in the forty years between *Trotacalles* and *Nocturno* served to diminish Landeta's relevance by making her less unique; yet it is also likely that in the 1990s as in the 1940s, Landeta was limited by a system of production that refused to take chances on a courageous, ambitious woman's vision.

Nevertheless, Landeta's body of work, and even more her notion of a feminist "other" cinema, remain an important influence and model for Mexican filmmakers today. At a time of national consolidation, when film served a key nation-building function, Landeta refused to believe that Mexican national identity could only be founded on female subservience; instead, she undermined stereotypes and made women heroes of national struggles. As Ruby Rich writes, "She laid the groundwork for the Latin American women's films of the 1980s, which began to incorporate women's struggles for identity and autonomy as a necessary part of a truly contemporary New Latin American Cinema" (11). Like Rosario Castellanos, Landeta searched for a way out of the uncomfortable roles to which women were confined:

Another way to be human and free.
Another way to be. (Castellanos, "Meditation on the Brink" 111)

The Limits of Commercial Film Production

In the preceding accounts of filmmaking by women in Mexico through the 1950s, I have tried to illuminate the complex relationships between government policies, ideology, production and exhibition practices, and the creative output of female directors whose context cannot be limited to the cinema milieu but must also include the historical situations in which they were both participants and observers. In so doing, I have tried to avoid portraying the chronological unfolding of history as seamlessly unidirectional, whether progressive or increasingly repressive, and have tried instead to portray the web of diverse and often conflicting factors in which these directors' work was inevitably imbricated. I have also tried to convey a sense of each filmmaker's individuality, the ways in which each crossed the boundaries of conventional cinema, the "how" and "why" of unique creative acts that, as Castellanos recognized, were exceptions proving the rule of the gender-imbalanced structure of artistic production.

What must also be taken into account in reviewing the first half-century of film production in Mexico and women's participation therein is the cinema's development as an industry within a nation-state undergoing a process of capitalist industrialization, with the political and economic complications that such a situation implies. I have already touched on some aspects of the industry which stand out as having been formidable obstacles to filmmaking by women, such as the generic triumph of the rural-patriarchal melodrama in the 1930s and the persistence of sexism within professional organizations and institutions, which increased as the industry reached a higher level of consolidation.

But the struggles of women within the industry were compounded by the struggles and contradictions of the industry itself, for instance: the constant threat of economic and cultural domination by Hollywood; monopolistic control of all aspects of the industry such that, by the 1950s, film production was in the hands of only a few powerful, family-based companies; and financing practices aimed at quick recovery of investments rather than at creating infrastructure. These problems had parallels in the economic development of the country as a whole, whose drive toward "modernization" was always fraught with contradiction. If the period of the "Mexican miracle" (roughly 1940–1968) produced a period of growth and a Golden Age of cinema, which for a time became the fifth largest sector of the national economy and whose sounds and images would influence all of Latin America for decades, it would also set the stage for a lasting and seemingly insurmountable crisis.[11]

To read Mexican women's cinema as *otro* or (to use a term suggested by U.S. and European feminist film scholars like Lucy Fisher, Ann Kaplan, Laura Mulvey, and Claire Johnston) "counter-cinema" requires an understanding of this broader context. For it was the very crisis in the industry, brought about by economic and political factors having little to do with gender as such, that would open a new avenue for women's filmmaking in the country. De la Vega notes that as the commercial film industry closed in on itself in the 1950s and 1960s, signs of a "cinematic counter-current" began to appear, first in the auteur cinema of directors like Luis Buñuel, Luis Alcoriza, Benito Alazraki, and Carlos Velo, aided by maverick producer Manuel Barbachano Ponce, then in the incorporation of film as a course of study at the national university, and finally in the rejuvenating impetus of the industry itself ("Origins" 92–93). These developments will be treated in the next chapter; for the moment, it is important simply to recognize that women's exclusion from the production side of the film industry was part of a larger tendency of that industry toward monopoly and exclusion, eventually to the point of stagnation. The changes that would come in subsequent decades were thus the result not only of women breaking boundaries but also of that model of production becoming exhausted, opening up fissures in which feminist and other critical and progressive points of view could flourish. The "jealously guarded borders" described by Castellanos would not disappear overnight, but as we shall see, their contours would significantly shift during the 1960s and 1970s.

Suddenly I woke up to find myself a filmmaker. I never thought things would turn out this way. I thought I would continue my writing and go into teaching, because I was married to a filmmaker, after all, and believed that he would be the one to advance in his career while I remained somewhat on the sidelines.

Marcela Fernández Violante[1]

We are part of the currents of thought that seek to give voice to those who fight for a better life, for dignity and respect. For human solidarity.

Berta Navarro[2]

CHAPTER 2

Student and Feminist Film, 1961–1980

The 1960s in Mexico saw the beginning of a cinema made outside or at the margins of the traditional industry. Like their counterparts in other countries, Mexican filmmakers at the end of the 1950s found themselves frustrated with a stagnant film industry whose resources were channeled into an impossible competition-through-imitation with far better-financed Hollywood product; at the same time, the advent of lower-cost filmmaking technology made it increasingly possible to challenge that industry's hegemony. Sixteen millimeter, for example, freed filmmaking from the studios' exclusive control and allowed it to be taken up in noncommercial arenas of expression, most notably the university. To an extent, filmmakers (male or female) no longer had to beg permission to make films; the blatant censure of Sequeyro and Landeta was not, during this period, repeated. Yet the new sites of production carried with them new constraints, particularly in the realms of distribution and exhibition and were also quickly enfolded into the state structure through such mechanisms as the famous experimental film competitions, which spawned a number of successful auteurs, if not the revitalization of the industry many sought.

But film history alone cannot explain the birth of feminist cinema in this period. The transformation of the cinema that took place during the 1960s and

1970s has to be seen in its historical and political context: the student movement and its repression, followed by the government's attempts at reconciliation and recuperation. In attempting to trace the development of women's
filmmaking in Mexico, we do not find a direct connection between the pio-
neers of the industrial era and their feminist descendants; rather, we find that
ideas considered radical in Sequeyro's and Landeta's eras—the notion of
an active, independent woman in control of her own body, sexuality, and
art—become much more widespread, thus enabling a feminist cinema to
emerge. The participation of women in the student movement and other social struggles, I believe, is what catalyzed the transformation of the early directors' individual struggles into a more collective and deliberate effort to create a woman-centered cinema.

Mexico and the New Latin American Cinema

At the beginning of the 1960s, the Mexican cinema was in crisis. While this di-
agnosis had been made in previous years and has been made almost ritually
ever since, the small number of films that were being produced by 1961 points
to a total breakdown in filmmaking activity. Salvador Elizondo, writing in
1962, lucidly summarized the crisis by attributing it to three factors: the producers themselves, the unions, and official institutions. According to Elizondo, producers had become accustomed to funding their products by ex-
porting them to Cuba, Venezuela, and Colombia, countries whose political
and economic situations now rendered them nonviable as markets. Meanwhile, the poor quality of Mexican films made them increasingly unattractive
to the U.S. Latino market. Perhaps most damaging was that producers had to
invest outside of the film industry in order to pay interest on and guarantee
their loans from the Banco Cinematográfico and therefore had not developed
the industry as a self-sustaining system. As costs soared, producers relied on
funding that the government could not provide (Salvador Elizondo 40).

As for the directors union, its closed status protected the privileges of
members while hampering the growth of the industry. Of its seventy members, only twelve to fifteen were actively working, yet the others were able to
maintain their exclusive status. The limited pool minimized the risks for investors but had created what most observers, especially aspiring filmmakers,
saw as an absurdly stagnant industry (41). Finally, the government had badly
mismanaged the film sector through arbitrary censorship, nepotism, self-
indulgent festival programming, and misguided policies such as a fixed max-

imum ticket price, which favored cheap commercial product and hurt higher-quality production (45).

Yet while the Mexican film industry seemed to be committing a slow suicide, movements were springing up all over Latin America to challenge the mode of film production it represented. Inspired in part by the French New Wave, Italian neorealism, and documentary experiments worldwide, the young directors of the New Latin American Cinema began producing passionate films whose intent was sociopolitical critique, and that made poverty of resources into a virtue—an "imperfect" cinema, a Third World "aesthetic of hunger"—rather than a weakness. In Mexico as elsewhere, young intellectuals flung themselves into this new movement, charging the formerly inert realm of film production with a new revolutionary fervor.

In April 1961, the first issue of the journal *Nuevo Cine* appeared, containing the "Manifiesto del Grupo Nuevo Cine." The twelve men whose signatures appeared at the end described themselves as "filmmakers, aspiring filmmakers, critics, and film club organizers"; they included film historian Emilio García Riera, writers Elizondo and Carlos Monsiváis, and director Rafael Corkidi. In their brief document, they outlined six objectives: 1) renovation of the Mexican cinema by opening it to new talent; 2) affirmation of the filmmaker's right ("like that of the writer, the painter, or the musician") to freedom of expression; 3) support for production and exhibition of films made at the margins of conventional, mainstream production, including shorts and documentaries; 4) six concrete measures to be implemented—the founding of a film school, active support for *cine-clubes* ("both in the Federal District and throughout the country"), the formation of a cinematheque, the publication of film journals such as *Nuevo Cine,* the study of all aspects of Mexican cinema, and support for experimental film groups; 5) a change in exhibition practices of foreign films, so that internationally recognized masterpieces (they named Chaplin, Dreyer, Bergman, Antonioni, and Mizoguchi) could be seen in Mexico; and 6) the revitalization of the Reseña de Festivales, an annual event that brought films from major international festivals such as Cannes and Berlin to Mexico ("Manifiesto del Grupo Nuevo Cine" 33–35).

The Nuevo Cine manifesto, which would subsequently be endorsed by eleven more participants (including Nancy Cárdenas, the sole female member of the group), is in retrospect extremely revealing of the situation of film culture as part of the cultural left in Mexico. As Moisés Viñas points out, the group did not take an explicit leftist or any other political position: "su opositor verdadero era el mal cine, con cualquier signo ideológico que se presenta" [their true opponent was bad cinema, under whatever ideological sign it appeared] ("Treinta años del Nuevo Cine" 16). Although the manifesto's advocacy of documentary and experimental filmmaking bore a resemblance to New Cinema practices elsewhere in Latin America, the model film culture it described was essentially based on the French example promoted by Truffaut, Godard, and others in the influential journal *Cahiers du Cinéma*. Film was seen less as a means of liberation than as what needed to be liberated—an end in itself. Most importantly, the manifesto was not a statement against existent institutions so much as a call for reform of those institutions. Its demands would thus be answered within the context of the state, under the rubric of *apertura*.

The program of the Nuevo Cine group would be realized first in a film—José Miguel García Ascot's *En el balcón vacío*—then in a series of state-sponsored film contests and finally under the administration of Luis Echeverría in the proactive film policy of the 1970s. *En el balcón vacío* (1961), based on texts by Spanish immigrant writer María Luisa Elío, showed the influence of the French New Wave in its low-budget mode of production and its subject matter, the Spanish Civil War as seen through the filter of childhood memory. García Riera, who collaborated on the script with Elío (who also starred) and García Ascot, explained that "en ningún momento pensamos en hacer una crónica de lo que son y representan la guerra y la emigración española como fenómenos políticos y sociales . . . el tema de la película no es la guerra de España sino la 'búsqueda del tiempo perdido'" [at no time did we think about making a chronicle of what the war and Spanish immigration were and represented, as political and social phenomena . . . the theme of the film was not the war in Spain but rather the 'remembrance of things past'] (Rossbach and Canel 50). The film was praised by critics, who saw it as the beginning of a new era in Mexican cinema.

In 1963, the filmworkers of the Sindicato de Trabajadores de la Producción Cinematográfica (STPC) went on strike for a month and a half over working conditions; the concessions they won would be met unevenly over the next decade. The following year, the STPC organized the first Concurso de Cine Experimental de Largometraje, or experimental feature film competition, whose aim was to create a channel by which new talent could be brought into the existing industry. Twelve films participated, with first prize going to Rubén Gámez's *La fórmula secreta,* an elegant non-narrative critique of capitalism. (Gámez, whose 1957 short *La China popular* was the first Latin American film shot in Communist China, was admitted to the directors union the following year but chose instead to remain on the outskirts of the industry.) Second prize went to Alberto Isaac's *En este pueblo no hay ladrones,* based on a story by Gabriel García Márquez, who along with Carlos Fuentes would become one of the literary figures most involved with the new cinema.

Although its impact was not as sustained as its sponsors might have hoped, the Concurso succeeded in reawakening interest in national cinema. For Eduardo de la Vega, it showed that Mexico indeed had directors who could take the cinema in new directions and could address problems more important than those of "los charros, los emascarados, los rockanroleros y un sinnúmero de prototipos más" [the *charros,* masked wrestlers, rock stars, and countless other prototypes] ("El cine independiente" 82). Yet overall, although the infusion of new blood into the moribund body of national film production was an important challenge to the established order's corruption, nepotism, and artistic complacency, the new Mexican cinema of the 1960s was arguably the least overtly political of the Latin American film movements of that period. Given the propensity of the Mexican left to be continuously absorbed by the institutionalized Revolution, the progressive film policy that followed the initial Concursos may be seen less as a democratization of a closed industry than as an ingenious attempt at co-optation—a co-optation, however, that the Nuevo Cine group itself invited when it demanded greater state support for film culture.

Film, the University, and *Echeverrismo*

Unlike the practitioners of popular filmmaking working in Bolivia, Cuba, and elsewhere in Latin America, the Grupo Nuevo Cine was motivated by what Viñas describes as "moral" rather than ideological concerns and emphasized artistic freedom more than social justice (17). However, its advocacy of film as an expressive medium did result in the development of a cinema that in many cases was motivated by social concerns: the cinema of the emergent student movement, whose base would be the Centro Universitario de Estudios Cinematográficos (CUEC) at the national university in Mexico City (UNAM). Founded in 1963 as a dependency of the university's Dirección General de Difusión Cultural, CUEC would in 1970 become a full department with its own budget and greater stability within the university system. As Marcela Fernández Violante (one of CUEC's first graduates and later its director) explains, the school emphasized social responsibility, film as a means of critical inquiry and research, and collective rather than individual (auteur) production ("El cine universitario" 84; "Objectivos" 11). Most of the Nuevo Cine members would serve, at one time or another, as instructors.

As Gustavo García points out, CUEC appeared at a critical moment for Mexican cinema, when its quality was declining due to the factors cited previously and when, at the same time, the growth of the country's educated middle class was contributing to the formation of a strong critical culture (4). The university setting, as well as the model of film production espoused by CUEC, enabled a different type of filmmaker to emerge: one less concerned with "film culture" per se and more involved in the use of the medium as a component of broader social struggles. The first explicitly feminist filmmaking in Mexico would come out of the university, and CUEC's first important film (Esther Morales's short *Pulquería la Rosita*, 1964) as well as one of its first features (Fernández Violante's *De todos modos Juan te llamas*, 1975) would be directed by women. Political militancy, pro-worker and pro-gay themes, and formal experimentation would all find a place in student films. Moreover, CUEC students, like most others at the nation's universities during the late 1960s, would be swept up in the student movement and the social turmoil that it generated. The frenzy of the times was documented in a film titled *El grito* in which students using CUEC's 16mm cameras bore witness to the day-by-day unfolding of events beginning in July 1968 and culminating with the horrific massacre of students by military forces in the Plaza de las Tres Culturas on 2 October of that year.

El grito, as Jorge Ayala Blanco describes it, is "el testimonio fílmico más completo y coherente que existe del Movimiento, visto desde adentro y contrario a las calumnias divulgadas por los demás medios masivos" [the most complete and coherent filmic testimony that exists of the Movement, seen from inside and in contrast to the calumnies put out by the rest of the mass media] ("El movimiento estudiantil" 59). Its footage taken before, during, and after the Tlatelolco massacre remains a singular testimony to an event that has not been clarified even today; for instance, the number of victims (officially around 25 but widely believed to be closer to 400) has never formally been established. The film's director, Leobardo López Aretche, was arrested that night in Tlatelolco and released months later; *El grito,* the first full-length film produced at CUEC, was banned by authorities and not exhibited until after López Aretche's suicide in July 1970 (Fernández Violante, "El cine universitario" 85).

Luis Echeverría was secretary of the interior at the time of the October massacre. When Echeverría became president in 1970, a crucial part of his agenda was making peace with the urban, educated middle class, much of which held him responsible for the tragic events of 1968 (Caletti Kaplan 71). One aspect of his program of reconciliation was the creation of a state-supported film sector under the personal direction of his brother Rodolfo, who became head of the Banco Cinematográfico. Rodolfo Echeverría's 1971 Plan for Restructuring of the Film Industry initiated and/or reinforced governmental participation in all facets of filmmaking, from financing and production to exhibition, distribution, and archiving. Nearly all of the objectives stated in the 1961 "Manifiesto del Grupo Nuevo Cine" became reality at this time. In public statements, the president affirmed the role of film in contributing to national culture and to the strength of the nation itself.

Yet, as Irma Serrano's failed effort to produce *Naná* indicates, the *echeverrista* vision was often as ideologically rigid and exclusionary as any that had preceded it. And as Aguilar Camín and Meyer point out, the regime's self-serving interest in mass communication did not preclude censorship of those voices that dared to criticize government policies (208–209). Camp similarly cites many instances of censorship by the Echeverría administration, including crude attempts to discredit the prominent historian and writer Daniel Cosío Villegas and an internal coup at the *Excélsior* newspaper apparently engineered by the president himself (Camp 198–204). While Echeverría's reforms certainly transformed filmmaking in Mexico by nationalizing nearly all facets of film culture (a process that would be reversed in the 1990s), they should not be taken at face value as a democratic opening, but rather as exemplary of governmental efforts to assimilate radical, potentially disruptive forces into the patriarchal, patrimonial state. For as Jaime Tello argues in his "Notas sobre la política económica del 'nuevo cine' mexicano," the democratization of previously rigid structures of film production created the illusion that the industry was now in the hands of its workers and creators, when in fact this very illusion served the interests of the state and the dominant classes in whose interests the "democratic" regime actually functioned (119).

Many of the changes of the 1970s were hardly more than rhetorical and stylistic; yet there is no doubt that filmmaking came much closer to being perceived as a social practice as well as a commercial medium or art form. In a manifesto issued in 1975, the Frente Nacional de Cinematografistas, which included former members of the original Nuevo Cine group and other young directors, declared that the Mexican cinema historically had been "uno de los soportes ideológicos principales de un orden social injusto y dependiente" [one of the principal ideological supports of an unjust and dependent social order] ("Manifiesto del Frente Nacional de Cinematografistas" 129). While the Frente praised the advances of the early 1970s, it also considered them incomplete; therefore, the signatories were announcing a movement fully committed to the development of cinema as a national art. Moreover, instead of *cine-clubes* and cinematheques, the Frente now spoke of hunger, infant mortality, and illiteracy. Instead of *renovación,* its members called for *solidaridad combativa* (131). Several of the manifesto's authors, such as Paul Leduc and Jorge Fons, would indeed go on to make important critical films; yet as we see in the 1990s, none fully succeeded in resolving the contradictions of cinema's compromise with what Mario Vargas Llosa famously called the "perfect dictatorship": a Mexican state that has counted on its ability to defuse opposition by means of absorption.

The Birth of Feminist Cinema

The emergence of the university as an alternative site of film study and production, the growth of a state-supported film sector, and the radical movements of the 1960s are the three crucial factors that converged to produce a scenario previously impossible in Mexican cinema: the sustained presence of women directors. Again, it is not so much the number of filmmakers who "happened to be women" that is significant but rather the particular context out of which they emerged. The kind of films they produced would be very different in content, purpose, and form from those imagined by a Landeta or a Sequeyro because, in effect, the world in which they were made had drastically changed.

Women had been a part of the social rebellions of the 1960s from the beginning, but their backgrounds were in many cases different from those of their male counterparts. While male student leaders came mainly out of the schools of political science, economics, and other disciplines traditionally closed to women, female students in the arts and humanities put their talents at the service of the movement. In her classic oral history *La noche de Tlatelolco* (published in English as *Massacre in Mexico*), Elena Poniatowska documents the creativity shown by young women such as actress Margarita Isabel,[3] who helped to stage street "happenings" consisting of heated political arguments designed to attract crowds, incite debate, and provoke bystanders into action on the "correct" side (21). Throughout the months leading up to the Tlatelolco demonstration, women students handed out flyers, provided transportation for demonstrations and meetings, delivered food and clothing to the leaders occupying the university, were arrested alongside their male *compañeros*, smuggled leaflets into prison in their brassieres, and cared for the wounded the night of the massacre.

For these women, the revolution was taking place on two fronts: the struggle against political tyranny, poverty, and repression on the one hand and on the other, the battlefield of gender. In the 1960s in Mexico as elsewhere, women's roles and the cultural models of femininity that governed them were in flux. The glorification of women's oppression that had been expressed and identified with *mexicanidad* in the artistic and literary forms of previous decades suddenly seemed outmoded. One mother told Poniatowska, "I spent my entire youth sitting on [romantic composer] Agustín Lara's white brocade sofa, with my tiny foot as slender as a needlecase, resting on a little cushion; the boys sang 'mujer, mujer divina' in my ear, and you won't believe how bored stiff we were" (16). Another woman spoke of living her whole life "on the sly, getting what I wanted in secret" and confided that "the life my daughter leads seems a thousand times better to me than the one I led. I know my daughter doesn't lie to me" (17).

As traditional patriarchal values crumbled, women began to carve out new spaces for activity and expression. In doing so, they were forced to confront not only a society which considered the students as a whole to be "degenerates" and "thugs" and (at its crankiest) believed that "it's the miniskirt that's to blame" (Poniatowska, *Massacre* 82), but also a male-dominated movement that was sometimes less than receptive toward women's participation. To the somber Strike Committee leaders, the miniskirted girl activists seemed frivolous. Salvador "Pino" Martínez's description of the gap between the students and the working class is as indicative of gender differences as of the communication gap he purports to analyze; critiquing some students' tendency to impose obscure theories on the uncomprehending workers, he ends up singling out the women students' ingenuousness:

> The girls from Philosophy would come back from the brigade meetings looking as cute as hell and with a big smile on their face and say "Comrades, we went to see the workers today! It was really great, really exciting! We passed out handbills: 'Come on, you workmen, take one, here you are, my good fellow.'" And the workers would say: "What the hell do those girls think they're doing?" (*Massacre* 20)

Whether or not the young women's "cute" style affected their political effectivity, they were forced to assert their commitment in ways that the men were not. Another leader, Eduardo Valle Espinoza, recalled that when a group of students went to investigate a right-wing takeover of a high school, he told the girls to stay behind: "They were highly indignant, and immediately replied that Che allowed women to fight in his brigade, and the hell with me" (*Massacre* 90).

Such incidents raised the consciousness of male activists but also ultimately contributed to the birth of an autonomous feminist movement in which women's rights would be prioritized and gender oppression would be confronted head-on. In "Déjalo ser," a 1993 television program made as part of the series *18 lustros de la vida en México en este siglo,* Busi Cortés looks at the beginning of feminism in the early 1970s, when "the women begin to come together"—a birth she symbolizes with the image of a raised fist displaying handsomely manicured bright red fingernails. At that time, women began to organize around issues such as abortion, rape, prostitution, and women's status in the home and the workplace. As in the student movement as a whole, film became both a document and a site of this struggle.

From 1963, when CUEC was founded, until 1970, Esther Morales and Marcela Fernández Violante were the film school's only female students. In the 1970s, however, the number grew rapidly and included the likes of Beatriz Mira, Alejandra Islas, Adriana Contreras, Dorotea Guerra, and later Maricarmen de Lara and María Eugenia Tamés. A second film school, the government-based Centro de Capacitación Cinematográfica (CCC), was founded in 1975 and graduated three women by the end of the decade. In the 1980s, it would be the training ground for directors such as Cortés, Dana Rotberg, and Marisa Sistach. But the increase in women's filmmaking was not simply a natural progression; as Angeles Necoechea reminds us, "Debemos tener presente que otras mujeres antes que ellas tuvieron que luchar arduamente por conquistar un espacio que ahora ellas disfrutan" [We should keep in mind that other women before them had to struggle arduously to conquer the space that (these women) now enjoy] (160). In the ongoing struggle for an *otro cine,* two combatants in particular stand out: Marcela Fernández Violante, whose lengthy career will be discussed shortly, and the Cine-Mujer collective.

Cine-Mujer

The Cine-Mujer collective began in 1975 as an association between CUEC student filmmakers and feminists working in other disciplines such as sociology and anthropology. Made up exclusively of women and focused on women's issues, the collective was also strongly Marxist in orientation, locating the oppression suffered by women within the broader context of class struggle. Its founder, Rosa Marta Fernández, explained the purpose of the group as *contra-ideologización:*

> Hay que desentrañar lo aparentemente "natural" en su marginación [de la mujer]; mostrar cuáles son los intereses políticos, económicos y culturales que hacen que la mujer esté en el estado en que se encuentra.
>
> [It is necessary to unravel what is apparently 'natural' about (women's) oppression; to show the political, economic, and cultural interests that cause women to be in the state in which they are in.] (Amado 13)

For the group, filmmaking was thus "a la vez que una práctica, un motivo de reflexión sistemática a propósito de la opresión femenina" [at the same time as a practice, a motive for systematic reflection regarding women's oppression] (Amado 12).

Its first film, *Cosas de mujeres* (1978), directed by Rosa Marta Fernández, dealt with the issue of abortion, which was and is an illegal practice in Mexico. Its subsequent films dealt with equally divisive and controversial topics, such as rape in *Rompiendo el silencio* (Fernández, 1979) and the domestic sphere as female prison in *Vicios en la cocina* (Beatriz Mira, 1977). Second-stage members María Eugenia Tamés and Maricarmen de Lara joined the group after having made *No es por gusto*, a documentary about prostitution in Mexico City, in 1981. That same year, the collective released *Es primera vez*, a documentary about a gathering of women's organizations that took place in Mexico City in October 1980. The gathering, the first of a series of such events involving women workers, *campesinas*, and community activists which would take place in the early 1980s, introduced the question of gender to social struggles previously understood solely in terms of class, thus contributing to the development of what Esperanza Tuñón refers to as "un feminismo de corte popular" [a populist or working-class feminism], in contrast to the perceived insularity of the self-defined feminist movement (73). Directed by Beatriz Mira, the title *Es primera vez* [It's the first time] suggests Cine-Mujer's recognition of the importance not only of the event filmed but also of their own participation in a movement which was then gaining strength in terms of numbers, visibility, and clarity of analysis.

For the members of the collective, each film was a learning process and one whose results would not always be well-received. In 1986, the newly founded film journal *Intolerancia* reprinted an excerpt from Jorge Ayala Blanco's book

La condición del cine mexicano titled "El parto de los montes feministas." The article harshly criticized this phase of feminist filmmaking and in particular *Vicios en la cocina, Cosas de mujeres, Rompiendo el silencio,* and *No es por gusto.* After attacking the formal and ideological weaknesses of these films, Ayala Blanco concluded:

> Desabrido y gratuitamente denigratorio, el cine feminista mexicano se extinguió como llegó. Por más que retumbaran los montes feministas, su parto dio como resultado un escuálido y asustadizo ratoncito.
>
> [Tasteless and gratuitously denigrating, the Mexican feminist cinema extinguished itself as it arrived. As much as the feminist mountains rumbled, their labor resulted in a squalid and frightened little rat.] (20)

Apparently in response, Angeles Necoechea wrote "Una experiencia de trabajo," a short history of Cine-Mujer that she pointedly subtitled "Pequeña contribución a la Memoria" [A small contribution to Memory]. Necoechea, a Cine-Mujer member who went on to work with the independent distributor Zafra, emphasized that in the 1970s, topics which are now more freely debated were barely mentioned aloud:

> Por aquellos años era (o había sido hasta el momento) imposible hablar sobre el problema del aborto ilegal, la violación, la división del trabajo entre hombres y mujeres, el trabajo doméstico (necesario pero invisible por no ser remunerado) y por supuesto de la sexualidad.
>
> [In those years it was (or had been until that moment) impossible to speak about the problem of illegal abortion, rape, the division of labor between men and women, domestic work (necessary but invisible because of not being remunerated), and of course sexuality.] (157)

Although she acknowledged the flaws and limitations of Cine-Mujer's filmic output, Necoechea argued that the early films were crucial in breaking barriers; the degree of repression, which only a few years later had already, for some, become difficult to imagine, made it necessary for filmmakers to work on a basic level, approaching their subjects in a way intended to generate maximum dialogue and debate. She concluded by saying that if, as Ayala Blanco had asserted, women film students of the 1980s were no longer interested in "feminist themes," it was precisely because of their predecessors' struggles, which had opened up a space in which greater freedom of expression became possible.

Not only did the collective break taboos in terms of content, however, but

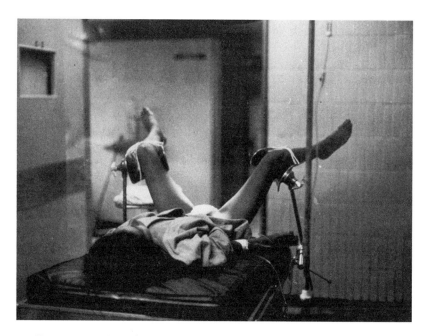

FIG. 2.1. Patricia Luke in Rosa Marta Fernández's pro-choice *Cosas de mujeres.*
Courtesy Cineteca Nacional.

it also broke with the cinematic and generic conventions by which women
had previously been represented. Women's struggles had been featured in
mainstream cinema, but only within the moralistic boundaries of the "fallen woman" melodrama; the language of the new feminist films, on the other
hand, was deliberately anti-melodramatic. *Cosas de mujeres* (Women's things)
emphasized the irony of its title—which invokes the feminine life "on the sly"
described by Poniatowska's informant—by writing it in "feminine" curlicue
letters that contrasted sharply with the harshness of its subject matter and approach. The dramatization of an emblematic story—a woman who finds herself pregnant and undergoes an illegal abortion—is intercut with real-life
statistics and interviews that attest to the prevalence of this dangerous practice
(Fig. 2.1). While the character suffers complications and eventually dies in
the hospital, the parallel documentary indictment becomes more and more
alarming: as newspaper clips demonstrate the government's rejection of legalization, we are told that one million abortions are performed annually in the
country, that most women who abort are mothers of three or more children

and cannot afford to support another child, and that complications due to abortion are the leading cause of maternal and female mortality.

Although as both Amado and Ayala Blanco point out, *Cosas de mujeres* could conceivably be read as a frightening argument against sex (by brandishing its potential consequences) rather than as an argument for legal reform, it is nonetheless a powerful depiction and indictment of what to this day remains "un secreto a voces" [an open secret] (Honey 35). *No es por gusto* similarly takes a topic that "everyone knows about"—prostitution—and puts it in feminist perspective. While prostitution has long been a privileged theme of the Mexican cinema, seldom has the prostitute been depicted without the romantic devices of melodrama. *No es por gusto,* however, takes this representational history as its point of departure; opening with 1930s music and a series of stills, it immediately delves into the banal lives of Mexico City's actual prostitutes, watching them on the street and interviewing them in their homes and in prison, where they discuss such issues as police harassment, contraception, and health care.

Again, Ayala Blanco's indictments of the film contain some truth. The then-popular notion that direct cinema is a purer expression of reality is clearly apparent. The prostitutes seem to be constructed as victims, shot in a filmic style that "lets" them talk as if doing them a favor, and the succession of interviews quickly becomes an unfocused babble (15–17). Yet *No es por gusto* can be seen as a response to decades of film production glamorizing beautiful, fallen *aventureras, ficheras* (dance-hall girls), and so on. The deconstruction of the prostitute stereotype that Landeta began in *Trotacalles* reaches a new stage in de Lara and Tamés's film; for once, women begin to speak—however "imperfectly"—for themselves.

Although the collective's principal contribution was in the documentary mode, some members of the group, including María Novaro, Lillian Liberman, and Guadalupe Sánchez, worked in fiction and even animation. The work of the collective was not limited to the content of its films; like other New Latin American Cinema filmmakers, the women sought avenues of exhibition and distribution outside the conventional movie-theater channels. Their concern was not with artistic recognition—though several members won Arieles and other awards—or with entering (much less revitalizing) the industry, but with communication, education, and dialogue, centered on social issues. Thus they showed their films in schools, public hospitals, and family planning clinics and to political organizations and neighborhood and workers' groups. According to Ana María Amado's 1980 interview with Fernández and other members, *Cosas de mujeres* was at that time being exhibited two or three times a week in schools and in hospitals where it often provoked a favorable reaction from medical personnel (15). The film was also utilized by the Frente Nacional de Liberación de la Mujer, a leftist-feminist coalition which waged a strong though ultimately unsuccessful campaign in 1979 for legalizing abortion. In the case of *Vicios en la cocina,* the film about the workday of a housewife was used with workers organizations as a point of departure for debate about the double workload inside and outside the home and women's socioeconomic role as unpaid reproducers of the labor force (16). In both cases, the post-film discussion was considered to be at least as important as the film itself, and the spectators became co-authors of the text as they selectively related its sounds and images to their own circumstances and experiences.

Cine-Mujer's final effort as a collective was *Bordando la frontera* (1986) about *maquiladora* workers in Ciudad Juárez, directed by Angeles Necoechea and produced by Beatriz Mira. By then, the collective was deeply divided over questions of strategy and purpose. Some members had moved on (Fernández, for example, emigrated to Nicaragua after the triumph of the Sandinista Revolution), while others were simply disillusioned by the enormity of their task and the failure of the left to achieve significant change. For María Novaro, the dissolution of the group was part of "el desánimo general, del desencanto de una época. . . . Realmente creímos que se iban a hacer una serie de cosas y que las cosas iban a cambiar y ni madres, no cambiaron, quedamos muy desilusionadas" [the general feeling of discouragement, the disenchantment of an era. . . . We really believed that a number of things were going to be done and that things were going to change and no way, they didn't change, we ended up very disillusioned] (quoted in Martínez de Velasco 105).

Oddly, the work of the collective has almost been forgotten, even though some of its members continue to work in film and television. De Lara has continued to explore the intersections of class and gender in her increasingly accomplished documentary work, while Novaro has become a successful director well known for her features *Lola, Danzón,* and *El jardín del Edén* (see Chapter 6). In his 1990 UNAM thesis, Enrique Palma Cruz rightly argues that the feminist filmmaking represented by Cine-Mujer was directly responsible for the debut of many women directors in the independent cinema of the 1980s (150). In analyzing the women-produced films of recent years, we would do well to remember their militant origins, even when, in some cases, those origins have since been repudiated. As Novaro (perhaps the collective's most ambivalent feminist) stated in 1994, "Reconozco que tengo personalmente una deuda con el feminismo en el sentido de que mi vida es muy diferente a la de mi mamá, mis tías y otras mujeres, porque bueno, me tocó ya una generación a la que el feminismo abrió muchísimas posibilidades" [I recognize that I am personally indebted to feminism in the sense that my life is very different from that of my mother, my aunts, and other women, because I belonged to a generation for whom feminism had already opened up many possibilities] (in Sarabia 25).

The Diversity of Women's Filmmaking

Apart from the Cine-Mujer group, many women entered the filmmaking field in the 1970s, working from a diverse array of approaches and paradigms. While not all of these directors can be discussed here, a few examples will illustrate the diversity of the period.

Writer, actress, and theater director Nancy Cárdenas, director of UNAM's *cine-club* and sole female member of the Grupo Nuevo Cine, made *México de mis amores* (1978). That documentary, a collaboration with Carlos Monsiváis, remains a comprehensive and valuable record of the classical Mexican cinema and its impact on the national imagination. Adriana Contreras, a student at CUEC in the mid-1970s, made five short films between 1976 and 1981, then directed the experimental feature *Historias de vida* in 1981. After moving to Uruguay, she made her second feature, *La nube de Magallanes,* as a Mexican-Uruguayan coproduction in 1989. Alejandra Islas emerged as an important testimonial filmmaker with the 1976 collaborative effort *La marcha* and continued with *La Boquilla* (1978), *Iztacalco: Campamento 2 de Octubre* (1978), *La indignidad y la intolerancia serán derrotadas* (1980), *Cerca de lo lejos* (1983), and *Veracruz 1914* (1987). In the 1980s and 1990s, Islas produced a large body of documentary work for television, including *Eisenstein en México: El círculo eterno* (1996), a reflection on the Russian director's unfinished yet influential *Que viva México!* Berta Navarro, the director of such socially conscious documentaries as *Crónica del olvido* (1979) and *Nicaragua: Los que harán la libertad* (1979), would play a further role in independent cinema as the producer of *Reed: México insurgente* (Paul Leduc, 1971), *Cabeza de Vaca* (Nicolás Echeverría, 1991) and *Cronos* and as cofounder of the New Latin American Cinema Foundation and collaborator in the Sundance Institute's Latin American cinema program (Moreno Ochoa, "Catálogo de directoras de cine en México" 581).

Although film production by women in the 1970s was overwhelmingly concentrated in the university sector, the decade also produced two interesting figures who would become commercial feature film directors at the beginning of the 1980s. Like their predecessors Derba and Sequeyro and unlike the film school graduates, Isela Vega and María Elena Velasco entered the field as actresses before taking control behind the cameras as well as on screen. Vega, stage and screen actress and sex symbol, began as a nightclub singer in the 1960s. By the mid-1970s, she was known as a provocateur of scandal both on and off stage; her national tours reportedly caused riots, and she and Irma Serrano were arrested while acting in a play in California after being denounced by a religious fanatic (Fernández Escareño 115). Vega was credited by fellow actress Silvia Pinal as the initiator of a new style in Mexican theater: a type of "theater of cruelty" constituted by nudity, violence, and provocation (Pinal 53). During the same period, Vega appeared in films by rising directors such as Jaime Humberto Hermosillo, Felipe Cazals, and Arturo Ripstein and worked in Hollywood, playing one of her most notable roles in Sam Peckinpah's *Bring Me the Head of Alfredo García* (1973).

Already recognized as the "author" of her theatrical spectacles, Vega made her debut as a *cineasta* in 1981, writing, producing, starring in, and unofficially codirecting *Una gallina muy ponedora* with Rafael Portillo. In 1984, she directed *Las amantes del Señor de la Noche,* a violent fantasy in which a young woman's use of witchcraft to continue erotic relations with her lover despite the distance which separates them eventually leads to madness and tragedy. Although Torres considers Vega's filmic ventures to be neither personal nor innovative ("La investigación" 42), Ayala Blanco's effusive essay in *La disolvencia del cine mexicano* describes an offbeat, delirious vision characterized above all by an overt sexuality not found in the films of any other Mexican woman director. For Ayala Blanco, *Las amantes* represented a deconstruction of the patriarchal ideology of national cinema (personified by Emilio Fernández in the role of the drunk and decrepit father) as well as a "mirada veladamente feminista pero estridenta" in which "todo Eros masculino es un Eros tanático y devastador" [a covertly feminist yet strident gaze, in which every masculine Eros is an Eros that is thanatological and devastating] (470).

Although Vega's work as a film director has been only a small part of her career—she has not directed a film since *Las amantes*—it is nonetheless an example of one of the ways in which women gained access to the medium outside of the university context. Although exceptional within the film industry, Vega can be seen as the product of a situation described by Pinal in which, due to the lack of a strong infrastructure, many stage actresses in Mexico found themselves from the 1960s on with both the liberty and the obligation to become their own producers and almost single-handedly take on the tasks of an entire production company. According to Pinal, actresses like herself, Angélica María, and Vega (and I would add Serrano), all to some degree critical of the system yet unable to break with it entirely, constituted their own "production systems," thereby gaining considerable control over their own images and the projects with which they were involved (54).

Such a notion of autonomy within the system likewise can be applied to the career of María Elena Velasco, who since the early 1970s had acted on stage, in films, and in the television programs *Domingos Espectaculares* and *Siempre en Domingo* in the role of "La India María," the quintessential poor indigenous woman in the city who triumphs over obstacles by means of her trickster humor and guile. By the end of the decade, she was an established comic figure in Mexican mass culture, a status which enabled her to become the successful producer and director of her own films in the 1980s, beginning with *El coyote emplumado* in 1982. Her 1987 *Ni de aquí, ni de allá* dealt with the provocative theme of illegal migration; produced by Televisa and clearly striking a chord with the Mexican public, it became the highest-grossing film of the year. By 1989, Velasco was one of only three women members of the directors union. In 1993, the thirteenth India María film, *Se equivocó la cigüeña,* was also an enormous box office success.

Derived from the comic traditions of popular theater, Velasco's unruly intervention in the terrain of commercial cinema eludes easy judgment. For Monsiváis, she represents "el indio recién aculturado como fuente de diversión . . . elemento conspicuo de colonialismo interno" [the recently acculturated Indian as a source of amusement . . . (a) conspicuous element of internal colonialism"] (quoted in Fernández Escareño 121), while Ayala Blanco sees her as "siempre oscilando entre la autodenigración de la imagen del indígena y la exaltación de hipotéticas cualidades inatas de la raza indígena" [always oscillating between the self-denigration of the indigenous image and the exaltation of hypothetical innate qualities of the indigenous race] (*La disolvencia* 461). While some critics have found her films denigrating, others have been drawn to what Carmen Huaco-Nuzum describes as "a tension between social forces of resistance and acculturation which are played out by the main character, the India María, who struggles to find a place in which to articulate her desires"—a struggle familiar to many poor and indigenous Mexicans whose interests have rarely been served by the ideology of modernization (143). The films seem to mix gross stereotypes with acute insights into the politics of race, class, and gender in Mexico and the United States; while crude representations of Blacks and other groups seem patterned on the worst Hollywood caricatures, María herself is a spirited figure of picaresque resistance. For Huaco-Nuzum, the India María provides "a voice which interrupts the established subaltern position of the indigenous female in popular Mexican film" (154).

While Velasco is certainly the most successful female director in Mexican film history in box office terms, she and Vega were exceptions to the persistent rule of male domination of the industry. Moreover, their work as directors was carried out not so much as a vocation per se as an extension of their creative ability as actors, which permitted them to gain more and more control over their own work. Yet it is safe to speculate that like female university graduates of the same period, Velasco and Vega were at least partially enabled in their careers by a feminist movement which had made it possible for women to assume positions of professional responsibility without suffering the levels of harassment and rejection experienced by previous generations. No longer isolated "trespassers," women filmmakers of the 1970s and early 1980s constituted a diverse group whose numbers and accomplishments would continue to increase over the next decade.

Marcela Fernández Violante: The Last "Contrabandista"

As late as 1989, the only women directors recognized by the film unions were Velasco, Matilde Landeta, and Marcela Fernández Violante. Whereas Velasco's work is unambiguously commercial, Fernández Violante has long remained on the borderline between industrial and university cinema. An always-controversial figure, Fernández Violante can perhaps best be described as a maverick; although she has been prominent in a variety of cultural institutions, her often precarious position, as well as the way she has stood up to entrenched obstacles with chutzpah and defiance, align her with the "contrabandistas" described in the previous chapter. Because of its length, scope and complexity, her career invites closer examination.

Fernández Violante's early trajectory as a filmmaker in the 1960s, as described to Julianne Burton in 1983, parallels that of the cinema of the era. She entered UNAM the year that CUEC was founded and began to study screenwriting along with more traditional philosophy and letters. When a screenplay she wrote became a "disaster" at the hands of a fellow student, she decided to go into directing. Her 1967 experimental short *Azul* won a Diosa de Plata, awarded by a panel of jurors that included Nuevo Cine members Carlos Monsiváis, Francisco Pina, and Emilio García Riera (Martínez de Velasco 106). In 1968, the school assigned Fernández Violante to direct its first feature-length script, to be called *Gayosso da descuentos,* but events of that year derailed the production. "With the country in such turmoil," she said, "nobody wanted to work on a fiction film. Everybody went out to participate and to film what was happening" (in Burton 197). The project was postponed, never to be completed. During that period, Fernández Violante married a fellow film student, became pregnant, and suffered an accident that provoked a miscarriage. In 1971, she went to work on her thesis film, the documentary short *Frida Kahlo.*

At the time *Frida* was made, Kahlo was not the ubiquitous icon she is today but was known mainly as Diego Rivera's wife. Having a personal connection to Kahlo through her father (who knew Kahlo) but denied access to Kahlo's personal papers, Fernández Violante decided to tell the artist's story by means of her intensely autobiographical paintings. What now (in the wake of Kahlo's posthumous ascent to superstar status in the 1980s) looks like a simple montage of familiar images would have been in 1971 an exciting work, one in which a promising artist at the beginning of her career paid homage to an undervalued female talent of a previous era. *Frida Kahlo* was exhibited internationally and won an Ariel and a Diosa de Plata, and on its strength, Fernández Violante secured funding from the university for her first feature, *De todos modos Juan te llamas.*

In *De todos modos,* the sometimes uneasy balance of conventional storytelling and political commentary that marks much of Fernández Violante's work is already apparent, as is her concern with history, gender, and nation. The film depicts the Cristero Rebellion of 1927–1929, a religious uprising that erupted in the wake of the highly contradictory "consolidation" of the 1910 Revolution (Figs. 2.2 and 2.3). Fernández Violante's description of her film's ideological position exemplifies her generation's disillusionment with the textbook version of history. "I don't believe in the Mexican Revolution as our historians present it to us," she told Burton:

> I have more faith in the artist's conception than in the historian's. Besides, with the same political party now in office for nearly seventy years, how are we to know what the truth is? *[De todos modos]* was an attempt

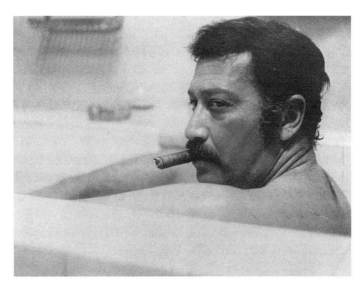

F I G . 2.2. The general in his labyrinth:
Jorge Russek in *De todos modos Juan te llamas.*

Courtesy Filmoteca de la UNAM.

F I G . 2.3. "La historia prohibida": Cristero rebels in *De todos modos Juan te llamas.*

Courtesy Filmoteca de la UNAM.

to demystify the Revolution. . . . Contrary to the conventional wisdom, the Revolution was not won. At that point of "consolidation" between 1917 and 1926, it was lost. (199)

Gustavo García, in *Intolerancia,* describes *De todos modos* as "la primera reflexión seria sobre la historia prohibida de la revolución mexicana, la guerra cristera" [the first serious reflection on the prohibited history of the Mexican Revolution, the Cristero war] (6). The "prohibited" nature of the Cristero conflict, as historian Jean Meyer suggests, lay in the way in which it exceeded the boundaries of an *historia patria* that sought to equate the government with the Revolution and the popular will it embodied:

> It was a terrible war of ordinary people rising against the state and its army, containing all the elements of both a revolutionary and of an anti-colonial war, though the government has since been depicted as representing the "left" and the insurgents the "counter-revolution." (213)

In the 1920s, anticlerical acts that were the product of myriad power struggles at the highest level of national politics were perceived by rural Mexicans in the southwestern part of the country as a threat to their freedom of religious practice; some twenty thousand rebels led by the Catholic Action movement took up arms against the government in 1927, and their number rose to fifty thousand by 1929, the year the conflict was finally settled. For Fernández Violante, the Cristero Rebellion was evidence of the Revolution's failure to satisfy the needs of the *campesinos,* materially as well as ideologically. Moreover, the story of the government's war against its own people (Meyer writes of "unarmed masses machine-gunned by the army" [214]) contained obvious echoes of the period in which her film was made—a period still haunted by the horrifying experience of Tlatelolco.

As the daughter of a general, Fernández Violante grew up in a military family that found itself deeply divided by the events of 1968. Her "rigid" father expelled her brother from their house for being a Marxist, she told John Mosier and Alexis Gonzales in *Américas:*

> Many families had this sort of split, and that was also an inspiration for the film. I knew that I couldn't make a film about 1968, since it was so recent that I wouldn't have the proper perspective, but I asked what happens in this same situation when religion is the main source of the conflict? It would have been much worse than in 1968. (16)

Using one family as a means of examining a larger conflict, *De todos modos* re-politicizes the melodrama's traditional displacement of social tensions onto the domestic sphere, making the personal political.

Fernández Violante recognized that her freedom to criticize such powerful institutions as the church and the military was due to her having the support of another institution, the university, and that the film would not have been made were it not for the *echeverrista* policy of rapprochement (Burton 198); however, she told Mosier and Gonzales that her film was criticized for focusing on the military family rather than on the *campesinos*—a detail reminiscent of Irma Serrano's experience and that once again points to the ideological rigidity of the period (Mosier and Gonzales 16). Nevertheless, after *De todos modos,* Fernández Violante was admitted to the directors union. Her next film, *Cananea,* dealt with the northern miners' rebellion that was one of the sparks leading to the 1910 Revolution. Shot by renowned cinematographer Gabriel Figueroa, *Cananea* examines the relationships and conflicts between U.S. property owners, Mexican mineworkers, and the anarchist intellectuals who organized the strike.

Once again, Fernández Violante's political analysis is complex and nuanced. In *Cananea,* the portrayal of the American mine owner Greene, played by Steve Wilensky, gives depth to the more typically one-dimensional "gringo" exploiter, while the anarchist is seen more as a necessary catalyst for change than as a conventional hero. In the film, the virtue of the strike was to lay bare the antagonistic class interests that the ruling class had attempted to disguise, addressing the workers as "compadre" and "brother" while underpaying them and subjecting them to dangerous, inhuman working conditions. The critique of Mexico's complicity with U.S. political and economic interests, already raised in *De todos modos,* is amplified; as Fernández Violante points out, Greene's property remained in his family until 1958, and events on Wall Street, not in Mexico, caused the loss of the Cananea mine (Mosier and Gonzales 16). Realistic in its evaluation of the historical significance of Cananea, the film avoids becoming a Golden Age-style elegy of the glorious Revolution. Instead, *Cananea* portrays "the history of Mexico writ small," in which "nobody wins and everybody loses" (Fernández Violante in Burton 200).

Since *Cananea,* Fernández Violante has made four more feature films: the humorous *Misterio* (1979), based on the novel *Estudio Q* by Vicente Leñero; *El niño raramuri* (1980), whose depiction of an urban mestizo boy's experience in a Tarahumara village interestingly reverses the pro-assimilation ideology promoted in Landeta's *Lola Casanova;* the urban melodrama *Nocturno amor que te vas* (1987); and *Golpe de suerte* (1991), an engaging comedy about one family's failed attempt to weather the economic crisis of the Salinas era that is unsparing in its critique of the contradictions and hypocrisy demonstrated by Mexico City's upwardly mobile lower-middle class. Besides being Mexico's most prolific female director, from 1978 to 1982 Fernández Violante taught in and served on the staff of CUEC and in 1985 became the school's director. She has taught in the United States, written articles, served on the juries of film festivals, and been an outspoken advocate for Mexican film at innumerable public events. Yet in spite of this recognition and achievement, her usual mode has been that of denunciation—a tone that, on closer examination, is justified in light of her experiences.

Like many filmmakers, Fernández Violante has long found herself entangled in a film establishment whose bureaucratic practices, far from fostering a healthy film sector, often function as a de facto form of censorship. In 1983, she told Andrew Horton that her films had never been censored (4); but a decade later, she explained to news reporters that her work had indeed been censored, not by cutting it or openly restricting its projection, but by premiering it at inadequate times and locations or by shelving it altogether (Quiroz Arroyo, "Marcela"). *Cananea,* for example, never opened commercially; *Misterio* opened during Mexico City's heavily promoted Muestra Internacional de Cine, a time when domestic debuts are likely to be ignored; and due to both the usual bureaucracy and the liquidation of the national film distribution company Películas Nacionales, *Nocturno amor que te vas* was not shown outside of the university until 1992, five years after its completion.

By the time *Golpe de suerte* was made, Fernández Violante was clearly fed up, with good reason: the governmental film institution IMCINE first agreed to support the production, then abruptly withdrew its support. With the Banco Cinematográfico now privatized, she was forced to borrow from the private bank Bancomer to finance the film, and the by-now-routine delay between the film's completion and its commercial premiere translated into a devastating accumulation of accrued interest on the loans. The film competed in the fourth Concurso de Cine Mexicano without success and, after a pre-screening in the Cineteca, was excluded from the Hoy en el Cine Mexicano film cycle and subsequently the annual Muestra de Cine Mexicano in Guadalajara.

Golpe de suerte, wrote *Esto* columnist Manuel Gutiérrez Oropeza, "ha dormido el sueño de los justos, es decir, está enlatada" [has slept the sleep of the just, that is, it's been canned], and "todo parece indicar que será nin-guneada y proyectada en cualquier cine de piojito" [everything seems to indi-cate that it will be ignored (literally, "nobodied") and projected in some flea-bag movie house]. In February 1992, Fernández Violante argued for her film's inclusion in the Hoy cycle as an homage to the actor Miguel Manzano, who had died shortly after completing the film; "no creo que afecte en nada," she told Enrique Feliciano of *Esto,* "si dentro de ese ciclo se programa una cinta más" [I don't think it matters if during this cycle they program one more film]. Manzano's family joined her in filing a formal request with the Consejo Nacional para la Cultura y las Artes.[4] The attempt to disrupt the bureaucratic hierarchy of film selection can be seen as an audacious "contrabandista" tac-tic, and one that probably did not endear Fernández Violante to the film es-tablishment. When *Golpe de suerte* was finally shown at the Cineteca in 1994, it was snubbed by the film journal *Dicine,* which condemned its "total absence of rhythm, interest, or hook," and advised readers to "avoid it like the plague" (del Diestro).

It is ironic that in the early 1990s, when the abundance of talented women filmmakers was constantly being celebrated, Fernández Violante's work would be ignored, "canned," and dismissed. Even more ironic is the way that the Kaf-kaesque bureaucracy depicted in *Golpe de suerte* was duplicated in the film-maker's own experience. The film deals with the fate of a civil servant (Sergio Ramos), whose dream come true of finally acquiring subsidized housing in the southern part of Mexico City quickly becomes a nightmare. By the end of the film, the civil servant has lost everything but a medal that was awarded him for his years of service—just as Fernández Violante herself has been rec-ognized as a pioneer but routinely denied the resources to meaningfully ex-hibit (and thus make a living from) her films. Bringing this point home, the scene depicting the award ceremony can be seen as a subtle but stinging in-dictment of the situation of the woman filmmaker in Mexico: the fictional protagonist receives his medal alongside none other than the real Matilde Landeta.

Landeta, it should be remembered, had said in 1990 that she would trade "todos los homenajes por media película" [all the homages for half a film] (Gallegos, "Cambiaría"). Attending the same event, Fernández Violante had intervened: "por una película, no solo media película" [for a film, not only half a film], to which Landeta, object of revisionist appreciation for nearly two decades, replied, "por media película . . . la mitad solamente" [for half a film . . . only half]. The poignancy of this exchange is echoed in *Golpe de suerte;* for what Fernández Violante shows us is that behind the homages and accolades, behind the speeches and pronouncements and awards and ceremonies, to be a filmmaker in Mexico—to be an artist, a social critic, a woman—is still a constant struggle.

"Una pequeña contribución a la Memoria"

While many of the barriers faced by earlier directors have been broken and many former taboos have disappeared, the road is by no means easy for women filmmakers. Berta Navarro writes of the limited access women still have to technological resources and training, pointing out that very few women work in technical areas such as sound, cinematography, and the emergent technologies of the electronic media:

> No es solamente el lenguaje para expresarse sino los medios que se utilizan para ese lenguaje. En este marco nuestra incorporación es difícil, nuestro aceso a la capacitación debe ser una exigencia prioritaria.
> [It's not only the language to express oneself but also the means which are used for this language. In this area our incorporation is difficult; our access to training should be a high-priority demand.] (153)

Navarro also points to lack of time—due to multiple roles and obligations—as a serious problem for women and concludes by emphasizing the urgency of women's struggle for access to the means of communication, saying:

> Las pocas mujeres que llegamos a desarrollar nuestras capacidades en este momento de tránsito histórico, estamos haciendo el camino para resolver el dilema que la mujer de hoy se nos presenta: libertad de elección y desarrollo en soledad o la negación de sí misma.
> [The few women who have been able to develop our capacities in this moment of historical transition are moving toward resolving the dilemma which the woman of today faces: freedom of choice and development in solitude, or the denial of herself.] (155)

In spite of continuing difficulties, the late 1960s and the 1970s were unquestionably a watershed period for women in Mexico and for women filmmakers in particular. No longer would life be lived "on the sly," and no longer would women be excluded from filmmaking solely on the basis of sex. Yet alongside the achievements of that era are its failures, complications, contradictions, and in particular the genesis of a new bureaucratic labyrinth in which many talented filmmakers would be hopelessly lost. While the Echeverría era has been lauded by many as a progressive and productive period for Mexican cinema, its supposed beneficiaries—the directors themselves—have more often than not found themselves battling the very institutions purportedly designed to enable and encourage their work.

Now that the *echeverrista* film infrastructure has been largely privatized to meet the ideological demands of neoliberalism, its most powerful and vibrant legacy may not be the films it produced through official channels but the films made at its margins: the "dirty" and "imperfect" films like *El grito* and *Cosas de mujeres* and *Es primera vez* that dared to document reality as the filmmakers experienced it. Although some of the modes of filmmaking they used have been rejected and their flaws laid bare, the issues they sought to address—abortion, rape, prostitution, gender oppression, social injustice— have not disappeared; their critiques are no less valid today. Their history, although recent, is almost as fragmentary and buried as that of the Ehlers sisters; by remembering their efforts, the obstacles they faced, and their struggles which continue into the present, we can better understand the complex situation of women filmmakers in Mexico in the 1990s.

PART TWO | Revisions

I believe that women have to invent, in our field of work, a new language that will be nourished by the common experiences of our individual histories. This woman's word should be inscribed in our culture. To destroy the false mirror of woman that is, in general, the cinema. . . . It means reappropriating our image and in doing so, seeking our identity.

Marisa Sistach[1]

CHAPTER 3

Marisa Sistach

The Other Gaze

During the 1960s and 1970s, the industrial cinema, along with the patriarchal ideology it had served to reinforce and reproduce, suffered serious challenges. During that period, the trappings of the genteel Mexican woman, whose movements were restricted to the family home and whose sexuality was safely curbed and hidden under white lace sheets, were thrown off by a new generation of middle-class youth who not only attended college in greater numbers than ever before but also participated in student rebellions, drove cars, wore miniskirts, listened to rock 'n' roll, idolized Che Guevara, and made passionate low-budget films attacking social problems and documenting their own experiences. The countercultural aesthetics that arose as the expression of a generational desire for change exploded the archetypes and stereotypes of previous decades; the cinema of the past, with its suffering mothers, fallen virgins and treacherous femmes fatales, had little to say to a generation that was waking up to its own potential for action and self-definition.

Many feature films produced during this era negatively manifested the influence of the changing times. In *Cinema of Solitude*, Ramírez Berg documents how many of the dominant myths of *mexicanidad*, particularly those with gender as their central component, could be observed to crumble in the cinema of the 1970s. In films such as *Fin de fiesta* (Mauricio Wallerstein, 1971),

Mecánica nacional (Luis Alcoriza, 1971), and perhaps most notably in the oeuvre of Arturo Ripstein, the sacred home of patriarchal melodrama became a suffocating prison, while its ruler, the nurturing and long-suffering mother, became "*smother,* pathologically overprotective, dangerous, violent" (*Cinema of Solitude* 70). Moreover, film after film exposed a crisis in masculinist ideology; the increasing visibility of homosexuality and a preponderance of tragic female protagonists who instead of being victims of fate's cruelty (like *Santa* and *Aventurera*) were portrayed as "victims of *machismo*" (77), suggested that "by the 1960s the authority of the *macho* figure in the movies had eroded. Like the state he mirrors, movie *macho* begins cracking" (102). Ramírez Berg argues that because of the ideological overlap between the Mexican state and patriarchy ("If there is a national male symbol in Mexico, it is the nation-state itself"), the sociopolitical crisis of the 1960s was inevitably also a crisis of gender (106–108).

By the 1980s, with the film industry undergoing one of the worst phases in its history, there was little for women to identify with on the mainstream Mexican screen. For in the movies as in real life, the stifling yet secure gender roles so well defined by the classical cinema were not replaced by images of freedom and equality but rather by ambivalence and confusion. The interventions effected by cultural activists in the women's and student movements had forcefully challenged the iconography of gender, including the symbolic links between gender and nation or *mexicanidad,* yet their impact was as yet limited. As Diana Bracho wrote in 1985, the fact that the state-supported film sector had brought many old stereotypes to an end did not mean that women were now adequately represented in the cinema:

> La mayoría de los nuevos cineastas que prometían salvar el cine mexicano, se interesó mínimamente por los problemas de la mujer, y muy a menudo lo hizo con una mentalidad misógina. Sus preocupaciones fueron otras.
>
> [The majority of the new filmmakers who promised to save Mexican cinema were minimally interested in women's problems and very often approached them with a misogynist mentality. Their concerns were different.] (422)

This situation is effectively encapsulated in a scene from Marisa Sistach's *Los pasos de Ana* (1988) in which the protagonist, Ana, and her friend Carlos's trip to a bookstore becomes the occasion for an examination of Ana's life. Carlos advises her to "cambiar tus esquemas" (change your schemes):

Modernízate, porque si no vas a acabar como Sara García en *Cuando los hijos se van.* ¿Te acuerdas? Eso ya no funciona. Hoy día tienes que concebirte de otro modo. No importa si el papel que te toca interpretar no tiene reflejo en el cine mexicano.

[Modernize yourself, because if you don't, you're going to end up like Sara García in *Cuando los hijos se van.* Remember? That doesn't work anymore. Today you have to think of yourself differently. It doesn't matter if the role that is yours to play is not reflected in the Mexican cinema.]

In response, Ana comments: "Hace tanto que no veo una película mexicana que ya no sé si existo" [It's been so long since I've seen a Mexican film that I don't know anymore if I exist].

In the wake of several decades of change and upheaval, women like Sistach's Ana—herself a filmmaker—found themselves not only alienated from the cinema but uncertain about their own roles as women in society. Although many of the old models had been dismantled, new ones had yet to be invented in practice, and many women found themselves caught in conflicting sets of expectations, including their own contradictory desires and needs as workers, mothers, wives, lovers, daughters, and so on. Women like Ana—striving to make ends meet but also to succeed on their own terms in professions of their own choosing, to be responsible and loving mothers without sacrificing themselves in the process, to be sexually assertive without making themselves vulnerable to male aggression, and to find support in others without becoming overly dependent—hardly experienced themselves as "liberated"; their hard-won autonomy still balanced precariously on the edge of social isolation.

Although *Los pasos de Ana* has been described as depicting a kind of postfeminist "hangover," the dialogue cited above more accurately describes the film's central problematic: if not Sara García and the traditional women's roles found in Mexican cinema, then what? Sistach addresses this question on a diegetic level, both by showing Ana's sometimes satisfying but often conflicted experiences with work, motherhood, and sexuality and by incorporating the quest for alternative forms of representation into the text, particularly through the use of Ana's video diary. At the same time, in her effort to arrive at a language adequate to describe Ana's experiences, Sistach takes her own steps toward the reconstruction of a feminine identity that would no longer depend on patriarchal "mirrors" to reflect and validate its existence.

For Sistach, the project of inscribing women's perspectives into film culture was one which necessarily involved the spectator, particularly the spectator construed as female. In interviews given from the beginning of her career through the 1990s, she spoke of the importance of addressing women and of creating images with which women could identify. In an interview conducted while she was still a student at the Centro de Capacitación Cinematográfica, Sistach explained her earlier rejection of anthropology in favor of film as a career, commenting that:

> me parecía terriblemente frustrante conocer los problemas de las personas, analizar su situación y después escribir un articulito que otros intelectuales leerían. Pensaba que lo importante es que la gente se entere qué problemas son semejantes y que existen formas de organización para luchar y resolverlos.
>
> [it seemed to me terribly frustrating to get to know people's problems, analyze their situation, and then write a little article that other intellectuals would read. I thought it was important for people to learn which problems were shared by others and that there exist forms of organization with which to fight and resolve them.] (In Martín and Pérez Grovas 34)

Film, she hoped, would be the ideal medium with which to replace the observer/observed dichotomy with a more equilateral form of communication that could give people tools with which to solve shared problems; the desired result would be collective action, but the necessary starting point was self-recognition (ibid.). More than a decade later, in a conversation with Patricia Torres that is quoted at length by Fernández Escareño, Sistach talked about the rebirth of "civil society" in the wake of the 1985 earthquake in Mexico City:

> A partir de eso la gente está ansiosa de reconocerse en el cine. Pero el cine que se le ofrece lo único que maneja ahora son los peores instintos, o los peores valores. De repente el simple hecho de ver a alguien tomando un camión en Tacuba, o ver a una chava caminando por la calle vestida de secretaria, ya son elementos de identificación muy buscados, muy necesarios para la gente en este momento de reencontrarse.
>
> [Since then, the public is anxious to recognize itself in the cinema. But the cinema that is available only deals in the worst instincts, or the worst values. Sud-

denly the simple fact of seeing someone catch a bus on Tacuba Avenue or seeing a woman walking down the street dressed as a secretary become sought-after elements of identification, very necessary for people in this moment of self-rediscovery.] (174)

This need for recognizable images is especially felt by women, whose history has long been distorted by a mainstream cinema heavily invested in upholding patriarchal ideology: "el no poderse reconocer en la pantalla es una carencia. Este era el cine que yo quería hacer, un cine con el que la mexicana pudiera identificarse" [not to be able to recognize oneself on the screen is a deficiency. This was the cinema I wanted to make, a cinema with which the Mexican woman could identify] (Arredondo 22).

What kind of film would put this theoretical ideal into practice? In an essay on "Aesthetic and Feminist Theory," Teresa de Lauretis suggests that a film which "addresses its spectator as a woman, regardless of the gender of the viewers" is one that "defines all points of identification (with character, image, camera) as female, feminine, or feminist" (180). Although de Lauretis is referring to the work of Belgian director Chantal Akerman (whose work, as we shall see shortly, was a model for Sistach's *Los pasos de Ana*), her discussion is helpful in approaching Sistach's films as well. For if Sistach's formal strategies are less radical than Akerman's in their break with filmic convention, her films nevertheless work, through character, image, and camera technique, to create a sense of complicity and recognition for the female viewer.

This is perhaps most readily apparent in an earlier Sistach film, *Conozco a las tres*. Made in 1983, *Conozco a las tres* was intended to be a feature but for economic reasons was limited to fifty-three minutes; nevertheless, it can be considered Sistach's professional debut, following her graduation from the CCC in 1980 (Vega, "Entrevista" 4). In this film, the difficulties faced by three women living in Mexico City are ameliorated somewhat by their friendship and mutual support. While the unemployed Julia (Chela Cervantes) awaits the return of her absent spouse, Ana (Irene Martínez), a divorced mother and copy editor, embarks on a romantic adventure with a journalist she meets at a party. The limitations of their relationship are revealed when Ana becomes pregnant and realizes that she cannot count on his emotional support. Meanwhile, María (Laura Ruiz), a sympathetic gym teacher who consoles her two friends through their daily dilemmas, suffers the worst experience of all when she is raped on the street and later undergoes a second violation at the hands of the arrogant and sexist judge in charge of her case.

Although María is somewhat vindicated when she stands up to the judge so forcefully that the perpetrators confess and she wins her case, the conditions that women face are depicted as bleak and almost hopeless, softened only by female solidarity and the ability to laugh in order to survive. During the film's final sequence, during which the three women celebrate Ana's birthday, they dare to ask themselves a penetrating question: "What if things were the other way around?" The film then dramatizes the role-reversal fantasy: Julia's husband alongside other men, knitting baby garments while awaiting the return of his absent wife; Pablo confessing to Ana that he is pregnant and her responding with indignation: "What? Didn't you take precautions?" The absurdity of these scenes, which with the genders reversed would appear "natural," forcefully emphasizes the double standards women still experience even after many years of feminist consciousness-raising and activism.

One of the most intriguing aspects of *Conozco a las tres* ("I know all three") is the "I" whose existence is announced in the title. Who is the "I" who "knows all three"? On one level, the observing I/eye is clearly Sistach herself, a trained anthropologist who tends to describe her films in terms of themes and issues rather than stories or characters. Indeed, the description of *Conozco a las tres* in the Zafra distributor's catalogue recalls the analytical essay-films produced by Cine-Mujer in the 1970s: its objectives are said to be "confrontar a las mujeres con su propia realidad y de analizar la situación femenina, no como una problemática individual sino colectiva" [to confront women with their own reality and to analyze women's situation, not as an individual but rather as a collective issue] (8F). Yet both the title and the film itself suggest a more overtly personal engagement; the "I" becomes a fourth character, constituted not only by the storyteller narrating the "common experiences of our individual histories" (Sistach in Martín and Pérez Grovas 35) but also by the spectator who shares the experience of "knowledge" and recognition.

This "I" is contrasted with the perspective of the journalist Pablo, whose well-intentioned article about rape is met with anger by María; victimized by rapists and then the legal system, she resents having her experience turned into a statistic in the press. Here Sistach explicitly raises the question of representation: which methods and media, which forms of narration, framing, and recording should be deployed in depicting social issues such as rape, single motherhood, unwanted pregnancy, abandonment? Consciously forgoing the distanced perspective that is standard in the social sciences and in journalism, Sistach opts for a more subjective form of communication which valorizes women's perceptions without idealizing their actions or obliterating their contradictions. Ana's affair with Pablo, for example, in spite of its negative dénouement, is portrayed in scenes fraught with a gentle eroticism; as the couple explores the city together, the sensation of rediscovering the everyday environment by means of a new passion is reproduced in the camera's lingering gaze. Similarly, a scene showing Ana's interaction with her young son foreshadows the intimate tenderness with which mother-child relations will be depicted in *Los pasos de Ana*. These and other scenes suggest such close complicity between the women portrayed on screen and the "I" which observes them that empathy is provoked in the spectator as well; as Ayala Blanco writes, "En efecto, yo también ya *Conozco a las tres* mas no como objetos, interrogadas como sujetos por un discurso femenino en plural, solidario y sobre la solidaridad entre mujeres" [In effect, I too know all three, but not as objects, interrogated as subjects by a plural feminine discourse that is in solidarity and about the solidarity between women] (*La condición del cine mexicano* 481).

The Other Gaze

Ayala Blanco's positive response reminds us that the concept of addressing the spectator as a woman does not necessarily exclude the male viewer but rather brings him to a position of complicity with the text—the polar opposite of his role in mainstream cinema, in which the spectator construed as male is placed in a position of identification with the camera, whose gaze at the women on screen is one of mystification and objectification. Without wishing to engage too deeply with the debates that took place in U.S. and European feminist film theory in the 1970s and 1980s over the issue of the gendered gaze, it is worth citing briefly the concept of dominant cinema's three "explicitly male looks or gazes" outlined by Laura Mulvey and summarized as follows by Ann Kaplan:

> There is the look of the camera in the situation being filmed (called the pro-filmic event); while technically neutral, this look is inherently voyeuristic and usually "male" in the sense that a man is generally doing the filming; there is the look of the men within the narrative, which is structured so as to make women objects of their gaze; and finally there is the look of the male spectator which imitates (or is necessarily in the same position as) the first two looks. (30)

In Mexican cinema, this system of gazes is precisely what has been used to contain and neutralize what superficially seem to be powerful representations of women. In the Golden Age films of María Félix, for example, her characters with their strong, independent personalities are gradually tamed: first by the male figures (such as the Pedro Armendáriz character in *Enamorada*) who resist her smoldering looks and ensnare her with their own and secondly by the camera which traps her in close shots whose effect is to reveal the erosion of her will and capitulation to masculine rule. Similarly, in the contemporary cinema to which Sistach attributes an appeal to the "worst instincts and values," action heroines like those played by Rosa Gloria Chagoyán in *Lola la trailera* and *Juana la cubana* are devalued by a filmic apparatus which constantly strips them down to their skimpy lingerie, exposing them to the objectifying gaze of male characters and spectators alike just at the moment when they seem to be most powerful. The question for feminist filmmakers thus becomes how to appropriate the gaze in order to create images of women which are respectful and with which female audiences can identify—in Sistach's words, how to "destroy the false mirror of woman that is, in general, the cinema . . . to re-appropriate our image and in doing so, seek our identity" (in Martín and Pérez Grovas 35).

This is precisely the project upon which Sistach would embark in *Los pasos de Ana,* her first feature. According to Itzia Fernández Escareño (175), Sistach conceived of *Los pasos de Ana* in part as an homage to Chantal Akerman's *Les Rendez-vous d'Anna* (1978), and indeed, the film shares many of the traits that characterize the work of that innovative director: a relaxed rhythm created by the use of long takes in which little apparently happens or in which the entirety of a conversation or action takes place within a single shot; an emphasis on domestic space as the scenario in which large portions of women's lives unfold; and in general, the conviction that the drama in women's stories need not come from the exaggerated plot devices of conventional narrative but rather emerges quietly out of quotidian encounters, daily labors, internal conflicts, disjunctures, and minor epiphanies—the material of everyday life, in short, that prior to feminist filmmaking and directors like Akerman and Sistach had rarely been deemed worthy of representation in the cinema.

Specifically, Sistach rewrites *Les Rendez-vous d'Anna*'s story of a film director traveling through Europe on a promotional tour for her latest movie in a way that better reflects Mexican reality: Sistach's Ana, played by animator, graphic designer, and former Cine-Mujer member Guadalupe Sánchez, is a film school graduate who, far from becoming a feature-film director, is sporadically employed as an assistant director on educational television programs. She is also a divorced mother of two whose primary affective relationship is with her children, unlike the European Anna whose most significant on-screen relationship is with her mother. Like her Belgian counterpart, the Mexican Ana experiences a series of disconcerting rendezvous or encounters with diverse men, but all of these take place in Mexico City, for Ana's is not a journey through a physical landscape but rather a quest for identity and wholeness within the context of her everyday life.

The question of the gaze is key for both Akerman and Sistach and in the films of both is posed in such a way that it cannot be avoided by the spectator. In Akerman's films, particularly her stunning early works like *Je, tu, il, elle* (1974) and *Jeanne Dielman* (1975), wide-angle shots taken with a motionless camera show women going about their business in scenes of such prolonged duration that we cannot help but become aware of the act of watching. Whether we are observing Jeanne Dielman peeling potatoes and making meatloaf or the "I" of *Je, tu, il, elle* eating sugar out of a paper bag and having sex with her lover, all in real or near-real time, our habitual voyeurism— apparently "natural" to the cinema—is exposed and undermined. While perplexing or boring to viewers accustomed to the physical and emotional pyrotechnics of conventional narrative cinema, these films construct, according to de Lauretis, "a picture of female experience, of duration, perception, events, relationships and silences, which feels immediately and unquestionably true" ("Aesthetic and Feminist Theory" 178). As Akerman herself comments,

> I give space to things which were never, almost never, shown in that way, like the daily gestures of a woman. They are the lowest in the hierarchy of film images. . . . But more than the content, it's because of the style. If you choose to show a woman's gestures so precisely, it's because you love them. In some way you recognize those gestures that have always been denied and ignored. (In de Lauretis, "Aesthetic and Feminist Theory" 179)

Akerman's approach is thus not only an aggressive rejection of the methods of dominant cinema but also a loving valorization of women's feelings, perceptions, and experiences.

If *Los pasos de Ana* is less radical in form, it is nevertheless equally concerned with challenging conventional cinema's objectifying gaze. At one point, explaining the purpose of her video camera, Ana philosophizes: "Algunas personas se preguntan cómo deben vivir. Yo me pregunto cómo debo mirar. Bueno, al fin y al cabo es lo mismo" [Some people ask themselves how they should live. I ask myself how I should see. Well, in the end, it's the same thing]. For Ana, who has not been able to realize her dream of becoming a film director and instead lends her skills to other people's commissioned projects, videomaking is a tool for making sense of her own life—not only a record of daily occurrences but also a method of interpretation. Turning her gaze on herself and on others, she begins to replace the dysfunctional mirror of patriarchal cinema with images that reflect her own thoughts, feelings, and questions (Fig. 3.1).

During the scenes that show Ana with her camera, we see her using it in two distinct ways: sometimes to record everyday events, but more often to film scenes which she has deliberately staged, either alone or with one or both of her children. The spontaneous recordings are often annoying to Juan and Paula, who perceive them to be an invasion of their privacy; Juan runs and hides when Ana tries to catch him on tape reading what she says are "lecturas eróticas," and Paula wonders why her mother insists on filming her on the toilet. In these examples, the camera is an instrument of power, with Ana's ownership of the gaze reinforcing a typical parental insensitivity to children's perceptions. But for the most part, the camera is incorporated into the games that Ana invents for her own and her children's amusement and satisfaction. Just before Juan and Paula leave for Tijuana, we watch them participate in a scenario in which Ana asks them on tape what color they are when they are sad (Juan confidently responds "yellow"). In videos she reviews while they are gone, we also see them playing and performing for the camera. Like more conventional home movies and photos, these tapes serve Ana as "consolation" in her children's absence, assuaging the solitude that the company of adults (as we shall see) has only reinforced.

Besides filming her children, Ana also uses the camera to record her own thoughts, creating expressive self-portraits that refer only indirectly to the events we see unfold in the film. In one shot, Ana's face peers through an empty picture frame, which she lifts up to her neck as if to hang herself while speaking the punch line "éste es el rostro de una mujer que tiene miedo de tener miedo" [this is the face of a woman who is afraid of being afraid]. In another clip, Ana leans toward the camera and says "éste es el rostro de una mujer que lo quería todo" [this is the face of a woman who wanted it all]. Although Ana may not in fact have it all, the making of these self-representations helps her at least to accept disappointments; as she comments to the camera while filming in her neighbor's empty apartment, "una también tiene sus soluciones, aunque no toda historia tiene final feliz" [one still has her solutions, even though not all stories have a happy ending]. Again we are brought

FIG. 3.1. "To see . . . to live": Guadalupe Sánchez in *Los pasos de Ana.*

Courtesy Cineteca Nacional.

back to Sistach's basic conviction as a feminist filmmaker: that reappropriating one's own image is the key to empowerment.

This conviction manifests itself in the larger film as well, particularly in the way that Ana herself is filmed within her everyday environment. It is interesting to consider *Los pasos de Ana* in terms of what de Lauretis describes as the "two logics" at work in Akerman's *Jeanne Dielman:* "character and director, image and camera, remain distinct yet interacting and mutually interdependent positions. Call them femininity and feminism, the one is made representable by the critical work of the other; the one is kept at a distance, constructed, 'framed' to be sure, and yet 'respected,' 'loved,' 'given space' by the other" ("Aesthetic and Feminist Theory" 179). This dynamic is different in *Los pasos de Ana,* since Ana is herself a filmmaker immersed in issues of representation. However, there is a similar distance between the logic of the protagonist and that of the filmmaker. Whereas Ana appears to be disillusioned with feminism, confused in her relationships with men and in Sistach's words "muy indefensa, con mucho miedo en varios sentidos" [very defenseless, with a lot of fear in various ways] (Arredondo 23), the same cannot be said of the camera: Sistach's representation of Ana is a lucid and confident portrayal that subtly challenges the conventions of patriarchal cinema, proposing instead other kinds of visual pleasure.

For the spectator whose notion of film feminism adheres to rigid stereotypes,[2] that challenge may not be readily apparent. Ana is conventionally attractive, favoring short skirts and blouses with low necklines, and is often seen in various states of undress. However, in the spare visual economy of the film, nothing is gratuitous and each shot of Ana works primarily to describe a relationship: how she is seen by others, how she sees herself. A few of these shots do seem to reinforce a voyeuristic gaze (for example, Vidal's look at the back of Ana's neck leads us to look at it too, identifying our gaze with that of the on-screen male who sees the woman as an object of desire without her knowledge or consent), but many others work to contest it. For instance, a shot which begins with Ana's bare legs pans up to show the feet of her daughter Paula and ends up focusing on the two of them playing together, the would-be erotic gaze diverted and transformed into a celebration of maternal affection. These and other scenes work to demystify the female image, replacing mainstream cinema's exaggerated emphasis on heterosexual eroticism with a sensuality grounded in motherly tenderness.

In the film's only sex scene, Ana is shown in the immediate aftermath of her hotel tryst with Luis (Enrique Herranz), a young man she picks up at a discotheque. The sexual act itself elided, the film cuts from a shot of the hotel's neon sign to one of Ana's naked body. She (actually a body double) is shown from her thighs to just above her breasts, lying on her side and facing the camera. Her own hand rests on her pubic area, lightly caressing herself. Her pleasure seems entirely self-contained, and it is only when she sits up that we see her companion behind her, smoking a cigarette. In the next shot, she is shown coming home in a taxi, Luis forgotten (his later attempts to re-enter her life will be met with irritation). Filmed differently, such a scene could indeed show Ana as an object of male desire and conquest. But seen by Sistach's empathetic eye, it is during this scene that Ana seems most complete, independent, and sure of herself, as if her very nakedness, far from making her a passive object, were a source of power. She defies the gaze just as she defies Luis's attempt to equate sex with ownership, for she is clearly her body's sole owner.

According to Márgara Millán, the main organizing principle of Sistach's cinema is *goce*—pleasure or enjoyment (5). In her films is an almost tactile engagement with spaces and objects as well as with people; her camera "gusta de recorrer el espacio, retratar los objetos, sostenerse en los colores como parte del contenido emotivo" [likes to move through space, describe objects, support itself in colors as part of the emotional content] (5), creating "un retrato fiel de lo cotidiano" [a faithful portrait of quotidian reality] (8). Millán breaks *Los pasos de Ana* into three types of shots: the long sequence shots such as the bookstore dialogue between Ana and Carlos; the close shots of the bodies of Ana and her children, linked to the "quotidian time" of the domestic sphere, which is qualitatively different than that of the streets or the workplace; and the shots belonging to the video within the film, "el ojo de Ana viendo (se)" [Ana's eye seeing (herself)] (Millán 8).

The second and third types of shots are particularly important, for both serve to conspicuously constitute the woman as subject: subject of her own desires in the first instance and of the filmic gaze in the second. But even the more neutral sequence shots contain a palpable element of *goce* with respect to the urban environment, which the long takes and camera movement seem to emphasize. The precisely delineated locations of each scene (Ana's apartment near the Chapultepec metro station, the Teatro de Ulises in the downtown historic district) convey clear meanings for many who will see the film in Mexico City, and although not as pronounced as in the films of María Novaro (see Chapter 6), there is an appreciation of the city as part of the subjective identity of its inhabitants, what Millán refers to as "una cierta intelectualización del espacio urbano como lúdico" [a certain intellectualization of urban space as ludic] (14).

These formal strategies, particularly of linking pleasure to a feminine/maternal domestic space with its own rhythms and proportions, coincide with Sistach's stated definition of feminism, which she contrasts with the moral puritanism of certain other feminists: "Me encantan los hombres y eso no me impide que piense que tiene que haber otra mirada sobre la vida y que el feminismo es esa otra mirada sobre las mujeres, los ancianos, los niños, incluso sobre los papeles de los hombres" [I'm delighted by men, and that doesn't stop me from thinking that there has to be another way of looking at life and that feminism is that other way of looking at women, at older people, at children, and also at the roles of men] (Vega, "Entrevista" 6). It is this *otra mirada* or other gaze, as much as the story Sistach tells or the thematic concerns she addresses, that creates in *Los pasos de Ana* a "picture of female experience" which "feels immediately and unquestionably true" (de Lauretis, "Aesthetic and Feminist Theory" 178).

The Opposite of Sara García

The emotional authenticity of the film is also the result of its autobiographical content, although Sistach describes it as autobiographical in terms of its emotions rather than the events it depicts. For Sistach, *Los pasos de Ana* was not about herself or any other specific woman but rather spoke to the common experiences of a generation: "Fuimos la generación que creímos en las izquierdas, en el feminismo, en muchas cosas que al final de los ochenta se vienen abajo. Y a mí, como a muchos, me quedó una sensación de soledad, de tener que enfrentar la vida más crudamente" [We were the generation that believed in the leftist movements, in feminism, in many things that went down the drain at the end of the 1980s. I, like many others, was left with a feeling of loneliness, of having to face life more harshly] (Vega, "Entrevista" 5). Yet far from being a sociological report, *Los pasos de Ana* seeks to create the same kind of complicity that Ayala Blanco found in *Conozco a las tres;* immersed in her emotional universe, the viewer, too, follows Ana's footsteps.

The fundamental axes around which *Los pasos de Ana* revolves are not so much narrative as thematic: motherhood, work, sexuality, and Ana's struggle for interpretive power as an artist and as a woman. The importance of motherhood as a source of both strength and conflict is apparent from the opening scene, a dream sequence in which Ana and her daughter appear submerged in water up to their necks, with Ana speaking in a voice that is slowed down and distorted: "De veras que da miedo, es como morirse, tú me lo decías, ¿verdad?" [It's really frightening, it's like dying, you've told me, right?]. Waking suddenly, Ana gets up and looks out the window; then, in reverse shot from outside the apartment, she is shown moving from room to room in her nightgown, sleep made impossible by the tensions evoked by the nightmare. In the next scene, Juan wakes up and turns off the lights that Ana turned on in her anxiety, suggesting familiarity with his mother's uneasy behavior. But Ana's fear of loss in relation to her children, expressed in these first moments of the film and apparently justified later on when her ex-husband claims custody of Juan and both children leave for summer vacation in Tijuana, is not only a psychological phenomenon; rather, it is the product of the contradictions of a culture which idealizes motherhood and yet makes it impossible for many mothers to live up to the ideal.

The simultaneous inventive spontaneity and material limitations of Ana's mothering are revealed early in the film. The morning after the nightmare, Ana and the children are playing in the bedroom as they prepare for the day ahead. On the street below, a vendor passes by selling balloons, and Ana buys one for Paula, sending the money down in a basket tied to a string, although not before arguing over the price—an action Ana will repeat several times during the film, indicative of her own financial straits if inconsiderate of the lower economic level of those with whom she attempts to bargain (a taxi driver and her housekeeper). Although she buys the balloon in spite of the price increase, it doesn't fit through the window frame, and Paula decides to let it fly away, a decision for which Ana will reprimand her. Ana's good intentions thus end, at least temporarily, in conflict and dissatisfaction.

This atmosphere of ludic play and maternal indulgence tempered by material constraint is contrasted in the next scene with the more conventional patriarchal model offered by the children's father, Lalo (José Roberto Hill), who has come from Tijuana to pick them up for the summer and who announces that he wants Juan to live with him during the year as well. Lalo clearly commands economic resources superior to Ana's, and his authority is further reinforced by the news that he has remarried, implicitly creating a secure family environment in contrast to Ana's perpetual instability. In arguing for custody of Juan, Lalo wields a discourse of "reason" that Ana cannot counter; her emotional attachment to her son holds little weight, and all she can do is attempt to cajole Juan to decide in her favor, an effort that ultimately fails. When Juan decides to move in with his father, Ana can only accept his decision with sad resignation.

In the scenes that follow, we see how the circumstances of Ana's life come into conflict with her obligations and desires as a mother. Because she has spent her savings on her video camera, she is behind in her rent and unable to meet her expenses. So when Carlos (David Beuchot) calls to offer her a job as assistant director on a television program, she expresses relief at finally having a source of income. For her children, however, Ana's employment means less time for them with their mother. As Ana showers and dresses to go out with Carlos and his boyfriend, Rafael, Juan complains that with her new job, they won't see her now for two months. Later, in a scene which we witness through the lens of Ana's camera, Paula, playing house with her stuffed toys, asks Ana to babysit them, explaining that she doesn't have anyone to leave them with. When Ana asks why, Paula explains that she is going to "make a film." In the scene that follows, in the supermarket where Ana in spite of her financial situation fills her cart with items for the children's vacation, Paula announces that she, too, wants to live with her father. Ana's frustration is palpable; for at the same time as she experiences discrimination in the workplace for being a mother, her effort to provide for her family has been interpreted by her children as abandonment.

Once Paula and Juan are gone, Ana consoles herself in their absence by watching her videotapes and apparently taking to heart Carlos's advice that "no hay nada peor en estos tiempos que el melodrama para sobrevivir" [there's nothing worse in these times than melodrama to survive]. Unlike the Sara García of *Cuando los hijos se van,* who remains essentially and exclusively a mother even when the children leave home, Ana throws herself into her work with visible enthusiasm and muddles her way through ambiguous encounters with men, including her neighbor Andrés (Andrés Fonseca) and Vidal, the director of the documentary on which she is working (Emilio Echeverría). Although her maternal role is central, it does not define the totality of Ana's existence. In a 1996 interview with Isabel Arredondo, Sistach elaborated on the comparison with García made by Carlos within the film:

Ana y Sara García son fundamentalmente madres. . . . Sin embargo, las separan los principios: Ana se divorcia, rompe la seguridad familiar, trabaja, tiene relaciones sexuales con varios hombres. En todo lo que podía creer Sara García, es en lo que no puede creer Ana.

[Ana and Sara García are fundamentally mothers. . . . However, they are separated by principles: Ana is divorced, breaks with the security of the family, works, has sexual relations with various men. Everything that Sara García believes in, that is what Ana can't believe in.] (23)

Sistach's "modernized" image of the mother is by no means a didactic construct yet is nevertheless one of the film's major revisions of Mexican film's feminine archetypes:

En el cine mexicano lo esencial es la madre abnegada y lo opuesto es la prostituta. Ana ejerece los dos papeles: tiene una sexualidad obvia y liberada y, por otro lado, es una mujer que ama tiernamente a sus hijos. Entonces, en ese sentido sí [Ana y Sara García] son los polos más opuestos. [In Mexican cinema the essential is the self-denying mother and the opposite is the prostitute. Ana plays both roles: she has an obvious and liberated sexuality, and on the other hand, she is a mother who tenderly loves her children. So, in this sense, (Ana and Sara García) are the most opposite poles.] (ibid.)

What the film conveys is that Ana is not a lesser or worse mother than the characters represented by García. In fact, the affection shown by her children, culminating in Juan's decision to come back to his mother, suggests that Ana's home is at least as healthy as any more conventional family environment. Nor is the maternal role itself denigrated or minimized. Instead, the classic "madre llena de virtudes y lágrimas" [mother full of virtues and tears] described by Bracho, which appeals to "los sentimientos supuestamente más nobles" of the "mentalidad machista" [the supposedly most noble feelings of the macho mentality] (419), is replaced by an image of the mother who fulfills that role without being subsumed by it, an image with which working women of the 1980s—beginning with Sistach herself—can more readily identify.

Dissonant Encounters

The issues surrounding motherhood in *Los pasos de Ana* were not limited to the film itself but were also raised during production, since both Sistach and Guadalupe Sánchez were working mothers. While Sánchez, with two small children, reportedly struggled to balance both roles, Sistach came up with a unusual solution, casting her real-life children, Pía Buil Sistach and Valdiri Durand Sistach, as Paula and Juan. The children's participation in *Los pasos de Ana*, along with the collaboration of Sistach's husband, José Buil, as screenwriter and editor, suggests a unique model for the integration of filmmaking with motherhood; for if Ana's television work signifies for the children her absence from the home, Sistach's film (like Ana's home videos) is a family project.[3] However, recognizing the difficulties faced not only by herself but by other women raising children while working in film, Sistach stated that one of her dreams would be to have a day-care facility attached to the set of any film production (Vega, "Entrevista" 4).

Such a woman-friendly film set imagined by Sistach is the polar opposite of the working environment depicted in *Los pasos de Ana,* ruled by Vidal. Ana's teacher from six years earlier, Vidal is an alcoholic who clearly considers his drinking to be part of his professional persona and who expects his crew to tolerate his moods and cater to his needs. He only vaguely recognizes Ana when she arrives for her job interview, then dismissively remarks that by now she must be married with children. When Ana objects to the question, Vidal brusquely explains that he will not tolerate "inefficiency," by which he means a mother missing work to care for a sick child or attend a meeting at school. Visibly angered, Ana keeps calm, responding that yes, she has two children but has never had a problem with her work for that reason. The tension subsides with the entrance of Carlos, but before Ana leaves, Vidal again warns her about "pretexts," to which she only answers, "When do I start?"

It is not surprising that Ana takes Vidal's patronizing attitude in stride; after all, it is only one example of the *machismo* that she encounters every day, not only at work but also in her personal life. Whereas *Conozco a las tres* emphasized the bonds that exist among women within an oppressive patriarchal context, Ana explores male-female relationships and in particular the difficulties that a divorced or single woman encounters when seeking to both preserve her independence and satisfy her need for companionship and physical affection. The novelty of portraying a nonmonogamous woman's sexuality honestly is illustrated in an anecdote from the film's production; according to Sistach, her producers at Canario Rojo tried to pressure her into calling the film "Confesiones de una mujer sola" [Confessions of a woman alone], an idea she rejected. When her crew subsequently took to calling it "Confesiones de una mujer fácil" [Confessions of an easy woman], she shrugged off the joke, considering it an expression of an "ideology that we all have inside us and that is very hard to overcome" (Fernández Escareño 173). Yet for Sistach, Ana's sexual dilemmas represented a problem shared by many women: "resolver tu vida amorosa . . . tu vida sexual en un país tan machista como éste cuando estás sola, es una cosa que le pasa a millones de mujeres en este país" [to resolve your romantic life . . . your sex life in a country as *machista* as this one when you're alone, is something that happens to millions of women in this country] (Fernández Escareño 174). Ana's responses to this situation are by no means idealized and in fact often seem ingenuous or careless, ringing true as the experiences of a young middle-class woman whose feminism, the political stance of a self-confident university student, proves more difficult to apply in a world whose dominant values have yet to change.

Ana, in describing her own worldview, repeatedly characterizes herself as a romantic. She chastises Carlos for being so "conventional" (the quality she seems to abhor most) as to live with someone whom he doesn't love for the sake of security, and in contrast, expresses envy of the doomed, one-sided passion found in writer Gilberto Owen's published letters to actress and dance promoter Clementina Otero, the text Carlos buys her to read in preparation for the television documentary on Owen's life on which she and he will work together and in which Otero will appear.[4] Captivated by the intensity of Owen's words, Ana videotapes herself reading the letters aloud in the bathroom and comments, "Me gustaría que me la hubieran escrito a mí" [I wish they had been written to me]. However, her professed "romanticism" never leads Ana to relinquish the independence she has won (after eight years of a difficult marriage) in order to pursue the impossible romantic ideals promoted by her culture. When Luis flirts with her at a discotheque, she willingly goes with him to a hotel for a one-night stand. However, she gives him a false name, tells him nothing about herself, and leaves without having arranged for future contact. Returning home to her sleeping children, it is clear that the impulse motivating her liaison with Luis was purely sensory, for her emotional needs are already met through the intense bond with her family.

However, by engaging in casual sex, Ana unwittingly exposes herself to the values of a patriarchal society which Luis personifies to a pathological extreme. Running into her by chance at the supermarket, Luis aggressively solicits her phone number and demands that they meet again. Ana tells him that she is too busy, that she doesn't have a phone—a lie that is loyally backed up by her son—and that since she's about to move, he can't have her address, either. When he refuses to take the hint, she escapes with the children into a taxi that she can't actually afford. A short time later, he calls her house, having somewhat improbably obtained the number from Carlos, and confronts her about having lied to him. Later on, he even waits for her in the stairwell of her apartment, demanding to be allowed in the door and into her life solely on the grounds of their having slept together once. Ana shoves him out of the way and bolts the door, threatening to call the police while at the same time reprimanding herself for getting involved with strangers. Although Luis leaves and does not reappear in the film, the threat of violence he represents calls Ana's freedom into question: although she reserves the right to determine the nature of her relationships with men, her power is limited, for such interactions are clearly not without risk.

Just prior to being ambushed in the hallway by Luis, Ana experiences another kind of confrontation with patriarchal values in an uncomfortable interaction with Vidal. Up to that point, their relationship has been tense due to his heavy drinking and authoritarian demeanor in the workplace—for example, humiliating Ana in front of the crew when she is late for work. This particular night, however, he drives her home from the shooting location and before letting her out of the van, confesses his attraction to her. They kiss, with Ana remarking that it is the first time she's been kissed by a teacher and giggling at the absurd situation that, for an instant, seems to reverse the power dynamics between them. However, as they begin to negotiate spending the night together, Vidal suddenly pulls away, explaining that he can't "break his promise." Caught off guard by such "conventional" reasoning, Ana leaves the van and runs into her building. The next day on the set, the source of Vidal's belated hesitation becomes clear when he introduces his very pregnant wife to Ana and Clementina, who has come to be interviewed for the program. As if to underscore Vidal's *machista* hypocrisy, the wife mentions to Clementina that at one time she, too, wanted to be an actress but that "la vida da muchas vueltas" [life takes many twists and turns]—the implication being that Vidal's career as a filmmaker depends on his having the support of a full-time wife and mother.

Given the outcomes of her flirtations with Luis and Vidal, frightening in the one instance and humiliating in the other, the only possible male partner remaining for Ana (within the limited social universe of the film) is Andrés, her mild-mannered, kind, and unthreatening (according to Viñas, "asexual") neighbor. A housepainter who resides only temporarily in the buildings in which he works, Andrés's declared abhorrence of owning property clearly applies to ties of any kind, in contrast to the proprietary Luis or the family men Vidal and Lalo. Andrés is portrayed as a kind of guardian angel watching over Ana and her family from a distance: we see him observing her from his window that faces her side of the building, sheltering Ana's cat, letting Ana shower at his apartment when the gas runs out in hers, and even buying her a new tank when he knows that she is too busy to do so herself. Yet, at least in the beginning, Andrés is made the target of all of the fear with which Ana fails to respond to more genuinely threatening men like Luis. Not knowing that he has moved into her building, Ana initially accuses Andrés of following her home.

Later, exploding with the rage provoked by Vidal's contradictory behavior and Luis's violent ambush, she orders him out of her apartment. In both scenes she quickly reconsiders and apologizes, but it is only later that she thinks to value his undemanding affection, and by then it is too late.

Following her final harrowing encounter with Luis, Ana spends the evening in Andrés's apartment, drinking mescal and singing along with the radio. The situation is purely platonic; by the time Andrés confesses his desire to touch her, Ana is sound asleep. The next day, she leaves hurriedly for work, ignoring Andrés when he calls out after her that he has something to tell her. At work, several events ensue that put the previous day's confusing encounters into perspective: the filming comes to an end, signifying the end of Ana's contact with Vidal; Vidal apologizes to Ana for his previous night's inappropriate behavior, and they part as mutually respectful colleagues; and Carlos arrives late and distraught, announcing that he has been abandoned by Rafael. No longer the pragmatic cynic, Carlos confesses that he did not know what he felt until it was too late and that now he does not know what to do. Fearing the same fate, Ana rushes back to her apartment building in search of Andrés, but he is gone, his apartment already empty. Ana is left with her video camera, with which she films the empty walls, because "al fin y al cabo, cada quien se consuela como puede" [after all, each of us consoles herself however she can].

Each of Ana's failed encounters with men is important to the film as a plot event and in illustrating the dilemmas faced by a heterosexual woman unwilling to give up the companionship and affection of men yet wary of the dangers that exist in a patriarchal society in which single women are seen as both "alone" and "easy," vulnerable to emotional manipulation and exploitation. As Sistach observes, "romper cierto tipo de esquemas sin tener realmente creados otros te deja muy indefenso" [to break out of certain schema without having really created others leaves you very defenseless] (Arredondo 23). But it is important to emphasize that, unlike relations in a conventional melodrama, Ana's relationships with actual or potential lovers are not the center of the story, much less the factor defining Ana's very existence as a woman. Apart from a certain level of discomfort, there is little at stake in the success or failure of Ana's rendezvous. On the contrary, it could be said that her identity emerges in part out of how she responds to the different situations, with the emphasis being on self-knowledge rather than on outcome.

Before leaving the subject of Ana's relationships with men, it is worth noting that Ana seems to have little or no interaction with women other than Clementina Otero. Unlike Novaro's Lola, for instance, her mother does not play a visible role in her life; her small family unit is entirely self-contained. (Her housekeeper, Mari, may be something of a mother substitute, since she is described as having known Ana forever and continues working even when Ana cannot pay her; nevertheless, she remains in the background and is never seen engaging in conversation with Ana.) Her colleagues at work are all male, and her only friend seems to be Carlos, who as a gay man does play a "girl-friend" role but whose advice is laden with ironic distance rather than the intimate solidarity shared by the protagonists of *Conozco a las tres*. (He is also responsible, if only indirectly, for her disastrous involvement with Luis, having given him Ana's name and phone number.)

A counterweight to the stifling *machismo* of characters such as Lalo, Vidal, and Luis, Carlos's role is also indicative of the increasing visibility and acceptance of homosexuality in the cinema of the 1980s; a particularly memorable sequence juxtaposes him distractedly caressing Rafael's hair while talking on the telephone to Ana, who is petting her cat. Ana's self-described solitude, emphasized by scenes such as this one, seems to be related to her isolation from other women, yet it is only the failure of her relationships with men and the persistent fear of losing her children that are actually depicted or alluded to on screen. The collectivity suggested by Sistach's extratextual remarks that Ana represents many women is strangely absent from the film itself: "Existen muchas Anas; a lo mejor son Anas secretarias o Anas proletarias, pero el hecho de tener que ganarse la vida en un mundo de hombre y tener que criar a tus hijos es cotidianísimo" [Many Anas exist; they are probably secretary Anas or proletarian Anas, but the fact of having to earn a living in a man's world and to raise your children is extremely quotidian] (Arredondo 22).

Contemporáneos

While written accounts of the film seem to agree that its main themes are motherhood, sexuality, and work (or cinema as a profession), they generally collapse the question of Ana's video diary with that of her work as assistant director on the educational television program about Gilberto Owen. No text that I have seen does more than mention the latter, even though Ana's investigation of Owen's life and the historical context of his work occupies much of the film. In the course of her research, Ana visits the Teatro de Ulises, where Owen and Clementina Otero first met, considered by Vidal to be the birthplace of the modern theater in Mexico but that is now in the abandoned and decrepit state typical of many colonial buildings in downtown Mexico City and is inhabited by genial squatters who are indifferent to the building's history. She also meets Clementina Otero, now aged and playing herself in the film, who shares her photographs and memories with Ana and with the public.

The television program, which Carlos calls "uno de esos programas cultos cultos que nadie ve" [one of those really cultured programs that no one watches], is in fact a re-elaboration of a real-life project on Owen that Sistach and Buil had directed while working for public television during the mid-1980s, an episode of the series *Los libros tienen la palabra* titled "Lo recuerdo olvidado, 1904–1952" (Fernández Escareño 171). Although the program's content is seemingly peripheral to Ana's story, the choice of subjects is an interesting one, for the cultural vanguard of the 1920s to which Owen belonged and which also included better-known figures such as Xavier Villaurrutia, Salvador Novo, and Carlos Pellicer bears a certain resemblance to the young filmmakers of Ana's/Sistach's generation; as the old models of national identity collapsed around them, both groups fervently hoped to "cambiar sus esquemas":

> Representan todos ellos la renovación, la posible modernidad de un espacio cultural (México) que tiene que ajustar su reloj local al reloj de la plaza universal.
> [All of them represent renovation, the possible modernity of a cultural space (Mexico) that has to adjust its local clock to the clock in the universal plaza.]
> (Coronado 11)

As Juan Coronado writes in his introduction to Owen's *De la poesía a la prosa en el mismo viaje,* the "Contemporáneos," as they were known, rejected the nationalist and folkloric aesthetics that effervesced in the wake of the Revolution, instead defending a universalist position that was both innovative in its breaking down of generic boundaries and elitist in its indifference to popular values, traditions, and sensibilities (11–12). By the 1980s, this avant-garde of the 1920s had become a respected part of national cultural history, and the unending debate over nationalism versus universalism was no longer cast in the same terms. Yet Sistach's appropriation of the European director Akerman as a means of calling into question the limited gender constructs of national cinema in some ways resembles the Contemporáneos' project insofar as cultural tendencies arising outside Mexico (in this case, feminist avant-garde cinema) are embraced as tools that can be used for national cultural renovation.

Nevertheless, the film's use of the Owen/Otero documentary is puzzling, even though their unconventional relationship dovetails nicely with the film's attempt to rethink male/female relations outside the boundaries of conventional romance. Otero appears simply as a respected elder, not as a feminist heroine or a diva with a well-known image inviting of revisionist deconstruction. It is possible that some spectators would have more than cursory prior knowledge of Owen and Otero and would therefore bring a richer intertextual interpretation to the viewing experience; yet the lack of readily available information about them, the fact that Sistach and Buil's original documentary was "Lo recuerdo olvidado" (The forgotten memory), that Coronado describes Owen as an "unknown" whose work circulated in limited editions and whose prestige was "construido por una élite intelectual que seguía su producción con fervor" [constructed by an intellectual elite who followed his production with fervor] (11), that Ana knows nothing about Otero or Owen before being hired by Vidal, and that no interviewer or critic writing about the film refers to the subject in any way all lead me to believe that the topic had little resonance for the majority of Mexican spectators.

Is *Los pasos de Ana* reverent toward, critical of, or in dialogue with the Contemporáneos and the Mexican literary tradition to which they belong? Instead of a response, the film offers only the following intriguing dialogue: Vidal, bringing Clementina to the present-day Teatro de Ulises for the first time, comments that "este país no tiene memoria, ¿verdad?" [this country has no memory, you know?], to which she replies, "Pues sí . . . pero esto nos salva, ¿no crees?" [True . . . but that's what saves us, don't you think?].

From "Sandwiches and Soda Pop" to the Mainstream

With antecedents in the Mexican women's movement of the 1970s, the feminist filmmaking it produced (including Sistach's own early efforts), and an international feminist artistic/cinematic avant-garde producing diverse "answers" to Silvia Bovenschen's provocative question, "Is there a feminine aesthetic?"[5] *Los pasos de Ana* was certainly an important event in Mexican film history. Yet unlike Busi Cortés's *El secreto de Romelia,* the other woman-directed feature to go into production during the breakthrough year 1988, Sistach's film received little attention, with good reason—it did not even exist as a film until 1991. As Sistach explains it, she began to shoot the film in 16mm with the intention of showing it in universities and other noncommercial cultural circuits. She developed the script in Cuba under the tutelage of Gabriel García Márquez and later at the Sundance Institute but received no monetary support for the film itself. Its production was completely independent, that is, without backing from either commercial producers or government agencies; Sistach received a loan from a businesswoman friend and donations of film from other friends; she borrowed equipment and put things together as best she could (Vega, "Entrevista" 6; Arredondo 18). Typical of conditions faced by filmmakers in the 1980s, Sistach called her mode of production "cine hecho de tortas y 'Chaparritas,'" [film made of sandwiches and soda pop], since that was what she fed her cast and crew, their only compensation (Vega, "Entrevista" 4). Postproduction on the film was done in video, but at that point, there was no money for its transfer back to film, and in 1989 (while *El secreto de Romelia* was being released and *Lola* and *Intimidad* completed), it circulated only privately in the video version.

Two years after its completion, *Los pasos de Ana* was invited to the Berlin Film Festival, at which point IMCINE financed its transfer from video to 35mm by purchasing partial exhibition rights. The film was then shown in the annual Muestra de Cine Mexicano en Guadalajara in March 1991 but inexplicably not exhibited commercially until 1993—a year after the successful release of Sistach's second feature, *Anoche soñé contigo.* In spring 1991, José María Espinasa wrote in *Nitrato de Plata:*

> Esta película está en camino de ser ejemplarmente sacrificada. . . . Después de la buena recepción en Alemania y el éxito de su exhibición en Guadalajara, se podía esperar que, si no se hacía el camino ideal: terminar la producción en 16mm y ampliar a 35mm, por lo menos se exhibiera tal como estaba. Pero *Los pasos de Ana* no existe para el IMCINE.
>
> [This film is on the way to being exemplarly sacrificed. . . . After the good reception in Germany and the success of its exhibition in Guadalajara, one might have hoped that, if the ideal thing—finishing the production in 16mm and blowing it up to 35mm—could not be done, it would at least be exhibited the way it was. But *Los pasos de Ana* does not exist for IMCINE.]

When the film was finally released, says Sistach, it did poorly, never reaching its intended audience. Not all of the blame lay with IMCINE, for by the 1990s, the *cine-club* circuit that had flourished in the 1960s and 1970s (the era of the Grupo Nuevo Cine and the Echeverría reforms) had largely disappeared. The only alternative was conventional movie-theater distribution, a circuit in which low-budget films like *Los pasos de Ana,* slow-paced and devoid of action compared to the average mainstream production, generally have a harder time competing. What Moisés Viñas described in his *Dicine* review as "el singular alejamiento cálido de sus imágenes, su cotidianidad a la vez extraña y sugestiva, y la sensual sinceridad con que observa y valora los más sencillos acontecimientos de una vida común" [the singular warm remoteness of its images, its quotidian quality that is at once strange and suggestive, and the sensual sincerity with which it observes and values the simplest events of an ordinary life] (36) were not easily marketable qualities, and *Los pasos de Ana* vanished quickly from Mexican screens.

Since *Los pasos de Ana*, however, Sistach's filmic output has been relatively prolific as well as varied in terms of style, content, and approach. *Los pasos de Ana*, it could be argued, was the last of Sistach's films to attempt a feminist mode of address; certainly, *Anoche soñé contigo* (1991) was a dramatic departure for a director whose stated commitment up to that point had been to demystify the images of women presented by mainstream cinema. The story of an adolescent boy's sexual awakening, the film was disconcerting to followers of Sistach's earlier work, given not only its focus on a male protagonist (Toto, played by Martín Altomaro) but also its reproduction of the latter's objectifying gaze vis-à-vis the object of his erotic longing, an older cousin named Azucena (Leticia Perdigón). Azucena, like so many other screen-fantasy females, is most often framed in poses that show off her body and sexy underwear. When she finally acquiesces to Toto's desire, she does so with defiance and contempt; yet even so, she is quickly transformed into a memory and absorbed into the mythology of male sexual initiation by an experienced older woman, her own motives and desires remaining a mystery.

In discussing the film, Sistach spoke enthusiastically to the press about exploring the mysterious world of the adolescent boy, a curiosity no doubt motivated by the experience of her own son Valdiri's adolescence; yet the fact that a teenage male perspective already informs much of Mexican and world cinema is perhaps what renders *Anoche soñé contigo* both conventional and even, in the opinion of Susana López Aranda, "misogynist": "El despertar sexual de un adolescente es el pretexto para incurrir en una visión tan vulgar y alburesca, tan cosificadora de la mujer y banalizadora, como la de las películas del Güero Castro" [The sexual awakening of an adolescent is the pretext for incurring into a vision as vulgar and mocking, as objectifying of women and as banalizing as the films of (Víctor) "El Güero" Castro]("VII Muestra" 3–4)— Castro being the director of lowbrow sex comedies like *Un macho en el reformatorio de señoritas* (1988) and *La fichera más rápida del oeste* (1991). Critical opinion notwithstanding, *Anoche soñé contigo*, produced and distributed by Clasa Films Mundiales, received widespread publicity and exhibition, reaching such commercial outlets as the U.S. Spanish-language television channel Univisión.

In 1995, Sistach again changed directions, codirecting *La línea paterna* with José Buil (who also wrote *Anoche soñé contigo*). A documentary compiled from footage shot by Buil's grandfather, *La línea paterna* is a decidedly non-commercial effort financed by grants and government cultural institutions. It is also a beautiful work of personal history, one which pays homage to Buil's Spanish roots, to provincial life in 1920s and 1930s Veracruz, to national history, to early cinema, and even to the directors' own relationship, when the two of them travel to the late grandfather's home in search of the historic footage. A home movie made by master artisans, *La línea paterna* represents a model of filmmaking that is neither overtly feminist nor, despite its title, particularly patriarchal; though primarily Buil's project, it also continues Sistach's effort to reinvent the family not as ideological institution but as a source of strength and even, at times, of wonder.

By the end of the 1990s, Sistach's place as a commercial director seemed secure, even though not all of her projects came to fruition. In 1996, she was slated to direct the first IMCINE/Televicine coproduction, *Cilantro y perejil*, but was forced to back out for health reasons. The film was directed by Rafael Montero. Next she was hired to direct a Televisa soap opera titled *La jaula de oro*. However, when she received news of IMCINE's acceptance of her next film project, she abandoned the *telenovela*. *El cometa* (1998), a likable if light feature set in northern Mexico during the early years of the Revolution, premiered in Mexico City movie theaters in January 1999 to wide media coverage and positive reviews. Following *Ana*'s model of revisiting one's previous footage in a new context, *El cometa* drew on *La línea paterna*'s fascination with early silent film to create an intelligent narrative about cinema's beginnings in Mexico. By featuring a French and a Spanish actor in major roles, it simultaneously honored Sistach's and Buil's heritages (Sistach's parents were French and Spanish) and their European coproducers. And by using the Revolution as background while emphasizing the "universal" romance of the movies, it told a story that, rather like Arau's *Como agua para chocolate,* seemed likely to please both Mexican and international audiences.

In these films of the 1990s, only traces remain of Sistach's earlier feminist project; one would be hard-pressed to recognize the film student of 1980 who asserted that "tendremos que aprender a vernos con una mirada descodificadora, que descubra y recorra toda una historia de las mujeres y en particular de las más explotadas" [we must learn to look at ourselves with a decodifying gaze that will discover and travel through all of a history of women and in particular of those who are most exploited] (in Martín and Pérez Grovas 35). Nevertheless, her career as a filmmaker stands as testimony to the fundamental changes that she herself helped bring about with films like *Conozco a las tres* and *Los pasos de Ana* that, to again cite de Lauretis, "engaged in the project of transforming vision by inventing the forms and processes of representation of a social subject, women, who until now has been all but unrepresentable" (de Lauretis, "Aesthetic and Feminist Theory" 192). In the work of directors like Sistach, women could finally begin to recognize themselves in the Mexican cinema.

As a woman filmmaker I am interested in presenting the vision, the way of being, feeling, and acting of the women of my era . . .

Busi Cortés[1]

CHAPTER 4

Busi Cortés

Telling *Romelia*'s Secrets

The career of Busi Cortés, like that of Marisa Sistach, shows a certain continuity with the recent past, even as it represents a new era for women filmmakers in Mexico. Born in 1950, Cortés began her career as a journalist in the 1970s, going on to work in educational television and finally to study filmmaking at the Centro de Capacitación Cinematográfica. Her 1988 debut feature, *El secreto de Romelia,* was also the CCC's first feature production. As a director, Cortés stood out as an ardent advocate of independent and university-based cinema. In the press, she boldly attacked not only the flaws in national production and distribution mechanisms but also the notion—almost masochistically insisted upon by Mexican critics—that Mexican cinema was inferior or in a state of stagnation. In an interview following the release of her 1991 feature *Serpientes y escaleras,* she commented on what by then was being called the "new Mexican cinema":

> Nuestro cine no ha cambiado ni en estilo ni en contenidos. La renovación no está en eso sino en la nueva actitud que los realizadores tenemos hacia el cine; es decir, ahora se hace cine con pasión; pasión proveniente del ímpetu de los egresados de las escuelas de cine, los que hemos aprendido a hacer películas con pocos recursos, método que aplicamos al cine industrial.

[Our cinema has not changed in either style or content. The renovation is not in (those aspects) but rather in the new attitude that we directors have toward the cinema; that is to say, cinema is now made with passion; passion emerging from the impetus of the film school graduates, those of us who have learned to make films with few resources, a method which we apply to the industrial cinema.] (Torralba)

In spite of her film school background, Cortés's work is in many ways reminiscent of Matilde Landeta's: for like Landeta, Cortés's self-described passion is not only for the cinema but for an *otro cine* that includes women as complex beings, not simply romantic or tragic icons. Her use of literary sources and her depiction of nationally resonant historical periods as contexts for stories with women at their center invite some of the same questions about revision and transformation that I addressed to Landeta's work in Chapter 1. In particular, her adaptation of Rosario Castellanos's 1964 short story "El viudo Román" (published in English as "The Widower Román") in *El secreto de Romelia* is a bold act of revision that, much like Landeta's *La negra Angustias,* replaces a bleak, disturbing tale with a narrative that begins to imagine the possibility of healing and redemption. Central to this imagining is the film's attempt to assess the nation's history, including the recent past of the 1960s student movement and its failure or dissipation, from a feminist perspective—a perspective which pointedly challenges the linkage between the nation-state and the ideology of *machismo* and its ritualized reenactment in, on, and through the bodies of women.

"The Widower Román": The "Inevitability" of La Malinche

The difference between Castellanos's short story and Cortés's film might superficially be detected in the changed title: "El viudo Román" refers to the vindictive don Carlos Román, who concocts an elaborate scheme to avenge himself on the family of his first wife's lover, Rafael, while *El secreto de Romelia* shifts the emphasis to Romelia, Rafael's young sister who becomes the semi-innocent victim of Román's vengeance (Fig. 4.1). Yet as a feminist writer, Castellanos was deeply concerned with the situation of Mexican women of diverse classes and backgrounds; her text, although centered on the widower, uses his remarriage as a way to examine the ways that women's lives are governed and circumscribed by social customs and values, particularly those regarding sexuality. What distinguishes her story more deeply from that told by the film is its profound pessimism, manifested in its almost literal illustration

F I G. 4.1. Romelia's return: Arcelia Ramírez in *El secreto de Romelia.*
Courtesy Cineteca Nacional.

of the thesis expressed by Jean Franco in *Plotting Women* as "the impossibility of Antigone and the inevitability of La Malinche" (129).

The problem of La Malinche, although perhaps more central to the work of Chicana feminist thinkers such as Gloria Anzaldúa, Norma Alarcón, and Cherríe Moraga than to Mexican feminism, is important insofar as it describes the problem of women's place in the Mexican nation. Franco points out that the historical woman known as Malinche was at first held in high esteem by Spaniards (as "exemplary convert") and indigenous people (who were certainly cognizant of the material and social rewards she received for her actions) but that her status fell as the narrative of nationhood developed after Independence (131). Although, like all myths, her uses and meanings have changed over time, Malinche has often been seen as at once victim (symbol of indigenous America's violation by Europe) and as traitor. The sexual nature of her treachery was given lasting emphasis by Paz in *The Labyrinth of Solitude,* and the notion of *malinchismo*—love of the foreign, implying betrayal of one's own community—is still particularly associated with women. "Malinche," wrote Castellanos, "incarnates sexuality in its most irrational aspect, the one least reducible to moral laws, most indifferent to cultural values"

(Castellanos, "Once Again Sor Juana" 223). As such, she represents a force against which the Mexican male subject is (defensively) constituted, while her own voice is necessarily silenced in the quest for national identity (Franco, *Plotting Women* 131).

According to Franco, writers of Castellanos's generation who attempted to plot women into the narrative of the Mexican nation were unable to create heroines; the construct of the nation itself denied women the power of the transcendent gesture and placed them in an impossible position analogous to that of Malinche herself, in which *any* action on their part could lead only to betrayal or self-destruction. In "The Widower Román," the Orantes women (Romelia, her sisters, Blanca and Yolanda, and their mother, doña Ernestina) attempt to transcend the oppressive pettiness of their provincial milieu by mourning their brother/son Rafael's death on an epic scale, like Antigone; Romelia even wears a locket guarding his last note to bed on her wedding night. Yet as the corruption of each one's relation to Rafael is revealed and as they become enmeshed in Román's plot of revenge, they betray themselves and each other. Unable to reinvent themselves as mourners—and thereby to claim a heroic subject position within the stifling context of small-town Mexican society—they end up inevitably repeating Malinche's tragedy. What is at stake, as Franco argues with regard to two other works by Mexican women (Castellanos's *Oficio de tinieblas* and Elena Garro's *Los recuerdos del porvenir*), is "whether a 'heroine' is possible at all within the terms of the epic or master narratives of the nation" (Franco, *Plotting Women* 132). For Castellanos, the response was clearly negative.

Many aspects of "The Widower Román" serve to illustrate the constraints imposed on women—and the ways in which they collude in their own and one another's oppression. The first story Castellanos tells is that of the servant, doña Cástula, whose experience as a poor indigenous woman serves as a counterpoint to that of both Carlos Román and the upper-class Romelia Orantes. For Cástula, love and betrayal are half-forgotten phantoms—real enough, yet in retrospect secondary to her memories of sickness, pregnancy, hardship, and finally stability and relative success as Román's housekeeper and substitute lady of the house. When Román asks Cástula what she would do if she were to meet the man who seduced and abandoned her when she was young, she realizes that she would not recognize him: "His features had faded from her memory many years ago. His name meant no more than any other man's. She did not dare confess as much, however, to a gentleman who from the moment he became a widower had never put off his mourning" (Caste-

llanos, "The Widower Román" 157).[2] To Román, his servant's indifference toward the past and her lack of anger ("Revenge is for men, not for me," she tells
him) are troubling, proving "nothing but her abject acceptance of her station"
(158). Yet by giving her narrative an explicit grounding in class difference—
she explains that Cástula did not have *time* for hard feelings, as "from morning to night there was nothing but work" (158)—Castellanos makes plain her
condemnation of the landowning class whose leisure, derived from the exploitation of indigenous men and women like Cástula, makes it possible for
them to engage in complex psychological dramas of nostalgia, revenge, and
self-destruction.

"The Widower Román" is not, however, an indigenist text, nor is it simplistic in its depiction of power relations and how they are played out in the
subjectivity of its characters. Cástula, for instance, is portrayed as an arrogant
woman who takes pride in her service in the Román household and resents
the territorial encroachment that comes with the widower's remarriage. Her
respect for her employer's bourgeois property and propriety, as well as her status as Román's confidante, preclude class or ethnic allegiance; she is offended
when Román resumes his medical practice, opening his home to an indigent,
abject, Indian clientele, and is only mollified when the widower orders the
house renovated and redecorated with the splendors of his ancestral wealth.
She also becomes his informant with regard to Romelia Orantes, thereby allowing him to carry out his private plot against the Orantes family.

Like Cástula, Romelia does not display solidarity with others of her class
or gender. Romelia, as Castellanos depicts her, is a spoiled youngest daughter
whose status as family pet is disrupted by the death of her brother Rafael,
which not only robs her of "perhaps the most devoted of her worshippers" but
also "changed those who had previously loved her into profoundly strange,
inscrutable, and hostile beings" (180). In order to attract attention, she exag-
gerates her grief, making it into a constant performance that distinguishes her
from classmates and others with whom she cannot compete on other fields.
Like Carlos Román, she dreams of "future revenge. Some time, in a manner
still vague to her, she was going to recover her privileged position. She was going to be raised to heights inaccessible to others; in sublime exaltation she was
going to be proclaimed the favorite" (182).

At puberty, she realizes that the instrument to achieve her ends will be the
only one available to women in her society and class milieu: her sexuality. Experiencing rejection from her family and craving love and "position" ("for
love must descend toward the chosen like light from a distant, powerful star"

[183]), she sets out to attract the widower Román and unwittingly forms an alliance with the man whose sole aim is to bring down her family—using, moreover, the very weapon she had thought to wield herself: her own body. Román's rejection of Romelia after their wedding night, on the grounds that she was not a virgin and therefore not worthy of his house, dramatically illustrates the limitations of women's ability to take action on their own behalf within the confines of patriarchy. Like the historical Malinche, who according to various interpretations may have collaborated with the Spaniards in order to achieve her own liberation from slavery or that of her people from Aztec domination, Romelia's scheming on her own behalf is ultimately overshadowed by her manipulation and objectification in a larger scheme of conquest; and like Malinche, she disappears—is disappeared—from the story's final pages.

Unveiling Romelia's Secret(s)

In Cortés's screen adaptation, however, Romelia no longer disappears but in fact displaces the widower Román as the title character. During *El secreto de Romelia*'s opening credits, an older woman (Dolores Beristáin) looks out a window, lost in contemplation. This woman cannot be immediately identified by readers of the Castellanos story; she is the adult Romelia, a grandmother, who is returning to her hometown accompanied by her divorced daughter, Dolores (Diana Bracho), and her three granddaughters, the teenage María, middle sister Aurelia, and the youngest, Romi. The occasion of this return is the death of Romelia's husband, the widower Román (Pedro Armendáriz Jr.), whose last moments are depicted in the first sequence. Yet for Dolores and her children, this event is shrouded in mystery, because Romelia has always maintained to them that their father/grandfather died long before, without even knowing of her pregnancy. The circumstances of their long-ago marriage and separation, obscured by Romelia's mysterious reticence about the past, will become the first of the film's secrets.

Beginning long after "The Widower Román" ends, *Romelia* is structured as a complex game of knowledge and concealment in which past and present overlap and memory constantly overtakes the ostensible present of the narrative. Returning to her childhood home, Romelia finds it populated with ghosts; and as she approaches the moment of her own death, she is increasingly unable to distinguish between temporal reality and memory. Her past is depicted as unresolved; over the course of the film, she is brought almost against her will into confrontation and, through her daughter, into revelation or confession. For it is primarily through Dolores's insistent questioning that Romelia is made to articulate her experience, and yet, because her experience exceeds or eludes any straightforward explanation, the film juxtaposes her fragmentary answers to scenes that only take place in Romelia's subjective memory.

Like the short story, the film begins with the exchange between Cástula (Josefina Echánove) and Román, only here it takes place just before his death. Romelia is not present; instead, the information about her former husband's death will come to her in a letter, the letter we have just seen him writing. From then on, we see him primarily in Romelia's flashbacks: a distant presence mostly glimpsed riding past on horseback, as in an early shot when she is characterizing him to Dolores as a "stranger." That this flashback occurs immediately upon her arrival in the village undermines Romelia's assertion that widowhood leaves one with "memories you can forget as you please," for in fact, unresolved issues from the past threaten to overwhelm her sense of the present. Chief among these is the death of Rafael, as well as her own dizzying trajectory from innocent child to disgraced bride, a trajectory determined less by her own will than by the weaknesses and machinations of those around her. Her own sense of resignation and lingering shame is contrasted to the ways in which she was victimized by circumstances; although she herself has created and sustained the mystery around her past, its gradual revelation is less a violation of her privacy than a process of healing.

Nearly everything on the property triggers Romelia's memories of Rafael, from the rain to the peaches which were the subject of his note guarded in her locket ("Enjoy them") and which she now sees her granddaughter pick. Yet ultimately, her affection is seemingly transferred to Román, whether for the reasons described by Castellanos or others; it is his ghost who visits her at the moment of her death and spirits her away, reclaiming what in real life he had rejected. In between, she relives the key moments of her girlhood: listening to her parents talk about politics in the garden; the revelation of Rafael's romance with Elena, Román's first wife, prohibited by their families and maliciously exposed by Romelia's sister Blanca; Rafael's departure and the older sisters' subsequent taunting; the *campesinos* returning Rafael's body; Román and Romelia's wedding; and the confrontation when she is returned in disgrace to her father's home. These recollections overlap with the present to such an extent that Dolores and the girls must continually ask her what she is saying or whom she has seen; by the end of the film, the present no longer exists. Watching for her ex-husband through the window, she brushes off María's objection that he is dead: "No, people don't die until we die." By revisiting the past and making peace with it, she herself is then able to die, yet her final vision suggests a redemptive fairy-tale ending that she herself never experienced.

Her journey back in time is not only a confrontation but a rewriting whose empowering effects, however, will only be felt in the future, by her descendants. As the plaque in the notary Joaquín's office reads, quoting Sartre, "El pasado es un lujo de propietario" [The past is a proprietor's luxury]. History, or rather, its interpretation, belongs to the victors, while victims such as Romelia find consolation only in forgetting. But when the proprietors' interpretation is contested, the seamlessness of historical "truth" gives way to the complexity and ambiguity of lived experience. At the film's beginning, the fiction that Romelia has told her daughter all her life (that her father died long ago) is already undermined by the scene of Román's recent death. As the film progresses, we see Romelia's life in flashbacks, but we also see scenes to which she had no access—most interestingly, Rafael's suicide, which is witnessed only by the boy Demetrio, the go-between for Romelia and Rafael, Rafael and Elena, and finally for Rafael's treacherous gift to Román, of Elena's letters, on Román and Elena's wedding night. Román's journal is the main source of these other scenes, yet if Rafael's death is described in the journal, it is reconstructed from the testimony of Demetrio, whom Román treats for shock following the incident. In other words, there is no single authoritative voice but rather a multiplicity of oral and written texts that narrate Romelia's story in much the same way that archeological artifacts narrate, by serving as clues whose meaning must be construed through juxtaposition and speculation.

The first clue is the letter written by Román to Romelia, in which he tells her that he has kept her secret until his death and that she is free to take what is hers and in which he asks for her forgiveness. Her secret, in this case, is his existence and their marriage, since his own daughter believes him long dead. The granddaughters find this letter in Romelia's purse, but Dolores learns of her father's recent passing from Cástula, who again plays a kind of Malinche role by appearing ghostlike in order to pass on hidden information. Serving Dolores tea in the now-empty study over which she still presides, she remarks, "I don't know why your mother always wanted to pretend he was dead. Don Carlos knew it; he used to laugh at his own death certificate."

Although Cástula adds charitably that "she must have had her reasons," Dolores returns suspicious, asking Romelia if she ever had a secret lover and demanding to know more about her father. As in much of the film, their discussion takes place in the close, intimate space of the bedroom, the bed serving as a metaphoric representation of the secrets being disclosed. The scene is blocked so that their distance from each other reflects their disagreement, while their shifting distance from the camera, making them larger or smaller, reflects their relative authority in the conversation. When at last Romelia confesses her "disgrace" and Dolores begs her pardon, they are seated together and equal in the frame, physically dramatizing their reconciliation.

In that scene, the mother alludes to an ancient bloodstain on a sheet as another piece of evidence, yet its value is questioned by her daughter, who argues from a contemporary perspective that "your virginity belongs to you, not to men." Dolores's counter-question—whether her mother ever loved a man—goes unanswered. Meanwhile, as the daughters find first Román's letter, then Elena's old dresses, and finally Román's diary, the mystery grows; Aurelia and María quickly adopt their mother and grandmother's tactics of "life on the sly," feigning illness, for example, in order to concentrate on the diary. Through their reading, we see scenes of Elena and Román—the delivery of her letters on their wedding night, her death shortly thereafter, Román's desperation. However, the contents of the letters are unavailable to the girls; it is once again Cástula, an ethereal and perhaps supernatural presence, who gives them to Dolores that night when Dolores sneaks out to "mass" and again visits her father's study. Before Dolores can ask for an explanation, Cástula vanishes. Upon her return to their room, Romi shows her the diary hidden under a pillow—the bed again the site of confidences. Later, Romelia herself reads in the journal the story of her betrayal by her husband, her manipulation in his elaborate plan of revenge.

As the texts that explain Romelia's secret are gradually discovered, their impact is felt in different ways by the different characters. Dolores, who is at first angered by the way her mother has concealed the truth about her father ("If I had had a father in my life, things would have been different," she accuses. "You stole him from me"), gradually comes to understand Romelia's tragedy. The difference in experience of the two generations at first causes conflict; Romelia disapproves of her daughter's divorce, while Dolores is astounded at the notion of Romelia's saving the sheet with the "proof" of her wedding-night virginity. But finally the gulf is bridged by empathy and compassion. Romelia's own confrontation with the past—her discovery that the shame she had tried for so long to conceal was in fact a contrivance used by Román to get revenge on her family—becomes a catharsis and means of self-reconciliation. In the beginning of the film, she is anxious to return to the capital, where she can forget the past. But by the end, she no longer wants to flee and dies in peace in her own hometown.

Meanwhile, the two older granddaughters, Aurelia and María, are intrigued by the stories of illicit romance and revenge delineated in the diary. They particularly giggle over the anecdote about their great-aunt Blanca's prudishness at the doctor's when she refuses to submit to a gynecological exam. The model of feminine behavior espoused by their grandmother's generation is clearly foreign to them, and they read the diary as if it were fiction. Mocking the others' immersion in the world of ghosts and secrets, they are perhaps the film's strongest rejection of the "inevitability" of feminine betrayal. Early in the film, a revealing exchange takes place around the dinner table: Aurelia asks her grandmother, "Which is better, to be married, a widow like you, or divorced like Mama?" Romelia responds by asking what she thinks. The youngest, Romi, blurts "The best is to marry!" but María, entering the room, counters: "Marry, no. To live with someone." "Who put those ideas in your head?" Romelia asks; María responds, "Just for a while—if it works, get married." The teenager's pragmatism is placed in sharp contrast to Romelia's viewpoint, which in keeping with the older woman's respect for convention is phrased as a collective assumption rather than personal opinion: "In my day, widowhood was considered the perfect state for a woman. It prevented one from suffering."

For Romelia's generation, marriage was an obligation, not a choice. And in spite of its mystification in both popular and elite culture, it was also acknowledged among women themselves not to bring happiness. Instead, one had to accomplish one's social role (marriage and motherhood) and only later enjoy relative independence as a widow. For Dolores, things have changed yet are far from perfect. Later in the film, when she is bathing after coming in at dawn, Romelia thinks she's gone to see Joaquín; Dolores laughs and says they're just friends. Her mother is skeptical: "Friends, at your age? In my day, those things had a different name." "Ay Mama, that's why they didn't work." "And they work now?" Romelia answers contemptuously; instead of having Dolores reply, the camera pans to her reflection in the mirror, smoking quietly. Although we are not told the details of Dolores's marriage and divorce, her inability to respond suggests that the more egalitarian understanding of romance held by her generation has not necessarily made things easier for women. However, the suggestion of a new start with Joaquín at the end of the film undermines any fatalism regarding heterosexual relationships; and more importantly, her daughters' openness indicates that the constraints and pretenses of "life on the sly" may be, by their adulthood, nothing more than a romantic anachronism.

Cortés's optimism on this point is conveyed through the mirroring of Dolores's three daughters and the three Orantes sisters, the former suggesting the rebirth and revindication of the latter in the present era. In the film, as in Castellanos's story, Romelia and her sisters are competitive, jealous, and vindictive. Blanca in particular devotes her energy to destroying Romelia's happiness; knowing of her sister's crush on their brother, Rafael, it is she who leads Romelia to spy on Rafael and Elena's illicit affair, and it is also Blanca who on her own initiative backs up Román's accusations and even names the circumstances under which Romelia might have lost her virginity. The second sister, Yolanda, is more forthright than Blanca, rather than falsely pious, but she also torments Romelia. In a scene just before Romelia's marriage, she reacts to Romelia's taking for herself the lamp that the three are embroidering by, commenting, "What a coincidence . . . we three have always wanted the same things. First our father, then Rafael." Over Blanca's protests, she continues, "I admitted it, you went to confession, and Romelia, who neither thinks nor feels, acted without asking, just as now with the lamp." Later, Yolanda seems to be supporting Romelia against Román's denunciation, pleading, "Have pity; think of what her life will be like here with us. Blanca will torture her night and day"—then suddenly adding the twist: "and I will never be able to forgive her. Because of her no man will ever look at me because my sister is a prostitute."

In this powerful scene, blocking and camera movement once again perfectly reflect power relationships. At first, the exchange between men (don Carlos and the girls' father, don Rafael) dominates the frame, with Romelia off to one side; then, the camera follows don Rafael to where the two sisters are seated and rise from the shadows to add, uninvited, to their sister's disgrace. By bringing up the possibility of incest and by exposing their own rivalries and frustrations with Romelia, they commit the film's most excessive and unwieldy act of betrayal—a betrayal committed not with the cold logic of patriarchy, but with near-hysterical passion.

Their revelation of their family's shame is self-destructive, but both sisters clearly believe that all the doors opened to them as women in their society have already closed and that they have nothing to lose. For the ultimate betrayal is not theirs of their sister but their culture's betrayal of all women—metaphorically, the original moment at which Malinche is sold into slavery by her own family, which prompts the later actions that will be read as treachery. (Their mother, attempting damage control, speaks up to deny Rafael's suicide: "But Rafael didn't kill himself, child. Everyone knows it was an accident. He was so good." By thus propping up her son's reputation, doña Ernestina damns her daughters even further, implying that any incestuous act or desire was theirs alone.) As if fleeing from the raw display of female despair, the camera follows Román, then don Rafael as they walk away from the women. Román, as husband and doctor, commands scientific as well as masculine authority and can therefore attest to the "truth" of female behavior far better than Romelia herself can, and don Rafael is forced to honor his word over that of his own daughter. Again facing one another, with Romelia looking on, the men conclude their "negotiation."

Among Dolores's daughters, no such competition or bitterness exists. Because they are not bound by rigid rules that dictate who should marry first and when and that hold them responsible for the honor of their family, the motives for betrayal are absent. The "inevitable" treachery is found, as Castellanos's text suggests but does not illustrate, to be a product of a social context that is stifling to women, a context which, Cortés's film seems to argue, has now passed into history. To say that the granddaughters represent a rejection of the ideological legacy of Malinche's betrayal does not mean that they totally reject the language of secrets, however. Throughout the movie, the two older sisters hide from the youngest, eavesdrop on the adults, and clandestinely read Román's diary. Yet for them secrets are simply a game and no longer a matter of honor and shame, life and death.

Romi, meanwhile, is party to another kind of secret; she forms a strong emotional and psychic bond with her grandmother to the point that she seems to "see" Romelia's memories (Fig. 4.2). In some ways, Romi is the film's most important character; as the youngest person in a film about generational differences, she most strongly represents the future, yet through her grandmother she is also linked to the past; she even stays behind with Romelia when the rest of the family leaves on the train. She believes not only in ghosts but also in love and romance—it is she who blurts out that getting married is the best option for a woman, with an optimism that reflects her age and probable immersion in fairy tales. "You've been watching the *telenovelas*," Dolores scolds her at one point. Yet after getting a glimpse into the world of real-life marriage (via the telling of her grandmother's secrets as well as her experience with her parents), she feels threatened by her mother's romance with Joaquín and confesses to Dolores that she does not want her to marry again. Romi's subjectivity is clearly in formation and will be shaped primarily out of the divergent messages she receives from her sisters, mother, and grandmother. In the moving penultimate sequence, during which grandmother and granddaughter walk back to the hacienda while the train fades into the distance, it is as if the story of Romelia, dropped so abruptly from "The Widower Román," has finally come full circle: for even as her story is ending, Romi's is about to begin.

Dolores's remark about the *telenovelas*, besides teasing her daughter, can be seen as a comment on the film itself, which repeatedly invokes *telenovela*-like elements of romance and intrigue while refusing their patriarchal implications. The romantic hacienda setting, the tales of loves thwarted and betrayed, the intimate language of diaries and love letters are all elements that could easily be woven into a generic melodrama, but in *El secreto de Romelia* they are politicized, contextualized as part of a gendered discourse that ultimately is exceeded by the complexity of women's lived experience. Foremost of these is the problem contained in the title itself: what, finally, is "Romelia's secret"? Her long-guarded bloodstained sheet? That her husband did not die early in her marriage but returned her to her family as unworthy? Her love for her brother Rafael, or the tryst she witnessed as a girl between Rafael and Elena, or his subsequent suicide? The secrets that were kept from her by others? Or the whole of the history that she has kept from her family out of pride and

FIG. 4.2. Grandmother and granddaughter revisit the past in *El secreto de Romelia*.
Courtesy Cineteca Nacional.

shame? Perhaps it is all and none of these: for unlike the classic "fallen woman" melodrama, this story holds no original secret that constitutes the truth about Romelia's experience, her downfall. Instead, the multiplication and revelation of secrets becomes testimony to the constraints imposed on women in a patriarchal context—a social rather than a personal tragedy.

As layer after layer of mystery is uncovered, the only secret that remains is that of the heart: locus of passion, desire, love, feelings which cannot be explained, let alone formalized, within the narrow confines of social custom and regulation. Romelia's adoration of Rafael, which may or may not transgress the boundaries of incest; the solitude she cultivates around the memory of her private tragedy; Dolores's hesitant romance with Joaquín, of which she is wary after a lifetime of implicit betrayal; and even the young Romi's wordless bond with her grandmother that leads her to remain with her in the village are secrets that cannot be easily rendered in language even when the patriarchal obligations of "life on the sly" are no longer in effect. By respecting the complexity and density of human experience and psychology, Cortés creates a film that is as much a work of beauty and emotion as a critique of oppression, in effect reclaiming the terrain of sentimental family melodrama for feminism.

Secret Histories: Women and the Nation

In discussing the impossibility of Antigone and the inevitability of La Malinche in "The Widower Román," I reiterated Franco's question about the possibility of inscribing women into the master narrative of national identity. In her chapter focusing on this question, Franco analyzes Elena Garro's *Los recuerdos del porvenir,* a novel that, like *El secreto de Romelia,* uses multiple temporalities and appropriates cultural forms traditionally associated with femininity, namely romance. For Franco, that novel "represents an impasse. Women do not enter history—only romance" (*Plotting Women* 138). She concludes that in Garro's and Castellanos's writings, "The woman acts in isolation, exploiting traditional women's spaces of romance and religion, yet without ever being able to institutionalize an alternative discursive practice outside oral tradition" (146).

My discussion of Romelia has thus far focused on precisely those elements which, for Franco, do not sufficiently challenge the patriarchal discourse of history: romance and emotion, feminine spaces, memory and oral tradition, and as an element of all of these, the notion of "the secret" as the privileged site of women's language and knowledge. However, as I suggested earlier, Cortés's film does in fact attempt to confront history as such and to reclaim the nation for Mexican women in a way that perhaps those earlier texts could not. She does this on two main levels: first, by showing what certain key moments in national history—Cárdenas's land reforms of the 1930s and the student movement of 1968—actually meant in the lives of the characters who lived them (as opposed to their usual abstract protagonist, "the nation"), and second, by displacing and decentering the customary meanings of politics and history themselves, weaving them in as elements of her seemingly private, intimate narrative.

The focus on the 1930s, besides being derived from Castellanos's story, is interesting for many reasons. Enrique Palma Cruz points out that 1988 was a year of unusual publicity for *cardenismo* due to the commemoration of the fiftieth anniversary of Lázaro Cárdenas's oil expropriation as well as to the presidential campaign of his son Cuauhtémoc; thus many of the year's films were set in that period (229). Moreover, the Cárdenas era was a period of intense feminist activity revolving principally around the struggle for the vote. As Enriqueta Tuñón has documented, women associated with socialism and especially with the socialist government in the Yucatan had been organizing congresses and demanding this right; in Chiapas, the state government actually recognized equal political rights for men and women in 1925. In 1935, the Frente Unico pro Derechos de la Mujer (FUPDM) was founded and claimed 50,000 members, many of whom were teachers. Under pressure from women, Cárdenas in 1937 promised to send a women's suffrage initiative to the national legislature, but the initiative was dropped in 1938. Tuñón argues that the failure of the suffrage initiative coincided with Manuel Avila Camacho's presidential campaign and that because of women's reputation for traditionalism and conservatism, it was not convenient for the Partido Revolucionario Mexicano (forerunner of today's PRI) to allow them to vote. The FUPDM aligned itself with the party, and its demands for women became secondary (184–186).

The film, however, does not address this aspect of women's history; in Romelia's environment, women's exclusion from the political sphere is not challenged. What *El secreto de Romelia* does consider are the land and labor policies implemented by Cárdenas that were aimed at carrying out the ideals of the Revolution by addressing inequities in land distribution and access to resources, particularly education. The *ejido* system of collective land cultivation, based on indigenous practices, had existed since 1922, but under Cárdenas it was greatly expanded: "The idea was to make the structural change in the Mexican countryside irreversible," with great expropriations of land throughout the country and with the establishment of an infrastructure for *ejido* management and agricultural organization (Aguilar Camín and Meyer 142–144). Although, as John M. Hart points out, the motives underlying the reforms as well as their goals and actual accomplishments continue to be debated by historians, what is certain is that between 1934 and 1940, the federal government distributed forty-four million acres to more than twelve hundred pueblos and transformed landholding patterns in the countryside, with far-reaching social and economic consequences (Hart 13–14).

Rosario Castellanos's family was among those who lost their property in that era and moved to Mexico City in 1941. In her 1970 essay "A Man of Destiny," she wrote of Lázaro Cárdenas:

> His was the first name that I heard my elders pronounce with fright, rage, and powerlessness. Not only because his policies were damaging to their economic interests—when he ordered the distribution of land throughout Mexico and made no exception of the state of Chiapas—but also because he was stripping them of all that certainty which had upheld them for centuries. (232)

For Castellanos, her family's loss became her gain, freeing her from the kind of fate she would depict with abhorrence in "The Widower Román," that of the respectable young lady confined to home and the obligations of motherhood and domesticity (234–235). Her personal independence as a woman was thus directly linked in her mind (at least in retrospect) to *cardenismo,* which also was a main influence on her professional career. In 1951, she became the director of cultural programs for the state of Chiapas and in 1956, the director of the National Indigenist Institute's educational puppet theater, which was based in San Cristóbal and traveled to indigenous communities throughout the state.

This history, which is only inferentially present in "The Widower Román," is brought to bear on Cortés's film (which, however, is shot not in Chiapas but in Tlaxcala). In the film, Román is portrayed as a socialist and Cárdenas supporter, while the Orantes family is conservative and balks at the presidential decree under which rural landowners are ordered to provide teachers for the children of their resident workers. Unlike Castellanos, Romelia does not revolt against her parents' conservatism but rather, as an adult, keeps alive their resentment at the loss of their properties. Blaming Cárdenas for her family's fate, she laughs bitterly when her granddaughter recites the popular view that "Cárdenas was the only good president that Mexico has had. They say he served the people." ("Yes," replies Romelia, "but which people?") Maintaining the prejudices of her class, Romelia considers Cástula unworthy of trust because she is a servant and ridicules Dolores's love of indigenous culture— "estos fandangos de la indiada." Romelia's political views, like her social values, separate her from her daughter, whose leftist values Romelia opposes and explains away by associating them with her father's lineage.

However, beyond the obvious class and generational factors shaping Romelia's politics, the film offers another interpretation which more subtly links politics and passion. The immediate outcome of the Cárdenas ruling on rural education is that the elder Rafael sends his son away as a teacher—both to comply with the law and to control Rafael's behavior. With this act, Romelia loses her beloved brother, who commits suicide at the school and whose body is returned to the hacienda by the workers, who tell the family he died in a hunting accident. Yet even before Rafael's death, an association is made between political discourse and personal loss in the scene in which Romelia's parents are in the garden discussing the new government decrees. Romelia, listening in on the conversation from a discreet distance, is distracted by her sister Blanca, who motions for her to follow. Blanca leads Romelia through the hacienda grounds to a wall overlooking the spot where Rafael and Elena are making love. The construction of the scene, with its progression from public to private *desgracias,* builds the association between the political turmoil during Romelia's youth and the personal tragedy of love and loss connected with her brother—an association that is seemingly confirmed by his death.

The film's juxtaposition and superimposition of conventional politics with sexual and romantic passions is continued throughout. In the past that Dolores and Joaquín share, the personal is inseparable from the political. They hadn't seen each other, Joaquín recites from memory, since "September 18, 1968—the night the tanks invaded the university." Dolores objects that they did see each other since on two occasions: "when you left Lecumberri"[3] and when Dolores got married. The two moments are well chosen, for beyond their personal meanings, the symmetry is obvious: the trajectory for men of their class and generation was rebellion, then conformity through government careers and assimilation into the establishment, while for women, it was rebellion, then conformity through marriage and child-rearing. Yet interestingly, Dolores retains her political convictions, chastising Joaquín's acquiescence to "the system." He responds by teasing her with her old nickname, "Lola the Guerrillera." [4]

Dolores also tells Joaquín that as a history teacher, she has had to struggle to explain the events of the 1960s to her students, who, whether due to official censorship or cultural amnesia, do not even recognize the names of then-President Gustavo Díaz Ortaz, Police Chief Luis Cueto, and other key figures of the era. She recalls a girl telling her that she thought "the movement" was an earthquake, since so many people had died. Given Cortés's self-proclaimed identification with the "generation of 1968" (in Gallegos, "Ha ganado la mujer"), one can speculate that Dolores's experiences are closest to the director's, whose contribution to the series *18 lustros de la vida en México en este siglo* vividly depicts the turbulent atmosphere of post-Tlatelolco Mexico, with its brutally repressed guerrillas, the continued imprisonment of political activists, the ascent of Echeverría to the presidency, and the birth of the feminist movement. Dolores's life is shaped by the historic events that have taken place around her, and like her mother, she displays strong political convictions. Since her life is not the focus of the plot so much as Romelia's, we don't know the details of her experiences. Yet through her discussions with Romelia and Joaquín, the notion of politics as conventionally defined is kept in a similar dialectical tension with her own history, the complexity of the latter calling into question the authority of the former as a sufficient explanatory discourse. It is not that her convictions are undermined but rather that her biography as a woman exceeds historiographic generalizations.

The trope of politics as a cover for or displacement of other kinds of experience is made most clear in the version Romelia gives of her marriage to Carlos Román. When Dolores finds out that the marriage was ended by separation and not by death, she pressures her mother for an explanation. Romelia repeatedly says that she was too old-fashioned and conservative for the socialist Román, and she only later reveals that he rejected her and claimed she wasn't a virgin. Political differences are thus used to cover intimate shame; moreover, Román's supposed progressive views are contradicted by his wielding of patriarchal power and privilege in the realm of sexuality. When we learn the story of his elaborate revenge on the Orantes household—in which his rejection of Romelia is planned long before the wedding-night test of her worthiness—it becomes clear that he, perhaps more than any other character, was motivated by passion, not reason. His socialism, like Romelia's conservatism, is a red herring, a surface explanation that in reality has little to do with their actual behavior. The political, as conventionally defined, becomes something impersonal, a subterfuge, while the personal, as the force behind material acts, becomes what is truly political.

Insofar as these intimate stories constitute the history of the Mexican nation, they are a radical challenge to *historia patria,* the patriarchal history in which events and transformations are caused by the actions of heroic fathers and in which women are only symbols (like Guadalupe) or vehicles for larger processes (like Malinche). Here, women's experience (and men's, for that matter) is shown to be complex and not relegated to the domestic sphere. In fact, the division between public and private is broken down, so that it is impossible to separate the personal lives of the characters from the political contexts of their respective eras. Franco asserts that "it is simply not possible to retain verisimilitude and make women into national protagonists. Women's attempts to plot themselves as protagonists . . . become a recognition of the fact that they are not in the plot at all but definitely somewhere else" (*Plotting Women* 146). Cortés's film begins to look at that "somewhere else" and to place it in a challenging relation to that national narrative from which women have been so forcefully excluded. In *Romelia,* official history is decentered and displaced, as it must be if it is to include women and their secrets.

Serpientes y escaleras

The release of *El secreto de Romelia* in September 1989, under the auspices of four federal and two regional institutions, could be said to exemplify the beginning of the Salinas-era "new Golden Age" insofar as it features several of the period's hallmarks: a young, university-trained director, a provincial location, and multi-institutional financing.[5] The first feature film to come from the CCC, *Romelia* was critically well received; in the ever-recalcitrant *Dicine,* Javier González Rubio wrote a positive review characterizing the film as an oasis of competent filmmaking in "el árido arte del cine mexicano actual" [the arid art of current Mexican cinema] (18). It also was showcased in a promotional ad campaign by the government of Tlaxcala, which sought to attract more film production to the state. One of only a handful of features directed by women in the 1980s, it received national and international recognition in spite of the fact that, as the director would later explain:

era una cinta que no tenía futuro; se hizo un poco a contracorriente, porque el ccc en ese entonces no estaba autorizado, por la normatividad del stpyc de producir largometrajes industriales. Fue saltarse la barda en todos sentidos y ese era su presente y su fin. Estábamos además, justo en el cambio de sexenio, y si no se terminaba corríamos el riesgo de que quedara enlatada.

[It was a film without a future; it was made a bit against the current, because the ccc at that time was not authorized by the norms of the stpc (the filmworkers union) to produce commercial features. It was jumping over fences in every sense and that was its present and its end. Also, we were right at the change of the *sexenio* (when government offices are reorganized), and if we didn't finish, we ran the risk that it would be shelved.] (In Peguero)

Although the film was not financially a success, its cultural prestige enabled her to make a second feature in 1991, *Serpientes y escaleras,* set in Guanajuato in the 1950s.

In *Serpientes,* co-written with her sister Carmen and with Alicia Molina, Cortés continued to explore the contradictions and connections between the personal and the political or, more precisely, between the "masculine" political arena and the "feminine" domestic sphere, between patriarchal power and the gendered body. Even more than in *Romelia,* the question of female agency becomes paramount: given a social structure created and run by men, how do women cope with, transcend, or change their situations? Once again, the Malinche model is explored and defeated, and the ability of women to chart their own trajectories is confirmed. And once again, the relentless persistence of an economic and political system deaf and blind to questions of social justice is juxtaposed with the true momentousness of the changes in consciousness that have taken place, particularly in women, across recent generations.

Serpientes depicts the adolescent experiences of Valentina (Arcelia Ramírez), the daughter of a powerful Guanajuato politician, and her best friend, Rebeca (Lumi Cavazos). While Valentina's self-sacrificing mother chooses to ignore her husband's many affairs and to preserve her marriage at all costs, the young women, although not consciously rebellious, become involved with young men who are members of the liberal opposition. These relationships give them an introduction to politics (a realm in which, in Valentina's father's home, women are more currency of exchange than participants) and spark divisions between the generations. At the same time, Rebeca, succumbing to conflictive desires, enters into an affair with her friend's father. As Alex Saragoza and Graciela Berkovich write, the pregnancy that results is "the symbolic fruit of her seduction by the powers and privileges of Valentina's father" and by extension of the government's powers to co-opt and assimilate opposition (29–30).

Josefina Echánove (Cástula in *El secreto de Romelia*) again plays a Pazian role, as the transmitter of patriarchal values from which women do not themselves benefit (Paz 35). As Oti the nanny, she explains that "we know much about politicians. If they are in love with their current mistress, everything is better for them. Women inspire them." Women enter into politics only as muses, diversions, and in the case of wives, as status objects and keepers of domestic harmony. The ultimate exemplar of these values and the suffering they cause is Adelaida (Diana Bracho), Valentina's mother, who endures her husband's flagrant affairs out of love, obligation, and the lack of practical alternatives. Rebeca's mother, Imelda (Pilar Medina), also finds her life defined by men; as the mistress of a hacienda owner who dies early in the film, she loses the property to his legal family but regains it through interventions by Gregorio, Valentina's father (Héctor Bonilla), on behalf of Rebeca. Imelda later marries Illades, whose political challenge to Gregorio is empowered by respectable matrimony. These women belong to the bourgeois class but actually have no socioeconomic status of their own—their "value," like that of Romelia in Castellanos's story, is defined solely in their relationships with men, which like the game of snakes and ladders that constitutes the film's primary structural conceit, are always tenuous and unstable.

The daughters, learning from their mothers' experiences as much as or more than from the social critiques they are exposed to through their radical journalist boyfriends, grow up determined to escape. Like Dolores in *Romelia*, Valentina and Rebeca sympathize with their mothers' pain but already belong to a different world. However, the traps of patriarchy are manifold, and before she can leave, Rebeca's attraction to the powerful politician Gregorio leads her to commit an accidental, but nonetheless *malinchista*, betrayal. A group of mineworkers entrusts her with documents to be handed to her fiancé, Raúl, whose muckraking newspaper columns are the chief threat to Gregorio's gubernatorial campaign. When she is seduced by Gregorio, she leaves the papers behind in his car—thereby putting Raúl's life in danger and the workers' organizing in jeopardy. Her seduction by power is a threat not only to herself and her friendship with Valentina but to the nascent possibility for social change.

Finding herself pregnant, Rebeca at first follows the conventional trajectory of a "fallen woman," isolating herself from her friends, attended only by Oti, while Gregorio goes on with his life and career. At first she hides her situation from Valentina; her subsequent confession tests the boundaries of their friendship. However, she is eventually reconciled with both Valentina and Raúl, who unlike the widower Román is liberal in his personal life as well as his politics and accepts her pregnancy. Cortés comments on this point: "La película hace consciencia también de que la liberación femenina no la lograron las mujeres solitas, sino apoyadas por sus compañeros" [The film also brings to light the fact that female liberation was not achieved by women all by themselves but rather with the support of their male companions] (Cortés, in Torralba). In the end, the two friends leave to join their boyfriends in Mexico City. The future is a question mark, but the dead end of provincial society—a semifeudal system run by and for a handful of men "cuyo poder se basa en el dinero y las mujeres" [whose power is based on money and women]—has been left behind.

Saragoza and Berkovich point out that "The father's transgressions are punished by the film's end: his gubernatorial candidacy is aborted by the party. But he is easily replaced. The father's posters are covered by those of another, seemingly indistinguishable, face." They conclude that "though the women have rejected the patriarchal system, the dominant order continues, apparently with scant visible damage" and that the film "applaud[s] the transformation in political consciousness, but understand[s] that its consequences are limited" (30). This is certainly valid, yet the effectiveness of the juxtaposition of discourses should not be underestimated. In both *Serpientes* and *Romelia,* patriarchal politics are shown to be sterile and hollow in their exclusion of women's lived experience, but what is empowering is the films' implicit argument that if the power structure cannot easily be overturned, it can at least be circumvented—that oppressive traditions and practices can be resisted and that women can take bold actions to change their fate.

Moreover, broad social struggle is an essential if understated element of both films. The *cardenista* legacy in *Romelia* and the miners' struggle in *Serpientes* each serve to widen and contextualize the principal stories, set as each of these is on markedly contested terrain. The leftist politics embraced by Dolores and by Valentina's and Rebeca's boyfriends (it is implied that the young women will join the cause as well) are not incidental. Rather, the exit the films propose to the seemingly inescapable edifice of the dominant order is a holistic integration of personal and public politics. While Cortés does not present a program or polemic, her films forcefully show that conventional politics are meaningless if paired only with personal hypocrisy and that women as well as men should be able to determine their own destinies and exercise control over their bodies and their lives.

"What interests me is what reaches the public"

In her two feature films, Cortés explored the world of secrets, intimacy, and near-clandestinity in which women, excluded from the nation's public discourse, have transmitted their knowledge and which has contained their histories, locked away from the master narrative of *historia patria.* In both films too, a more open, public, active, and liberated role for women was proposed—an end, as it were, to life on the sly. Although *Romelia* and *Serpientes* are beautifully lit, designed, and filmed examples of so-called quality cinema, honored with accolades and festival prizes, their existence by no means signified an end to the obstacles faced by Cortés and other women filmmakers. Following *Serpientes,* Cortés often mentioned her plans for a third feature as well as her interest in making films for children. By 1996, however, Cortés had apparently left feature-film production behind (Lazcano).

The reasons for her departure are not difficult to discern, in spite of the enthusiasm and energy she had demonstrated during her involvement with the cinema. In a 1992 interview in *La Jornada,* Cortés told Raquel Peguero that what interests her is not so much the cinema as the communications process:

> Por ello voy a buscar otro tipo de proyectos en radio, televisión, porque a partir de *El secreto de Romelia* me reconcilié con mi carrera de comunicación que había dejado de lado por esta veneración al cine de arte y como ya dejé de creer en el cine como expresión artística y me interesa más el que llegue al público, a ése estoy encaminada.
> [For that reason I am going to look for other kinds of projects in radio, television, because after *El secreto de Romelia,* I reconciled myself with my career in communication that I'd put aside because of this veneration for art cinema, and as I've already stopped believing in cinema as artistic expression, and as what interests me more is what reaches the public, I'm moving in that direction.]

Frustrated with a working environment in which films were badly projected and distributed and ineptly marketed (for instance, packaging *Romelia* for its video release as an action movie with the generic title *Herencia de sangre,* meaning "blood inheritance") and in which commercial success—or even recovery of costs—was most often a pipe dream, Cortés looked toward other media for the freedom of action, of expression, and above all for the rapport with a broad audience that even the reinvigorated cinema of the 1990s could not, in her opinion, provide.

While it remains to be seen whether Cortés will return to work as a film-maker, her films nevertheless occupy an important place in the history of women's film production, above all for their insistence on disrupting patriarchal narratives by telling the women's stories or "secrets" that such narratives conceal. It is fitting that Matilde Landeta, in 1992, praised Cortés's work and called her "de las más representativas de esta nueva generación de cineastas mexicanas" [one of the most representative of this new generation of Mexican women filmmakers] (Gallegos, "Matilde Landeta"). Like Landeta's work, Cortés's takes on Mexican nationalism and dismantles stereotypes, not with anger but with compassion, beauty, and empathy. Although the subtlety of these qualities may make such work particularly susceptible to appropriation and dismissal, its fundamental critique should nevertheless be recognized: the history of women demands the rewriting of History.

I wanted to make a film about how it felt to be part of a cultural minority. And all the inside fights that I have had—that I think that anybody who belongs to a cultural minority has had—about how you have to forget about your personal heritage in order to belong. That conflict, that's what I wanted to talk about. And it seemed as if all of a sudden, there was an eruption in the world, where all this was happening.

Guita Schyfter[1]

CHAPTER 5

Guita Schyfter

The Chicken and the Egg

In the beginning of her family autobiography, *Las genealogías,* cultural critic Margo Glantz lists a number of items that she, a second-generation Mexican and a secular Jew, has in her home: a shofar and some inherited candelabras rest next to images of Catholic saints, Christ, and pre-Hispanic deities, a juxtaposition that causes a cousin to comment that she does not seem Jewish, "porque los judíos les tienen, como nuestros primos hermanos los arabes, horror a las imágenes" [because Jews, like our first cousins the Arabs, have a horror of images]. The author, however, concludes otherwise: that "todo es mío y no lo es y parezco judía y no lo parezco y por eso escribo—estas—mis genealogías" [all of it is mine and isn't, and I seem Jewish and don't, and for this reason I write—these—my genealogies]. (20)

The mixture of religious traditions on Glantz's home altar is, on the one hand, emblematic of the cultural phenomena that perhaps most deeply characterize the Americas: *mestizaje,* hybridity, syncretism. The fusion of indigenous and Catholic beliefs is at the heart of Mexican religious practice, whose preeminent icon is the brown-skinned, Nahuatl-speaking Virgin of Guadalupe. The Jewish elements, however, disturb this otherwise commonplace mixture. While the veneration of holy objects is seemingly universal, Glantz explains only the significance of the shofar and candelabras, implicitly presuming her readers' unfamiliarity; moreover, the Jewish "horror of images" indicates a fundamental incompatibility between the traditions. To be Mexican and Jewish, Glantz seems to be saying, requires an embrace of contradiction that is potentially threatening to guardians of tradition on either side.

This embrace is the theme of Guita Schyfter's first feature film, *Novia que te vea,* based on Rosa Nissán's novel by the same name. Nissán, the sister of a prominent leader in Mexico City's Jewish community, used a semiautobiographical narrative to bring to light the diverse and contradictory experiences of that community, thus building on Glantz's work of a decade earlier. Schyfter, a Costa Rican-born Jew of Polish and Ukrainian descent, adapted Nissán's novel in 1992, bringing one of the first representations of Jewish experience to the Mexican screen. The ambitious work, which encompasses gender and generational conflict as well as religious and cultural difference, raises important questions about Mexican national identity—specifically, about the myth of a "mestizo nation," official notions of *mexicanidad,* and the patriarchal understanding of the nation as a single "family."

Jewishness and *Mexicanidad*

As the film itself indicates, the history of Jews in the Americas is inextricably linked with that of the conquest of these continents; the year of Columbus's first voyage, 1492, is also the year that the Jews were expelled from Spain. Banished by the Inquisition, Jews arrived in the New World as early as the fifteenth century; as Solange Alberro explains, their faith was kept alive with the support of *conversos,* supposed converts who practiced Judaism in secret (85).

The Inquisition, however, followed the Jews to Mexico; its first trial, on February 28, 1574, targeted Jews along with Lutherans and other heretics (Lerner 86). Many were burned to death in the Mexico City plaza that is the present-day Alameda; yet many were able to survive. Phenomena such as remote, predominantly indigenous communities that adhere to the Jewish faith attest to the persistence of this diaspora (Stavans, *Tropical Synagogues* 5; Lerner 123). More recent immigration of both Ladino-speaking Sephardim and Eastern European Ashkenazim has created an important Jewish minority in the country.

Yet in spite of its deep roots, Mexico's Jewish population has been largely invisible and overwhelmingly excluded from the foundational ideology of Mexico as a mestizo nation, part indigenous and part Spanish. Mexican-born writer Ilan Stavans, like Glantz, understands the seemingly inclusive notion of *mestizaje* as one which fails to include the waves of immigrants, Jewish and otherwise, that over 500 years have "created a mosaic of racial multiplicity" (*Tropical Synagogues* 1). In "Lost in Translation" he writes, "Bizarre combination—Mexican Jews: some 50,000 frontier dwellers and hyphen people like Dr. Jekyll and Mr. Hyde, a sum of sums of parts, a multiplicity of multiplicities" (492).

The sense of liminality and exclusion he describes is echoed by Schyfter, who says of her childhood, "When I was a little girl and studied the history of Costa Rica, and they said 'Then the Spanish came' and then 'He was our president . . .' I never felt that had anything to do with me. So I became an observer" (Presner 13). After moving to Mexico and becoming a documentary filmmaker, she read an interview with Isaac Bashevis Singer in which he encouraged writers to look into their own roots. This advice inspired her to make the more personal film *Novia que te vea,* which she adapted along with Nissán and Hugo Hiriart and submitted to IMCINE. With government backing, she was able to make a film which directly addressed her own experience of outsiderness and exclusion, as well as the history of Mexican Jews as a whole.

That Schyfter's reexamination of *mexicanidad* through Jewish eyes came to the screen in the 1990s has everything to do with larger changes taking place during this period: the collapse of myths of national unity in the wake of successive economic and political crises and the emergence of contestatory discourses such as feminism, gay activism, and *campesino* and indigenous resistance to centralized state power (culminating in the Zapatista uprising of 1994), with their direct and indirect consequences for national filmmaking. As a privileged site of national self-articulation, the classical Mexican cinema tried to define "Mexican" in sweeping terms that implied very specific, limited constructs of gender, race, class, and ethnic identity. Ramírez Berg documents how political and economic disruptions have undercut the viability of those constructs; but if, as he argues, "by 1969, the problems of the dominant ideology overwhelmed the classical narrative's ability to contain them" (32), that breakdown also opened the way for new, potentially oppositional projects. As the foundational ideologies of the Mexican nation continued to collapse, it is not surprising that new voices, such as those of women, gays, and Jews, began to emerge in the cinema.

What is profound about *Novia que te vea* is not so much its making visible of a cultural minority but rather the challenge that it poses to the dominant construct of *mexicanidad.* Although its characters repeatedly argue that minorities are "the salt of a country," its reexamination of Mexican history goes beyond Stavans's plea for acknowledgment of difference and diversity. Its analysis of gender divisions within the communities it portrays (Ashkenazim, Sephardim, Gentile) complicates its speaking position still further, positing a representation of marginalization within marginalization. Rather than substituting one tradition for another (in this case Jewish for Catholic) at the center of filmic representation, it calls all hegemonic tradition into question.

Between Traditions: The Persistence of Exile

The opening sequence of *Novia que te vea* situates the film within the tradition, affirmed each year at Passover, that links all Jewish stories to the original Exodus. A conventional framing device has the protagonists, Oshinica Mataraso (Claudette Maille) and Rifke Groman (Maya Mishalska), looking at Oshi's family album showing her family's arrival in Mexico and her own childhood, which the film will go on to dramatize. In voice-over, Oshi comments that the sepia-tone photos of her immediate ancestors once seemed to her to be "illustrations of the Bible" and that in a way, they are: "Why not?" What ensues is thus firmly located in a larger history that transcends its immediate context and becomes global, even as it details the particular experiences of two young Jewish women in Mexico.

Unlike the work of some of her contemporaries, Schyfter's film is largely conventional in form; the concise chronological editing, framed within an extended flashback, attests to the director's background in documentary production. Black-and-white footage at the beginning tells the story of Oshi's family's arrival in Mexico City in the early 1920s, following an already established route to La Lagunilla, the marketplace where many Jews kept shops. The stories of Oshi's and Rifke's childhoods show, by means of brief vignettes, what it was like to grow up Jewish in Mexico City: the fear and fascination of being taken to a Catholic church by an Indian nanny, speaking Ladino or Yiddish at home, being teased and harassed by other children, hearing heated debates over politics, Israel, and socialism; in short, childhoods both typically Mexican and constantly marked by difference.

In *Las genealogías,* Glantz talks about the feelings of deprivation she experienced at being excluded from Catholic celebrations like the Día de los Reyes, when the children around her all received gifts; Hanukkah and other Jewish rituals could not compensate for that feeling of loss. In *Novia,* Oshi too remembers having "a foot in both worlds": "I used to cross myself, just in case."

Early in the film she is shown visiting a church with her nanny; she is amazed by the plaster Christ's wounds and begs the nanny not to tell anyone that she is Jewish. Rifke, the daughter of liberal Ashkenazim, exhibits an even more tormented longing toward mainstream Catholic culture. Like Glantz, she is fascinated by the rituals of the other, and her pride in her heritage does not totally compensate for a desire to erase the feeling of difference that the dominant culture imposes on her. We see her as a child run from her parents' house yelling that "the baby Jesus does too exist!" But looking back as an adult, she recalls that "I wanted to belong. To say 'we' this, 'we' that, 'we.' I believed that you had to choose between Jewishness and the rest, but you can't choose. You stay in limbo. You're not here, you're not there, you're not, period."

Because much of her family was killed in Europe, Rifke never knew her grandparents and believed she "had no history . . . [and] had sprung from nothing, like a mushroom." Her interest in national history as well as her eventual marriage to a Gentile are firmly grounded in this early monologue. Moreover, the ambivalence that surrounds her—her family's silence on the subject of the Holocaust, her father's enthusiasm for Israel, and her uncle Meyer's profound pain, vehement anti-Zionism, and solemn allegiance to his adopted country—virtually mandates her forging of a new path, the creation of her own identity out of the confusing material of the Jewish diaspora.

Although similarly marked by childhood experiences of difference and discrimination, Oshi as she matures is torn less between Jewish and Gentile worlds than between the requirements of her strict upbringing and her own desire to be an artist. While seemingly accepting her preordained trajectory toward marriage and domesticity, she struggles to convince her parents to let her study painting—an undertaking they find unsuitable for a daughter. In her family, a young woman's only thoughts should be of her wedding, as the compliment "novia que te vea" (I hope to see you a bride) implies. Scenes in her home depict a feminine sphere whose only objective is its own survival and reproduction—and thereby that of the Sephardim as a whole (Fig. 5.1).

But Oshi's rebellious spirit is inflamed by her contact with Ashkenazi Zionist and leftist youth, who in the early 1960s were influenced not only by the political currents informing Mexican youth culture in general but also by the utopian promise of the Israeli Kibbutzim, to which many Mexican Jews flocked in hopes of finding a true homeland or a better future. Interestingly, while Nissán's novel ends in 1957, Schyfter chose to set the bulk of the film in the late 1950s and early 1960s, contemporaneous with the first years of the Cuban Revolution and with the growth of a pro-Cuban, anti-U.S. and anti-

F I G. 5.1. The destiny of a Sephardic daughter: *Novia que te vea*'s feminine sphere.
Courtesy Instituto Mexicano de Cinematografía.

imperialist left whose critique of the postrevolutionary status quo in Mexico would bring it into conflict with the PRI government. Although anti-Communist repression is shown in the film, the fact that *Novia* unfolds prior to the massacre of 1968 allows it to depict the ideals of its characters without bitterness, as wellsprings of hope and personal empowerment. The young Jews' idealization of Israel and of the kibbutz mode of social organization becomes a variant of this, a kind of Jewish "translation" (to borrow Stavans's term) of Che Guevara's dream of the "new man" (Fig. 5.2). The influence of such thinking is shown as extending beyond the circles of organization or party militants; in the context of the revolutionary ideas espoused by Rifke, Shomer youth leader Ari (Daniel Gruener), and their Gentile Communist friends, the more conservatively raised and less intellectual Oshi finds the support she needs to fight for her own self-determination.

Again, the film echoes Glantz in its portrayal of the idealistic Jewish youth milieu, although Glantz came of age more than a decade before the characters in the film. For like Glantz, *Novia que te vea*'s characters grow up and find their identities in the central city, among the living remnants of a culture which places them at a paradoxical distance. Scenes of Rifke painting pro-Cuba banners, restoring Mesoamerican artifacts, and flirting shyly with Saavedra (Ernesto Laguardia) in the cobblestone streets around the National Preparatory School (Fig. 5.3) seem to illustrate Glantz's reminiscences as well:

> Alguna vez yo fui sionista. Y lo fui durante mis mejores años, los que pasé en San Ildefonso junto a los frescos de José Clemente Orozco, que me dejaron tal impresión que a veces cuando me miro al espejo me doy cuenta de que así, ojerosa y pintada, soy el vivo retrato de algunas de las inmisericordes que dejó por el muro el magnífico manco.
>
> [At one time I was a Zionist. And it was during my best years, the ones I spent in San Ildefonso, beside the frescos of José Clemente Orozco, which made such an impression on me that sometimes when I look at myself in the mirror I realize

FIG. 5.2. Ari Telch and Maya Mishalska as young idealists in *Novia que te vea*.
Courtesy Instituto Mexicano de Cinematografía.

Fɪɢ. 5.3. Rifke (Mishalska) and Saavedra (Ernesto Laguardia) painting
pro-Cuba banners in *Novia que te vea.*

Courtesy Instituto Mexicano de Cinematografía.

that like this, with circles under my eyes and blotchy, I am the living replica of
those miserable women that the magnificent one-armed painter left on the wall.]
(Glantz, *Las genealogías* 207)

In the murals to which she refers, which appear in *Novia que te vea* as well,
Orozco attempted to connect modern Mexicans to their past by portraying
the onset of European domination and subsequent moments of national formation in the crucible of race and class conflict. But Glantz's identification
with the painted figures is not based on an imagined line of heredity; it is an
embodiment that is necessarily arbitrary, an identification with "miserable"
women who are "ojerosa y pintada" rather than members of a particular race
or class, and also with the city itself ("ojerosa y pintada" being an allusion to
the urban landscape in both Agustín Yáñez's 1959 novel of that title and the
Ramón López Velarde verse which inspired it). Moreover, the murals are associated in Glantz's memory with Zionism. Through the murals, Mexico City
becomes both patria and site of subjectivity for Glantz and, by extension, for
Jewish women. This passage, like many in *Las genealogías,* displaces the surface subject matter of the book, her family's specific history, in favor of a

broader, richer, more flexible but also more ambivalent and elusive notion of identity (or genealogy).

Such a rethinking of Jewish *mexicanidad* is an important subtext of *Novia* as well—most obviously through the character of Rifke but also in Oshi's attempt to mediate between her family's traditionalism and the modernist environment in which she finds herself. In this respect, the choice of painting as Oshi's vocation becomes quite significant, for painting is perhaps the expression par excellence of Mexican nationalist culture. The visual arts in Mexico are rooted in indigenous traditions of pictorial language, mural painting, and decoration; in the colonial era, the fusion of Catholic and indigenous styles produced some of the world's most baroque religious art; and in the 1920s and 1930s, the muralist movement led by Orozco, Diego Rivera, and David Alfaro Siqueiros secularized the form and made it the privileged public expression of the modern nation. In Jewish tradition, however, visual images are prohibited in religious contexts and thus not especially privileged in the secular realm. Yet it seems almost inevitable that the Jewish presence in Mexico would give birth to new syncretisms, and indeed, Arnold Belkin's painting of a mural in the city's first synagogue took place under the vigilance of a rabbi, a community leader, and the poet Jacobo Glantz, Margo's father, who calmed the painter's fears of controversy by telling him "pinta lo que te dé la gana" [paint whatever you feel like painting] (Glantz, *Las genealogías* 169).

In Belkin's mural and that painted by Fanny Rabell at the Jewish Sports Center (both realized during the 1950s), the influence of "Los Tres Grandes" (Rivera, Siqueiros, and Orozco) is brought to bear on Jewish subject matter, creating art that is unique to its cultural context (Lerner 22, 39). Thus although Oshi's art itself (as opposed to her desire to study) is not represented as transgressive per se in *Novia que te vea,* it can nevertheless be seen as one of the film's tropes of fusion and syncretism. It identifies Oshi with a generation that does not reject the past so much as it embraces a more encompassing vision of identity and individuality.

Along similar lines, but more overt as both a political choice and a narrative device, is Rifke's immersion in anthropology as a means of reconciling her sense of betweenness and marginality. It is here, I would argue, that the film moves farthest beyond a narrative representation of Jewish history and toward a conscious analysis of the consequences of that history for Mexican identity. Rifke's study of her country's indigenous roots is cleverly used to revise the role of Jews in the cultural construct of the nation, which during the period addressed by the movie was labeled the "great Mexican family."

At the university, Rifke learns of the settlement of central Mexico by tribes arriving in waves from the north, ending with the Aztecs in 1325. In a brief classroom scene, Rifke's professor explains that "the brilliant Tenochtitlan was the product of successive migrations. . . . Culture after culture imposed itself on and merged with earlier cultures." While by no means revisionist, the emphasis on migration gives the film a way to relocate the Jewish diaspora within canonical notions of Mexican nationhood. The dominant view of Mexican origins stresses the originality of indigenous peoples and the transgressor/invader status of Europeans and culminates in the fusion of the two: the resolution of the Hegelian master/slave dialectic via the creation of a new "cosmic" race. But by delving into the region's pre-Cortesian history, the stage is set for conceptualizing Mexico as an immigrant nation, the "mosaic of racial multiplicity" described by Stavans. The dialectical synthesis that underlies the concept of the mestizo nation is found to be inadequate, not only for describing Mexico's sizable indigenous population (which retains ethnic specificity even as it is immersed in the nationalist discourses and policies of the patria) but also in accounting for the nation that continues to evolve after 1521 and that includes Blacks, Germans, successive waves of Spaniards, and many other immigrants, including Jews.

Rifke's study of indigenous Mexico is repeatedly utilized to elucidate not only her own Mexican identification but also to make an argument for the centrality of Jewish experience within the construct of the nation. In a campfire discussion during a Shomer outing, Oshi and Ari remark that although their parents are from Turkey and Poland, they themselves feel no connection with those countries. Rifke, whom we have seen frequently upset at being treated as a foreigner by non-Jews, joins the conversation: "I was born in Mexico. I study archeology and I'm learning Nahuatl." For Rifke, learning an indigenous language and immersing herself in Mexico's long pre-Cortesian history cements and solidifies the Mexican identity that is already hers by birth but which is constantly called into question by Gentiles who assume that she does not fully belong.

In a later scene, Rifke is invited to dinner at her boyfriend Saavedra's lavish family home, where she is forced to confront the exclusionary views held by segments of the Mexican bourgeoisie. Saavedra's father is an official in the López Mateos government, and their other dinner guest is a conservative journalist. Pleased by Rifke's diplomatic response to a point of contention between his son and himself, Saavedra Sr. comments that he has some very close friends who are "Israelis." This disclosure of Rifke's Jewishness provokes hostility from the journalist, who asks her how many Jews there are in Mexico, (about forty thousand, she responds) and comments, "Is that all? Are you sure? I thought there were about two million. . . . They seem like a lot because they're everywhere, but they don't integrate."

The camera, framing Saavedra and Rifke as the reverse shot of the close-up of the journalist, emphasizes their unity, and it is Saavedra who responds. "Integrate into what? The 'gran familia mexicana'?" Seeing the affirmative response, Saavedra lashes out at the dominant ideology: "There are few ideas that disgust me as much as that of the 'gran familia mexicana.' Because it presumes that we all want the same thing, and it's not true. Some want to exploit, others want not to be exploited." Here we are shown clearly how the leftist thought of the 1960s, critiquing from a Marxist perspective the myth of national unity based on shared patrimony, provides an opening for the embrace of diversity as well. But the politics of ethnic and cultural identity are, of course, not identical to the class struggle, and the journalist insists: "In this class society, where are the Jews? Among the exploited?"

Saavedra's mother attempts to keep the peace by naming examples of Jewish achievement: Einstein, Freud, Marx. But Rifke, exasperated by references to her people as other (the constant marker of difference conveyed in the distinction between "ustedes"/other and "nosotros"/Mexican), again invokes the discourse of *indigenismo* to align herself with her country's roots. Wielding her knowledge of indigenous populations, she argues that "the great Mexican family also has its cultural minorities: the Otomí, the Cora, the Tarahumara, the Huichol, the Nahua . . . the Jews."

"All are Mexican," adds Saavedra, "but with different traditions." Rifke explains that minorities enrich and are "the salt of a country." The father mutters something noncommittal, and the party, now shown in a nonpartisan wide shot, falls into a silent stalemate. As the two older men excuse themselves, the scene is resolved in an interesting way. Saavedra, trying to smooth over Rifke's indignation, tells her that his mother was a teacher during the Cárdenas years and can sing the socialist "Internationale" anthem. Suddenly a common ground is established that transcends the ethnic divisions imposed by the two conservative men: Rifke, previously seated next to Saavedra, steps out of the frame and reappears in the next shot with his mother, singing and embracing. In this moment, the bitterness provoked by the journalist's antiSemitism (and its more benign manifestation in the notion of the "gran familia mexicana") is replaced by a vision of progressive idealism as the leveler of differences.

Such a vision clearly informs Rifke's entire relationship with the young Communist Saavedra. Their politics bring them together in ways that would not happen otherwise, given both the latent anti-Semitism of the Catholic culture and the separatism of the city's Jewish community. Although at first Rifke is defensive and self-protective, she comes to trust and respect him, just as he comes to accept that her participation in the Communist party will always be secondary to her Zionist activities. Although Rifke defies her family by falling in love with a Gentile (a trajectory that the film foreshadows in its portrayal of her boundless curiosity that leads her as a child to demand Nativity scenes at Christmas and insist on the Christ child's authenticity), she never compromises her Jewishness but rather repeatedly demonstrates that it is possible to live the hybrid reality that is, after all, the reality of the Americas even though (she says) "they always want to make you choose."

In her portrayal of the couple, Schyfter uses several striking visual devices to place them within a larger context of Mexican historical representation. Much of their early courtship takes place in and around the National Preparatory School on San Ildefonso Street; its stairwells are decorated with the Orozco frescos mentioned in *Las genealogías.* Prominent among these is his "Cortés y la Malinche," which depicts the Spanish conqueror and his indigenous translator, adviser, and companion as Adam and Eve. The painting is noteworthy for its ambivalence; the couple is naked, connoting innocence, yet at their feet is an amorphous body, and Cortés's arm is outstretched in a gesture of restraint, holding Malinche back from some ambiguous movement or impulse. Although its details are not visible on the screen, it is an image that many Mexican spectators would recognize when Saavedra pauses underneath it, watching Rifke walk away after refusing yet another of his invitations. Later, they will walk down these stairwells together, displacing the canonical historical images of European male conqueror/indigenous female conquered with the joyous alliance of Jew and Gentile on their way to protest Yankee imperialism.

The connection between Rifke and Saavedra's romance, national history, and contemporary political struggle is also reinforced visually in the classroom scene mentioned earlier. While the professor lectures on the interpretation of codices, Saavedra enters and asks permission to interrupt. Standing in front of the class, he announces the next day's meeting time; a slide from an Aztec codex is superimposed on his face, and in the next shot, we see Rifke beaming. According to the professor, the slide shows Chiconomostoc, the place of the seven caves, which is the birthplace of the Nahua tribes; thus it is no less than the birth of the Mexican nation that is being graphically fused with both radical activism and romantic desire.

In these scenes, the film makes a subtle yet audacious statement about the utopian possibilities unleashed by the progressive movement of the 1960s and its rejection of patriarchal notions of national identity. Politics are a catalyst for romance, and both are set against an historical narrative that goes back hundreds of years and over which both the left and Jews must claim interpretive control in order to achieve their empowerment. Importantly, Rifke's journey of self-discovery by means of Mexico's ancient history is balanced by Saavedra's acceptance of their differences. In fact, it is ultimately Saavedra who at the end of the film agrees to raise their children in the Jewish tradition; a jump forward shows their son's barmitzvah. Through Rifke and Saavedra, the dialectical concept of *mestizaje,* as it is deployed at the service of the false unity of the "gran familia mexicana," is replaced by a celebration of diversity and multiplicity.

Although the film is an affirmation of Jewish culture and history as part of the nation, it is important to note that its message was not welcomed by the official institutions of Mexican Jewry. When Nissán's novel was published, her brother objected to its semi-autobiographical representation and spoke out against it. As president of the Jewish Central Committee and an important member of the community, he influenced Jewish organizations not to support the film (which went into production almost simultaneously with the novel's publication). Schyfter was refused permission by the president of the Ashkenazi community to film at the old synagogue and the Jewish cemetery, on the grounds that the film included an intermarriage—thus replicating the very conflict portrayed in the film.

Clearly the conservatism of some segments of the community still persists; yet other segments have become much more open to change. A group of independent Jewish investors helped to finance the film, indicating that not all Jews were offended by its inclusive politics; more broadly, the appearance of works by writers and artists like Glantz, Nissán, Sabina Berman (whose eloquent 1991 novel *La bobe* similarly narrates a Jewish childhood), and Schyfter indicates that younger Jews are questioning aspects of the tradition from within, without abandoning Judaism as a touchstone of identification. Anecdotal evidence, such as discussions on the interactive website *Israel en español* and articles published in the Mexico City Jewish newspaper *Kesher,* indicates that the issue of separatism versus integration continues to be controversial and tends to split on generational lines. For many Jews, as Elba Szclar wrote in *Kesher* in 1997, "No es necesario escoger una identidad y tener que desechar la otra; somos judíos y somos mexicanos a la vez. . . . La riqueza espiritual no divide; al contrario, suma y multiplica" [It's not necessary to choose one identity and have to throw out the other; we're at once Jews and Mexicans. . . . Spiritual wealth doesn't divide, on the contrary, it adds and multiplies]. Rifke and Oshi may still be threatening to some guardians of orthodoxy, but the choices they make in the film are much like those made by many contemporary men and women for whom the boundaries between ethnoreligious cultures are less significant than the commonalties derived from centuries of coexistence.

Defying Gender Prescriptions

In her public discussions of *Novia que te vea,* Schyfter has indicated that her primary concern was to represent the history of her generation as well as the internal conflicts often suffered by members of an ethnic or cultural minority. In an interview in *Dicine,* she explained to Patricia Torres the collaborative process of adaptation and her intended focus in the script:

> Yo discutía los momentos más importantes de la historia: el tío Mayer [sic], estos socialistas viejos que no creen en el estado de Israel; el papá, que es el sionista que los judíos necesitaban, etcétera. . . . Yo quería dar todo ese mundo socialista judío que la gente no conoce.
> [I argued for the most important moments of the story: Uncle Meyer, these old socialists that don't believe in the state of Israel; the father, who is the Zionist that the Jews needed, et cetera. . . . I wanted to show all of this socialist Jewish world that people don't know about.] (in Torres, "Entrevista con Guita Schyfter" 26)

Schyfter also reveals the difficulties she confronted in adapting Nissán's novel, since as a Sephardic Jew Nissán's experience was far from familiar to the director. Nissán, a photographer, wrote her novel in a workshop led by Elena Poniatowska, who Nissán says "sacó esa novela de adentro de mí, porque jamás pensé escribirla" [brought this novel out from inside of me, because I never thought of writing it] (in Gallegos, "Guita Schyfter"). Poniatowska later recommended *Novia que te vea* to Schyfter, who was looking for material with which she could carry out Isaac Bashevis Singer's mandate to "look for your roots"; Nissán, Schyfter, and playwright Hugo Hiriart then forged the script. The collaboration resulted in a synthesis that is rich and multilayered: characters—most significantly that of Rifke—were added, dropped, and modified; the time period was moved up to the early 1960s; and the social conflicts of that period were made central rather than peripheral. In the novel, an early boyfriend of Oshi becomes a Shomer activist and introduces her to Zionist-Socialist thought, but Becky, the character on which Rifke is most based, is not politically active although progressive and daring in other ways. In general, the film combines the story of Oshi's coming of age with other experiences that together form a broad panorama of Jewish experience. What remains of Nissán's novel, however, is a deep questioning of gender roles from a perspective that is both specific to the Sephardic community and familiar to feminists everywhere, who cannot but empathize with Oshi's struggle to resist a preordained fate and to determine her own destiny as a human being.

"I was born to marry," Oshi explains to Rifke, "and according to custom, the sooner the better." As a child she is put to work preparing her trousseau, and the gossip that accompanies her female relatives' constant embroidering revolves around the engagements and weddings of others. Although her grandmother, who migrated to Mexico alone with her daughters, provides an example of female strength and independence, the model of femininity that is imposed on Oshi involves running the household, gossiping, playing cards with other women for diversion, and replicating this model in the next generation. Education for girls is not valued, and even an innocent activity like drawing becomes suspect when Oshi pursues it too stubbornly. As an adolescent, Oshi's activities are only permitted to the extent that they enhance her marriageability.

However, early in the film, Oshi's grandmother teaches her a lesson that (according to the tightly woven logic of the narrative) will have repercussions later, when Oshi decides to follow her heart rather than custom. The grandmother, a strong and sympathetic woman who teaches, in the Jewish tradition, "by telling stories," puts young Oshi to bed one night and tells her the story of a Jewish girl who married a rich king and went away from her homeland to live in luxury. Once there, she realized that she didn't fit in, that she didn't understand her new country, nor did it accept her. "She thought she had found a treasure," explains the grandmother, "but it was a poisoned treasure." She cautions Oshi that, if the poisoned treasure should appear, she should "let it go."

Like many parables, the grandmother's story is ambiguous. On the one hand, it can be read as a cautionary tale against straying from one's own clan, and thus as an endorsement of the community's prohibition on intermarriage, not only with non-Jews but with non-Sephardim. However, because the key to knowing whether the treasure is poisoned is looking into one's own heart, the story is also an indictment of marriage for external material reasons and a validation of the right of an individual to free choice and the pursuit of her own happiness. It is the latter lesson that Oshi ultimately absorbs, though not without struggle.

When Oshi meets a medical student at a dance, her fate is immediately sealed; her enthusiastic mother sets the wedding date almost before Oshi has a chance to realize what is happening. In a series of comic scenes, Oshi gradually realizes that she will never be happy married to the authoritarian Leon Levy, whose jokes and mustache she comes to despise. A sequence involving such iconic 1950s date elements as a convertible and a drive-in restaurant illustrates the incompatibility of the couple whose union, on the surface, is the realization of their families' and culture's dream. After Leon and Oshi order their food and soda, Leon outlines with terrifying precision the boundaries of their immediate future. After they marry, he will complete his social service and go into pediatrics. Their house, conveniently located near the emergency room, is already picked out; what is less clear is where Oshi's desires fit into his plan.

Throughout much of the film, Schyfter uses framing to reflect degrees of conflict; when characters are in agreement, they are framed together, whereas when they disagree, they are shot in close-ups which are then edited against one another, intensifying the sense of confrontation. In this sequence, though, the two-shot from the front of the car reflects Oshi's complicity; when she realizes what Leon is actually saying, she sits up quickly, as if to remove herself from the frame. Learning that he wants to continue his professional training, she tells him that she too wants to study. He laughs and asks what for.

Oshi is crushed: clearly her marriage will not help her realize her dream of becoming a painter. Moreover, Leon's authority over his future wife is even more oppressive than that exercised by her family. When she tries to order more food, he stops her, warning her that he doesn't want her to get fat. Then he laughs at her announcement that she is going to the Holy Week festivities in Malinalco with her anthropologist friends. After demonstrating his indifference to her views, he presumptuously tries to kiss her; she pulls away and takes a bite of cake instead. The two-shot that ends the sequence is no longer about romance but rather distance and the patriarchal prison that, at this point, seems to be Oshi's destiny.

Troubled, Oshi nevertheless goes along with the plans for the wedding. But when Oshi's mother learns that she is taking painting classes and makes her stop, Oshi realizes that her own dreams are more important than her family's wishes. Talking to the sympathetic Ari, she decides to break the engagement—an extremely defiant and taboo act in her community. She confesses her feelings to her father, who seems sympathetic yet unable to conceive of breaking so abruptly with custom. He tells her that love comes later, that no one is in love in the beginning. His examples, like the story of her aunt Zafira's betrothal to someone she'd only seen in a picture and disliked on sight, but whom she had to marry in order to be allowed off the boat from Turkey, have the opposite of the intended effect. When Rifke leaves town to escape the personal crisis triggered by Saavedra's arrest, Oshi decides to accompany her.

Like Rebeca and Valentina in Busi Cortés's *Serpientes y escaleras,* the two women must physically separate themselves from their families and communities in order to achieve their own liberation. In this case, however, the journey is brief and temporary, easily achieving a resolution of both women's conflicts. They go to the home of Oshi's grandmother, whose poisoned-treasure parable years earlier foreshadowed Oshi's dilemma. In Oshi's absence, Leon so irritates Oshi's father that he throws his would-be son-in-law out of the house, effectively breaking the engagement. Meanwhile, Saavedra's pursuit of Rifke all the way to Guadalajara cements their union and convinces Rifke that in spite of her family's disapproval, she cannot leave him.

The idea that love overrides social custom is brought home by two conversations. First, at the kitchen table in her home, Oshi's grandmother repeats the poisoned-treasure story. This time it is Rifke who asks how one knows if the treasure is poisoned. The grandmother again answers that the truth is in the heart but elaborates that most people don't know what they really feel. Seemingly contradicting her own advice, she counsels Rifke not to marry a Gentile. However, a few minutes later, as she and Oshi watch the happy couple from the window, she will pronounce the final verdict: "It is her destiny."

Meanwhile, Saavedra's eloquent declaration to Rifke as they walk out of the garden again locates their relationship within national and universal history and reinforces the notion of the couple as something like the Adam and Eve of a brave new world:

Do you realize all that had to happen so that you and I could meet? A pogrom in Russia, a train dynamited in Puebla, a ship arriving late in Danzig, the son of Alvaro Saavedra studying medicine . . . Hitler in Munich and Obregón assassinated . . . a world war, millions of lives, and millions of trivial incidents, all fitting into the immense geography on one side or other of the ocean. In Hamburg and Tuxpam, the gigantic mechanism of universal history bearing down on a single point so that I could say, "I love you, Rifke."

The film ultimately proposes that Rifke's and Oshi's defiance of some their community's most important laws is part of an unstoppable larger force, namely destiny. This notion of destiny draws on the conventional romantic notion that love conquers all and on the melodramatic convention of romance across class lines or other social boundaries. It also invokes the Talmudic teaching that human destiny is written at the moment of creation but that it is nevertheless up to the individual to make moral choices. This idea is referenced both in the grandmother's admonition (made in front of a prominent menorah that metonymically lends the weight of an ancient tradition to her words) that the angels arrange the weddings of children before they are born and that Rifke and Saavedra's marriage could not have been made in heaven, and in her later pronouncement that in fact Saavedra is Rifke's destiny. But most of all, it makes the case that what is good for the individual and for the community at certain times—such as using marriage restrictions to ensure Jewish survival during times of intense anti-Semitism—is open to change.

When we finally return to the adult Oshi and Rifke, we see that they have not abandoned their Jewish roots but rather have found ways to integrate the different sides of their lives into a harmonious whole. Oshi has married Ari, has children, and paints. Rifke has continued her scholarship, writing about Aztec as well as Jewish history. With her son raised as a Jew and her husband in the national legislature, her earlier daring break with convention seems to have resulted in a comfortable outcome. The protagonists, it seems, live happily ever after; but more importantly, as Oshi's remark that the family photos are like "illustrations of the Bible" is reiterated, what had seemed to be profound cultural conflicts are resolved, and the notion of a conciliatory Jewish *mexicanidad* is affirmed. As in the films by Busi Cortés, the destinies of individual women cannot be separated from those of the nation whose former patriarchal boundaries are successfully stretched to include them.

Novia que te vea's many didactic elements attest to the filmmaker's impulse to educate and to her assumption that Jewish history is unfamiliar to most of her audience and must be directly told, not simply evoked as diegetic context. These essay-like elements invite an analysis of the film as a commentary on the role of Jews in Mexican history and ideology; however, of equal importance is the film's deployment of generic melodramatic conventions, such as those of generational conflict and romance across social barriers.

In her essay "Tears and Desire: Women and Melodrama in the 'Old' Mexican Cinema," Ana López discusses the privileged relation of melodrama to Mexican culture, citing its intersections with the "three master narratives of Mexican society: religion, nationalism, and modernization" (150). Rendering social issues as personal moral conflicts, melodramatic films defined the models of sexuality and femininity that were—or were not—compatible with the national project. As Silvia Oroz writes:

> El melodrama cinematográfico latinoamericano fue la educación sentimental de más de una generación, consolidando y sublimando, a través de su propia convención lingüística, las conductas y modelos motivados por el dicho popular: "El amor lo puede todo." Es entonces cuando, por vía indirecta, entra en juego el pecado. El melodrama constituirá un eficaz modelo de comunicación, donde el inseparable binomio amor/pecado, fundamental en la escala de valores patriarcales, queda homologado.
>
> [Latin American film melodrama was the sentimental education of more than a generation, consolidating and sublimating, through its own linguistic conventions, the behaviors and models that arise from the popular saying: "Love conquers all." It is then that, indirectly, sin comes into play. Melodrama constitutes an efficient model of communication in which the inseparable binomial love/sin, fundamental in the scale of patriarchal values, is replicated.] (34–35)

The popular *telenovelas* of today uphold this same value system, in which sexual attraction is an all-powerful force that one often resists at first but ultimately succumbs to—sometimes with tragic results, but all for the better when the object of desire turns out to be heroic rather than evil and, in the best of cases, rich rather than poor.

As feminist film scholars have often pointed out, the subduing of the melodramatic heroine's will becomes the key to her own happiness; Linda Williams, for example, writes in her discussion of female spectatorship that "the divided female spectator identifies with the woman whose very triumph is often in her own victimization" and that "the melodrama's impulse towards the just 'happy ending' usually places the woman hero in a final position of subordination" (320). In *Novia que te vea,* on the contrary, the union between Saavedra and Rifke is a choice for which the heroine has struggled and which has implications beyond the personal narrative. In fact, the placement of their steamy bedroom scene just after Saavedra's appeal to universal history suggests that their sexual union is itself an historically significant act, one with the potential to replace the ambivalent heritage of Cortés and Malinche with a new foundational myth of Mexican identity based on acceptance rather than violence.

Both Rifke's and Oshi's choice of partners implies a certain politics and an investment in their own futures, which will be emotionally supported, not decided, by their husbands. In Rifke's case, she insists on raising her children as Jews, while Oshi's marriage is contingent on her following her first love, painting. Although the happy ending, with its Hollywood-style intimations of a double wedding, has an overly simple, fairy-tale aspect to it (the fact that the once-censured Saavedra goes on to become a legislator may or may not be an intentional injection of irony), it nonetheless represents the reclaiming of popular feminine fantasy from a political perspective emphasizing female agency and choice.

Just as in Cortés's *Serpientes y escaleras,* the feminist vision put forth in *Novia que te vea* is concerned with questioning not the institution of marriage as such, but rather the injunction to marry for reasons other than love. Liberal men are seen as allies, and the social construction of desire within patriarchy is not addressed. In other words, the premium that conventional melodrama puts on love is retained, although its terms are radically changed. The representational strategy that results from this brand of feminism lets viewers have their cake—their escapist/romantic/feminine fantasy—and eat it too: Cortés's and Schyfter's heroines escape the confines of patriarchal tradition and end up with the young men who will help them realize their personal dreams. In both films, liberal or radical politics are integrally linked to individual freedom and to narrative romance: the first linkage implies that men and women will be free when oppressive institutions, be they political machines (in *Serpientes*) or outmoded customs (in *Novia*), are overturned, while the second implies that the fairy-tale scenarios of popular feminine melo-drama need not be completely rejected by feminists.

The Chicken and the Egg

The association of *Novia que te vea* with melodrama is reinforced, albeit prob-lematically, by one of its ads (printed on the back cover of *Dicine* 55), which features a close-up of Oshi with her eyes aimed upward, seemingly gazing at the film's title above her head. In the title, the letter "u" is enlarged to form a menorah with candles of red, white, and green, the colors of the Mexican flag. The graphic style evokes the posters of the 1960s. The copy reads: "Oshinica está en la edad de descubrir todo. Sólo una cosa se lo impide . . . ser judía mex-icana en los turbulentos años sesentas" [Oshinica is at the age to discover everything. Only one thing stands in the way . . . being a Mexican Jew in the turbulent 1960s].

Ironically, this ad's assertion epitomizes rather than explicates the entire problematic of the film and, more broadly, of gendered Jewish identity in Mexico. For the "one thing" standing in the way of Oshi's "discovery" is not, in fact, one but rather several, or a compound of several factors: being Jewish and Mexican and female *(judía mexicana)* and in the turbulent 1960s. Yet the preferred reading, reinforced by the large menorah which in turn is empha-sized by Oshinica's gaze, points to being Jewish as the obstacle, since it is Jew-ishness, after all, that constitutes the film's singularity.

But what is it that Oshi would discover if she were not Jewish, or if she were not any of these things? Viewing the film does not yield an answer, but both novel and film make it clear that Oshi's overprotected upbringing results not from Jewish tradition per se but from specifically Sephardic cultural tradition and within that, from the values of her particular family. In the novel, for ex-ample, the permissive upbringing of Oshi's future sisters-in-law is contrasted to that of Oshi herself, who is so sheltered within her house that she is shocked the first time she realizes that there are stars in the sky (Nissán 160). Other Jewish characters in the novel and film are shown as enjoying varying degrees of personal freedom from and within their families. In this respect, the char-acterization of Oshi as held back by her Jewishness is misleading and coun-terproductive vis-à-vis the film's project.

Although even *Novia que te vea*'s own advertising poses Oshi's minority sta-tus as an obstacle, the film itself makes a strong case for the adaptability of the

"Mexican family" to include a "multiplicity of multiplicities," thus under-cutting the melodramatic emphasis on individual conflict and resolution. Moreover, the displacement of social concerns such as anti-Semitism onto the characters' personal circumstances is only partial; although the film works within the conventions of a coming-of-age melodrama, the dis-covering of Mexico's multifaceted Jewish culture ultimately takes precedence over the in-dividual dilemma stressed in the ad.

The word "discovery," however, is particularly interesting in this context. In the writings of Jews on Mexico, the "discovery" or conquest of the Ameri-cas is a recurring theme and one that is addressed in ways notably different from non-Jewish literature. In key texts from Jacobo Glantz's *Kristobal Kolon* to Ilan Stavans's *Imagining Columbus,* the issue of conquest is almost brack-eted; the voyages that historically led to the devastation of a continent instead become voyages of the imagination and of the imaginary. They are inevitably touched by the horror of the Inquisition and the recurrent Exodus, the dream of a promised land, the Jerusalem still to be found, the chronic state of home-lessness that is the Jewish condition. In *Las genealogías,* this motif occurs re-peatedly; it is, moreover, personalized, gendered, feminized. Glantz writes:

> Todas las mujeres tenemos algo de Colón (o mucho). Todas tenemos que ver con el huevo, a todas se nos ha ocurrido, antes que a Colón, resolver el famoso enigma placentario. A todas se nos ha pasado, si no por la ca-beza sí por otra parte, resolver practicamente la dicotomía y hemos con-juntado huevo y gallina hasta en la escritura.
>
> [All women have something of Columbus (or a lot) in us. We've all dealt with the egg; all of us, before Columbus, have had to resolve the famous placentary enigma. All of us have had, if not in the head then somewhere else, to resolve the dichotomy in practice and have joined the chicken and the egg even in our writing.] (183)

According to Margo Glantz, women are compelled to explore the world and acquire knowledge, not for gold or material gain but because it has been denied to them for so long. But associating women's liberation with the male conquistadors displaces historical fact and substitutes a utopian vision in which women, and Jews, can conquer the world from inside themselves and in which power need not negatively determine human relations. In this sense, Oshi and Rifke's "discovery" of the world in *Novia que te vea* is not a discov-ery (much less a conquest) but a creation or a remaking: a promised land.

What distinguishes this act of imagination/creation from the conventional happy ending of cinematic melodrama is that in it, contradictions are embraced rather than resolved. In one of the film's most salient moments, the Groman family tests out the latest audio technology—the 33⅓ rpm record—by playing Bach's "Concerto for Two Violins." Rifke comments in voice-over, "It was a puzzle I could never forget. How could Heifetz play the two violins at the same time?" This, of course, is exactly what Rifke will go on to do: juggle identities, worlds, desires, traditions. Like Glantz's reconciliation of the chicken and the egg, *Novia que te vea* asserts that one can be Jewish, Mexican, and female and still discover everything, especially if it is the "turbulent 1960s." For in that decade, as we have seen, canonical notions of national identity and gender boundaries began to break down, allowing the emergence of new social formations and new subject positions. The cinematic interventions made in the 1980s and 1990s by women like Cortés and Schyfter are both a result and a continuation of this dissolution; if their films retain many of the conventions of mainstream cinema, they also use those conventions to further a feminist agenda in which the trope of feminine sacrifice (for the greater good of the nation as well as the patriarchal family) is replaced with an inclusive vision that affirms rather than eradicates women's capacity for self-determination.

Coda: *Sucesos distantes*

In 1994, Guita Schyfter directed a second feature, *Sucesos distantes.* Written by Schyfter's husband and longtime collaborator, Hugo Hiriart, and featuring members of the cast of *Novia,* this film took the director's work in a somewhat surprising new direction. The documentary impulse informing *Novia* is almost completely absent from *Sucesos,* which tells the story of Arturo Fabre (Fernando Balzaretti), an entomologist tormented by the mysterious past of his wife, Irene (Angélica Aragón), a stage actress whom we mostly see playing a female Faust in a highly stylized theater production.

Irene, a Russian immigrant and the widow of a Cuban, is subject to episodes of insomnia and weeping that she refuses to explain to Arturo, who thus is reduced to expressing his frustration and "retrospective jealousy" to his mentally ill mother as well as in comically portrayed sessions of group therapy. When the mysterious Russian Victor Ivanovich Fet (Emilio Echeverría) suddenly appears and declares himself to be not only Irene's former spouse but one of her two living ex-husbands, her secret seems to be revealed as a shocking betrayal. In reality Victor is actually pursuing Irina, a colleague of

Irene now using the name Svetlana, but before Arturo realizes this, he has uncovered the stranger's jewel-counterfeiting operation and thereby placed himself in danger. Luckily, a poisonous centipede—the danger of whose escape is foreshadowed in the beginning of the film—saves the day by killing Victor and biting Arturo, who survives by lying still while the poison dissipates.

His immobile condition provides an opportunity for Irene to deliver a lengthy monologue revealing her true past: her youthful affair with the Cuban Fernando that was forcibly broken up by her parents; a marriage of convenience to a political functionary, whom she later left when Fernando reappeared and convinced her to follow him to Cuba; his death and the lingering tragedy of two children left behind in Russia. The children appear in Irene's dream that opens the film, but Arturo is unaware of their existence. Although the moral ambivalence of the abandonment is part of the reason for her pain, Irene's story absolves her of the charges of treachery, and any possible bargain with the devil on her part is safely contained on the stage.

Although this convoluted plot leaves little room for the kind of character development and social analysis we saw in *Novia*, a few continuities can be observed. First, just as Rifke's anthropology classes provided rationalization for the conceptualization of Mexico as a nation of immigrants in *Novia*, Arturo's entomology lectures and the observations of insect behavior he shares with his assistant Heberto function to develop the thesis that human behavior is not always readily understandable, and one cannot explain another person's actions simply by projecting one's own emotional structure onto the other. Just as the markings of a nonpoisonous butterfly species make it look poisonous to potential predators, so too might signs of marital treachery and deception turn out to be benign or to have some other explanation. Yet insect behavior is contrasted with that of humans; the lecture that introduces us to Arturo deals with an insect that lays eggs, leaves food for the young that will hatch, and never returns. For human mothers, guided by reason and feeling rather than instinct, such a separation is more likely the result of a difficult decision and a decisive action that, even if perceived as necessary, leaves painful scars.

Second, Schyfter's interest in the central city milieu is apparent in the scenes that take place around a small clothing factory run by Ludmilla (Svetlana Makoveva), the aunt of Irene's sought-after colleague. Seeking information about his wife's past, Arturo arrives in the old colonial sector of the city, crossing the central plaza with its costumed neo-Aztec dancers, pushing past the crowds that fill the narrow streets, and upon reaching his destination in the garment district, stopping a woman to ask directions. In a strange visual joke, the woman directs him to "Jaibo," a young street vendor whose dress and appearance is indeed that of Jaibo in Luis Buñuel's *Los olvidados* (1950). Making his way through a dark yet bustling fabric shop to the back courtyard of a colonial building and up the back staircase, Arturo finally locates his wife's alleged relative, who accepts his claim of being her niece's husband, since the women have not seen each other for some time.

Ludmilla is portrayed as both a shrewd, aggressive businesswoman and as a colorful character typical of the downtown garment district, many of whose merchants are traditionally of foreign descent. In contrast to *Novia que te vea,* however, the sociology of this milieu is not deeply examined. Off screen, class-based conflicts among central city businesspeople, street vendors, and other urban groups have often produced repugnant expressions of both xenophobia and anti-Semitism (Davis 86, 123; Cross). The portrayal of the aunt as associated with smuggling and possibly exploitative labor practices, and as proudly disdainful of the word *maquila* to describe her export business, in some ways seems to perpetuate the image of the exploitative "foreigner." But at the same time, the matter-of-fact treatment of Ludmilla, Svetlana, Irene, and the other Russian characters, who speak to each other in Russian several times without translation, underscores the claims made in *Novia:* that Mexico is not made up of a single mestizo race but is in fact the product of many cultures and many intertwining and overlapping histories.

Finally, Irene's story revisits in brief some of *Novia*'s major themes: the rejection of imposed convention implied in her abandonment of a dysfunctional marriage in pursuit of personal happiness; and the romance with revolutionary Cuba, here literalized as a past personal relationship with a Cuban, the intensity of which caused Irene to leave her homeland and cross geographical and cultural boundaries. Yet in *Sucesos* these themes are tragic: the undesired marriage in Russia produces children whose abandonment is the bitter price of the mother's freedom; and the Cuban dies in Angola, his revolutionary commitment thus destroying rather than creating the possibility of personal fulfillment for the couple. Although Irene's third marriage in Mexico constitutes a partial reconciliation, the sense of "having it all" is absent, for the "distant events" of the title are in fact not distant but quite present, reinforcing her constant sense of loss and transforming her into a strangely literal version of La Llorona, the legendary ghost-mother perpetually wailing for the children that she herself once sacrificed. Moreover, if *Novia* constituted a nostalgic look at the optimism of the Mexican left prior to Tlatelolco, *Sucesos* shows instead the disillusionment represented by the collapse of the Soviet

Union. As Arturo discovers through his encounters with Victor and Ludmilla, "immense fortunes" are being amassed in 1990s Russia through capitalist exploitation, and socialist ideals live on only in the images of Marx and Lenin displayed in an UNAM Russian professor's office—images now infused with an odd nostalgia, as their distant lives have little to do with contemporary reality.

While Schyfter's interests have gone beyond documenting Mexican Jewish experience, she continues to portray a Mexico that is heterogeneous, multiethnic, and multilingual. She herself has explained that her discovery of the Russian presence in Mexico was the film's starting point and that "la mirada que tiene una cultura sobre otra es lo que siempre me ha interesado" [the view that one culture has toward another is what has always interested me] (Silva Martínez 26). Even within the confines of a rather theatrical and forced narrative, her mise-en-scène seems to convey a love of Mexico City and its inhabitants, and her interest in nondominant populations leads her to show the city in interesting ways. Most of all, her two feature films convey the sense that neither national nor personal history can be conceived of in schematic or one-dimensional terms; each is the result of many seemingly arbitrary events, *sucesos distantes* that leave traces on the flesh of the present. While externally imposed choices, especially the choice between desire and duty, convert these into painful wounds and scars, Schyfter argues for the refusal of false dichotomies and transforms the screen into a space in which social constructs and conventions can be questioned and the reconciliation of both individuals and cultural communities, within the larger community of the nation, can be imagined.

I love to play with clichés. However, you have to take them on, break them, spin them around, take pleasure in them. In *Danzón* are almost all of the clichés of the Mexican cinema: the music, the rumba dancers, romanticism, melodrama, kitsch, and in the end, they're all put into play.

María Novaro[1]

CHAPTER 6

María Novaro

Exploring the Mythic Nation

In 1991, María Novaro's second feature, *Danzón,* starring María Rojo, became the first Mexican film in fourteen years to be invited to the Directors' Section of the prestigious Cannes Film Festival. Still in postproduction, the film was hurriedly finished and subtitled; it premiered in France, where its director saw it for the first time in its entirety. Following its successful reception at Cannes, *Danzón* played at two commercial cinemas in Paris, toured the festival circuit, and soon became an international success; in the United States, it was bought for distribution by Sony Classics, the "prestige" film division of Columbia Pictures. In Mexico, after its premiere during the newly inaugurated Hoy en el Cine Mexicano cycle, *Danzón* went on to do what few "quality" films had done in recent memory: make a profit at the box office.

As journalists such as Ysabel Gracida of *El Universal* observed, such success boded well for the future of Mexican filmmaking; for Gracida, the fact that three examples of "quality cinema" *(Danzón, La mujer de Benjamín,* and *Cabeza de Vaca)* had achieved box office returns in Mexico and recognition abroad that year could be seen as a sign that the national cinema was indeed undergoing a renaissance, perhaps even a new Golden Age. Furthermore, the appearance of a second strong feature by Novaro, whose earlier *Lola* (1989) had also been received well, seemed to confirm and strengthen the hard-won

167

acceptance of women at the forefront rather than the margins of national film production. Novaro herself expressed surprise at the film's positive reception outside of the country, having assumed that its strong cultural identification would limit its appeal. Instead, she said, its *mexicanidad* seemed to be the factor that most attracted and intrigued foreign audiences (in Michel).

In spite or because of its success, *Danzón* generated widespread critical disagreement. Was the film feminist? Was it political? Or was it nostalgic and escapist? What was it trying to say about Mexico, about women, about the traditional music and dance form called the *danzón?* While writers about the film agreed on its basic themes and qualities, many differed in their response to these questions. Novaro herself, as a highly vocal and active "author," perhaps contributed to the confusion with her own ambiguity vis-à-vis her film's politics. Yet the very fact that the film repetitively provoked these particular questions suggests an interface between *Danzón* and issues of broad concern in contemporary society.

As we have seen in previous chapters, women-centered stories, to the extent that they displace a masculinist national narrative, raise doubts about conventional versions of *mexicanidad.* Filmmakers of Novaro's generation have intensified these doubts by enacting a literal displacement—their shifting of focus to underrepresented geographical, cultural, and/or psychological terrain and their rewriting of conventional genres and what Novaro calls "clichés." While *Danzón*'s critics have tended to narrow the field of interpretation in their attempts at categorization, I will argue for a broader view, in which feminism becomes more like what Marisa Sistach called an *otra mirada,* a way of seeing more than a dogmatic ideology, and in which Novaro's simultaneous articulation of key issues—gender, nostalgia, cultural identity, liberation—can be seen as a powerful intervention in the social context of the 1990s.

Penelope's Journey

Like Matilde Landeta's 1951 *Trotacalles, Danzón* opens with a close shot of a woman's feet clad in ankle-strap high-heeled shoes. Such glamorous shoes have an established iconic history: they suggest women's confinement and oppression (in *Trotacalles,* their wearer, a prostitute, is knocked to the ground by a car) but simultaneously the possibility of escape—whether through the temporary oblivion of the dance hall or a "Wizard of Oz"-like transformative journey. As it turns out, all of these evocations are brought into play during the course of the film.

As the camera moves around a crowded dance floor, it continues to show only the feet of the dancing couples until it pans up from ground level to the face of protagonist Julia Solórzano (María Rojo), a telephone operator and single mother with a passion for dancing and especially for the *danzón*. This opening sequence takes place in the Salón Colonia, one of Mexico City's popular dance halls, where despite the encroachment of European-style discotheques on the one hand and the hardships of the economic crisis on the other, traditional orchestras still summon elegantly dressed couples to the dance floor with the cry of "¡Hey familia!" to dance steps brought to Mexico from the Caribbean at the end of the nineteenth century. Angel Trejo's *¡Hey, Familia, Danzón Dedicado a . . . !*, documents the *danzón*'s trajectory from its European prehistory to Haiti and Cuba, then to Mérida and Veracruz, and finally to the dance halls of Mexico City. In Trejo's interviews, musicians and aficionados acknowledge the *danzón*'s Cuban roots; yet *danzón* and dance hall culture, immortalized in films from Emilio Fernández's classic *Salón México* (1948) to a recent remake with the same title, has long had a privileged place in the representation of urban *mexicanidad*. For Julia and her friends, this is a treasured ritual, their only escape from otherwise difficult and mundane lives. Yet even before the ritual has completely ended, ordinary time and space take over. As the dancers change into their ordinary shoes, they chat about their lives, their worries, and the unreliability of men, who are pleasant dance partners but not very trustworthy off the dance floor ("They're all married," complains Julia's friend Silvia, played by Margarita Isabel). And soon it is the next day and they are back at work.

The rupture in this routine comes when Julia's dance partner, Carmelo (Daniel Regis), suddenly disappears. Although Julia is not romantically involved with him and indeed knows little of his life away from the dance halls, she becomes obsessed with finding him, wandering through forgotten corners of the city pursuing vague connections and clues. She still goes to the dance halls but does not dance. She is grouchy at work, and her friends suspect menopause. A card reader she consults, who claims to reunite couples, foresees a young man, then an older man, boats, trains, and journeys. At the Salón Los Angeles, Julia sulks and dismisses the young men who ask her to dance, explaining to Silvia that one should never dance with a younger partner; then she tells Silvia that she is going to Veracruz.

As Margo Glantz aptly points out, it is "como si Penélope abandonara su lugar sagrado, la casa donde fabrica su inagotable tejido, para buscar a Ulises; como si Penélope rompiera el encantamiento de la espera, como si convirtiera en Telémaco y recorriera el ancho mundo en busca de su padre" [as if Penelope had abandoned her sacred spot, the house were she weaves her inexhaustible cloth, to go look for Ulysses; as if Penelope had broken the enchantment of the wait, as if she had turned herself into Telemachus and had traversed the wide world in search of her father] ("Danzón" 21). In going to Veracruz, Julia not only goes toward Carmelo (she hopes) but also toward a fuller engagement with the mythic ethos of the dance that heretofore has sustained her as a temporary ritual. Veracruz, the most Caribbean and African-influenced region of Mexico, is considered the birthplace of the Mexican *danzón*. When Julia's train arrives at the station, we see another close shot of her high heels descending onto the platform; she exits the train into a warm and tropical environment where she is greeted by the admiring smiles of non-threatening male onlookers. The possibilities that she has sensed in the dance (as Glantz would have it, in her feet) have suddenly become concretized in a new and unfamiliar landscape, via the alchemy of travel.

Although we know little of Julia's life before Carmelo's disappearance, it is clear from her reactions (conveyed well by Rojo's expressive acting) that each situation is new, amusing, and enchanting to her. Novaro's optic is a poetics of detail: the way Julia's movements are less constrained once she leaves Mexico, the way her clothes flow differently and she smiles at each novelty her eye encounters. When a Russian tries to pick her up in a café using outrageous lines in a mixture of languages, she giggles and makes eye contact with other women in the cafe, who are also laughing. She has begun to welcome such arbitrary and unpredictable encounters. At night, she runs toward the water and dances in the sand.

By the next day, however, she is not at all sure what she is doing there and breaks down crying in front of doña Ti (Carmen Salinas), the gruff proprietor of the hotel where she is staying. The latter softens, says she knows Julia is crying for a man—an analysis not entirely accurate but which universalizes Julia's situation as a typical female dilemma, enabling her to bond more readily with other women. Taking doña Ti's advice, Julia enlists the local prostitutes in her search. La Colorada (Blanca Guerra) asks whether the man she's looking for gets an erection easily and is surprised when Julia says she doesn't know. Instead, Julia talks enthusiastically about dancing and is sent to the Par-que Zamora, where she meets one of the customers who appeared earlier in the café scene; only the "woman" is now clearly a man. Susy (Tito Vasconcelos) is referred to throughout the film as an "artista," an actor both in her tropical-themed nightclub show and in daily life. This label and the character herself invoke the faded glamour of the cabaret and the pleasure and danger of masquerade.

Prostitutes (who help to naturalize and universalize her predicament) and transvestites thus become the agents of Julia's transformation. In Susy's backstage dressing room, Julia notices with delight a pair of false breasts, which she picks up and examines. The nude female sculptures in the nightclub, as the backdrop of a transvestite stage show, suggest the social construction of femininity itself. When Susy convinces Julia to buy a new, flashier wardrobe, it is as if Julia too is putting on drag—which, it may be pointed out, is a costume whose conscious adoption is paradoxically an expression of what one experiences as one's true or inner self. In the merging of exterior appearance and interior desire, masquerade and self-discovery are the same.

Julia's voyage is by no means the stereotypical tale of an innocent inducted into a seedy yet seductive underworld. On the contrary, Julia takes her new acquaintances in stride, making them seem anything but marginal. She participates in the free play of gender roles that Susy initiates; although she is reluctant to break with tradition and teach him (in this scene Susy is wigless and in masculine attire) the woman's part in the *danzón*, she eventually gives in, realizing that Susy's living participation in the dance ritual is more important than the dance's formal conventions (Fig. 6.1). While initially she hesitates about the bold red outfit that she thinks might make her look like a whore, she goes on to wear it with relative confidence, emboldened by the romantic atmosphere of the dock and its brightly painted ships.

There is a tense moment at a café when Susy suggests that they pretend to be *novios* (sweethearts) and attract the attention of other patrons. Susy explains that when she wants to she can be *muy varón* (very masculine) but makes the statement campy by fanning herself haughtily. Instead of the expected complicity, Julia's expression makes Susy ask if she is embarrassed; Julia says no, of course not, but immediately gets up to dance with a male patron. Reinforcing her earlier comments about appropriate dance partners, this action seems to suggest that however open she might be about friendships, she is still rigid about correct roles in the *danzón*. (Later, upon trying to dance with Rubén, she runs off the dance floor rather than tolerate his

FIG. 6.1. Dancing around gender constraints: Julia (María Rojo) teaches Susy
(Tito Vasconcelos) the woman's part in *Danzón*.

Courtesy Instituto Mexicano de Cinematografía.

FIG. 6.2. Julia contemplates Rubén (Víctor Carpinteiro) and
her own mixed feelings in *Danzón*.

Courtesy Instituto Mexicano de Cinematografía.

inexpertness.) Yet Julia's commitment to traditional gender relations on the dance floor is constantly undermined by the other social interactions captured by Novaro's camera: the young girl dancing with her grandmother in the same scene, for example, or later on, a shot of the male hotel porter holding the bottle of polish while doña Ti paints her nails. While these are not radical challenges to the social order, they do offer counterpoints to the *danzón*'s patriarchal allegory in which the man leads and the woman follows and is put on display.

Her fling with the young Rubén (Víctor Carpinteiro) is another manifestation of this; while not entirely out of the bounds of acceptable behavior in contemporary Mexico, Julia's active expression of desire is clearly novel and surprising to herself (Fig. 6.2). Although we know nothing of her prior romantic life, her separation from her daughter's father and her lack of interest in the men she meets at the dance halls suggest that her experiences have been less than gratifying, and it is with bemusement that she enters into a relationship with Rubén—who, perhaps because he doesn't dance as much as because of his age, seems quite outside of the world to which she is accustomed. She comes away from the affair not having met the love of her life but rather with a deeper understanding of herself and her own desires and capacities.

Aventurera Revisited

The story and characters described above are enmeshed throughout in Novaro's lush mise-en-scène, captured by a cinematographic gaze that is uniquely observant and almost excessive in its overt self-referentiality and intertextuality. The film is brilliantly colored, and the brightest color of all is red, as in the high heels worn in the *danzón,* the lighting in the Salón Los Angeles, Julia's new dress, earrings, and lipstick in Veracruz, Susy's and doña Ti's fingernails. Julia's fear of being mistaken for a prostitute is reinforced when La Colorada, putting on a tight red shift and black lace stockings, says that red is a good color for working; yet the modest Julia dares to wear it anyway. This use of color reinforces the link between passion and masquerade and posits desire as a kind of preexistent free-floating quality as well as a force belonging to or felt by individuals.

The elegant and flashy costumes and decor of the dance halls are part of a clearly circumscribed ritual, but over the course of the film, they exceed the latter's boundaries and become the colors and textures of the utopian environment of Veracruz, an almost make-believe land of sea and shore, glamorous nightclubs and outdoor dance floors, brightly painted boats, and friendly cafés. The color blue also is used extensively, balancing the red of passion with a bittersweet sense of destiny and inevitability. The blue of sea and sky suggest a timelessness that is beyond the social realm; yet the song "Azul" humanizes this association and relocates it in the sphere of melodrama, where it is the color of sadness, longing, and lost love.[2] A beautiful shot of Julia in her red dress against the blue sky, throwing a bottle containing the lyrics of a Juan Gabriel song into the ocean, poetically brings all of these associations together, expressing visually the romantic essence of the culture of *danzón*.

Equally important are the references to Mexican popular culture that occur throughout the film. Susy's name is taken from a 1960s comic book, *Susy, secretos del corazón* (published by Novaro's family's press). The boats in the Veracruz harbor are named for songs and refrains such as "Amor Perdido" and "Lágrimas Negras," which also appear on the soundtrack; Rubén's boat is called "Me Ves y Sufres" [See me and suffer], mocking his youthful attractiveness which both frightens and captivates Julia. The music itself invokes intertextual associations and comments on the story, absorbing Julia's contemporary journey into archetypal formulae. These references, which would be of little import to a foreign audience unable to recognize them, add another layer of meaning to the film, not only providing pleasure for spectators who "get" the allusions but also embedding *Danzón* in a history of popular expression which is as stylized, romantic, sentimental, and emotionally cathartic as the story we are watching.

In fact, *Danzón* can be seen as a response to and reinvention of one of the most important genres of Mexican cinema: the *cabaretera* film. The dance halls and cabarets where key moments of the film take place are two of the sites Monsiváis has described as the quintessential "mythic atmospheres" of the films of the Golden Age ("Mexican Cinema" 144–145). At that time, an entire genre evolved focusing on their female inhabitants, a genre which for Diana Bracho reflects Mexican cinema's lingering fascination with the iconic and melodramatic figure of the prostitute. For along with Landeta's *Trotacalles,* countless tragic and comic streetwalkers and their only slightly more reputable *fichera* sisters have strolled across the screen since at least 1931 in *Santa,* one of Mexico's first sound films—so many that Bracho refers to the cinema's "pimping" of its female characters (413).

Bracho's description of the character *Santa* encapsulates the fate of Golden Age screen women, not only prostitutes but any who found themselves by choice or circumstance outside of the domestic sphere:

Su triste vida nos muestra como la inmoralidad se paga con la enfermedad y la muerte, aunque quede claro que esa inmoralidad ni siquiera es un acto de voluntad propia sino fruto de un destino cruel de ser objeto del deseo de los hombres y víctima de la maldad de otros que se han divertido a su costa y que se han chingado, término perfectamente literario desde Octavio Paz.

[Her sad life shows us how immorality is paid for with sickness and death, although it is clear that said immorality is not even an act of personal will but rather the fruit of a cruel destiny of being the object of men's desire and the victim of the wickedness of others who have enjoyed themselves at her expense and haven't given a fuck—a term that's perfectly literary ever since Octavio Paz.] (414)

The flippant reference to Paz reminds us that the influential author of *The Labyrinth of Solitude* believed that in the construct of Mexican identity derived essentially from the European conquest, women were inevitably passive victims of male violence and at the same time *malas mujeres* guilty of the original betrayal, that committed by Hernán Cortés's lover, La Malinche. In the classical Mexican cinema, the independent will of women such as *Doña Barbara* (1943) and even *La negra Angustias* resulted from originary rapes, and the tragedy of the fallen woman was always inevitable.

The *cabaretera* or *rumbera* cycle that emerged during the sexenio of President Miguel Alemán (1946–1952) was, in spite of its cosmopolitan veneer, no less morally punishing of its heroines. As Ana López points out, the liminal space of the nightclub posed a formidable challenge to the constrained moral order of the home and family: "Nowhere else have screen women been so sexual, so willful, so excessive, so able to express their anger at their fate through vengeance" ("Tears and Desire" 158). Yet in the quintessential *rumbera* film, *Aventurera* (Alberto Gout, 1949), the protagonist, played by Ninón Sevilla, falls into prostitution through an originary tragedy, suffers numerous traumas and violations, fights back, and in the end is domesticated through a love affair that, predictably, fails to resolve the film's contradictions. According to López, the prostitute in this era became an iconic figure whose shameful association with Malinche was partially eclipsed by her transformation into a symbol of modernity and a challenge to Porfirian sexual ideology (159). For Bracho, Sevilla can be seen as "potentially subversive," but overall the screen portrayal of the prostitute had less to do with reality than with an ongoing tradition of exploitation (416).

As both Bracho and López argue, the prostitute was the flip side of another stereotypical female character: the mother "llena de virtudes y lágrimas" [full of virtues and tears] (Bracho 419). As the moral center of the family, the Mexican mother must suffer and suffer. Yet like the Virgin of Guadalupe (and unlike the always-troubling Malinche), she is exalted by her suffering. Although, as López points out, the maternal melodramas of the Alemán era showed the fragility and fragmentation of the modern family structure, the mother's role as martyr and pillar of values was never questioned.

While *Danzón* clearly draws on these classic woman-centered melodramatic genres, it does so obliquely. Whereas, for example, Arturo Ripstein and his scriptwriter and collaborator Paz Alicia Garciadiego explode melodramatic conventions in their 1990s films by pushing them to extremes,[3] Novaro simply captures an atmosphere and a style, discarding the framework of overarching moral conflict. As a mother, Julia is singularly unburdened by the trappings of maternal ideology; nor is the absence of a husband/father portrayed as particularly problematic, let alone tragic. Julia's relations with her daughter, Perla, are not idealized (they quarrel and have separate goals and interests), nor are they a source of conflict. Her quest is not in itself an urgent one, nor do her encounters (even with Rubén) have serious moral consequences: in *Danzón*'s world there is no sin and thus neither damnation nor redemption.

Yet in spite of its atmosphere of freedom, the film is neither a hedonistic celebration of "liberated" female sexuality nor a role-reversal fantasy like *Juana la cubana,* in which Rosa Gloria Chagoyán's character is both tough rebel commander and Cuba's sexiest showgirl. Although not moralistic, Novaro's revised *aventurera* is clearly aware that her choices have consequences, that her sudden flight from Mexico City has implications for her job and her daughter, and that on some level her search for Carmelo makes no sense. She is also aware of the relationship between small, seemingly inconsequential gestures and the obscure project on which she has embarked almost accidentally, of self-knowledge and transformation; Rojo projects this weight in each of her dazzled, confused, and delighted reactions. Moreover, Julia's experiences do not happen to her alone as if in a vacuum. They are marked by interactions that affirm the value of friendship, generosity, and solidarity.

Again, the comparison with *Trotacalles* is revealing. In Landeta's film about the conflict and the parallels between two sisters, one a prostitute and the other a "respectable" woman who has married for money, the most moving element is the solidarity between the streetwalkers, who show each other the care and concern that they are obviously missing from family and other sources. Yet the prostitutes' solidarity is through misery: when one becomes deathly ill, the other women take care of her but can do little to ease her suffering, and what sacrifices they do make are punished by their pimps, who resent the interruption in commerce. The women's unity is expressed visually in moving two-shots, lingering close-ups, and eyeline matches, yet the affective bonds that Landeta seems to want to celebrate are not powerful enough to halt the narrative's fatalist trajectory.

If the characters of *Danzón* are not bound by the punishing logic that determines the fate of the women in *Trotacalles,* it is because they are, to a greater or lesser degree, outside of the patriarchy's immediate grasp. The Veracruz prostitutes do work for a male pimp, but when a violent argument breaks out, doña Ti explains to Julia that the women defend one another and can take care of themselves. Similarly, the Mexico City telephone operators watch out for one another and protect young Perla when she joins their ranks. In the relative absence of male authority, friendship becomes a force which can console but also guide one's actions. This is especially the case because outside of male-centered frameworks, women's actions do not have a predetermined pattern to follow but must be invented, albeit not in a vacuum and not without the possibility of danger. Although it could be argued that the absence of menace in *Danzón,* in spite of Julia's vulnerability vis-à-vis the omnipresent male gaze, is the film's most fantastic aspect, the implication nevertheless persists that Julia's fate rests on the generous assistance and complicity of those who surround her.

The notion that Julia and the other characters inhabit a liminal space, within a patriarchal system but not under the authority of particular men, helps to explain why Julia follows Carmelo in the first place, since they have no particular attachments off the dance floor. For a Mexican woman of Julia's class, it would be unusual to take a vacation by herself, spontaneously and without motivation. But following her dance partner allows Julia to approximate a comprehensible action: everyone understands that she is looking for a man, and if she protests that he is neither a relative nor her lover, it doesn't matter, the idea is the same. The quest, while genuine enough to bring Julia to tears of frustration and despair, is also a kind of masquerade.

When she returns to Mexico City with new clothes, souvenirs, and a relaxed appearance, it is exactly as if she has been on vacation, especially when Carmelo turns up of his own accord, thereby erasing the urgency of the pursuit. In a roundabout way, Julia has simply given herself the freedom to take care of her own needs—needs that are forgotten in the daily routine of work and family and that are not wholly fulfilled at the dance halls. For in spite of the glamour suggested by the film's title and packaging, ballroom dancing is actually somewhat demystified. Unlike the screen cabarets of the Golden Age, the dance halls Julia frequents are not overwrought scenarios of sin and redemption, nor are their inhabitants the seductive and decadent sirens of the songs of Agustín Lara. Rather, they are pleasant, inviting arenas of play, pleasure, and release or escape in which the dance itself (not the milieu) is central and transcendent. If Julia, Silvia, Carmelo, doña Ti, and Susy are the heirs of the scandalous originators of the *danzón,* the slaves, sailors, whores, political radicals, impoverished composers, and *ficheras* who gave what Monsiváis calls the "waltz of the poor" (*Los rituales* 154) its legendary aura prior to its acceptance by high society, they are also nothing if not ordinary.

It is this ordinariness that is finally what is extraordinary in *Danzón* as in much of Novaro's work. Her refusal to impose traditional narrative conflict or an overarching moral structure on the film leaves us focused on its details, its ritualization of time and space, its visuality, and its rhythms. As Glantz points out, the opening dance sequence builds from close-ups, while the parallel sequence that ends *Danzón* is made up of full shots that allow us to see the dancers, Julia and Carmelo, and the full dance floor as a harmonious whole (21). Rather than creating a clear conflict in order to arrive at a final resolution, *Danzón* begins with the almost invisible fragmentation that pervades Julia's life, so naturalized that she herself is hardly aware of it, and works almost magically toward the restoration of wholeness.

Feminine or Feminist: The Politics of Reception

In an interview about the film in *Cine Mundial,* María Rojo, *Danzón*'s star, referred to the film as "intimista, pero sobre todo altamente feminista" [intimist, but above all highly feminist] ("María Rojo llegó").[4] But judging by documented response to the film, not all viewers agreed. While the *intimista* label was almost universally applied, published criticism and a sociological study of the film's reception indicated a deep ambivalence over the meaning of "feminism" as applied to the film text.

For some writers, the celebration of *danzón* was inherently nonfeminist, since the dance assigns specific, different roles to men and women, presumably as a metaphor for a gendered division of labor. Glantz, who did not mention feminism, seemed to uphold a certain essentialism when she suggested that:

Julia busca a Carmelo porque juntos forman una figura . . . en ese es-
fuerzo, en la conjunción de sus dos cuerpos que se unen para bailar, se
genera un placer, se inscribe una elegancia, se produce una forma, una
forma evanescente, que es necesario recobrar en la incesante repetición
de una coreografía.

[Julia looks for Carmelo because together they form a figure . . . in that effort, in
the conjunction of their two bodies that unite to dance, a pleasure is generated,
an elegance is inscribed, a form is produced, an evanescent form, which must be
recovered in the incessant repetition of a dance movement.] ("Danzón" 21)

Although she was careful to point out that this harmonious union was different from and even transcended sex and that Carmelo and Julia completed
each other as a ritual "figure" rather than as a couple, there remained the sense
of a union of essences based on opposition and complementarity.

Glantz's interpretation was apparently similar to that of Novaro herself,
who told Victor Bustos of *Dicine*:

A mí me gusta mucho ir a los salones de baile y me gusta mucho bailar.
Y particularmente, me gustaba hablar acerca del danzón por el tipo de
baile que es, muy tradicional, con reglas muy precisas para los hombres
y para las mujeres; me parecía un buen marco para la historia.

[I very much like to go to the dance halls and I very much like to dance. And in
particular, I enjoyed talking about the *danzón* because of the kind of dance that
it is, very traditional, with very precise rules for men and women; it seemed to
me a good frame for the story.] ("María Novaro" 10)

A 1992 article in *El Heraldo* reports that "su idea de 'Danzón' nació de lo con-
sidera un ritual: el hecho de que el hombre guíe, pero la mujer sea la pro-
tagonista del baile" [her idea for *Danzón* emerged out of her considering it a
ritual: the fact that the man leads, but the woman is the protagonist of the
dance]. The article then quotes Novaro: "Es lo que les gusta a los hombres, y
no se trata de sentimientos primitivos, sino esenciales, en al ámbito de estos
cínicos y escépticos mexicanos post modernos. Es algo que debemos preocu-
parnos por conservar" [It is what the men like, and it is not about primitive
feelings but rather about essential ones, in the context of these cynical and
skeptical postmodern Mexicans. It is something that we should make an effort to preserve"]. (In "La prensa de N.Y.")

Called upon to clarify the ambiguity of this statement, Novaro's mentor,
Gabriel García Márquez,[5] suggested that the director tried to show something

of the condition of Latin American women, not because she was a feminist but rather "por su cuenta y su deseo," that is, because of her personal inclinations (ibid.). Yet in *Proceso,* Susana Cato implied (without mentioning feminism) a more conscious agenda, suggesting that Novaro and screenwriter Beatriz Novaro, the director's sister, "toman una posición cómplice al lado de las mujeres, no en el discurso, sino en el quehacer de lo cotidiano" [take up a complicit position on women's side, not rhetorically but in (representing) quotidian activity]. For Novaro herself, however, this was not necessarily a feminist act; in 1990, she said that although her films had women as protagonists, "No hay una postura feminista, sólo estoy al lado de ellas y tomo partido por ellas" [There isn't a feminist stance, I only stand beside (women) and take their side] (García Cruz in *El Nacional*). While this may in itself be a workable definition of feminism, Novaro refused the label. Interviewed by Sarabia in *Nitrato de Plata,* she explained that while she considered herself a feminist in her personal life, she was not one in her work, as she did not want the latter to be limited or to be reduced to a didactic pamphlet (25).

If Novaro herself was ambivalent toward the feminist label, other observers were simply divided. Ignacio Escárcega wrote in his description of *Danzón* in *Dicine,* "Parece lo anterior discurso feminista. No lo es. Más bien quiere resaltar una reflexión sobre la magia, el ocultismo y la cachondería de cierto aspecto de relación de pareja" [The above resembles feminist discourse. It isn't. Rather, it tries to bring out a reflection of the magic, the occult, and the sexiness of a certain aspect of the relations between a couple]. The grounds for this clarification were not made clear, other than that *Danzón* was not about feminism (as if feminists cannot speak about magic or romance or other topics). Tito Vasconcelos, similarly, spoke of a "sentido femenino, que conste, y no feminista. Es una película femenina" [feminine sense, that (the film) would demonstrate, and not feminist. It is a feminine film] (Carrera). María García-Torres de Novoa of *Uno Más Uno* also wrote of a feminine sensibility but seemed unsure as to its relationship to feminism; she remarked on the diverse ways that women can be happy, such as through beauty and heterosexual love, apart from "the archetype of liberation and power." Yet Alejandro Leal of *El Universal* was equally convinced that Novaro's cinema revolved around "su visión de la intimidad feminista (que no femenina)" [her vision of feminist, not feminine, intimacy].

Whatever their conclusions, the binarism of these statements reveals how narrowly "feminism" was construed by critics, for whom the term seemed to connote a pejorative, cartoonish "man-hater" rather than the valorization of women and rejection of oppression. Hence García-Torres de Novoa's peculiar assertion that Novaro's film rejects "liberation," when what she clearly means is that it rejects the cliché of "women's lib" in which women must find fulfillment by assuming positions of power and control traditionally held by men and by denying all traits traditionally thought of as feminine. That few Mexican feminists have advocated such a stance has not prevented it from becoming the dominant stereotype of feminism.

The ambiguity and ambivalence with which viewers reacted to the gender politics of the film comes out even more strongly in Norma Iglesias's experimental study of *Danzón*'s gendered reception. In order to examine masculine and feminine subjectivity, Iglesias conducted a study with four focus groups at an unnamed university in Madrid in 1994. One group was all women, one all men, and a third was mixed; the fourth, which she labeled a "conversation" group to call attention to its less rigorous selection process and structure, consisted of a smaller group of somewhat older women, some of whom were previously acquainted and thus were able to express themselves more freely than the other groups. Each group watched the film together and then discussed their emotional and intellectual responses.

In analyzing her findings, Iglesias discovered many differences between the groups—some broad and immediate, others more subtle and complex. To begin with, men and women differentiated themselves even in the screening; while the male group watched in silence, the women laughed and demonstrated enjoyment of the movie. In the subsequent discussions, male and female discursive styles also differed dramatically. The women spoke in personal voices, citing their own moments of pleasure and identification with the film. They addressed one another as women rather than as "experts," for example asking one another what they would do in Julia's situation. Iglesias characterizes their response as emotional and stresses their experience of "complicity" with the film (6).

The men, on the other hand, tended toward a rationalist discourse which presupposed a barrier between themselves and the film (8). Instead of personal reactions, they raised issues: the film's relation to Mexican and international cinema (for instance, comparing it to Jane Campion's *The Piano*) or the problematic of feminine identity. They also assumed the role of experts describing objects of study, sometimes referring to characters by first and last names. Whereas the women interrupted one another and continued one another's thoughts, the men's comments were orderly and self-contained. Finally, the mixed group displayed a mixture of these two approaches, although in more moderate responses than either, and seemed to exemplify a tendency toward negotiation and avoidance of conflict (9).

Yet when the discussion focused on specific questions, such as whether the film reflected a "feminine gaze" or could be considered feminist, the women seemed to retreat from their position of emotional engagement and become more critical, while the men revealed an emotional response centered mainly on the film's treatment of men. When the younger women argued over whether the film had clearly been made by a woman, their previous complicity was replaced by simplistic stereotypes: the film, some said, was obviously directed by a woman because men played a peripheral role; the absence of men made it feminist; or alternatively, its lack of male-bashing made it not feminist. Iglesias comments, "Desde esta perspectiva parece decirse que lo característico del feminismo es básicamente el rechazo a los hombres, más que un cuestionamiento de la situación de opresión de la mujer, y más ampliamente del rechazo a cualquier opresión" [This perspective seemed to say that what characterizes feminism is basically rejection of men, more than a questioning of the situation of women's oppression, and more broadly the rejection of all oppression] (14). The older women, however, seemed much more willing to accept the film as a subjective and critical portrayal of the "female condition" (16).

The all-male group overwhelmingly rejected the notion of a feminine aesthetic or sensibility, which, as Iglesias notes, manifested itself in the emotional reactions of viewers but not in the form of verifiable evidence demanded by rationalist discourse. Yet when they discussed the film's male characters, the men conveyed a feeling of being personally attacked by the "marginalization," "stereotyping," and "ill treatment" of men (19). At the same time, they chose to see the film as a vindication of traditional values, reading the ending not in terms of Julia's psychic liberation (as did the female viewers) but rather as her renunciation and submission to the patriarchal order. Like many of the film's Mexican critics, they concluded that the film was "femenina pero no feminista" [feminine but not feminist] (19).

In the end, notes Iglesias, all of the discussions were conflicted and contradictory, although the groups even diverged in their response to contradiction: the female discussants examined their conflicts, while the men did not acknowledge them (36). While no group or individual expressed an overtly *machista* perspective, the self-generated structure of the debate and what she refers to as "symptoms" and "lapsus" revealed severe differences between men's and women's unconscious assumptions about power and knowledge.

While the difference in discursive styles that Iglesias reports is almost shockingly stark, what is most significant for our present purposes is the groups' ambivalence toward what constitutes feminism. It would appear that in the minds of many spectators, a woman-centered text or a rich viewing experience based on complicity and gender solidarity have little to do with an ideology understood to be based on "scandalous" militancy and rejection of men.

María Rojo's willingness to call the film "muy positivo, muy vital y muy feminista" [very positive, very vital, and very feminist] (in Leñero Franco 4) comes, we can therefore conclude, not only from her reading of the film and its production history but also from her personal politics. One of the most respected actresses in contemporary Mexican cinema, Rojo has acted in many of the most audacious and critical films of recent years, including *Rojo amanecer, La tarea,* and *Tequila* (Rubén Gámez, 1991). She has also appeared in *telenovelas* but has criticized the self-censorship of Mexican television: "me gustaría que hubiera una televisión con más apertura en la que se pudieran presentar escenas más reales en las que la gente fume, o se pueda decir la palabra violación o se pueda hablar de homosexuales" [I would like it if there were television with more openness, in which more real scenes could be presented, where people smoked, or one could say the word rape or talk about homosexuals] (Quiroz Arroyo, "Me gustaría"). In October 1994, she and fellow actress Ofelia Medina hosted a night of *danzón* in which attendees paid to dance with the celebrities of their choice, with proceeds benefiting the indigenous children of Chiapas; the advertisement, naturally, read "¡Hey Familia!" At this event, the Mexican "family" was invited to celebrate its cultural traditions, honor its stars, fulfill its media-inspired fantasies—"Cuántas veces," Claudia Nayeli of *Tiempo Libre* asked, "fuimos partícipes imaginarios de aquellas noches de danzón al ver alguna película de Ninón Sevilla o Andrea Palma" [how many times were we imaginary participants in those nights of *danzón,* watching a Ninón Sevilla or Andrea Palma film] (21)—and to aid a group whose marginality had become unavoidably politicized in the wake of the EZLN uprising. A political act was thus staged via the integration of a popular cultural practice with mass-media star discourse, enhanced not only by Medina's activist reputation but by Rojo's prior association with *Danzón.*

For the politically progressive Rojo, who would later enter formal politics as a PRD congresswoman, feminism was not a negative term, and therefore she applied it easily to a film made by women in which women's experiences were central. Leal, on the other hand, used the same term as an epithet. For Leal, Novaro's earlier exploration of single motherhood in *Lola* was a distasteful tribute to "maternal irresponsibility." In *Danzón*, he complained, "the man is an object of reference, not a character." Although Leal praised the music and Vasconcelos's acting in the role of Susy, the terms *feminista* and *antimachista* used in the headline turn out to be put-downs in the context of his article—which, befitting his patriarchal values, he dedicated to his son.

Leal's reaction should not be construed as an isolated one; in an environment in which the very assertion that women's stories are interesting material is enough to offend a certain fraction of the audience, García-Torres's and others' defenses of a "sensibilidad femenina" (feminine sensibility) begin to seem less conciliatory and more subversive. Yet even a cursory reading of the feminist periodicals *fem* and *Debate Feminista* or the works of feminist writers like Castellanos and Poniatowska would reveal that this sensibility is perfectly compatible with Mexican feminism. The displacement of the term by a more conciliatory euphemism is a strategy of containment that serves to negate what is powerful and empowering in the film text, making it into an affirmation of the status quo.

The Politics of Appropriation

Different criticisms of the film have been made by film scholar Nissa Torrents and by *Dicine* writers Ignacio Escárcega and Tomás Pérez Turrent. Although Torrents described *Danzón* favorably as a "pleasant reworking of a fairy tale, reworked with modern ingredients," she wondered whether it might not be too soft: "the acceptable face of feminism?" (226). Escárcega, meanwhile, suggested that the film's use of clichés was not as distanced as Novaro would like to think and that at times it in fact vacillated between *Aventurera* and *Saturday Night Fever*.

Pérez Turrent, in a scathing indictment of the complacent and complicit visage that Mexican and global cinema of the 1990s had turned toward the New World Order, suggested that *Danzón*, in spite of its charms, exemplified the current ideal of a cinema "que no cuestione, que no moleste, que no corte la digestión, que no tenga contradicciones, que no cree polémicas, que no ofrezca suciedad ni desesperación y en determinados casos que ni siquiera haya un conflicto, como exigían las viejas normas" [that doesn't question, doesn't annoy, doesn't disturb the digestion, doesn't contain contradictions, doesn't create polemics, doesn't offer dirt or desperation and in certain cases doesn't even have a conflict, like the old norms demanded]. Its success, he argued, was due to its contagious optimism, its lack of "sucios, feos y malos" [dirties, uglies, and bad guys], how it leaves the viewer with the sensation that, in spite of everything, we live in the best of all possible worlds (6).

To a certain point, this critique was valid in the context of the "democratic" Mexico of the 1990s, where in spite of government rhetoric, films that were perceived as being truly critical were indirectly yet systematically censored, where journalists' lives were threatened, and where foreign priests and human rights workers documenting military abuses in Chiapas were expelled from the country. The makers of "quality cinema" chose to ignore the country's misery to a large extent and tended to deal with middle-class characters and concerns. Whereas Novaro's short film *Una isla rodeada de agua* invoked the legacy of rebellion in Guerrero and *Lola* attempted to reveal what Novaro called "los lados oscuros de la maternidad" [the dark sides of motherhood] against an alienating urban landscape (Velásquez), *Danzón* could be seen as little more than a sophisticated *churro,* an innocuous and sexy dance movie nostalgic enough for domestic audiences and exotic enough for foreign consumption.

In countering these objections, it must be pointed out that the urge for escapist entertainment is often a response to rather than a denial of despair and that a fairy tale does not necessarily affirm that ours is the best of all possible worlds but in fact may be an outlet for otherwise impossible desires. Uruguayan writer Eduardo Galeano, in his *Book of Embraces,* coined a term which may aptly describe the cinema of the former Maoist Novaro: "magical Marxism"—"one half reason, the other half passion, and a third half mystery" (223). Provisionally, however, I will suggest that Novaro's "game" of cultural appropriation and revision is a powerful intervention in the field of nationalist discourse which, whatever its specific form in a given moment, has traditionally aligned *mexicanidad* with masculinity and patria with patriarchy.

I have already argued that Julia as well as the other characters do not fit into the Mexican cinema's dualistic vision of femininity, in which Woman is either mother or whore, noble Virgin or treacherous Malinche. (Nor do we find in *Danzón* the depersonalized sex objects who are so ubiquitous in the lowbrow commercial cinema of the 1970s through the present.) Ramírez Berg suggests in his discussion of the changing image of women in the cinema of the 1970s that by then those archetypes were breaking down; but in the examples he gives, women who do not fit into traditional roles were still punished, albeit by a tangible power structure rather than by destiny. It is only with *Doña Herlinda y su hijo,* directed by Jaime Humberto Hermosillo in 1984, that he sees Mexican film potentially going from the critique of patriarchy to the projection of alternative visions. Describing *Doña Herlinda*'s "utopia of tolerance," he describes how that film uses gentle scenes of personal interaction "to depict a new social order based on the politics of cordial communal interest and mutual respect" (132). Such utopian politics, I would argue, also inform *Danzón;* for any project of change must not only recognize oppression but also imagine its demise. A film about pleasure and desire need not affirm the status quo; it may also help us think through new ways of imagining (for example) motherhood and sexuality, beyond the confines of patriarchal ideology.

In *Plotting Women,* Franco (in reference to Elena Garro's novel *Los recuerdos del porvenir*) argues that popular song, cinema, orally transmitted culture, and later *fotonovelas* have been vehicles for romantic narrative, "the most persistent mode of representing female desire," and further, that "romance is one way in which Utopian feelings repressed by tyranny and machismo can be expressed" (135). While these media and genres have often been considered inferior, they have spoken more directly to female audiences than has elite culture, in which male authors and artists have represented Woman as a transcendent symbol, leaving real women invisible. If *Danzón* is indeed a contemporary fairy tale, as Torrents labels it, it is a highly self-referential one; its utopian desire is not one of rescue by a handsome prince but rather that of building a space for female desire to be expressed, using materials already existent in urban Mexican culture. As Cato put it, "*Danzón* es la ingenuidad, la razón de ser de lo banal, lo yin, lo femenino, lo romántico, lo kitch y lo telenovelero que todos los mexicanos llevamos dentro" [*Danzón* is the ingenuousness, the raison d'être of the banal, the yin, the feminine, the romantic, the kitsch, and the soap-operatic that all Mexicans have inside us].

The ideas and feelings evoked by these formal aspects of the film render its diegetic ending, which some viewers have criticized, somewhat superfluous. In the end, Julia leaves her new friends, gives up the affair with the younger man, and goes back to her daughter, her friends from the capital, and her divided life as service sector employee and dance hall habitué. Surprisingly, Carmelo turns up right where she left him at the beginning of the movie. As we have seen, some viewers read this ending as feminism's defeat and as valorization of the patriarchal order. For Saragoza and Berkovich, Julia's changed consciousness is merely a subversive gesture within a social order that inevitably remains intact. "Read as an allegory of the state," they argue, "*Danzón* suggests that the state is an unavoidable presence, although one can find dignity and integrity within its rigid boundaries" (30).

Yet *Danzón* is not, per se, about the state. In fact, one could argue that its journey into nostalgic and marginal pockets of popular culture reflects a broader movement away from the state as the locus of intellectual inquiry and activism: the emergence of the *sociedad civil* in the wake of the September 1985 earthquake and the economic catastrophes of that decade. As Elena Poniatowska has written, inhabitants of Mexico City, stricken by disaster and faced with inadequate and disorganized assistance from the government, were forced to mobilize on their own and in the process discovered their own collective strength.[6] In the aftermath of the earthquake, women garment workers who for decades had tolerated their unjust lot became aware of their oppression and began to organize against workplace tyranny, a process documented in Maricarmen de Lara's 1985 film *No les pedimos un viaje a la luna* as well as in Poniatowska's texts ("Report from Mexico" 74; "Women, Mexico, and Chiapas" 100–102). All across the country, women and men, including prostitutes, gays, lesbians, AIDS victims, indigenous people, workers, and *campesinos,* began to organize locally, to struggle as communities and as civic groups to try to see their needs met. These struggles had little to do with the cycle of corruption and self-perpetuation that is Mexican politics, and they did not turn to nationalist mythography for vindication.

The cultural parallel to this development of an alternative public sphere could be found in the fragmentation of the master narratives that formerly guided Mexican artistic expression. The notion of an unbroken line of "fathers" stretching from Cuauhtemoc to Lázaro Cárdenas and encompassing Juárez and the heroes of the Independence and the Revolution had certainly run its course, ruptured by the traumatic events of 1968 and rendered parodic by the crises and corruption of subsequent decades. (The celebrity of the iconic Subcomandante Marcos in the 1990s was already a new phenomenon, characterized by self-referentiality and the assumed anonymity that allowed supporters to proclaim, "todos somos Marcos"—we are all Marcos.) The notion of national unity was more than symbolically ruptured by the January 1994 uprising in Chiapas, but well before then, it had become a hollow myth. The heroic murals and patriotic melodramas of previous Golden Ages were no longer adequate, if they ever had been, to depict the fragmentation and confusion of a nation undergoing crisis and uneven change.

Given the choice between a sterile nationalism (best embodied in state pageantry and in an atemporal veneration of the folkloric) and an uncritical embrace of the mass culture that now bombards Mexican cities and countryside alike across geographical borders, many artists have chosen a third path: a vindication of popular culture that embraces modernity and syncretism but remains on the side of ordinary people, whose creativity is recognized as an act of survival. Jesús Martín Barbero writes of a "rediscovery of the popular" in Latin America not as a static or pure essence but as an evolving counter-hegemonic process. This reevaluation implies "the perception of new dimensions of social conflict, of the formation of new subjects—ethnic, regional, religious, sexual, generational—of new forms of rebellion and resistance" ("Communication from Culture" 453). Furthermore, the rediscovery of the popular "refers us not only to the past but to the present, uncovering its conflictuality and creativity for us, its non-contemporaneity, which is not merely backwardness but an open breach with modernity and with the logic with which capitalism seems to exhaust the reality of the present" (454).

Novaro's comments in *El Heraldo* that "it's not about primitive feelings but rather about essential ones, in the context of these cynical and skeptical postmodern Mexicans" can perhaps be read in light of Martín Barbero's discussion of the temporality of popular culture. Whether or not romanticism is "essential," it has a place, possibly a subversive one, in a "postmodern" context. The *danzón* ritual central to the film invokes the past but is not a timeless tradition; the film is not a nostalgic appeal to an earlier era but rather an attempt to deploy certain traditional elements in defense of the liberty of a heroine who is nothing if not modern.

The film's fairy-tale logic may be juxtaposed to that of many *telenovelas* in which the poor heroine's salvation comes through the discovery of concealed noble parentage and/or alliance with a wealthy man. While the latter excuses socioeconomic inequality (by resolving it through fantastic means) and does not question male domination, *Danzón* suggests that desire itself, as well as the cultural expressions it has produced within and against the discourse of the monolithic, patriarchal nation-state, is a potent force that must be recuperated for any transformative praxis.

The Mythic Nation

The themes developed in *Danzón* can be seen in Novaro's earlier work as well as in her subsequent feature, *El jardín del Edén* (1993). Her 1985 short film, *Una isla rodeada de agua,* deals with a young girl's search for her mother in the conflicted coastal region of Guerrero, location of the famous vacation destination Acapulco but also of the armed uprisings of the 1970s led by Lucio Cabañas and Genaro Vásquez, whose officially repressed legacies are nevertheless preserved in graffiti that the camera records. Another short film, *Azul celeste* (1987), also revolves around an inconclusive journey, this time that of a young woman who arrives in Mexico City eight months pregnant, looking for the baby's father with no information other than the color of his house. Her search becomes the pretext for an exploration of the city that would be continued in Novaro's first feature, *Lola*.

Lola further developed the theme of a woman's ambivalent relationship to place and of the family ideal that rarely matches reality, which imposes separations, ruptures, and loss. The title character, a street vendor and young mother (Leticia Huijara), is shown raising her daughter Ana almost single-handedly; the father, a rock musician, is constantly away on tour and at the beginning of the film leaves to spend a year in Los Angeles. Although a loving mother, Lola is overwhelmed by the obligations of parenthood (she is reprimanded by Ana's teacher for the girl's poor hygiene and sloppy homework) and by the pressures of the city: frequent raids on the street vendors, male aggression, poverty, and loneliness. Unlike the mother archetypes of the classical cinema, Lola is shown as a complex human being who experiences pleasure and desire, ambivalence toward motherhood, depression, frustration, and longing for escape. Like Julia in *Danzón,* Lola finds solace on the beaches of Veracruz; from the depths of her despair, Lola is rejuvenated and, at the end of the film, reunites with her daughter at the edge of an ocean that, unlike the stifling streets of the city, promises infinite freedom.

Novaro has described her frequent use of water imagery as part of an effort to depict "el concepto de México que yo veo, un país tropical donde el mar es su rostro, y no magueyes y parcelas como se ha retratado en el cine nacional" [the concept that I see of Mexico, a tropical country whose face is the sea, and not maguey plants and plots of land as has been portrayed in the national cinema] (Solís 27). The ocean reappears as a symbol of liberty in *El jardín del Edén,* this time even more sharply in contrast with the constraints of human existence. Set this time in Tijuana, the film explores the impact of the U.S.-Mexico border, refracted as a multiplicity of physical and psychological barriers, on the lives of a diverse set of characters. Whereas these are each constrained by sociopolitical limitations not of their own making, the whales that swim up and down the coast without regard to national law suggest the utopian possibility of a world without borders.

Instead of concentrating on a single protagonist as in Novaro's previous films, *El jardín* attempts to convey the experiences of a range of women — an Anglo-American wanderer, a Chicana artist and curator, an indigenous

woman from Oaxaca, and a recently widowed Mexican mother of three—
as well as several men. Through these diverse characters we are shown the
myriad effects of what Gloria Anzaldúa has called the "*herida abierta* [open
wound] where the Third World grates against the first and bleeds" (3). Although interesting and ambitious, this strategy (as Maldonado points out in
her *Dicine* review) impedes the development of strong characters with whom
viewers can identify, falling instead into overly broad generalizations. Moreover, although it continues the themes of physical journey and quest for self
that are so important to Novaro's work, by eliding the (filmmaker's) central
starting point of Mexico City, the film risks mystifying the borderlands; it
eliminates the distancing effect by means of which, in *Danzón* and *Una isla
rodeada*, Veracruz and Guerrero become mythic sites with symbolic resonance in the national psyche. Although not explicitly stated, it would appear
that for Novaro as for other Mexico City-based intellectuals who took up this
theme, Tijuana was the ground zero of national identity in the 1990s, a liminal and transitory gray zone between countries and cultures, as prefigured in
Lola when Omar, Lola's partner, returns from an extended engagement in Tijuana only to leave for an even longer one in Los Angeles. In this scenario, the
fact that people are born, work, participate in politics and culture, live, and die
in Tijuana just like in any other urban area is of little import. In *El jardín del
Edén,* Tijuana (like Veracruz in *Danzón*) is less a city than the mythic setting
for the exploration of the "borderlands" of identity.

Indeed, although the locales in which her films take place have varied,
Novaro's perspective (as she herself has stated) can be best said to reflect that
of the Mexico City progressive intellectual sector, a perspective developed
through the conflicts and idealism of 1968, the feminist and guerrilla movements of the 1970s, the disillusioning aftermath of the latter, and the emergence of an organized civil society after the 1985 earthquake (Solís 27). In *Lola,*
the effects of the earthquake are omnipresent in the form of crumbling buildings that mimic the crumbling emotional state of the protagonist. Near Lola's
home in the still-devastated central city, signs painted by the government attempt to reassure the populace: "México sigue en pie" [Mexico is still stand-
ing]. Yet the Mexico of yesterday, the imagined community filled with contradiction yet eulogized in the countless patriarchal narratives of the classic
Mexican cinema, has in fact been falling apart for decades, and in *Danzón,* all
of its tenets are turned playfully inside-out.

With the Mexican edifice in crisis, it makes sense that artists like Novaro
would seek hope among the ruins. In focusing on characters who are margin-

alized socially and sexually, by means of a music with strong regional and subcultural associations, and in inverting generic conventions and playing with cherished clichés, *Danzón* alters the meaning of *mexicanidad*. The challenge to existent power relations symbolized by such gestures as the reversal of male-female positions in Susy and Julia's *danzón* is perhaps no revolution; but with the Revolution as a dim legacy whose few small gains continue to be reversed by the policies of a government which still acts in the Revolution's name, it is a small step in the direction of a more genuine and effective liberation.

Mexico is living on absolutely apocalyptical levels, in all senses, in terms of the immediate quality of life of the people there. It's a visual part that we just don't see in the cinema.

Dana Rotberg[1]

CHAPTER 7

Dana Rotberg

Modernity and Marginality

In Dana Rotberg's 1991 *Angel de fuego,* a rundown circus and an evangelical puppet show on the outskirts of Mexico City serve as the setting of spatial and social marginality. The beginning of the published screenplay by Rotberg and Omar Rodrigo not only indicates the circus's poverty but also places it in relation to the city's more prosperous center:

Un circo instalado en la periferia del DF. A un lado de la vieja carpa parchada con múltiples remiendos, hay tres dormitorios móviles, un rudimentario comedor al aire libre y un viejo camión que hace las veces de bodega. Un par de destartaladas jaulas móviles están a un costado de la carpa. Al fondo, los edificios dibujan el contorno de la ciudad. Más allá se observan las montañas que rodean el Valle de México. Empieza a llover.

[A circus installed on the periphery of the Federal District (Mexico City). To one side of the old, much-repaired tent are three mobile dormitories, a rudimentary open-air kitchen, and an old bus that is also used for storage. A pair of ramshackle mobile cages are alongside the tent. In the background, buildings sketch the outline of the city. Beyond them can be seen the mountains that surround the Valley of Mexico. It is beginning to rain.] (Rotberg and Rodrigo 13)

The Circo Fantasía, whose name does little to disguise the misery shared by performers and spectators, doubles as a brothel to make ends meet, while its inhabitants live out a story of suffering more akin to a Biblical parable of divine retribution than to the *salinista* fable of social and economic modernization. Just as Luis Buñuel's 1950 *Los olvidados* opened with postcard panoramas from the world's "great and modern cities" to contextualize the misery and insularity of the poor *barrio* Tepito, the outline of the city in the background (shown about ten minutes into the film, after the nighttime opening scene)reminds us that what we are looking at is not exotic or distant but simply the forgotten periphery of what sociologist and historian Diane Davis has named, in her study of Mexico City's rapid and unruly development, the "urban Leviathan."

For former CCC student Dana Rotberg, the film was a striking departure from her debut feature, *Intimidad* (1989). The latter was a romantic comedy written by film critic Leonardo García Tsao from a play by Hugo Hiriart which Rotberg subsequently explained as a piece that gave her the opportunity to direct but did not reflect her personal interests (López Aranda, "Dana Rotberg" 8). *Angel de fuego,* on the other hand, was a highly personal vision of the urban squalor in which, in a period of alleged economic recovery and prosperity, millions of Mexicans found themselves living. Although emerging from the context of the national film renaissance of the early 1990s, it can be seen to an extent as a recuperation of some aspects of the politically and formally confrontational Latin American cinema of the 1960s, or what Glauber Rocha called "sad ugly films, these screaming films where reason does not always prevail" (70).

Rocha, in his famous 1965 essay, applied Franz Fanon's theses on colonialism and violence in *The Wretched of the Earth* to the cinema, describing the brutality of his own films and those of his colleagues as an "Esthetic of Hunger"; later Brazilian underground filmmakers would attempt to replace Rocha's Cinema Novo with the even more violent and excessive "Marginal Cinema" or "Cinema of Garbage" (Stam 312–313). Although such terms have seldom been used by Mexican filmmakers, a "garbage aesthetic" would seem to be particularly appropriate to Mexico City, whose colonial beginnings were forged on the ruins of the Aztec capital: in the early sixteenth century, the wreckage of Tenochtitlan would help fill in the lakes upon which the Spaniards would construct their new city (Wolf 6; Kandell 128). In recent years, with the metropolitan population swelling to twenty million, the Federal District's huge landfills have almost become cities unto themselves where thou-

DANA ROTBERG   193

sands of workers called *pepenadores* spend their entire lives sorting garbage as a means of survival. Moreover, in the city's constantly expanding squatter settlements, families without access to even basic services build homes of found materials, while their children play in streams, lakes, and gullies thick with raw sewage and industrial pollution.

In 1969, director Rogério Sganzerla addressed similar conditions in São Paulo and their influence on his filmmaking, writing:

> I will never deliver clear ideas, eloquent speeches, or classically beautiful images when confronted with garbage—I will only reveal, through free sound and funereal rhythm, our own condition as ill-behaved, colonized people. Within the garbage can, one must be radical. . . . No one can think purely and esthetically on an empty stomach. (85)

But in the Mexico of the early 1990s, such confrontational positions were rare. Under the administration of President Salinas, "modernization" had become the key term of the era. Mexico, according to proponents of neoliberal economic development, was poised for economic uplift via foreign investment and free trade; and even if not everyone believed the president's promises of prosperity, the highly acclaimed "new Mexican cinema" from which *Angel de fuego* emerged, itself bolstered by renewed government support, tended to be apolitical if not optimistic, reflecting the sensibilities of an insular middle class. In a polemical essay in *Dicine*, Tomás Pérez Turrent criticized the predominance of superficial, trivial themes in national and international cinema of the period and accused film spectators, critics, festival judges, and "film professionals" of being "in perfect agreement with the so-called new world order, the end of History, of the class struggle and of utopias" and of "not want[ing] trouble" ("*Angel de fuego* y otros asuntos" 6).

Pérez Turrent recognized that the absence of representations of the underclass from the Mexican screen was due in large part to filmmakers' desire for a personal, self-reflexive cinema that reflected—de facto, due to economic constraints on who is able to make films and who is not—the preoccupations of the middle class. However, he continued:

> Sólo espero que esto no implique que la nueva generación haya decidido que dentro de nuestro *milagro económico* thatcheriano-aspiano y todo lo que sigue, ya no cabe más que hablar de nosotros, los que (las) podemos . . . . ¿Para qué hablar de los marginados, los explotados, los sucios, los malos y los feos, cuando éstos ya tienen nada menos que Soli-

daridad? Sería terrible que la nueva generación se convirtiera en el retrato hablado del cineasta adolescente salinista. Espero no ver pronto
(ni nunca) una película sobre la torre de cristal de la Bolsa que tanto en-
vidian los franceses de *izquierda*.

[I only hope this doesn't imply that the new generation has decided that within
our Thatcherite-Aspean economic miracle and everything that follows, there is
room for nothing more but to talk about ourselves, those of us who can . . . . Why
talk about the marginalized, the exploited, the dirty, the bad, and the ugly, when
these already have nothing less than Solidarity? It would be terrible if the new
generation turned into the speaking portrait of the adolescent *salinista* filmmaker. I hope not to see anytime soon (or ever) a film about the crystal tower of
the Stock Exchange, which the leftist French so envy.][2] (7)

For Pérez Turrent, *Angel de fuego* was a striking exception to that vacuous optimism: a film whose aestheticized yet brutal vision was not so much dystopic
or apocalyptic as an appropriate response to contemporary national reality.

Other critics, however, considered the film more "surreal" than political,
and some accused Rotberg of having produced a distorted, exotic image of
Mexico. In the remainder of this chapter, I will argue that the film's religious
themes and circus setting, far from detracting from its realism, are deployed
in ways that amplify its social critique. Just as the stories of Exodus are said
within the film to resonate with the experience of present-day urban squatters, so too are the characters' messianic and apocalyptic visions portrayed as
a comprehensible reaction to an urban landscape that decades of misguided
development has rendered toxic, barren, and frightening. The decrepit circus,
while invoking a cultural institution familiar to Latin American audiences, is
also used as a graphic representation of the social construction of marginality.
For what the film makes plain is that concurrent with and even essential to the
program of economic modernization that created extreme wealth for a small
number of Mexican businessmen in the early 1990s was the persistence and
expansion of a vast, alienated, "ill-behaved," and "colonized" underclass.

This marginal sector, as anthropologist Carlos Vélez-Ibáñez pointed out in
his study of political processes in nearby Ciudad Nezahualcóyotl, is "not a
population of waste but one unfortunately wasted by the industrial forces
responsible for its creation" (54). For Jesusa Palancares, the protagonist of
Elena Poniatowska's 1969 semifictional biography *Hasta no verte Jesús mío*, this
"wasted" condition brought about a renunciation of Mexico, of nationality,
and of identity itself:

Al fin de cuentas, yo no tengo patria. Soy como los húngaros: de ninguna parte. No me siento mexicana ni reconozco a los mexicanos. Aquí no existe más que pura conveniencia y puro interés. Si yo tuviera dinero y bienes, sería mexicana, pero como soy peor que la basura, pues no soy nada.

[After all, I don't have a country. I'm like the Hungarians: from nowhere. I don't feel Mexican nor do I recognize the Mexicans. Here nothing exists but pure convenience and self-interest. If I had money and property, I would be Mexican, but since I am worse than garbage, I'm nothing.] (218)

In her analysis of *Hasta no verte,* Jean Franco writes that the marginalized Jesusa has no place in either the patriarchal system into which she was born or in the modern capitalist nation state that Mexico was then becoming. Instead, "Jesusa creates a transient self, a self that is mobile"; her experience "is linked to the formation of a consciousness, not a consciousness of individuality nor a consciousness of feminine solidarity, but rather a stray consciousness whose solidarity is with the dead, and which leads to her repudiation both of the present and of Poniatowska herself" (*Plotting Women* 180–181). Her story "has no moral," as Franco points out: "It does not lead us to any particular conclusion about the state of the nation or the poor" (181). Yet, I would argue, it is this very alienation from discourses about the nation and the poor that poses such a radical challenge to the concept of *mexicanidad,* in *Angel de fuego* as well as in Poniatowska's text. During the Salinas era as during Palancares's adult lifetime, the ideology of modernization resulted for many in poverty and misery which in turn produced extreme alienation as the dark underside of nationalism. *Angel de fuego* can be read as a radical critique of this situation, placing the most marginalized of Mexicans at the center of a narrative whose moral and theological themes never mask or supersede the social reality in which the story takes place. The nation—that mythic unified entity presumed to be on the triumphant verge of First World status—is absent, and its place is filled by garbage.

The Lake of Fire

And whosoever was not found written in the book of life was cast into the lake of fire. (Revelations 20:15)

Angel de fuego's title character is Alma (Evangelina Sosa), a fire-eating trapeze artist who, at thirteen, has reached the age where she is expected to join the other women in prostitution to supplement the circus's meager box-office receipts. She refuses this work to spend time with her father, the clown Renato (Alejandro Parodi), with whom she is incestuously involved. At the beginning of the film, amidst the dismal squalor of a performance carried out with little enthusiasm and for few spectators, Alma's estranged mother, Malena (Gina Moret), slips into the tent and watches the show, causing tension among the performers and paralyzing Renato in the midst of his act. We soon learn that Renato is fatally ill and that Malena, a former member of the circus, is trying to claim her daughter. Yet Alma, who is pregnant with Renato's child, deeply resents her mother for having abandoned her earlier in life. A later encounter between Malena and Alma takes place on top of a garbage heap, emphasizing the alienation between mother and daughter.

Upon her father's death, Alma is no longer protected within the circus hierarchy. When her pregnancy is revealed, she is given the same choice that countless women employed in marginal occupations face: to give up the baby or to be dismissed. Moreover, because the fetus is the product of incest, she is warned that it will be a monster. But for Alma, her child to come is the only possible source and object of love in her harsh world. She thus leaves the circus and takes to the streets in her costume, swallowing fire at intersections and begging for coins from passing cars. Wandering through the city's barren outskirts thinking only of her and her fetus's survival, Alma comes across an evangelical puppet show which promises redemption and the return of the dead to life. Fascinated, she lingers and is soon taken in by the strange family consisting of the prophetess Refugio (Lilia Aragón), her adult son Sacramento (played by Evangelina's brother, Roberto Sosa), and Noé, a formerly abandoned child now living with the evangelists.[3] In this second family, all interaction is displaced onto the realm of religion and penance. Alma, eager to free her unborn child from the sin of its conception, submits under Refugio's direction to escalating forms of self-mortification (Fig. 7.1).

The circus and the puppet show are modes of marginal survival with similarities to any other workplace; but as sites of visual spectacle (analogous to the cinema), both are stylized or aestheticized in ways that differentiate them from other commercial enterprises. The circus community is populated by dwarves, deaf-mutes, and other marginalized figures whose relationships are mediated to some extent by self-conscious masquerade and performance, while Refugio's group is focused exclusively on achieving purity and divine forgiveness. The emotions that simmer within Refugio and Sacramento in spite of their devotion are forbidden; emotions and body processes that one

FIG. 7.1. "The radical loneliness of the subaltern classes": Evangelina Sosa
in *Angel de fuego.*

Courtesy Instituto Mexicano de Cinematografía.

could consider natural are denied in acts that the characters perceive as demonstrations of faith but which also suggest an alienation even more extreme than that which, in Franco's speculation, led Jesusa Palancares to embrace an occult spiritist religion and which Franco (paraphrasing Gayatri Spivak) called the "radical loneliness of the subaltern classes" (*Plotting Women* 181). Like the similarly marginalized Jesusa, Rotberg's characters find little solace in human communities and no meaning in human actions. Far from building solidarity, they practice a radical negation that can only culminate in death.

Scenes of play between Noé and Alma remind the viewer that both are children, but the apocalyptic faith in which they are enmeshed, like the apocalyptic setting which denies them all but the smallest material comforts, negates conventional childhood. Parents are absent, menacing, or construed in terms of sexual/incestuous rather than conventional parental bonds; the trope of filial sacrifice is the film's insistent biblical motif. The puppet play tells the story of Abraham and Isaac, a story that Alma learns she will have to repeat if she is to be purged of her sins. Although Noé and her unborn child present the possibility of love and affection, this possibility has little chance of coming to fruition. For in the world they inhabit, love can only be expressed as the sacrifice of innocents, a paradoxically nihilistic form of redemption.

By the end of the film, the fire-eating, costumed circus angel has become the exterminating angel of Revelations, inflicting God's wrath on an earth that has been found unworthy of his pardon. Although the hell that the penitents are all trying to escape is assumed to exist after death, its blueprint is already inscribed in their present. The lake of fire predicted in Revelations could, in Rotberg's rendering, just as well be that now-dry lake system upon which the Aztecs once built their capital, which in the late twentieth century carries waste and pollution in what remains of its waterways. (In the rapidly expanding Ciudad Nezahualcóyotl of the 1970s, for instance, winds would blow dust contaminated with dried fecal matter off Lake Texcoco during the dry season, while floods brought waste and sewage into inhabitants' homes during the rainy months [Vélez-Ibañez 71].) By the end of the film, Alma has lost her fetus and in revenge has first provoked Sacramento's suicide and then destroyed the circus tent and herself with it. Alma's self-immolation, which is preceded by two gestures of intense tenderness (freeing the caged animals and bidding a silent farewell to her sleeping friends), can be seen as a biblical-scale attempt to cleanse a land that has been overrun by corruption and horror.

The religious dimension of Alma's story, beyond its direct references to the Bible, is thus closely connected to the film's sense of place. Rotberg has commented extensively on the influence of her Jewish upbringing on the film, describing the "hallucinating" and "fantastic" nature of the stories she was told as a child. The visual quality of the film, she says, was what was most defined for her at the beginning of the project: "La quería polvosa, como el desierto que me imaginaba cuando me contaban las historias de la Biblia" [I wanted it dusty, like the desert that I imagined when they used to tell me stories from the Bible] (López Aranda 8). Yet *Angel de fuego* is not a modernized Old Testament tragedy; it is syncretic and skeptical, for like that of Guita Schyfter, Rotberg's Mexican Judaism necessarily becomes a kind of double consciousness, manifest in a fascination with the unique religious expressions that flourish in what she calls "el país más pagano del planeta" [the most pagan country on the planet] (López Aranda 9).

Whereas *Novia que te vea* attempts to create space for Jewish identity within *mexicanidad* (albeit transforming the latter in the process), there is little that is overtly Jewish about *Angel de fuego*. Rather, on a personal level, the film's religiosity becomes an attempt to remedy the isolation that Rotberg says she felt growing up in a context so different from that of most Mexicans that "a veces siento que mi percepción de la realidad y mis códigos no tienen nada que ver con la realidad de este país" [at times I feel that my perception of reality and my codes have nothing to do with the reality of this country] (López Aranda 9). In the film, stories of Genesis and Exodus are superimposed on the Mexican landscape; Refugio at one point comments on the resonance of Exodus with the experience of the squatters who populate the city's outer boundaries to whom she hopes to bring a small measure of solace. The character of Refugio herself, interestingly enough, is described by Rotberg as an expression of her own "pagan-Jewish-Mexican religion" and as an attempt to reconcile herself with a culture which has often excluded her (ibid.).

Although extreme and, in the view of many commentators, "surreal," the cult led by Refugio contains many historically grounded elements. Sacramento's self-mortification with *nopales,* for example, evokes both Catholic penitence and the ancient rituals of mutilation practiced by indigenous priests before the Conquest. Judeo-Christian notions of sin and forgiveness and the emphasis on the written word as exemplified in the *Libro de Perdón,* in which Refugio inscribes the names of her followers, blend with a pre-Christian approach to bodily cleansing and purification in rituals that, if stylized and exaggerated, nevertheless reflect in spirit the syncretism and diversity of Mexican folk religion. The notion of sacrifice is certainly common to all three belief systems, although in all three it has ceased to have the literal meaning which with the film invests it when Alma is made to abort her child as a condition for redemption.

But ultimately, the religious virtue and necessity of all sacrifice, whether of human children (Isaac) or of Christ himself, is called into question, and this questioning extends to the very existence of God. "¿Por qué el sacrificio tiene que ser la única prueba, la primera y la última, a los ojos de un Dios que igual te abandona siempre?" [Why does sacrifice have to be the only proof, the first and last, in the eyes of a God who always abandons you anyway?] asks Rotberg, describing one of the film's underlying questions (López Aranda 8). In another interview, Rotberg links religious thought with totalitarianism: "Any totalitarian thought that excludes the free exercise of thinking and action by human beings inevitably is going to lead to death—death of the senses, of the mind, or of the body" (Rufinelli and Tanner 14). The notion of self-denial as a measure of faith is taken seriously in the film but is ultimately shown to be tainted by self-interest and untenable as a solution to the problems of individuals whose social marginalization is compounded by a stark, extreme condition of radical isolation.

Although the film does not suggest communal or collective values as a solution, their absence is striking. Leaving the corruption of the city for the squatter settlements that extend from its outer edges into what remains of the countryside, the messianic group encounters mounted policemen dragging a prisoner on a dark road in the dead of night—a testament to the sinister and arbitrary operation of "justice" in this environment. Less literal ropes bind the *campesinos* who line up to receive Refugio's blessing; their worn, mute faces suggest the exhaustion of any capacity for resistance and the profound need for consolation. But the redemption promised by Refugio's faith is one to be achieved in the hereafter; on this earth, it is little other than a call to suicide. The conservation of life, as represented in Alma's struggle to keep her unborn child, arises as an alternative to the cult of death—but an alternative that is not tenable in an environment that has become, due not to the wrath of God but rather to the relentlessness of urban economic development and consequent marginalization, a lifeless lake of fire.

The New World Order's Forgotten Ones

Angel de fuego's circus and religious themes, with their surrealist associations, led many critics to compare the film to Alejandro Joderowsky's 1989 *Santa sangre*—some criticizing what they saw as a too-heavy debt to the work of the quirky Chilean-born director, others pointing out the obvious differences in sensibility. However, a somewhat less noted but equally apt precedent can be found in the Mexican work of Luis Buñuel. *Angel de fuego*'s fusion of a highly aestheticized tragic narrative with a documentary-like critique of social reality is just one of its many similarities to Buñuel's *Los olvidados,* which can be read as both a harshly realistic indictment of conditions in Tepito and as an artistic masterpiece rich in Freudian imagery.[4] In both films, "the modern is grafted onto archaic and destructive death drives, and the adventure unfolds with all the inevitability of classic tragedy" (Franco 153). Although the two filmmakers' specific uses of what Franco refers to as Eros and Thanatos are perhaps quite distinct, many elements are similar—the monstrous mother, for example, or the way in which food loses or exceeds its nurturing quality and becomes charged with sinister symbolism. (A pineapple that Alma carries at one point and that, as described in the script, she can clearly "neither peel nor eat" recalls the pineapple carried by the priest at the end of Buñuel's 1958 *Nazarín.*) However, it is important to note that Rotberg's focus on women leaves more space for identification than in Buñuel's vision, which as Franco points out tends to align women with nature and makes them "helpers and opponents in the male quest for identity" (155). In *Angel de fuego,* the viewer can readily sympathize with Alma's struggle for life in an environment permeated by death and even with Malena's and Refugio's misguided and futile maternal impositions. Yet in both films the archetypal long-suffering and therefore saintly mother of the Mexican cinema is replaced by a vision of parenting debased by socially unacceptable desires and by physical and psychological violence.

Beyond textual similarities, what is interesting about these two films in particular is their status within Mexican cinema as films that are at once highly regarded and anomalous. In 1950, *Los olvidados* stood as a harsh repudiation of the benevolent paternalistic state and its ideology of modernization—that is, of the version of *mexicanidad* most frequently represented in the Golden Age cinema. In the most acclaimed films of the era, such as those of Emilio "El Indio" Fernández, social problems were not only rectified through the devices of melodrama but were transformed cinematographically into beautiful and exotic images suitable for export. In contrast, an often-repeated anecdote about Buñuel recounts the time he hired Gabriel Figueroa, the cinematographer acclaimed for his masterful compositions, to shoot *Nazarín* in 1958: Buñuel allowed Figueroa to set up his perfect shot, only to order him to turn around and capture the far less composed and painterly landscape which, to Buñuel, more honestly reflected his film's conception of Mexican reality (King 130). Like the New Latin American Cinema directors who would come after him, Buñuel subverted the myth of economic development and progress in *Los olvidados* by telling a sordid story on a "dirty screen."[5]

Angel de fuego stands similarly apart from the bulk of films produced during the Salinas era. While the best of those films dealt in innovative and compassionate ways with middle-class experience, Rotberg's film suggested that at least part of Mexico City's population was barely surviving a savage and dystopic present. Interestingly, the favorable international reception of the film, culminating in its triumphant screening at Cannes and purchase by Columbia Pictures, led some writers to accuse Rotberg of crafting an exotic, unrealistic spectacle of Third World misery aimed at foreign audiences. In *La Jornada,* Julia Elena Melche criticized "una propuesta pintoresca y anticuada que únicamente podría interesar al público extranjero" [a picturesque and antiquated concept that could only interest the foreign public]; in the same newspaper's weekly magazine, José María Espinasa implied that Rotberg had become more concerned about "la posteridad efímera de los festivales" [the ephemeral posterity of the festivals] than about communicating with an audience (9). In *El Sol de México,* Guadalupe García accused Rotberg and other independent directors of making movies for "snobs" and called *Angel de fuego* "una cinta sin vida, como casi todo de nuestro nuevo cine, pero vamos a Cannes o casi nos nominan para el Oscar. Gran consuelo" [a lifeless film, like almost all of our new cinema, but we go to Cannes or they almost nominate us for the Oscar. Great consolation].

While this criticism was by no means universal, it did elicit the above-mentioned rebuttal in *Dicine* from Pérez Turrent, who pointed out that the international market of the 1990s was hardly rewarding images of misery: that in the foreign press, journalistic exposés of violence and corruption in Mexico went unpublished in favor of praise of the neoliberal economic "miracle," and that if Rotberg had wished to please Europe, "debería haber hecho un ángel pero de los salones de baile" [she should have created an angel but from the dance halls]—a reference to *Danzón* as well as to the Australian film *Strictly Ballroom* (6).

In spite of Pérez Turrent's essentially accurate assessment, *Angel de fuego* was embraced by the same international cinema circuit that had similarly welcomed the far more upbeat *Danzón.* When Rotberg's film inaugurated the noncompetitive Directors' Fortnight at Cannes in 1992, the international market appeared hungry for Mexican product. *Danzón* had been picked up for distribution by Sony; Alfonso Arau's *Como agua para chocolate* would be released internationally that year and become an enormous success; *El mariachi,* Robert Rodríguez's Spanish-language Chicano film frequently mislabeled Mexican, was bought by Columbia at the same time as *Angel de fuego,* both for release in U.S. theaters, (although only Rodríguez's film would actually be exhibited and would be dubbed in English for its video release). Upon her return from France, Rotberg regaled Mexican reporters with stories of a European public taken by surprise—one that imagined Mexico to be a Sam Peckinpah landscape populated by outlaws with huge mustaches, and that, she said, had no idea that Mexican women were directing films. According to Rotberg, the European exhibition of her film not only was a personal honor but also meant the chance to sustain the Mexican cinema's newfound vitality, attracting investment and demonstrating its vigor on a worldwide scale.

Rotberg's appraisal to the contrary, however, the accolades lavished on the film were by no means proof that the world was interested in Mexico. In the context of international cinema, *Angel* could easily be placed alongside many other "art" films dealing with the circus (from Cecil B. de Mille's *The Greatest*

Show on Earth to Fellini's *Clowns* to Tod Browning's *Freaks,* as Flavio González Mello pointed out in *El Economista*) or with incest, in either case losing its historical specificity. Critics could speak of its "surrealism" and/or "universality," thereby minimizing its social content. The film's reception, in fact, recalled Rocha's observation in "An Esthetic of Hunger" that "for the European it is a strange tropical surrealism. For the Brazilian [read "Mexican"] it is a national shame" (70). Yet for Mexican critics, even those writing in conservative newspapers, Rotberg's critique of the Salinas "miracle" was unmistakable. In a favorable review in *El Universal,* Jesús Ortega Mendoza wrote that "sin ser panfletaria, la realizadora propone una visión entre asombrada y paradójica de un México de enormes contradicciones y pobreza que ningún milagro económico ha podido eliminar" [without pamphleteering, the director puts forth an astonished and paradoxical vision of a Mexico of enormous contradictions and poverty that no economic miracle has been able to eliminate]. In a subsequent piece in *El Universal,* Moisés Viñas referred to the "mundo marginal y desamparado" "casi muerto" [marginal and vulnerable, almost dead world] that the film's characters inhabit and to their religious mysticism as an escape from misery and marginalization.

In *El Día,* Eduardo Leyva commented on Rotberg's fusion of reality and imagination: "personajes reales, suburbanos, pobres, jodidos, a la vez que míticos y mágicos"; "un mundo de pobreza y crudeza, un mundo circunscrito a la marginación de la gran ciudad que sin embargo no pierde su magia popular"; "una cineasta poco optimista acerca del futuro de la naturaleza humana, a la vez que rígida en mirar las miserias de un México que está aquí, y existe aún en tiempos del 'liberalismo social'" [characters who are real, outlying slum dwellers, poor, screwed, but at the same time mythic and magical; a world of poverty and harshness, a world circumscribed on the margin of the big city that, nevertheless, does not lose its popular magic; a filmmaker hardly optimistic about the future of human nature, yet at the same time severe in looking at the misery of a Mexico that is here and continues to exist even in times of "social liberalism"]. Gustavo Suárez Ojeda's review in *Cine Mundial* was titled "'Angel de fuego', historia citadina con enorme contenido crítico-social" [city story with enormous social-critical content]; its caption for a photo of Evangelina Sosa contrasted her role in the film with her supporting work in a then-current *telenovela* starring Televisa superstar Thalia: "la antítesis de [the antithesis of] 'María Mercedes.'"

Regarding this context of misery, Rotberg herself has commented:

the worst thing is, it's not all in my imagination. It's what is really there. That's what is here in Mexico now. It's already reached this point, as of years ago, and really, at least in terms of the urban space in Mexico, 80 percent of Mexico City is like this. . . . The movie, in set design terms, doesn't have any work to it. All is done on real time, and we filmed everything as it is. (Rufinelli and Tanner 14)

Although critics such as Melche objected to the film's "decorative" and distanced portrayal of the urban poor, the profundity of Rotberg's recognition of "what is here in Mexico now" should not be underestimated. Leonardo García Tsao, who at the time of production was Rotberg's husband and who was present during its filming, has spoken revealingly about the experience; presenting the film in Olympia, Washington, in 1996, he recalled the disturbing feelings brought on by the poor and devastated locations that, were it not for the film, an intellectual like himself would have little cause to ever visit. Although he stressed that the film was a work of imagination and personal vision rather than documentary, one can see the circumstances of its production as symptomatic of the gulf between two Mexicos, one rich, the other poor—a gulf which at its best the cinema can reveal, but rarely bridge. For once the cameras are gone, the inhabitants of the poetically named *ciudades perdidas* (lost cities) resume their role as urban Mexico's *olvidados* or forgotten ones, mere statistics in the ongoing narrative of the country's disturbingly uneven and unequal modernization.

The Circus and the City

To simply show poverty, however, is not the same as developing a critique or analysis. The varied critical reactions to the film, some of which I have discussed here, attest to the role of the spectator in creating meaning: where some observers saw mysticism, exoticism, or classical tragedy, others found the harsh indictment of *salinismo* that is only present by implication. In fact, *Angel de fuego,* like Poniatowska's *Hasta no verte Jesús mío,* "does not lead us to any particular conclusion about the state of the nation or the poor" but rather describes "the radical loneliness of the subaltern classes," a loneliness that Franco tells us "should not be confused with individualism" but is nevertheless quite removed from the consciousness of collectivity (i.e., solidarity) that would be necessary to initiate change (Franco, *Plotting Women* 181). Yet just as Jesusa Palancares's life experiences serve to assert, in Poniatowska's text, a "heterogeneity, beyond all the great, overarching, and homogenous notions such as class, race, and nation" (ibid.), Rotberg's use of the circus milieu, far more than a simply aesthetic choice, is a key element which enables the film to be read as radical social critique, both from a sociological standpoint (as I will discuss below) and from a perspective that draws on Bakhtinian-influenced theories of clowning, parody, masquerade, carnival as a social institution, and the "carnivalesque" as a mode of representation.

For Russian literary theoretician Mikhail Bakhtin, the festivals and celebrations of preindustrial Europe were privileged spaces for invigorating community ties and for rebelling symbolically against the dominant order, since in the carnival, social class, gender, and all other social hierarchies could be temporarily overturned. Although Bakhtin applied his analysis of carnival to literature, it was grounded in concrete social practices that were part of his own cultural history. Contemporary academics have drawn upon his ideas to formulate more general (and often ahistorical) arguments about textual practices; but as Stam points out in *Subversive Pleasures: Bakhtin, Cultural Criticism, and Film,* Bakhtin's analyses have had particular resonance in Latin America, where carnival is a living tradition which, in spite of commercialism, retains many of its popular elements (123). Latin American scholars such as Brazilian anthropologist Roberto da Matta have fruitfully analyzed present-day festivals and spectacles in Bakhtinian terms, and Latin American cultural studies as a whole has increasingly turned its attention to popular cultural practices in order to rectify what are now perceived to be elitist errors of earlier methodologies (such as the Marxist notion of "false consciousness") and to arrive at a deeper understanding of culture and power in the Americas.

One could argue that it is by means of the circus that Rotberg aligns herself most closely with Mexican popular culture and a tradition of critical social expression rooted in indigenous societies in which ritual humor was the area par excellence not only for the acting out of social taboos and forbidden desires such as incest but also for criticizing authority. In many traditional cultures, parodic performance (clowning) accompanied official ceremonies, with the implicit purpose of deflating the artificial importance placed on human actions and rechanneling respect toward the realm of the divine. After the Conquest, ritual humor satirized the Spaniards and later the Criollo / Ladino population that had usurped both land and political power. Parodic and often obscene rituals were ways of confronting dissent within communities and of affirming community cohesion in an increasingly besieged environment.[6]

The European circus, as John Townsen makes clear in his history *Clowns,* served many of the same functions and at different times met with varied levels of official acceptance or repression. Although the late-nineteenth-century-style circus that took root and has endured in Latin America had no overt links to the sacred clowning of indigenous ritual, its popularity was surely based on many of the same elements: that is, on its ability to create a temporary "other" space, removed from quotidian concerns and limitations, and at the same time invert and mock the conventions—and repressions—found in the everyday world.

Although the Latin American circus is a commercial spectacle rather than a community celebration, it is deeply associated with popular rather than elite culture and retains certain aspects of the traditional carnival. In recent years, it has been represented frequently as an entrepreneurial, independent form of entertainment and commerce, symbolic of older ways of life threatened by contemporary transnational mass media. Yet at the same time, it is very often portrayed as sinister; in literature and film, its clowns are more often than not harbingers of tragedy, and its more sordid elements, especially its association with prostitution, infuse it with ambivalence. More than the subversive, resistant utopia some scholars might wish to see in carnival, the circus is more akin to what Franco, drawing on Foucault, describes as *heterotopias*—other spaces that exist within society yet in which some of society's norms and structures are radically altered (Mathews 159).

In *Angel de fuego,* this otherness of the circus allows for a visual poignancy that enhances the emotional quality of the narrative and, I would argue, facilitates the treatment of taboo subjects, particularly incest. As Patricia Davalos points out, the denizens of the Circo Fantasía are "desdichados, pero a la vez revestidos de la personalidad de 'alegre' que debe tener un circo" [miserable, but at the same time dressed up in the 'happy' personalities that a circus should have]. Although Rotberg is by no means the first filmmaker to exploit the distance between the clown's painted-on grin and his actual marginalized or tragic condition, the pseudo-glamorous masquerade serves to heighten the film's central theme of alienation. When Renato dies, for example, he is laid out for burial in clown makeup, emphasizing not only his history with the circus but also his isolation from any other community (Fig. 7.2). The makeup is the equivalent of the smell that (as described in Rogelio Martínez Merling's compelling 1992 documentary *Pepenadores*) clings to garbage workers who try to leave the closed world of the landfill, binding him symbolically to an insular and marginal world whose dismal fortune is synonymous with his own.

On the other hand, Alma's stage costume, which becomes her everyday

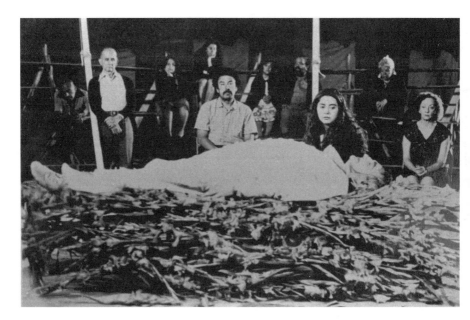

F I G . 7 . 2 . Renato (Alejandro Parodi) is buried in his clown makeup in *Angel de fuego*.
Courtesy Instituto Mexicano de Cinematografía.

attire after leaving the circus, emphasizes her rootless, displaced status. Having rejected both the psuedofamily of the circus and the degraded connection
sought by her prostitute mother, she is essentially cut off from the everyday
world, even as she wanders its streets and depends on its inhabitants for survival. Although Alma's "angel" designation is little more than a costume, a
learned skill, and a choreographed act, it comes to signify her radical repudiation of and by human society.

The foundational act of that repudiation is, of course, her incestuous relationship with her father, resulting in her pregnancy. The circus provides a fertile ground for this relationship, not only because of its insularity but because
its essential other-worldliness already places it outside of social convention.
Its inhabitants belong to it precisely because of their outsider status, whether
as dwarves, bearded women, exotic foreigners, or persons with supernatural
powers, dubious moral standing and other-worldly inclinations; and even
when these qualities are manufactured, their presence presupposes a distancing from social norms. As in other heterotopic situations, alliances are formed
out of necessity that do not always correspond to what the dominant culture

considers normal. It is the liminal, marginal status of the circus that, perhaps paradoxically, permits behavior that could be described as more free, such as the unremarked-upon gay relationship between the magician Lidio and the ringmaster/circus manager Rito, as well as Alma and Renato's incestuous relationship. Thus when Alma finally leaves the circus, it is not because of having committed incest but because of a pregnancy that will destroy her economic value as a performer. For if the morality of the outside world is transformed within the Circo Fantasía, the measurement of human worth in monetary terms is, if anything, exaggerated; such is the condition of marginality.

In the circus, both natural and human laws are subverted: the acrobat defies gravity, the magician cuts bodies in two and causes objects to vanish, frightening wild animals are shown to be tame and eager to please, and wily clown tricksters outwit bumbling clown policemen and pompous, patriarchal authority figures. The clown is an underdog who temporarily triumphs, but only within the ring; for just as the ritualized mockery of the hated ruling class does not restore their land and freedom to subjugated indigenous communities, the circus not only does not effect change but comes to be seen as a sinister symptom or symbol of degradation. In an era dominated by television and other communications technologies, the "circo de mala muerte" or down-and-out circus, is the entertainment par excellence of the *ciudad perdida* even as the city itself, in the words of the popular rock band Maldita Vecindad, becomes "a giant circus." [7]

Maldita's characterization of Mexico City as *El Circo* on the album of that name refers to more than the chaos and disorder of an overcrowded environment populated, in spite of Salinas's attempts at regulation, by thousands of street vendors, beggars, musicians, thieves, snake-oil salesmen, preachers, and prostitutes; it is also a depiction of a city in which poverty takes on aspects of the circus. A 1995 UNICEF study of street children in the Federal District estimated that 13,373 boys and girls were working in the streets and that of these, 3 percent made their living as clowns (Equipo de Ciencias Sociales/CAM). Other occupations included begging (26 percent), washing windshields (20 percent), and selling something (10 percent). Although the UNICEF figures are considered conservative, they verify the entrenchment of clowning as an occupation of indigent youth; if 3 percent is a comparatively slight figure, it is still significant given the demands of costume and at least rudimentary training in comparison to the other activities named. Occasional governmental attempts to repress street entertainers—clowns, musicians, and magicians—also indicate the pervasiveness and visibility of this sector.

While the spectacle of clowns and magicians that confronts Mexico City residents daily in parks, metro stations, and busy intersections may indeed appear surreal, it is nevertheless a byproduct of economic need. Thus in response to Jorge Rufinelli's question about the "almost purely Mexican significance of the fire-eaters," Rotberg emphasizes the social realism as well as visual symbolism they provided her film:

> I wanted to use [something] that all of us inhabitants of Mexico City know on a daily basis in order to transport my film in some way to people. And also it really helped me to visually and dramatically use this symbolism. (Rufinelli and Tanner 14)

By choosing the circus milieu and making her protagonist an "angel of fire," Rotberg generates visual beauty and explores mysticism and theological questions without leaving behind sociological reality. Like Carlos Monsiváis, who observes in his *Los rituales de caos* that "en buena medida, la crisis económica *es* la cultura urbana" [to a great extent, the economic crisis *is* urban culture] (121), Rotberg focuses on a seemingly extreme situation and uses it to create an allegory for the whole.

The Return of the Dirty Screen

Before making *Intimidad* in 1989, Dana Rotberg codirected with fellow CCC student Ana Diez Díaz the short documentary *Elvira Luz Cruz: Pena máxima* in 1985. For Eduardo de la Vega, their portrayal of the well-known case of a woman accused of murdering her children was a brilliant illustration of Foucault's analyses of the penal system in *Discipline and Punish,* exposing "una realidad sofocante, densa, permeada de violencia cotidiana y de ensañamiento que manifiesta a su vez una irrecuperable crisis de valores" [a reality that is suffocating, dense, permeated with everyday violence and rage, that at the same time manifests an irrecoverable crisis of values] ("Tercera Muestra" 4). Through the simple technique of multiple on-site interviews, the filmmakers depict in detail and without commentary the circumstances leading up to the jarring final image of Cruz behind prison bars, producing a powerful indictment of her oppressed condition.

Although Rotberg claims to have had little to do creatively with the documentary, it is this same "suffocating reality" that she recreates in *Angel de fuego.* In fact, an Elvira Luz Cruz figure appears briefly in *Angel:* Refugio's group, traveling along a road at night, passes a group of four policemen on horseback holding ropes tied to a woman prisoner who walks among them on foot. Refugio stops them and demands to know why the woman is being held. Told to back off, she curses the officer who threatens her, and she approaches the woman, who protests "no los maté" [I didn't kill them]. Refugio kisses the woman's forehead before being pushed away by the police. Although the gesture is tender, it is also impotent, for whatever the extent of Refugio's power to damn or forgive lost souls, it does not even pretend to address conditions on earth.

It is this portrayal of impotence in the face of gross injustice that distinguishes *Angel de fuego* from the other films discussed in this study. Whereas the films of Sistach, Cortés, Novaro, and Schyfter in various ways rehabilitate Mexican history and claim *mexicanidad* for women, Rotberg's film forces us to confront the radical alienation that is the underside of nationalist discourse, in which "history" is little more than the *puros trancazos* (pure blows) described by Jesusa Palancares, "cada vez más desmadejada en esta chingadera de vida" [weaker all the time in this fucked-up life] (Poniatowska, *Hasta no verte* 148). Profanity, the sociolinguistic analogue of the "dirty screen," is key; for rather than drawing on the ambivalent legacy of Malinche, the mythic indigenous mother of the Mexican nation whose characterization as La Chingada (the fucked one) has been disputed and revised by feminists, *Angel de fuego* aligns itself with such marginalized citizens as the Mexico City youth interviewed by Monsiváis in *Los rituales del caos* who says that "Digo chingada tantas veces al día que más que palabra me parece mi familia" [I say "chingada" so many times a day that more than a word, it seems like my family] (123).

The parallels with Rocha's "Esthetic of Hunger" as well as with the "Cinema do Lixo" (garbage cinema) that developed in Brazil in the late 1960s and 1970s are clear; for like the works of the Brazilian directors, Rotberg's film responds to conditions of physical and psychic hunger with aesthetic violence and transgression. But where does this seeming pessimism leave us in our study of strategies of feminist representation? Interestingly, in the criticism and discussion surrounding the film the question of feminism never arose, in contrast to the experience of the other filmmakers discussed—although like them, Rotberg has been a strong advocate for women in the cinema, having argued that a larger female presence would invigorate the industry and bring in new perspectives (Aviles Duarte; Camarena). Although Rotberg relocated to Europe shortly after *Angel de fuego*'s release and at the time of writing has not returned to play a role in Mexican cinema, her activities in war-torn

Bosnia indicate a strong commitment to cultural activism: in collaboration with Bosnian filmmakers, she helped stage an international film festival in Sarajevo in 1993, brought Bosnian films to Mexico City in 1994, and produced Ademir Kenovic's 1996 antiwar film *The Perfect Circle.* This proactive stance, with its implicit collectivism, contrasts with the unmitigated isolation depicted in her film.

But the central role of women in *Angel de fuego* and the sympathy shown for downtrodden figures (such as Alma, Malena, and the woman prisoner) who are morally complex, rather than innocent victims, reveals Rotberg's feminist understanding of oppression. Alma's experience graphically illustrates how in a context delineated by social injustice, the body—and particularly the female body—becomes a terrain of struggle. Her joyful celebration of her fertile womb at the beginning becomes a drive toward destruction when that same womb is forcibly emptied and when upon her return to the circus, she finds herself unable to perform on the trapeze and fit only for prostitution. The control that economic and theological forces exert over Alma's body lead inexorably to death and annihilation; the converse (suggested by her liberation of the animals prior to her suicide) is the repudiation of these forces in an affirmation of life.

As I have indicated, many critics considered *Angel de fuego* surreal; while I believe that the description is for the most part facile, it is perhaps worth recalling the political dimension of Surrealism, a movement that produced revolutionary manifestos as well as dreamlike imagery. The Surrealist movement's exploration of the unconscious and its break with bourgeois aesthetic convention were conceived as radical acts aimed at liberating not only art but the human mind from social structures of oppression: "to change our perception of the world and hence to change the world itself" (Bigsby 39). André Breton, in 1947, summarized the three goals of Surrealism as "the social liberation of man, his complete moral liberation, and his intellectual rejuvenation" (quoted in Henning 58). Although the movement was unable to find a strong political base with which to ally its artistic experiments and ultimately collapsed due to conflicts among its members regarding the Soviet Union and the split between Trotsky and Stalin, its insistence on psychological and artistic freedom as a prerequisite of social liberation remains its enduring legacy.

Breton, moreover, was influenced by Mexican art, both Mesoamerican and contemporary. Among the first to recognize the value of Frida Kahlo's paintings, he proclaimed her work "surreal," a label she refused. Although the association is tangential, something of the connection between the mutilated, oppressed, and yet sanctified female body and the larger social world and cosmology of modern Mexico that we find in Kahlo's work can be perceived in *Angel de fuego* as well. Kahlo's strong yet rarely explicit political sensibility—her diary is filled with allusions to Stalin and revolution, yet her paintings were hardly ever doctrinaire—also finds echoes in Rotberg's film. For as we have seen, although benefiting fully from the cinematic renaissance encouraged by the Salinas government, Rotberg does not use "surreal" imagery to sell exotic visions of Mexico but rather to undermine the illusory pretensions of *salinismo,* by showing the results of its modernization strategies.

While the Salinas regime hoped to clean up the Federal District through increased regulation—for example, by forcibly moving vendors off the streets into designated market buildings whose high rents few vendors could realistically afford—it did little to address the problems that had created the mess in the first place. Neither Salinas's nor any other government has been able, or willing, to answer the challenge posed by an alienated multitude whose relationship to the nation was starkly expressed by Palancares when she told Poniatowska that "soy basura a la que el perro le echa una miada y sigue adelante" [I'm that garbage that the dog pisses on and goes on its way] (*Hasta no verte* 218). Although *Angel de fuego* presents no concrete solutions, it nevertheless defies complacency in its powerful revitalization of the mandate of oppositional Latin American cinema: that "within the garbage can," that "forgotten" yet rapidly expanding urban zone where crisis has become culture, "one must be radical."

Mexican cinema died a while back. . . . The people don't have enough money to eat, how are they going to go to the movies?

Ofelia Medina[1]

I want all the women to wake up and sow in their hearts the need to organize. The free and just Mexico of which we all dream cannot be built with our arms folded.

EZLN Comandante Ramona[2]

Conclusion

Borders and Boundaries of National Cinema

The second half of the Salinas *sexenio* was a relatively optimistic period for filmmakers in Mexico. The proactive policies of IMCINE under Ignacio Durán had replaced the torpor of the 1980s with a vibrant cinema that was winning back domestic audiences and attracting attention abroad, leading some observers to speculate about a "renaissance" or "new Golden Age." For some this was marked by the international success of Novaro's *Danzón* and Arau's *Como agua para chocolate;* for others, what was most impressive was the entrance of new directors into the industry and, in particular, directors who were women. Conferences, festivals, international tours, journal issues, and academic theses proliferated, all paying homage to the suddenly booming *cine de mujer.* The new face of Mexican cinema, it seemed, would be tolerant, pluralist, and substantially guided by the creative presence of women.

Although the directors in question remained for the most part cautious and even skeptical with respect to the phenomena of "women's cinema" and a cinematic "boom" in Mexico in general, many interviews and press statements from the period reveal an implicit faith in the viability of filmmaking as a career. During the climactic year of 1992, in which four films by women challenged one another in the Ariel competition and in which the exhibition of Rotberg's *Angel de fuego* at Cannes reinforced the impression of global acceptance created by the presence of Novaro's *Danzón* the previous year, each of the directors mentioned in this study spoke confidently to the press about their anticipated next projects—only one of which, Novaro's *El jardín del Edén,* would actually be realized.

From 1992 to 1994, women continued to maintain a strong presence in the cinema. Marisa Sistach, following the relatively obscure *Los pasos de Ana,* reached a wider audience with the mainstream comedy *Anoche soñé contigo,* released in 1992. Eva López Sánchez, a CCC graduate, joined the ranks of feature directors with *Dama de noche* in 1993, while María Novaro made *El jardín del Edén* as a Canadian coproduction the same year. In 1994, Guita Schyfter directed her second feature, *Sucesos distantes,* and Sabina Berman codirected with Isabelle Tardán a film version of Berman's popular play *Entre Villa y una mujer desnuda* for Televicine. Other women continued to be active as documentary makers, video artists, and directors of short films, mostly within the university environment.

Although often exhibited together, the work produced by women during these years was far from constituting a unified school or wave, feminist or otherwise; in many cases, the directors' oeuvres were not even particularly cohesive in themselves. The films of Novaro and Cortés showed strong thematic and stylistic consistency, yet the films of Sistach, Schyfter, and Rotberg varied enough in style, genre, content, and overall approach that it would be difficult to construct an authorial signature for any of them, apart from the directors' own personal testimony (for instance, Rotberg's assertion that *Angel de fuego* was a personal film, whereas her earlier *Intimidad* was not). Asked repeatedly by the press to comment on their colleagues' work and its possible connections to their own, the directors understandably protested their individuality. "Porque somos mujeres creen que tenemos que hacer cosas parecidas," commented Novaro in *Nitrato de Plata.* "Me da gusto que digan que no tenemos mucho en común entre nosotras" [Because we are women, they think we have to do similar things. I like that they say that there isn't much in common among us] (in Sarabia 24). Nevertheless, while recognizing the stylistic diversity of women's filmmaking, several observations can be made about women's contributions to Mexican cinema during this period.

Women's Filmmaking as Intellectual Endeavor

First, while the aesthetics of the various films differed, the women directors of the 1990s were seen as belonging to a generation of directors whose commitment to the cinema was personal and artistic in nature—that which Cortés has variously described as "passion" and "veneration for cinema as art" (Torralba 7; Peguero). Not only did they not belong to a factory-like system of industrial production, but they, along with male directors from similar university backgrounds, effectively constituted a second film sector that had little in common with the commercial form of production, which, although similarly traceable to a small number of directors, was organized primarily around genre (the replication of almost identical sex comedies, action dramas, and so forth). Although much work produced during this period may *not* have reflected the choices of its makers (since, as in the case of Rotberg with *Intimidad,* novice directors seized any opportunity to gain experience in the medium), the films of Novaro, Rotberg, and others, like those of Arturo Ripstein, Jaime Humberto Hermosillo, Carlos Carrera, Alberto Cortés, and other male directors, were widely understood to reflect a personal vision rather than the demands of the marketplace.

This perception of the cinema as personal helps to explain a certain ambivalence that directors and commentators alike expressed in discussions of whether a given film (or director) was "feminist." For unlike the overtly political films of previous eras (such as the films of Emilio Fernández or Roberto Gavaldón in the Golden Age or Felipe Cazals in the Nuevo Cine period), most of the films of the 1990s were not "social issue" films. They did not dramatize sweeping national themes such as the Revolution, exploitation of indigenous peoples and *campesinos,* or urban misery, nor were they prefaced with titles situating the story within the glorious narrative of the nation's history. Their characters were idiosyncratic rather than archetypal, and any presence of the Mexican flag tended to be incidental or perhaps mildly ironic (as in the Independence Day paraphernalia visible in the background in *Danzón* before Julia's flight from Mexico City). Their feminism, such as it was acknowledged to exist, was likewise not associated within the text with a larger social movement and, as we have seen in individual cases, could be ignored by viewers who preferred an apolitical reading.

At the same time, the idea of film as the expression of a personal vision enabled filmmakers to participate in the public life of the nation in a way not unlike that of other intellectuals such as journalists and writers. In *Intellectuals and the State in Twentieth-Century Mexico,* Camp defines an intellectual as:

> an individual who creates, evaluates, analyzes, or presents transcendental symbols, values, ideas, and interpretations on a regular basis to a broad audience. (38)

Camp goes on to discuss the various ways in which intellectuals have been specifically characterized in Mexico, citing as salient traits "the use of the intellect to live, the search for truth, the emphasis on the humanities, the creative bent, and the critical posture" (ibid.). Although he sees Mexican intellectuals as somewhat divided between those who participate in society by working for the government and those whose critical outlook leads them to seek other means of survival and expression (such as in academia or oppositional organizations), Camp and his informants—intellectuals and political leaders—considered the role of the intellectual not to be confined to a particular discipline but rather to be involved in commenting on, analyzing, critiquing, and shaping the public life of the nation.

At the time of Camp's research in the early 1980s, he did not consider film production to be a particularly viable arena for intellectual activity, noting that government control, a lack of private funding, inability to compete with foreign product, and a general lack of interest on the part of the public had contributed to Mexican cinema's overall mediocrity and insignificance (191–192). In the 1990s, however, many filmmakers were engaged in what could be considered intellectual production. With the financial support of the government, universities, and other institutions supplementing private investment, noncommercial or semicommercial filmmakers created narratives that broke with generic formulae and spoke to the prevailing concerns of the contemporary nation (or segments thereof) from the perspective of a well-defined creative consciousness.

To the extent that film was still a viable medium, filmmakers in this period were in a position to be the intellectuals par excellence of their generation. For the written word, whose instrumental role in defining and perpetuating what Foucault called "regimes of truth" in Latin America from the moment of colonization through the twentieth century was persuasively delineated by Angel Rama in *The Lettered City,* had long been in decline. While this devolution was not quantitative—García Canclini points out that more books are printed today than ever (*Culturas híbridas* 17)—print culture could be said to be losing importance in Latin America, where high rates of illiteracy had always made it the exclusive province of a privileged elite. Whereas the literate intelligentsia had previously been able to act at times as "mediators for the popular classes and advocates of social change" (Franco, "What's Left" 16), its significance diminished in recent decades, while the power of the mass media grew. Following García Canclini, Franco describes a "reconversion" of the cultural field in which not only has print culture become "only one, and not the most important, of the resources of advanced capitalism" (*La cultura moderna* 350), but also "music and the television image, rather than the printed word, have become the privileged vehicles for the exploration of Latin American identity and the nature of modernity" ("What's Left" 17).

If this is indeed the case, then the ascent of visual and electronic culture can be seen as a potential refutation of Roger Bartra's critique of the quest for *mexicanidad* (in Ramírez Berg, *Cinema of Solitude* 4–5) as a game played only by privileged elites, as the mass media make the collective "exploration of identity" accessible to a far larger audience. Yet to locate the project of collective self-definition within this realm is also extremely problematic, insofar as television and radio (if not music as such) are expensive and tightly controlled media, far less accessible than print from the standpoint of production. Camp's discussion of censorship distinguishes between broadcast media, which are heavily regulated precisely because of their accessibility to a broad audience, and print media, which enjoy greater freedom but far less influence (182–192). And as Cynthia Steele notes, the subversive creativity of grassroots popular culture is vulnerable to misappropriation by the wealthy and powerful corporate media, making effective critical intervention even more difficult (150).

Nevertheless, many of the most interesting and potentially influential cultural figures of the 1990s were those who stood somewhere in the interstices of established elite traditions, 1960s-style counterculture, and contemporary commercial media: performance artists (Jesusa Rodríguez, Guillermo Gómez-Peña, Superbarrio), musicians (Sergio Arau, Eugenia León, José de Molina, Astrid Hadad), *cronistas* (Monsiváis, Poniatowska, Cristina Pacheco), cartoonists (Ruis, El Fisgón), and filmmakers. While sometimes suffering the drawbacks of the traditional intellectual professions (ghettoization in specialized forums such as the Cineteca Nacional, where their audience is limited to the "converted"), these individuals had the potential to reach a large and not necessarily educated or elite audience without compromising their personal aesthetic or political ideas. In the film industry in particular, as Isabel Arredondo points out in her study of film schools and women directors, the shabby and disorganized state of commercial cinema in the early 1990s facilitated the entrance of university-trained professionals, with the self-perception and sensibility of artists rather than technicians, into the industry as a rejuvenating force (17). The commercial success of films like *Danzón* shows that in some instances, a complex and progressive text can breach the gap between "popular" and "elite" discourse, constituting a significant intervention in the nation's ongoing conversation about—that is to say, invention of—itself.

The Body Politic

If we put to one side the formal and generic diversity of women's filmmaking, we can begin to sketch a coherent if tentative outline of an *otro cine* in which film is an intellectual endeavor, at once the expression and the on-screen representation of Landeta's "woman as thinker." From this perspective, what unites the filmmakers discussed here is their critical engagement with the concept of *mexicanidad*—an engagement which, although in different ways and with different emphases, brings each of them toward a more inclusive vision of the Mexican nation. In each case, this vision goes beyond a liberal feminist advocacy of tolerance and equality within a preexisting framework ("Mexico") and demands the transformation of the existing nation into one which not only permits but which actually emerges from the diverse subject positions of its constituent populations—women, religious minorities, social and sexual dissidents, indigenous peoples, the urban poor. The filmic liberation of these subjects from the schematic and objectified roles to which they were previously confined is itself a significant contribution to national cinema.

Of course, male filmmakers also have called into question some of the tenets of official nationalism. The names of Jaime Humberto Hermosillo, Arturo Ripstein, Gabriel Retes, and Jorge Fons, mentioned in previous chapters, may be specifically emphasized here. Since the 1970s, Hermosillo has produced representations of gay men that challenge commercial cinema's offensive caricatures and, as Ramírez Berg suggests, subvert the association of *mexicanidad* with a narrow notion of male heterosexuality (*Cinema of Solitude* 131–133). Ripstein, often in collaboration with screenwriter Paz Alicia Garciadiego, has made films that deconstruct such patriarchal genres as the family melodrama and the *cabaretera* film, showing how rigid social/moral environments tend to produce cannibalistic exploitation and self-destruction, especially for women. Retes has satirized the neoliberal era in *El bulto* (1991) and *Bienvenido/Welcome* (1994), while Fons broke the silence surrounding the 1968 Tlatelolco massacre with his 1990 film *Rojo amanecer,* based on the famous eyewitness testimonies collected by Poniatowska. Yet it has been women writers and filmmakers who have most dramatically revised, within their creative work, the relationship between the nation as a space of collective identification and the bodies that inhabit it. They have done so first by inserting an explicitly female perspective into the public sphere (as opposed to the "neutral" yet gendered subject of conventional discourse) and second, by insisting that the female body not be sacrificed to the interests of the nation, but rather that the nation become a place in which all bodies can survive and flourish.

In emphasizing the centrality of the body to feminist film practice, I seek to call attention to the specifically visual dimension of this work and the extent to which filmmakers have expressed feminism less as an explicit stance than as a visceral extrapolation of lived experience. This expression is aesthetic as much as theoretical: the films in question rarely position their characters in relation to an unchanging Mexican landscape (that timeless terrain captured or invented in the heroic compositions of Gabriel Figueroa during the Golden Age), but rather frame their protagonists in shots that emphasize subjectivity and the power dynamics of the human environment. Like experimental literature that searches for a language capable of expressing a physical realm for which existing linguistic codes are inadequate, feminist film has used the medium to resist the conventional objectification of the female body and to centralize that body as subject, while simultaneously embedding it in a time and space that give it broader social implications.

Thus *Danzón* addresses female desire and working-class experience in Mexico City; *El secreto de Romelia* explores mother-daughter bonds, conventions of femininity, and historical transformations in Mexico; *Angel de fuego* is at once a study of religious belief and transgression and a denunciation of urban marginalization; and so forth. As Franco writes of contemporary Latin American women novelists, "It is not 'daddy, mummy, and me' who dominate their novels, but precarious and often perilous alliances across generations and social classes" (*Plotting Women* 186).[3] Yet the traditional format of the social novel or film, in which most often an educated, urban, middle- or upper-class intellectual denounces from the standpoint of an "objective" outsider the plight of a given oppressed group, is replaced by one in which subjective experience is valorized, private and public are integrally related, and a holistic politics emerges as the organic result of everyday life practices.

Women filmmakers in Mexico can thus be seen as part of the larger social phenomenon of Latin American feminism. Franco notes that the specificity of feminism in Latin America lies in its alignment of "gender politics and other forms of struggle without subordinating gender and without sacrificing politics" (*Plotting Women* xxiii). Scholarship produced by and about women's movements in the region, as well as the concrete labor carried out by women's organizations, demonstrates an indivisibility of gender and other identifications (particularly class) that is not equaled in the United States.[4] Women's issues are not separate but rather a dimension of all social struggle; moreover, gender becomes a kind of ground zero upon which social structures, institutions and ideologies are tested and from which they can be challenged and resisted.

The feminist movement that emerged in the 1960s and 1970s was often documented on film by women who were at once participants and cinematographic observers. Filmmakers who began working during that era have continued to document women's political participation, not only in Mexico but also in revolutionary struggles and resistance movements in South and Central America. While, in contrast, women's feature films of the 1990s did not participate directly in the struggles of an organized movement or of women's organizations, they did express a feminist politics in their depiction of the female body as something other than object and symbol: as regulated and constrained by patriarchal tradition *(Romelia, Novia que te vea)* and by contemporary social contradictions *(Los pasos de Ana);* as embedded in popular culture in ways that are both confining and potentially liberating *(Danzón);* and as the terrain of struggle on which not only religious battles but also the low-intensity wars of poverty and marginalization are waged *(Angel de fuego).* This treatment of the female body—that is, of the female subject whose body is both a source of pleasure and strength and a battleground—recalls Rosario Castellanos's self-admonition to maintain "contact with my carnal and historical roots" ("If Not Poetry" 258) and challenges the cinematic regime described by Matilde Landeta as of "la mujer explicada a través del hombre" [women explained through men] (in Martínez de Velasco 64), instead clearing a space from which women can begin to speak by and for themselves.

Approaching Dialogue: Gendered Reception

In the preceding section, I have suggested some of the ways in which women film directors in Mexico, as intellectuals and producers of artistic texts, have participated in what Franco calls "struggles for interpretive power." But as many scholars (notably Janet Steiger in her book *Interpreting Films: Studies in the Historical Reception of American Cinema*) have persuasively argued, film spectators are also participants in such struggles: the circumstances in which producers and consumers are imbricated give meaning to films, and viewers' interpretations of a film may not coincide with the meaning intended by its producer, especially if there is a shift in context. What constitutes a film's feminist stance (or lack thereof) must therefore be at least partially determined in the process of reception.

The vagaries of interpretation in this regard are clearly perceptible in the critical response to the films analyzed in this study; a given critic's reaction to *Los pasos de Ana, Romelia,* or *Danzón* frequently revealed more about his or her own beliefs and opinions about feminism than about the film in question.[5] How the general public, as opposed to professional critics, perceived these films has thus far only entered into the discussion peripherally, in the form of quantitative data such as box-office statistics and cinema attendance. Unlike published criticism, general audience response is difficult to gauge and even more difficult to evaluate. More often than not, scholars have used box-office figures to confirm their own readings of films: we infer, for example, that *Allá en el Rancho Grande* was popular because 1930s audiences were tired of politics and nostalgic for an unreal past, even though such fatigue and nostalgia cannot be empirically demonstrated. But Norma Iglesias's study of the gendered reception of *Danzón* discussed in Chapter 6 bears further mention here; its revelation of the different ways of experiencing and interpreting Novaro's film adds the dimension of polysemy to our understanding of feminist film as a social practice.

Iglesias, as we have seen, used *Danzón* as a means of approaching the cultural construction of gendered identity. Working with all-female, all-male, and mixed-gender focus groups, Iglesias and her colleagues recorded and analyzed the reactions during screenings of the film as well as the groups' discussions afterward. While the artificiality of this method, as well as the fact that the study was done in Madrid rather than Mexico,[6] limits its usefulness for our purposes, many of Iglesias's observations were quite revealing. For example, the all-male group tended to approach the film as detached observers and "experts" in sociology and film history, commenting on such aspects as the protagonist's attainment or loss of "feminine identity" and on the film's location in cinema history (7–8). In contrast, the female viewers entered into the film, identifying with the protagonist and referring complicitously to "nuestro punto de vista" [our point of view] (6, 11). Overall, Iglesias observed that in spite of some divergences that emerged upon further reflection, the women overwhelmingly enjoyed the subversive experience of a film which broke patriarchal codes of representation, depicted female experience with which they could identify, and allowed their complicity with what they very much perceived as a "feminine" story (11–12).

What is suggestive about this microstudy of *Danzón*'s reception is its implications for the potential social impact of feminist cinema. Iglesias's initial premise—that film has been an important factor in the perpetuation of gender roles and identities for many decades—has been articulated by many film scholars and writers in Mexico, notably Monsiváis, who has written extensively about the role of film in easing audiences through the social, cultural, and economic transformations of the twentieth century.[7] Although perhaps an obvious point, it is worth remembering that altering the images of masculinity and femininity presented to the public and offering alternative models of what it means to be a woman or man in Mexican society (Castellanos's "another way to be human and free") is cultural labor that does not only concern critics and scholars but also—especially if sustained over time rather than confined to single films—can empower and transform audiences. For as Steiger argues, films are not fixed containers of meaning but rather the terrain of situational interpretation whose lack of rigidity can translate into the positive value of dialogue.

Falling Stars: The End of *Salinismo*

In the early 1990s, such a dialogue was more or less readily imaginable; the willingness of the government to fund and promote film provided openings even for points of view that had emerged out of a culture of opposition. But by the end of 1994, the social and economic landscape of the country had drastically shifted—or rather, contradictions that the Salinas regime had attempted to cover over had erupted with stunning violence. As film, like all other sectors of society, was deeply affected by the new situation, it is worth reviewing the events of the mid-1990s before going on to assess their direct and indirect implications for the cinema.

On 1 January 1994, the North American Free Trade Agreement went into effect. That same day, a guerrilla army in the state of Chiapas declared war on the federal government of Mexico, launching an impressive rebellion that—as the entire nation seemed to immediately recognize—dramatically exposed the *salinista* program of "modernization." Drawing on the legacy of Revolutionary hero and martyred *campesino* leader Emiliano Zapata, the Zapatista Army of National Liberation (EZLN) rapidly became Mexico's expression par excellence of discontent among urban intellectuals as well as among rural indigenous and *campesino* communities. Some of the former attended the National Democratic Convention (CND) convened by the guerrillas in August;

others, generally more conservative, formed the Grupo San Angel, an informal think tank which gathered in Mexico City to analyze the political situation and formulate recommendations. As even mainstream historian Enrique Krauze later noted, the Zapatista movement as a political phenomenon strengthened the demand for a democratic transition in Mexico and awakened the nation's "dormant" consciousness regarding ethnic inequality, particularly with regard to indigenous peoples (Vega, "Krauze").

The EZLN's struggles on the cultural front, as I will discuss below, provided new arenas and new challenges to journalists and artists, including film and video makers based primarily in the nation's capital; moreover, the strength and popularity of the rebellion (disproportionate to its actual resources and lasting long after the few initial days of overt confrontation) made it troublesome to the government, which was fighting to achieve an image of stability and prosperity that would continue to attract foreign investment and foster approval of its policies. Although the result of ten years of clandestine organizing, the EZLN rebellion seemed to emerge out of nowhere; yet it has since been revealed that both the U.S. and Mexican governments were aware of the existence of a guerrilla movement in Chiapas prior to 1994. Such knowledge was thus deliberately kept from the public, thereby preserving the illusion of tranquillity in the light of NAFTA and of the PRI's desire to retain control during the upcoming election year.

During that final year of Salinas's rule, however, the illusion of stability began to crumble at an astonishing speed. In March, the PRI's handpicked presidential candidate, Luis Donaldo Colosio, was assassinated in Tijuana, in full view of security guards and national television cameras. While the alleged gunman was quickly arrested, Byzantine conspiracy theories proliferated, investigations stalled, investigators were dismissed and replaced, and no satisfactory explanation (as of this writing) was found. In the fall, a second assassination precipitated the definitive downfall of the Salinas dynasty: José Francisco Ruiz Massieu, former governor of Guerrero and secretary-general of the PRI, was shot in Mexico City, and (after another round of investigations, speculations, and bizarre sideshows) the crime was pinned on a number of individuals connected with the government, including Raúl Salinas de Gortari, the president's brother.

When newly elected President Ernesto Zedillo opted to imprison Raúl Salinas in an open break with the tradition of immunity for the nation's power elite, Carlos Salinas followed the example set by hundreds of peasant and working-class activists protesting his regime and went on a brief hunger strike, to little effect. Soon afterward, the ex-president left the country. Meanwhile, the public revelation of the crimes of the Salinas clan (Raúl has also been investigated regarding embezzlement of public funds and has been accused by Swiss investigators of deep connections with the drug trade) was compounded by the realization that the *peso* devaluation that devastated the economy at the end of 1994 was the result of deliberate planning: Salinas had kept the currency artificially afloat in order to secure a PRI victory in the August elections while cynically promising ever-increasing prosperity and "well-being for your family" and leaving his successor to deal with the consequences of those empty promises.

Although a full analysis of Mexican politics in the 1990s clearly exceeds the scope of the present study, it is crucial to understand that in many parts of the country, the PRI's "bienestar" had been imposed by force in the first place, using open bribery and manipulation backed up by military occupation and intimidation. Entangled with overt political violence was the U.S.-sponsored war on drugs, which became a routine pretext for military activity in conflictive areas. (For instance, soldiers and tanks entered the coastal and mountain regions of Guerrero on the very eve of the elections; PRI and PAN representatives in Chilpancingo explained the maneuver as a drug-related operation.)[8] But in 1995, the hollowness of the government's economic promises was definitively exposed, as across the country businesses closed, individuals fell from prosperity into poverty and from poverty into desperation, food prices rose, subsidies on basic necessities such as tortillas and milk were cut, food consumption dropped, and in an ironic parody of NAFTA's supposed stimulus to production, the balance of trade with the the United States came to be weighted dramatically (if temporarily) in Mexico's favor, simply because importing products from the north was no longer feasible.

Although the poor certainly suffered the most in an absolute sense from the economic crisis, the hope and the failure of *salinismo* were illustrated most dramatically among the middle and even upper classes. At the end of Salinas's presidency, for example, a widely cited survey in *Forbes* magazine listed twenty-four billionaires in Mexico; a year into the Zedillo *sexenio,* that number had dropped to ten. For the less wealthy, the accouterments of "modernization" so heavily promoted during the previous decade became nightmares overnight; having been encouraged to borrow money and rely on credit cards, middle-class consumers saw interest rates soar overnight to untenable levels, which forced many people to take second and third jobs just to pay the interest on their purchases of the previous few years.

Many members of this sector would align themselves with a movement called El Barzón (the yoke), which used militant tactics to try to gain some relief for debtors with proposed solutions such as payment plans tied to family income levels, a grace period for payments by unemployed debtors, and cancellation of interest imposed in an illegal (usurious) manner. In September 1996, a number of prominent film and television actors announced the formation of El Barzón de las Verdaderas Estrellas, a branch of the organization made up of actors who claimed that, like the thousands of small business owners, farmers, and blue- and white-collar employees who faced legal action and loss of their property, they were no longer able to pay their debts (Nájar).

The organization was led by Ana Colchero and Demián Bichir, both then protagonists of *Nada personal,* a *telenovela* with political overtones produced by leftist journalists Epigimenio Ibarra (of *Argos*), Hernán Vera (a founder of El Salvador's Radio Venceremos), and Carlos Payán (of *La Jornada*). Colchero, a former Televisa actress, had helped propel *Nada personal* (aired by rival mainstream network TV Azteca) to a surprising level of popularity. In December 1996, however, she would quit the program, citing differences with producers over the nature of her role, which she felt had gone from being an "honest and gutsy" feminist role model to being an undignified coward (Preston 1). Although the producers thought otherwise (and accused her of letting personal relationships on the set undermine her professionalism), her public position was a strong feminist statement—and an indictment of lingering sexism on the Mexican left. Bichir, for his part, had been among several celebrities to appear on posters promoting the EZLN "Consulta" of the previous year, an alternative national plebiscite designed to both demonstrate and build support for the Zapatista program. In joining the Barzón, Bichir, Colchero, and their colleagues demonstrated that their political activism was not simply a fashionable celebrity cause but a response to a crisis that had the potential to affect them personally as workers and as consumers.

But the economic crisis that began in 1994 affected the media as an industry along with film and television workers as consumer-debtors. In her discussion of the 1995 Muestra de Cine Mexicano en Guadalajara, *Dicine*'s Susana López Aranda wrote that "entre devaluaciones, escándalos políticos, crimenes sin resolver, indefiniciones y para resumir, crisis en dosis masivas, se sentía en Guadalajara, que de alguna manera, un ciclo llegaba a su fin" [between devaluations, political scandals, unresolved crimes, indefinition, and in short, crisis in massive doses, one felt in Guadalajara that somehow a cycle was coming to an end] ("X Muestra" 9). Even the giant Televisa, whose future under neoliberalism had seemed assured, had been forced to cut back on its plans for film production; the variable and vulnerable state-supported film sector was devastated, causing López Aranda to wonder, "si no hay películas, ¿qué sentido tiene la muestra?" [if there aren't any films, what is the point of the festival?] (ibid.).

Only a few months into the crisis, it was clear that most directors in the country would not have sufficient work, much less produce another *Como agua para chocolate* any time soon. As if to symbolically underscore the crisis and its relationship to the false promises of the free-trade agreement, Arau's 1995 Hollywood debut, *A Walk in the Clouds,* would be rejected by U.S. critics for its "formulaic" delivery of the so-called magic realism that many of the same critics had lauded three years before. In Mexico, meanwhile, production dropped to almost zero, and many directors, including such rising stars as Alfonso Cuarón and Guillermo del Toro, sought work outside the country. The "new Golden Age" had been cut short before it even began.

Yet like *salinismo* itself, the notion of the "new Golden Age" was, as we have seen, highly problematic even during its most optimistic moments, especially if we focus on women as creators of alternative representations of self and nation. Therefore, although the economic situation at the end of 1994 worsened dramatically, with very real material consequences for the cinema as well as for almost all Mexicans, I do not wish to portray that moment as a break so much as a watershed in our understanding of the previous *sexenio.* What the events and revelations subsequent to 1994 force us to do is to reevaluate those optimistic moments and to replace the early 1990s' uncritical celebration of women's cinema with a more profound understanding of the borders and boundaries of a cinema materially (through funding and infrastructure) and symbolically understood to be "national." To begin with, we must consider more closely what was and was not possible to articulate during this period: who spoke, who was silenced, and what interests such voices and silences served.

Censorship and Struggle

Addressing the question of Mexican cinema's future at the end of *Cinema of Solitude,* Ramírez Berg wrote of the need for a new community:

> The immediate task, it would seem, is to find a progressive, not regressive, way to resurrect the community. What is being proposed is a

new, communal redefinition of *mexicanidad*—I call it *la nueva comunidad*. (212)

He went on to cite Carlos Fuentes, who wrote in *Tiempo Mexicano*, "Let us hasten to create . . . a Mexican socialism . . . Not a paradise, but simply a community."

But what kind of community could be imagined in the mid-1990s? At a time when human rights workers, PRD members, and *campesino* and indigenous activists were routinely arrested, disappeared, and assassinated, when (according to organizations such as Amnesty International) torture was on the rise and human rights abuses were legion, truly critical media-makers received few funds from IMCINE or private producers and instead faced harsh censorship. In an era of supposed political reform, President Salinas's commitment, delivered on videotape in 1992 to a union of radio and television workers, bore little relation to the reality of media production in Mexico: he pledged to "respetar plenamente la libertad de expresión, proteger los derechos y la seguridad de los comunicadores mexicanos, crear y recrear las condiciones de su desarrollo y cerrar el paso a toda forma de intolerancia" [fully respect freedom of expression, protect the rights and security of Mexican communicators, create and recreate the conditions of their development, and put an end to all forms of intolerance] (CEPROPIE 29). Although government funding sometimes enabled the production and diffusion of art and information that was unacceptable to commercial producers such as Televisa, a few examples will indicate the variety of forms of censorship imposed on media producers that did not serve the needs of either the business sector or the government during this period.

According to Alex Cox, the end of formal government censorship came about by force in 1990 with the release of Jorge Fons's *Rojo amanecer*. Made with private financing and filmed "in strictest secrecy" in a Mexico City warehouse, the film was banned upon completion, supposedly by order of the army. But protest on the part of filmmakers and other intellectuals led to the rescinding of the ban, and in spite of its exclusion from important venues like the Muestra in Guadalajara and the Havana Film Festival, the film became one of the best-selling domestic features ever, circulating to this day in video stores and market stalls throughout the country (Cox 33). For Cox, the government's acquiescence to public demand meant greater freedom for all filmmakers; for other observers, however, the gatekeeper function carried out by IMCINE and other institutions was simply censorship by another name. For Víctor Ugalde, filmmaking in Mexico was a "labyrinth" which one could best negotiate with the help of wealthy or powerful connections, without which one's movie would probably never get off the ground. In an essay bitterly attacking a film establishment he saw as corrupt and exclusionary, Ugalde concluded that "tal y como soplan los vientos neoliberales dentro de la industria cinematográfica mexicana, la verdadera y más cruel de las censuras se ejerce al momento de seleccionar los proyectos para su filmación" [the way the neoliberal winds are blowing in the Mexican film industry, the real and most cruel form of censorship is exercised at the moment of selection of projects to be filmed] (62).

For those films that did reach completion, whether through IMCINE or with some other form of financing, the most effective mechanism of control was unquestionably distribution, a fact about which nearly every Mexican filmmaker has at some point justifiably complained. Marcela Fernández Violante's public disgust in the wake of IMCINE's bad-faith negotiations over her film *Golpe de suerte* was equaled by Ofelia Medina's complaints about treatment of her film *Gertrudis Bocanegra* (1991), an historical drama which she starred in and coproduced and which her brother Ernesto directed. Although IMCINE had financed the expensive period feature, its weak distribution strategies caused Medina to denounce the institute's sabotaging of filmmakers:

Sí voy a seguir haciendo películas pero no con el Imcine, prefiero perder sola que mantener una burocracia inútil e inepta que condena al suicidio a los productores que buscamos hacer un cine diferente.
[Yes I'm going to keep making films but not with IMCINE; I would rather lose alone than maintain a useless and inept bureaucracy that condemns producers who seek to make a different kind of cinema to suicide.] (Quiroz Arroyo, "No estoy dispuesta")

Whether treatment such as Medina experienced was deliberate or simply negligent, what is certain is that the bureaucratic mechanisms of the industry could easily be manipulated for political ends; for instance, while the independent collective Canal 6 de Julio, makers of *Crónica de un fraude*, was not explicitly prevented from showing its video about the 1988 elections, the Department of Radio, Television, and Cinema simply never responded to its repeated formal requests for distribution authorization, thus imposing a de facto ban on its public exhibition (Quiroz Arroyo, "Existe censura").

Such slippage between inefficiency and deliberate censorship produced a level of frustration that in turn encouraged the emergence of small-scale film and video makers outside of the establishment. One of these was the Argos group, whose documentary on the Zapatista uprising, *Viaje al centro de la selva,* was sold directly to the public on video and also shown in various sites in autumn of 1994. In February 1995, when President Zedillo ordered a crackdown on the EZLN and when thousands of copies of the video had reportedly been sold, Argos journalist Javier Elorriaga was jailed as a Zapatista collaborator. Elorriaga's wife, María Gloria (Elisa) Benavides, likewise employed by Argos, also was arrested.[9]

Elorriaga claimed that his only relationship with the Zapatistas was that of a sympathetic journalist and witness; he later revealed that in mid-1994 he had been the go-between for a series of secret messages between Zedillo and the EZLN (that is, that Zedillo knew of, condoned, and made use of his access to the Zapatistas during the making of the video). After more than a year of imprisonment in Chiapas, Elorriaga was released in June 1996 and, paraphrasing Emiliano Zapata to proclaim that "freedom of expression belongs to those who work it," aligned himself with the Zapatista National Liberation Front (FZLN), a civilian organization independent of although linked to the Zapatistas. Given that no evidence of criminal activity on the part of the Argos journalists was ever found, it would seem that they were persecuted solely for having exercised their right of free speech on behalf of the Chiapas rebels.[10]

Like film and video, radio has been subject to censorship, not only because of its content but because of its adaptability to unregulated use in rural areas and access to dispersed and/or illiterate populations. In August 1994, Voz de la Montaña, an indigenous station in the impoverished and turbulent mountain region of Guerrero, was incapacitated when its equipment was stolen (Reyes Morales et al.). In May 1995, the low-wattage Mexico City radio station Radio Pirata was shut down for broadcasting without a permit (Gómez and Molina); months earlier, Marco Rascón had pointed out the hypocrisy of the government's attempted "expropriation" of Radio Pirata and its parent organization, Televerdad, in contrast to its tolerance of and complicity in Televisa's monopoly over broadcasting. In Veracruz, Radio Huaya was persecuted for allegedly broadcasting encoded pro-guerrilla messages; these messages turned out to be broadcasts in the indigenous languages of the region (Vásquez). Journalists at the station received repeated death threats, and all of these stations experienced indirect censorship via manipulation of licensing and other bureaucratic requirements.

The print media, by virtue of their inherent decentralization, have more successfully eluded government control, abetted by the demise of a longstanding government monopoly on newsprint. Yet the dependence of newspapers on paid advertising, both commercial and political (often in the form of stories called *gacetillas* which are indistinguishable from other articles), hampers free expression (Russell 132). Moreover, although newspapers like *La Jornada* have emerged as voices of independent journalism, violence against journalists (especially outside of the capital) is not unheard of, and manipulation occurs on many levels, from bribery to coercion. Finally, as Camp points out, the fear of government censorship leads editors and publishers to practice an arbitrary self-censoring that is in many ways more effective and detrimental than any overt, official practices would be in curtailing critical expression and producing "vagueness, contradictions, and superficiality" (Camp 197). In film and video as well, says Canal 6 de Julio's Carlos Mendoza, the "great triumph" of authoritarianism lies in the internalization of censorship by media producers, even in such supposed zones of free expression as the university (Mendoza 60).

Given these conditions, it would seem problematic (to say the least) to look to the cinema for the seeds of a "new community," when off-screen, real communities are being devastated and deterritorialized by state violence at the service of capital, and when journalists and videographers who seek to document this reality are risking their lives. Yet—without wishing to speculate excessively on a history that is still unfolding—I will reiterate that in the context of an increasingly vocal and organized civil society, films that rewrite the master narratives of the nation constitute an important part of the struggle for what Matilde Landeta saw as not only an "other cinema" but an "other world."

Crafting a Culture of Resistance

To speak of the "context of civil society" is not only to read films in their specific historical contexts, as earlier chapters have done; it is also to broaden the notion of what might constitute a feminist *otro cine*. Although the phenomenon of a women's cinema and the questions it raises about such issues as the particularities of the female gaze or the formal similarities and differences between directors continue to interest scholars in the United States and Mexico, such an approach tells us little about the role these films play in society and elides the strong social impulse that motivates many of the artists in question. The extratextual activities of cinema workers, from Landeta's lifelong involvement with labor unions to Ana Colchero's work with the Barzón and Medina's organizing on behalf of indigenous children in Chiapas and other states, are not separate from those women's work in film, but come to be an extension of it.

Medina, in fact, has continually used her clout as a stage and screen actress, especially the international recognition gained by her starring role in Paul Leduc's 1984 film *Frida* and the resulting association between herself and the politically committed painter she portrayed, to further a variety of political causes. Active in environmental groups, Medina cofounded the Indigenous Children's Health Fund of Mexico in 1990 in response to a measles epidemic that was exacerbated by an extreme undercounting of indigenous children in official vaccination statistics. At the time, Medina tried to gain the support of President Salinas, with whom she apparently had good connections (Gayoso; Quiroz Arroyo, "No estoy dispuesta"). By the mid-1990s, however, she had become a prominent advocate of the Zapatistas, frequently leading protest marches, organizing human rights delegations, serving on the state of Chiapas's electoral commission in 1994, and speaking on platforms alongside opposition figures like Rosario Ibarra de Piedra, Cuauhtémoc Cárdenas, and Superbarrio. Although still acting, she often staged plays and other performances as benefits for the organizations with which she was involved rather than pursuing high-profile film roles. When Medina and María Rojo organized a *danzón* benefit for Chiapan children in Mexico City in October 1994, they capitalized on the success of Novaro's film and on their recognizability as actresses to conduct an event that was simultaneously a means to an end (raising funds) and a performative act of resistance.

Such acts are not the exclusive province of women in the film world, however. One significant example of an *otro cine* was EZLN Comandante Ramona's video, which circulated in February 1995, at a time when the Zapatistas were under threat of arrest and their usual spokesperson, Subcomandante Marcos, had retreated into silence. The exact date and location of production were unknown; yet the tape reached the national and international press, which reported its message worldwide the day after its distribution in Mexico City on 19 February.

The video consists of a single medium shot in which Ramona is shown seated at a table with a newspaper in front of her and a white banner reading "EZLN" in the background (Fig. 8.1). She is a small woman whose face is almost completely covered by her black knit ski mask, which contrasts with her bare arms and red and white embroidered blouse. No one else appears, although noises in the background indicate the presence of the anonymous

videographer. Looking at the camera, Ramona announces her location as "un lugar en la Selva Lacandona" [someplace in the Lacandon jungle] and proceeds to address the people of Mexico, whom she specifies by group: women, youth, and men, and finally "all the inhabitants of our country."

Implicitly responding to government accusations that the Zapatista movement was led by nonindigenous outsiders, she describes the life of indigenous women in Chiapas. She explains that there is little to eat, that they regularly go hungry, and that they are often ill. She herself, she says, is very ill and "may die soon." (Instead, she would again make history in October 1996 by defying government prohibitions and appearing in Mexico City, where she would attend the first National Indigenous Congress and afterward receive a successful kidney transplant.) Women and men, she says, are exploited as workers in the marketplaces where they sell their crafts, in the cities where they go to work as domestic laborers, and in the fields. As she speaks, her soft voice goes up and down, its rhythm emphasized by the constant movement of her small clenched fists. Proclaiming the Zapatistas' desire for peace, she asks that the federal troops go back to their barracks, that the refugees be allowed to return and rebuild their communities, and that Bishop Samuel Ruiz (whose commitment to the practice of liberation theology in Chiapas had attracted death threats) be protected. Concluding her three-minute-long message, Ramona expresses her hope that women would become conscious of the need to organize in order to build the "free and just Mexico of which we all dream."

Born of urgency, the formal simplicity of the short video adds to its power. While probably not intentionally symbolic, the white sheet used as a backdrop seems to stand in for the movie screen, a space in which indigenous Mexicans had long been invisible. Its surface now marked with the letters of revolution, this space is forcibly occupied in the video by a woman whose quiet strength and dignity shatters all "India María" stereotypes. *Comunicado del Ejército Zapatista de Liberación Nacional en voz de la Comandante Ramona* hardly implies a new movement in feminist filmmaking, but the implications of Comandante Ramona's and other guerrilla and activist women's interventions in the realm of political imagery and spectacle are profound. Just as feature film directors have sought to create and project images of women previously unknown to and excluded from the Mexican screen, so too have women like Comandante Ramona, Comandante Trinidad at the San Andrés negotiations in May 1995, and EZLN delegate Dalia in Spain in July 1997 deliberately performed female indigenous identity for a national and international audience. Entering into arenas long denied to indigenous women, they have played on racist and sexist expectations of themselves as submissive and inarticulate in order to gain the moral high ground.

Trinidad, for example, addressing government negotiators in her native Tojolobal, "apologized" for not speaking Spanish or knowing how to read or write, while at the same time articulating a forceful claim for recognition and justice in the name of "todas las mujeres mexicanas, indígenas, y de Chiapas" [all Mexican, indigenous, and Chiapan women] (Zuñiga and Bellinghausen). Challenging the nation to see and hear them for the first time, these Zapatista women have used not only their words but their physical presence, their bodies, to call attention to a long history of marginalization which they say must now come to an end. Instead of complying with conventions of public discourse which have long functioned to exclude them, they have staged performative acts that, much like the best work by feminist filmmakers, seek to construct new spaces for women within the nation and to insist: "never again a Mexico without us."[11]

A Different Kind of Country

By going beyond the traditional understanding of national cinema and looking at feminist cultural interventions such as those of Ofelia Medina and Comandante Ramona, we may be able to construct a model of feminist film as part of civil society, as a popular medium that can and has avoided the traps with which intellectual discourse has so often been captured and co-opted. While the traditional film sector is again in crisis, alternative media have emerged in direct response to the governmental and corporate control of communication. These media are diverse and heterogeneous and include such phenomena as the feminist performance artists associated with the El Hábito cabaret founded by Jesusa Rodríguez, the Mayan women involved with the Chiapas Photography Project documenting the daily lives of their families and communities,[12] and video teams such as Canal 6 de Julio, made up of women and men, that market their footage of protests and current events in the plazas and bookstores of Mexico City and other regional capitals.

The founding of Telemanita in 1991 was an especially important step forward for feminist media production in Mexico. A nonprofit center providing equipment access and training in video and multimedia production to women at low or no cost, Telemanita has enabled women of many different backgrounds to represent themselves, their organizations, and their experiences on videotape. The active involvement of Telemanita staff with each production, along with the center's strong commitment to empowerment and demystification of media technology, has resulted in videos of extraordinary quality as well as diversity: productions range from Susana Quiroz and Inés Morales's urban documentaries, *Gritos poéticos de la urbe* (1995) and *Angeles de la ciudad obscura* (1997), to the Organización de Mujeres Madre Tierra's *Hoy las mujeres mayas* (1997) about a Guatemalan refugee community in Mexico, to a series of programs documenting Mexico City's lesbian community, filmed by Alejandra Novoa for the organization Enlace Lésbico and distributed under the title *teta-teta t.v.* Moreover, clearly aware of the problems posed by distribution and exhibition, Telemanita has worked to promote feminist media nationally and abroad, organizing festivals and developing links to organizations worldwide, thus making it possible for information and images produced by women with few economic resources to reach national and international audiences.

On a different level, the links between film and political participation have been concretized in the off-screen activities and in the very bodies of figures like Irma Serrano (senator from Chiapas in the 1990s), María Rojo (who became a congresswoman in 1997), Ofelia Medina, Ana Colchero, and even Gloria Trevi, the mainstream pop star contracted to Televisa who told *fem* magazine that "when I am president of Mexico," one of her first acts would be to legalize abortion (Hernández Carballido, "Gloria Trevi" 14). If Trevi's candidacy is unlikely in the near future,[13] and if Serrano's performance on the senate floor has been more colorful than politically transformative, each of these women has nevertheless contributed—through conventional activism but also and inseparably through imagery and performance—to the creation of a feminist public sphere, within which substantive change can be at last imagined.

For these and all women—and men—who have dared to imagine a country better than the one in which they now live, the present moment poses enormous obstacles, even as it offers enormous opportunities for change. In an interview in *Américas* magazine, novelist Angeles Mastretta commented that the years in which she was writing *Mal de amores,* 1994 and 1995, reminded her very much of the years right before the Revolution, especially in terms of people's ability "to dream about a different kind of country and their willingness to take up arms in order to bring about something different" (Mujica 39). In fact, even as globalization and consequent increased economic stratification pushed some Mexicans to the point of armed rebellion and threatened the cultural and material survival of many others, the nebulous outline of "a different kind of country" began to appear on the movie and television screens of the 1990s, above all in the work of women writers and directors. As old certainties collapsed and the construct called Mexico faced myriad epistemological and material challenges, women filmmakers offered critical reflections on the nation's past and present and imaginative visions of its potential future. It is in this sense that Sistach, Cortés, Novaro, Schyfter, Rotberg, and others could be said to share the project articulated by Comandante Ramona in the citation that opened this chapter: that of both "waking up" and "dreaming," that is, of awakening spectator-citizens into new awareness in order to dream a new nation into being.

The images these directors produced served as a powerful intervention into public discourse, especially on the terrain of gender politics; for regardless of how well they were received, their films forced critics and the moviegoing public to consider, from a perspective understood to be "female" if not "feminist," such issues as single motherhood, divorce, incest, abortion, female sexuality, women's paid and unpaid labor, and many other themes previously foreign to the national screen. The women's cinema that Landeta envisioned decades earlier, that of the *mujer pensante,* a cinema aimed at creating an *otro mundo,* came to be aligned in the 1990s with a larger project of democratic transformation.

For this reason, we may conclude by reframing the problematic described by Isabel Arredondo in her study of women directors and the film schools:

> A menudo, entrar en el cine comercial también significa formar parte de la normativa del país, lo que obviamente impone ciertos límites en el tema de las películas. En el caso de las directoras la producción de películas cuyo tema sea mujeres construidas como sujetos tiene que entenderse, a menudo, como un ataque a la normativa.
>
> [Often, to enter the commercial cinema also means forming part of the country's normative structure, which obviously imposes certain limits on the theme of the films. In the case of the women directors, the production of films whose theme is women construed as subjects has to be understood, often, as an attack on the norm.] (20)

For in fact, the attack on the country's norms has not been the work of filmmakers alone, as Arredondo indeed recognizes; rather, their protests of present conditions, vindications of women's experiences, in contrast to imposed standards and expectations, and visions of feminist alternatives transcend the boundaries of the film industry—commercial or otherwise—to become part of the collective "dreaming" that is transforming the Mexican nation. The outcome, however, remains to be determined; for the terrain of this new country, the Mexico described by Fuentes as "not a paradise, but simply a community," is still being charted, and its history has only begun to be written.

Annotated Filmography

This appendix is intended as a resource for readers seeking further information about women filmmakers in Mexico. The first section, "Highlighted Filmmakers," provides biographical data and filmographies for the directors whose works are discussed in chapters 1 through 7: Dolores and Adriana Ehlers, Adela Sequeyro, Matilde Landeta, Marcela Fernández Violante, Marisa Sistach, Busi Cortés, Guita Schyfter, María Novaro, and Dana Rotberg. The second section, "Additional Filmmakers," lists other directors from four time periods: 1900–1960, 1961–1980, 1981–1990, and the 1990s. Students appear under the heading for their schools, and the members of the Cine-Mujer collective also appear under a separate heading; otherwise, listings are alphabetical.

The following abbreviations are used:

Type of film: S = short film, M = medium length, F = feature (35mm unless otherwise indicated), D = documentary, Fic. = fiction, V = video, A = animation. D/Fic. indicates a film combining documentary and dramatized footage.

Schools: CUEC is the Centro Universitario de Estudios Cinematográficos, established in 1963 at the Universidad Nacional Autónoma de México, while the Filmoteca de la UNAM is the university's film archive. Other university departments are listed as UNAM; and STUNAM is the university workers union. CCC is the Centro de Capacitación Cinematográfica, established in 1975. CIEC refers to the Centro de Investigación de Estudios Cinematográficos, established in 1987 at the Universidad de Guadalajara, and UAM is the Universidad Autónoma Metropolitana. Student films are 16mm and fiction unless otherwise indicated.

Government institutions: IMCINE is the Instituto Mexicano de Cinematografía, established in 1983, and FFCC is the Fondo de Fomento a la Calidad Cinematográfica, established in 1988. UTEC is the Unidad de Televisión Educativa y Cultural belonging to the Secretaría de Educación Pública. CONACULTA is the Consejo Nacional para la Cultura y las Artes. INI is the Instituto Nacional Indigenista.

Highlighted Filmmakers

1. EHLERS, DOLORES AND ADRIANA (Chapter 1). Silent-era photographers and filmmakers. Under the sponsorship of President Venustiano Carranza, they studied in the United States, then returned to Mexico in 1919 and worked in all aspects of film production, including governmental regulation. Later they worked in their own shop as well as making newsreels. Films: *La industria del petróleo* (c.1921); *Documental sobre las pirámides de Teotihuacan y las piezas arqueológicas del Museo de la calle de Moneda* (c.1921); *Real España vs. Real Madrid* (c.1921); *Revistas Ehlers* (newsreels 1922–1929).

2. SEQUEYRO, ADELA "PERLITA" (Chapter 1). Born in Veracruz in 1901. Journalist, poet, actress in theater and silent film. In 1935, Sequeyro and colleagues formed the film production cooperative Exito. In 1935, she wrote and starred in *Más allá de la muerte*. In 1937, she founded her own company, Carola, and wrote, adapted, directed, and starred in *La mujer de nadie*. In 1938, she directed and wrote *Diablillos del arrabal*, an attempt at a more mainstream style and theme; faced with financial problems, she was unable to make another film, and retired from the cinema in 1943. Sequeyro died in 1992.

3. LANDETA, MATILDE (Chapter 1). Born in Mexico City in 1913; grew up in San Luis Potosí, then came back to live in the capital. Studied in the United States, where an early sound film, *Old San Francisco,* awakened her interest in cinema. In 1933, with the help of her brother, actor Eduardo Landeta, she went to work as a script clerk. In 1945, she became an assistant director, working with most of the major directors of the Golden Age; finally she applied to join the directors union and was accepted. She filmed Francisco Rojas González's novel *Lola Casanova* in 1948, and in 1949, adapted the same author's *La negra Angustias.* In 1951, she directed the urban melodrama *Trotacalles.* Her next script, *Tribunal de menores,* was purchased by the Banco Nacional Cinematográfico (the arbiter of funding for film production) but given to Alfonso Corona Blake to direct. Retitled *El camino de la vida,* its script won an Ariel, yet Landeta was effectively shut out of directing. She worked for a U.S. company making Howdy Doody shorts and co-wrote *Siempre estaré contigo* (Julián Soler, 1958) with Janet Alcoriza, as well as several scripts that were never filmed. In the 1970s, she was rediscovered by feminists, and her films began to be screened again. She wrote the adaptation for Carmen Toscano's *Ronda revolucionaria* in 1977; worked with Luis Spota's widow Elda Peralta on *El rescate,* a 1983 documentary compilation of footage shot by Spota; and in 1991, returned to directing with *Nocturno a Rosario,* a period melodrama. Landeta remained active in the Mexico City film community until her death in January 1999.

Landeta's Films

Lola Casanova. Técnicos y Artistas Cinematográficos Mexicanos Asociados (TACMA), 1948. Screenplay Landeta and Enrique Cancino from the novel by Francisco Rojas González. Cinematography Ezequiel Carrasco. Editor Gloria Schoemann. Performed by Meche Barba, Isabela Corona, Enrique Cancino, Armando Silvestre, José Baviera, Carlos Martínez Baena, Ernesto Vilches, Guillermo Calles, Ramón Gay, Jaime Jiménez Pons, César del Campo, Rogelio Fernández, Agustín Fernández, Salvador Godínez, and the Ballet Nacional.

La negra Angustias. TACMA/Eduardo Landeta, 1949. Screenplay Landeta from the novel by Francisco Rojas González. Cinematography Jack Draper. Editor Gloria Schoemann. Performed by María Elena Marqués, Agustín Isunza, Eduardo Arozamena, Gilberto González, Enriqueta Reza, Fanny Schiller, Ramón Gay, Carlos Riquelme, Elda Peralta, Rogelio Fernández, Agustín Fernández, Salvador Godínez, and the voices of the Trío Los Panchos.

Trotacalles. TACMA/Eduardo Landeta, 1951. Screenplay Luis Spota, adapted by Landeta and José Aguila. Cinematography Rosalío Solano. Editor Alfredo Rosas Priego. Performed by Miroslava, Elda Peralta, Ernesto Alonso, Isabela Corona, Miguel Angel Ferriz, Aurora Izquierdo, Enedina Díaz de León, Juan Orraca, Rogelio Fernández, Salvador Godínez, and Wolf Rubinskis.

Nocturno a Rosario. CONACULTA/IMCINE/FFCC/Cooperativa José Revueltas, 1991. Screenplay Landeta, adapted by Landeta and Tomás Bernardo de León. Cinematography Henner Hofmann. Editor Carlos Savage. Music Amparo Rubin. Performed by Ofelia Medina, Patricia Reyes Spíndola, Evangelina Sosa, Simón Guevara, Horacio Vera, Uriel Chávez, Manuel Ojeda, Ernesto Gómez Cruz, Mario Iván Martínez, José Luis Avendaño, Sergio Sánchez, Eloisa Capilla, and Tomás Pérez Turrent.

4. FERNÁNDEZ VIOLANTE, MARCELA (Chapter 2). Born 1941 in Mexico City. Entered CUEC in 1964, where she made her first films. She was accepted into the directors union in 1975, worked at CUEC from 1978 to 1982, and became its director in 1985.

Fernández Violante's Short and Student Films

Azul (1966, S); *Gayosso da descuentos* (1968—unfinished); *Frida Kahlo* (UNAM 1971, S, 35mm, D).

Fernández Violante's Feature Films

De todos modos Juan te llamas. Dirección de Actividades Cinematográficas-UNAM, 1975. Screenplay Fernández Violante, Mitl Valdez and Adrián Palomeque. Cinematography Arturo de la Rosa. Performed by Jorge Russek, Juan Ferrara, Rocío Brambila, Patricia Aspíllaga, José Martí, Pilar Souza, and Salvador Sánchez.

Cananea. CONACINE/Churubusco, 1977. Screenplay Fernández Violante. Cinematography Gabriel Figueroa. Editor Raúl Portillo. Performed by Steve Wilensky, Carlos Bracho, José Carlos Ruiz, Víctor Junco, Yolanda Ciani, and Milton Rodríguez.

Misterio. CONACINE, 1979. Screenplay Fernández Violante based on the novel *Estudio Q* by Vicente Leñero, adapted in collaboration with Leñero. Cinematography Daniel López. Editor Jorge Bustos. Performed by Jorge Dizan, Jorge Fegán, Juan Ferrara, Víctor Junco, Ramón Menéndez, Helena Rojo, and Beatriz Sheridan.

El niño raramuri or *En el país de los pies ligeros.* CONACITE II, 1980. Screenplay Antonio Noyola, adapted by Fernández Violante and Noyola. Cinematography Lorenzo Contreras. Editor Max Sánchez. Music Leonardo Velázquez. Performed by Pedro Armendáriz Jr., Helena Rojo, Ernesto Gómez Cruz, Aurora Clavel, Francisco Mauri, Arturo Adonay, Jesús Bernave Quinteros, and Ramón Menéndez.

Nocturno amor que te vas. UNAM, 1986 (released 1992). Screenplay Jorge Pérez Grovas, adapted by Pérez Grovas and Fernández Violante. Cinematography Arturo de la Rosa. Editor Ramón Aupart. Music Leonardo Velázquez. Performed by Patricia Reyes Spíndola, Sergio Ramos, Leonor Llausas, Uriel Chávez, Dunia Saldivar, Eduardo Ocana, Alberto Rodríguez, Ernesto Yáñez, Leonardo Trebole, Carlos Saaib, Jorge Fegán, Evangelina Martínez, and Alejandro Flores.

Golpe de suerte. Riat Asesores/FFCC, 1991. Screenplay Fernández Violante and Luis Eduardo Reyes from the play *De interés social* by Reyes. Cinematography Alex Phillips Jr. Editor Saúl Aupart. Performed by Lucha Villa, Sergio Ramos, Miguel Manzano, Bruno Bichir, Odiseo Bichir, Margarita Isabel, Patricia Reyes Spíndola, Martha Padilla, Carlos Bracho, Tiaré Scanda, Jorge Fegán, and Martha Aura. Distributed by Cine del Mundo.

5. SISTACH, MARISA (MARYSA) (Chapter 3). Born in Mexico City in 1952. Studied anthropology in Paris and communications at the Universidad Iberoamericana. In 1975, entered the CCC, where she often collaborated on projects with fellow student José Buil, a partnership that continues to this day. Later worked for UTEC, serving as assistant director on Jorge Fons's series *Diego Rivera, vida y obra* in 1984 and writing and directing episodes of the series *De la vida de las mujeres* and *Los libros tienen la palabra.* Sistach also directed documentary films on the environment for Imevisión (Fernández Escareño 171).

Sistach's Short and Medium-length Films

Habitación 19 (CCC 1979); *¿Y si platicamos de agosto?* (CCC 1980); *Conozco a las tres* (1983, cinematography Maripí Sáenz, sound Penélope Simpson, editor Sonia Fritz).

Sistach's Feature Films

Los pasos de Ana. Canario Rojo/Feeling/Tragaluz, 1988. Converted to 35mm with funding from IMCINE in 1991; 16mm/video. Screenplay Sistach and José Buil. Cinematography Emmanuel Tacamba. Editor Buil. Performed by Guadalupe Sánchez, Emilio Echeverría, Clementina Otero, David Beuchot, Roberto Cobo, Valdiri Durand Sistach, Pía Buil Sistach, Andrés Fonseca, Enrique Herranz, José Roberto Hill, Carlos García, and Sergio Torres Cuesta. Distributed by IMCINE.

Anoche soñé contigo. Clasa Films Mundiales/Tragaluz/Francisco and Pablo Barbachano, 1991. Screenplay José Buil, based on the story "La venganza creadora" by Alfonso Reyes. Cinematography Alex Phillips Jr. Editor Sigfrido García. Performed by Leticia Perdigón, Socorro Bonilla, Moisés Iván Mora, Patricia Aguirre, Martín Altomaro, and José Alonso. Distributed by Clasa Films.

La línea paterna. Tragaluz/Cineteca Nacional/FONCA/IMCINE/MacArthur and Rockefeller Foundations, 1995. Codirected by José Buil. Based on archival footage shot by Buil's grandfather, José Buil Belenguer. Cinematography Buil and Servando Gajá. Editor Buil. Distributed by IMCINE.

El cometa. IMCINE/FFCC/Fondo Sud/Resonancia/Tragaluz/Multivideo SL/Alhena Films/Tabasco Films/Estado de Tlaxcala, 1998. Codirected by José Buil. Screenplay Sistach, Buil and Consuelo Garrido. Cinematography Gabriel Beristáin. Editor Guillermo Maldonado. Sound Juan Carlos Prieto. Performed by Patrick Le Mauff, Carmen Maura, Diego Luna, Ana Claudia Talancón, Gabriel Retes, Manuel Ojeda, Arcelia Ramírez, Fernando Rubin, Juan Carlos Colombo, Alfredo Gurrola, José Antonio Cora, Rodolfo Arias, and Juan Claudio Retes. Distributed by IMCINE.

6. CORTÉS, BUSI (Luz Eugenia Cortés Rocha)(Chapter 4). Born 1950 in Mexico City; studied at the Universidad Iberoamericana and CCC (1979–1984). Worked in television as assistant director to Alfredo Joskiwicz and Felipe Cazals on *Historia de la educación* and director of six episodes of *De la vida de las mujeres* (UTEC 1984–1985) as well as "Déjalo ser," the episode covering 1970–1974 in the series *18 lustros de la vida en México en este siglo* (Filmoteca de la UNAM 1993).

Cortés's Short and Medium-length Films

Las Buenromero (CCC 1979); *Un frágil retorno* (CCC 1980, based on a story by Kate Chopin); *Hotel Villa Goerne* (CCC 1982); *El lugar del corazón* (CCC/Universidad Iberoamericana 1984, based on a story by Juan Tovar).

Cortés's Feature Films

El Secreto de Romelia. CCC/IMCINE/FFCC/Consejo de Radio y Television del Estado de Tlaxcala/CONACITE II/Universidad de Guadalajara/Eduardo Maldonado and

Gustavo Montiel Pagés, 1988. Screenplay Cortés from "El viudo Román" by Rosario Castellanos. Cinematography Francisco Bojórquez. Performed by Dolores Beristáin, Pedro Armendáriz Jr., Diana Bracho, Josefina Echánove, Arcelia Ramírez, and Alejandro Parodi. Distributed by IMCINE.

Serpientes y escaleras. IMCINE/FFCC/Producciones Romelia/Universidad Iberoamericana, 1991. Screenplay Cortés, Carmen Cortés and Alicia Molina. Cinematography Francisco Bojórquez. Performed by Lumi Cavazos, Arcelia Ramírez, Héctor Bonilla, Diana Bracho, Bruno Bichir, Ernesto Rivas, Josefina Echánove, Pilar Medina, and Luis de Tavira. Distributed by IMCINE.

7. SCHYFTER, GUITA (Chapter 5). Born 1947 in Costa Rica. Completed her bachelor's degree at UNAM in psychology and her master's degree in social psychology before studying audiovisual production and working with the BBC in London in 1975. From 1978 on, Schyfter directed television and video for governmental agencies in Mexico, including weekly programs on health and arts education, twenty historical videos for the Archivo General de la Nación, and documentaries on Rufino Tamayo, Vicente Rojo, Luis Cardoza y Aragón, the fighter Cavernario Galindo, and Héctor Mendoza for UTEC's *Los Nuestros* series during 1983–1984. Schyfter has produced theater and worked in various administrative and academic positions at UNAM and SEP since 1973.

Schyfter's Documentaries

Decentralización, desarrollo regional y Lago Texcoco (Archivo General de la Nación 1985); *Los caminos de Greene* (Secretaría de Agricultura/Estado de Tabasco 1986, docudrama on Graham Greene in Mexico, screenplay Hugo Hiriart, performed by Alejandro Parodi, María Rojo, John Edmonds); *Xochimilco: Historia de un paisaje* (1990); *La fiesta y la sombra (retrato de David Silveti)* (1991, about bullfighter Silveti); *Tamayo a los 91 años* (1991).

Schyfter's Feature Films

Novia que te vea. IMCINE/Producciones Arte Nuevo/FFCC, 1992. Screenplay Schyfter, Rosa Nissán and Hugo Hiriart, based on the novel by Rosa Nissán. Collaboration on screenplay Raquel Lubezki, David Grinberg, Judith Boxer. Cinematography Toni Kuhn. Editor Carlos Bolado. Performed by Claudette Maille, Maya Mishalska, Angélica Aragón, Ernesto Laguardia, Mercedes Pascual, Veronica Langer, Miguel Couturier, Nathan Grinberg, Leslie Hoffman, María Safati, and Daniel Gruener. Distributed by IMCINE.

Sucesos distantes. IMCINE/Cooperativa Conexión/Universidad de Guadalajara/Arte Nuevo, 1994. Screenplay Hugo Hiriart, Guita Schyfter and Alejandro Lubezki from a text by Hiriart. Cinematography Carlos Marcovich. Editor Sigfrido Barjau. Sound Salvador de la Fuente. Music Eduardo Gamboa. Performed by Angélica Aragón, Emilio Echeverría, Fernando Balzaretti, Mario Iván Martínez, Claudette Maille, Martha Verduzco, Jesús Ochoa, Lucila Balzaretti, Jorge Zárate, Abraham Stavans, and María Pankova. Distributed by IMCINE.

8. NOVARO, MARÍA (Chapter 6). Born 1951 in Mexico City. Studied sociology at UNAM before entering CUEC in 1980, where she was part of the editing team "las Ninfas" with Marie-Christine Camus and Silvia Otero and a member of the Cine-Mujer collective. Novaro was the fourth woman admitted to the directors union, after Landeta, Fernández Violante and María Elena Velasco.

Novaro's Short Films

Lavaderos (1981, super8); *Sobre las olas* (1981, super8); *De encaje y azúcar* (1981, super8); *Conmigo la pasarás muy bien* (CUEC 1982, codirected by Marie-Christine Camus); *7 AM* (CUEC 1982); *Querida Carmen* (CUEC 1983); *Una isla rodeada de agua* (1985); *Pervertida* (1985—Novaro's thesis film at CUEC, not completed due to conflicts with the administration); *Azul celeste* (UNAM 1987, episode of collective film *Historias de ciudad*); *Otoñal* (1992).

Novaro's Feature Films

Lola. Macondo Cine-Video/Cooperativa José Revueltas/CONACITE II/Televisión Española, 1989. Screenplay Beatriz Novaro and María Novaro. Cinematography Rodrigo García. Editor Sigfrido Barjau. Sound Carlos Aguilar. Music Gabriel Romo. Performed by Leticia Huijara, Alejandra Vargas, Martha Navarro, Roberto Sosa, Mauricio Rivera, Javier Zaragoza, Cheli Godínez, and Gerardo Martínez.

Danzón. IMCINE/Macondo Cine-Video/FFCC/Televisión Española/Tabasco Films/Estado de Veracruz, 1991. Screenplay Beatriz Novaro and María Novaro. Cinematography Rodrigo García. Editors Nelson Rodríguez and Novaro. Performed by María Rojo, Carmen Salinas, Blanca Guerra, Tito Vasconcelos, Victor Carpinteiro, Margarita Isabel, Cheli Godínez, and Daniel Regis. Distributed by IMCINE.

El jardín del Edén. Macondo Cine-Video/IMCINE/Verseau International/Universidad de Guadalajara/FFCC, 1993. Screenplay Beatriz Novaro and María Novaro. Cinematography Eric A. Edwards. Editor Sigfrido Barjau. Performed by Renee Coleman, Bruno Bichir, Gabriela Roel, Rosario Sagrav, Alan Ciangherotti, Ana Ofelia Murguía, and Joseph Culp. Distributed by IMCINE.

9. ROTBERG, DANA (Chapter 7). Born 1960 in Mexico City. Worked at the Filmoteca de la UNAM in 1980 and at the Cineteca Nacional from 1980 to 1984. Entered the CCC in 1982, leaving before graduation to work as an assistant director with Felipe

Cazals. Rotberg moved to Europe in 1994, where she worked with filmmakers in Sarajevo and produced Ademir Kenovic's *The Perfect Circle* in 1996.

Rotberg's Short Films

Teresa, ¿Bailamos?, Juego de pelota, and *El vomitado* (all CCC 1982–1984); *Elvira Luz Cruz: Pena máxima* (CCC 1985, M, D exploring well-known murder case, codirected by Ana Diez Díaz).

Rotberg's Feature Films

Intimidad. Producciones Metrópolis/Léon Constantiner, 1989. Screenplay Leonardo García Tsao, based on a play by Hugo Hiriart. Cinematography Carlos Marcovich. Editor Oscar Figueroa. Performed by Emilio Echeverría, Angeles González, Lisa Owen, Alvaro Guerrero, Juan José Nebrada, and Ana Ofelia Murguía.

Angel de fuego. IMCINE/FFCC/Metrópolis/Otra Productora Más, 1991. Screenplay Omar A. Rodrigo and Rotberg. Cinematography Toni Kuhn. Editor Sigfrido Barjau. Music Ariel Guzik. Performed by Evangelina Sosa, Lilia Aragón, Roberto Sosa, Noé Montealegre, Mercedes Pascual, Alejandro Parodi, Salvador Sánchez, Farnesio de Bernal, Marta Aura, and Gina Moret. Distributed by IMCINE.

Additional Filmmakers

1900 – 1960

During the first half of the century, Mexican cinema developed as an ideological apparatus of patriarchal nationalism, and films directed by women were rare; the few women to make films demonstrated great ambition and determination that, however, did not ensure their success in a field that was overwhelmingly male-dominated.

1. BELTRÁN, CANDIDA. Born in 1899 in Mérida, Yucatán. Moved to the capital and worked in social services; wrote, produced, directed, and acted in the feature *El secreto de la abuela* in 1928, based in part on her own experience as an orphan. Also wrote popular songs.

2. DERBA, MIMI (MARÍA HERMINIA PÉREZ DE LEÓN). Theater actress; cofounded Azteca Films, which produced five features during 1917. Of these, Derba wrote the script for *En defensa propia* and *En la sombra,* acted in these and *Alma de sacrificio* and *La soñadora,* and unofficially directed *La tigresa.* Her sixth film, *Chapultepec,* was never finished, and after an unsuccessful attempt to market Azteca's films abroad, she dissolved the company and retired from production. She continued to act and appeared in *Santa,* one of Mexico's first sound films, in 1931.

3. LIMIÑANA, EVA "LA DUQUESA OLGA." Pianist, of Chilean origin. During the 1930s, she wrote and/or produced twelve films, all directed by her husband, José Bohr (also Chilean): *La sangre manda* (1933), *Quién mató a Eva?* (1934), *Tu hijo/Amor de madre* (1934), *Sueños de amor* (1935), *Luponini de Chicago* (1935), *Marihuana, el monstruo verde* (1936), *Así es la mujer* (1936), *Luz en mi camino* (1938), *Por mis pistolas* (1938), *El latigo* (1938), *Herencia macabra/La traicionera* (1939), and *Borrasca humana* (1939). When Bohr left Mexico in 1940, Limiñana stayed and codirected *Mi Lupe y mi caballo* with Carlos Toussaint in 1942. The film was suspended during production due to lack of resources and *enlatada* (shelved) for two years after completion; Limiñana then retired from the cinema.

4. RAHON, ALICE. French expatriate, poet and painter. Made an experimental puppet film, *The Magician,* around 1947, in collaboration with her husband Edward FitzGerald, a set designer for Luis Buñuel. The film ran into funding problems and was never released, but is noteworthy for its experimental techniques and its subject matter: the sole survivor of a nuclear war, a magician who lives on the bottom of the sea, is charged with recreating the human race (Deffebach 181–183).

5. TOSCANO, CARMEN. Born in 1910, the daughter of silent-era filmmaker Salvador Toscano. Began her career as a writer, first in poetry and literary criticism and later for television. In 1950, she edited her father's footage of the Revolution and life in the early years of the century into a full-length documentary, *Memorias de un mexicano.* In 1977, she wrote and directed *Ronda revolucionaria* using historical footage and fictional reconstructions, with an adaptation by Matilde Landeta. Although the film was produced by the government (CONACINE), it was never released.

1961–1980

During the 1960s and 1970s, the newly established film schools became the crucial factor in enabling the emergence of women directors, including the feminist collective Cine-Mujer; documentary films flourished, bearing witness to the era's social upheavals and cultural transformations; and an intellectual film sector reflecting the political and the aesthetic values of a growing middle class was constituted outside the boundaries of the commercial industry.

Centro Universitario de Estudios Cinematográficos at UNAM

Founded in 1963, CUEC became the training ground for a large number of women working in all areas of film production. In the late 1960s, it became involved with the student movement and helped to document the social struggles of the era. Esther Morales Gávez was the first woman admitted to the school, in its founding year; in 1964, she directed one of its first productions, the short film *Pulquería "La Rosita."* Morales went on to direct a short documentary for UNAM's biology department (*El jardín botánico*, 1967) and to teach at the Universidad Iberoamericana. In 1964, Marcela Fernández Violante became the second female student at CUEC and the last to enter during the 1960s.

CUEC students and their films during the 1970s included:

1. ALBERS, KARIN. *El motor principal* (1981, S, D about support efforts of wives of striking workers); *Tigrito* (1982, S, D about *campesino* struggle in Zacatecas); *Juntos hacia la felicidad* (1983, S, D/Fic.); *Flor de corazón* (1984, S). German; later moved to Chile.

2. ALVAREZ, MARÍA ANTONIETA. *Ensayos* (1978, S, D); *El blues* (1981, M, D filmed at Mexico City blues festival). Later taught and worked for the newspaper *La Jornada*.

3. CAUDILLO, ROSA DELIA. *Tlayacapán en la mirada* (1979, S, D, codirected by Rafael Rebolloar, Marco Aurelio Sosa); *Un crucero* (1981, S, D, codirected by Irma Carrión); *Fratricidio* (1981, S). Subsequent work: *Otra manera de hablar* (STUNAM 1987, M, D about meeting of women university workers, codirected by María Eugenia Tamés). Producer, writer, and assistant director on independent films.

4. CONTRERAS, ADRIANA. *Un gesto social* (1976, S, super8); *Desayuno* (1976, S, super8); *La sagrada familia* (1976, S, super8); *Otro sobre navidad (imagen y sonido)* (1977, S, collective exercise); *Lecciones de poesía* (1978, S); *Naturaleza muerta* (1979, S); *Historias de vida* (1981, F). Contreras later moved to Uruguay, where in 1989 she directed the feature *La nube de Magallanes* as a Mexico-Uruguay coproduction.

5. CUENCA, BRENY. *No nos moverán* (1972, M, D about the history of the workers movement in Chile). Cuenca later returned to her native Chile.

6. GILHUYS, PATRICIA. *VII Juegos Panamericanos* (1976, S, D); *La improbable Susanita* (1980, M).

7. GUERRA, DOROTEA. *Acaso irreparable* (1976, S, super8); *Desesperanza* (1976, S, super8); *El niño y el tren* (1976, S, super8); *Dos más uno son cuatro* (1979, S); *Ratón* (1980, S); *Hacer un guión* (1981, M). Guerra subsequently directed episodes of the television program *De la vida de las mujeres* (UTEC 1984–1985) and the short film *La muchacha* (Didecine/IMCINE 1991, based on texts by Elena Poniatowska).

8. HERNÁNDEZ, ROSARIO. *El encuentro* (1976, S); *El desayuno* (1977, S); *La hermana enemiga* (1979, S, based on a text by José Revueltas).

9. ISLAS, ALEJANDRA. *La marcha* (1977, S, D, codirected by Alberto Cortés and Juan Mora); *La boquilla* (1978, S, D); *Iztacalco: Campamento 2 de Octubre* (1978, M, D, codirected by José Luis González Ramírez and Jorge Prior); *La indignidad y la intolerancia serán derrotadas* (1977–1980, M, D, codirected by Alberto Cortés). After graduating, Islas continued as a documentary filmmaker, directing *Cerca de lo lejos: Elías*

Nandino (Filmoteca de la UNAM 1983) and *Veracruz 1914* (UNAM/Estado de Veracruz 1987) and more than thirty programs for television and video between 1985 and 1996, including "Tina Modotti," "Paul Strand," "Edward Weston," "El caso Molinet," "Polvo en el viento" (an episode of the 1993 series *18 lustros de la vida en México en este siglo,* produced by the Filmoteca de la UNAM), and *Eisenstein en México: El círculo eterno,* a three-part series based on research by Eduardo de la Vega, produced by CONACULTA, IMCINE, Canal 22, and the Cooperativa Salvador Toscano in 1996.

10. LANGARICA, MARÍA TRINIDAD. *Nostalgia* (1970, S); *Despertar* (1973, S) (both shorts made prior to entering CUEC); *Chihuahua, un pueblo en lucha* (1974, M, D, directed by Langarica and three others for Taller de Cine Octubre); *Mujer, así es la vida* (UNAM/Taller de Cine Octubre 1980, codirected by Armando Lazo); *Te digo que no es un animal (brevísima historia de la Revolución Mexicana)* (Taller de Cine Octubre 1982, S). From 1976 to 1978, Langarica studied cinematography in Romania and later worked mainly as a cinematographer. She subsequently directed *Tetraedero* (1982, D) and *La química del oro negro* (1984, M, D about the oil industry, directed by Langarica and five others for Taller de Cine Octubre).

11. MOLTKE HOFF, LISKULLA. *Iscuracha* (1977, S, D about violin legends in Michoacán and Sweden); *El reto* (1978, S, D about the traditional play *El reto de Don Gonzalo* performed in Puebla).

12. MORA, MARTHA. *Otro sobre navidad (imagen y sonido)* (1977, S, collective exercise).

13. PIAZZA SUPRANI, MILVIA. *La mujer que llegaba a las seis* (1979, S); *Los horcones* (1980, S, D about repression of a *campesino* group in Honduras); *Carta a un niño* (1981, M). Piazza later returned to her native Venezuela.

14. SORIANO, HILDA. *El principio del placer* (1981, S). Studied at Cuba's ICAIC in 1978; later worked as a producer with Canario Rojo (1980–1982) and Canal 13.

15. VARGAS, MARIBEL. *Más te vale San Antonio* (1977, S); *La misma vieja historia* (1978, S). Originally from Guatemala, Vargas later moved to Honduras.

16. VELASCO CARABÉS, MARÍA ELENA. *Angela* (1976, S); *Desempleo* (1978, M, D). Later worked at UNAM.

Cine-Mujer

This leftist-feminist collective, founded by CUEC students in the late 1970s, can be considered the first instance of explicitly feminist filmmaking in Mexico. Active until the mid-1980s, its members included:

1. CAMUS, ELLEN. *Got to push* (1973, D about women garment workers in Boston, made at Harvard University in association with the International Ladies Garment Worker Union).

2. DE LARA, MARÍA DEL CARMEN "MARICARMEN." Although de Lara was not a member of Cine-Mujer until the mid-1980s, her early films share the collective's feminist vision. At CUEC, she directed *Amor, pinche amor...* (1980, S, codirected by Alfonso Morales, María Eugenia Tamés); *No es por gusto* (1981, M, D, codirected by María Eugenia Tamés); *Preludio* (1982, S, performed by Margarita Isabel); and *Desde el cristal con que se mira* (1984, S, co-written and assistant-directed by Angeles Necoechea, performed by María Rojo). After graduating, de Lara studied film in Moscow, then continued her filmmaking career in Mexico, directing programs for Canal 11, UNICEF, and Univisión in the 1980s. In 1986, she founded the Fundación Mexicana de Cineastas. De Lara directed some of the strongest feminist documentaries of the 1980s and 1990s: *No les pedimos un viaje a la luna* (1986, M, D about Mexico City garment workers in the wake of the 1985 earthquake); *Las que viven en Ciudad Bolero* (1992–1994, D series about women composers and singers of Mexican romantic music, codirected by Leopoldo Best); *Voces y VIHsiones* (1994–1996, three-part D on various aspects of AIDS and HIV in Mexico).

3. FERNÁNDEZ, CAROLINA. According to Moreno Ochoa, the Chilean CCC student Fernández's documentary about domestic workers, *La vida toda* (1978), was made as a project of Cine-Mujer.

4. FERNÁNDEZ, ROSA MARTA. Founder and leader of the collective. Films: *Cosas de mujeres* (CUEC 1978, M, D/Fic. about abortion, cinematography Arturo de la Rosa, Mario Luna, and Víctor Viala, performed by Patricia Luke, Angeles Necoechea, and Martín Lasalle); *Rompiendo el silencio* (CUEC 1979, M, D); *Nicaragua: Semilla de soles* (1984, D, made in Nicaragua); *Cuatro días después (documento no. 1)* (1985, D, TV); *El problema está en el aire* (1985, D, TV); *La casa dividida* (n.d., F, V). Fernández left the group to live in Nicaragua in the 1980s but after returning to Mexico, became the director of TV-UNAM in 1989.

5. FRITZ, SONIA. Director, producer, and editor. Films: *Yayaltecas* (1984, D about women in a Oaxacan community, distributed by Zafra); *Bandas, vidas, y otros sones* (Archivo Etnográfico Audiovisual-INI 1985, M, D). Later moved to Puerto Rico.

6. LIBERMAN, LILLIAN. *Espontánea belleza* (CUEC 1980, S); *Lugares comunes* (CUEC 1983, S); *Amanecer* (CUEC 1984, S). After graduation, worked as an assistant director and made public service videoclips for Canal 11.

7. MIRA, BEATRIZ. *Herbolaria y medicina* (1977, D, codirected by Scott Robinson, Gonzalo Infante, and Deborah Shaffer); *Vicios en la cocina* (CUEC 1978, S, D about women's work in the home, based in part on a poem by Sylvia Plath); *Es primera vez...* (1981, D, made by Mira, María Novaro, Sonia Fritz, Angeles Necoechea, and Guadalupe Sánchez). Mira later returned to her native Brazil.

8. NECOECHEA, ANGELES. Documentary film- and videomaker, later associated

with the independent film distributor Zafra. Films: *Vida de ángel* (1982, M, D about poor women and domestic labor); *Amas de casa* (1984, S, D involving poor Mexico City women in a role-play situation to prepare them to deal with a real-life eviction, V); *Memorias de ella* (1984, D, V); *8 de marzo* (1984, D, V); *Primer encuentro nacional de mujeres campesinas* (1985, D, V); *Bordando la frontera* (Zafra 1986, S, D about women workers in Ciudad Juárez). Martínez also cites a documentary titled *Villa Arenje* (102).

9. ROSSETI, LAURA. *Circunstancias* (CUEC 1983, S); *Vamos al cine . . . te lo disparo* (CUEC 1983, S, D about Mexican cinema); *Don Tato y sus milagros* (CUEC 1985, S); *Si no puedes vivir rockanrolea* (CUEC 1986, S). Later worked as a journalist and industrial film producer and with the Cooperativa José Revueltas.

10. SÁNCHEZ, GUADALUPE. Graphic designer and animator. *Mentirosa* (1979, S, A); *Y si eres mujer . . .* (1979, S, A). Later starred in Marisa Sistach's *Los pasos de Ana* and worked in graphic design, special effects, and animation with the company Animarte.

11. TAMÉS, MARÍA EUGENIA. CUEC student from 1979–1983; member Cine-Mujer in the mid-1980s. Tamés later worked in audiovisual production for government institutions including the Instituto Mexicano de Petróleo and the Banco Nacional de México. Films: *Amor, pinche amor . . .* (CUEC 1980, S, codirected by Alfonso Morales and Maricarmen de Lara); *No es por gusto* (CUEC 1981, D, codirected by Maricarmen de Lara); title unknown: documentary video about women in Chiapas (1982); *Quién es ella* (UAM 1983, D, V); *Mi vida no termina aquí* (CUEC 1983, D about cabaret performer Fuensanta Zertuche); *¿Y por qué no?* (CUEC 1984, S, Fic. about divorce); *Construcción del puerto petrolero Salina Cruz* (1985, D); *Otra manera de hablar* (STUNAM 1987, D about a meeting of women university workers, codirected by Rosa Delia Caudillo); *Testimonios de petróleo* (1988, S, D about the 1938 oil expropriation); *Sexo seguro* (CONASIDA 1991, D); *De chile, dulce y manteca* (CONASIDA 1991); *Una esperanza de vida* (TV-UNAM/CONASIDA/ Wellcome, 1996, S, D/Fic. about pregnant women infected with HIV).

12. Other Cine-Mujer members included: the French sound engineer Sibille Hayem, anthropologist Amalia Attolini, sociologist Pilar Calvo, Ana Victoria Jiménes, Mónica Mae, and María Novaro.

Centro de Capacitación Cinematográfica

Founded in 1975 by the federal government with the goal of renovating the national film industry, the school quickly became a bastion of independent filmmaking. The CCC's first women students were Magdalena Acosta (*Sólo un grito solo*, 1978), Olga Cáceres (*Goitia*, 1980, S, D; *Lejos de las fiestas*, 1982, S), Cine-Mujer member Carolina Fernández *(La vida toda)*, Gloria Ribé (*Monse*, 1978), and Maripí Sáenz (*A rezar*, 1979), along with Marisa Sistach and Busi Cortés. Of these graduates, Acosta went on to work in television in various creative, technical, and administrative positions; Cáceres later worked with Alejandro Pelayo on the series *Los que hicieron nuestro cine* (UTEC 1983) and directed episodes of the series *De la vida de las mujeres* (UTEC 1984–1985), while Ribé worked for IMCINE, founded her own video production company, and continued to direct, making *Tepito* (n.d., shown 1987), *Plegarias* (IMCINE 1991) about the cult of the Virgin of Guadalupe, and *El efecto tequila* (1995), an imaginative documentary about Mexican politics and culture produced by Cooperativa de Producción Alternativa (COPAL). Maripí Sáenz worked as cinematographer on many feminist films of the 1980s, including Sonia Fritz's *Yayaltecas,* Maricarmen de Lara's *Preludio* and *No les pedimos un viaje a la luna,* María Eugenia Tamés's *Mi vida no termina aquí,* and Marisa Sistach's *Conozco a las tres.*

Individual Directors

1. CÁRDENAS, NANCY. Member of the Nuevo Cine group and director of UNAM's *cine-club;* also playwright, theater director, producer, and actress. Directed *México de mis amores* (CONACINE/PECIME 1978), a feature-length documentary about the history and myths of Mexican cinema, with texts by Carlos Monsiváis.

2. CARRIÓN, OLIVIA. Documentary filmmaker. *Xantolo (fiesta de la muerte)* (1973, D, codirected by Scott Robinson, Epigimenio Ibarra); *Virikuta (la costumbre)* (1976, D, codirected by Scott Robinson, Carlos Sáenz).

3. NAVARRO, BERTA (BERTHA). Independent documentary filmmaker and producer. Founder and president of Producciones Iguana; chief of production at CONACITE 1 in 1976; cofounder with Gabriel García Márquez of the New Latin American Cinema Foundation; instructor in the Sundance Institute's program for Latin American directors (1986–1989). Producer of Paul Leduc's *Reed: México insurgente* (1971), Nicolás Echeverría's *Cabeza de Vaca* (1991), and Guillermo del Toro's *La invención del Cronos* (1993), among others. Films: *Crónica del olvido* (1979, M, D about Mexico City combining statistics, interviews, and texts by Juan Tovar); *Nicaragua: Los que harán la libertad* (1979, M, 16mm, D about a Sandinista family); *Victoria de un pueblo en armas* (1980, M, 16mm, D about the Nicaraguan revolution, codirected by Quincho Ibarra); *Los pescadores* (1981, M, 16mm, D about fishermen); *México: Historia de su población* (CONAPO 1987, S, 35mm, D/Fic. about Mexico City youth).

4. SUZÁN, MARGARITA. Documentary filmmaker. *La carta de deberes y derechos* (1976, D); *Nuestra democracia* (1976, D, codirected by Gonzalo Infante); *La social democracia* (1976, D); *3 mujeres 3* (1976, D); *Historia del cine mexicano* (1977, D); *El tiempo del desprecio* (1977, M, D); *Pirámide* (n.d., M, V); *Clausura de la conferencia de las mujeres científicas* (1987, D, V, made in Nicaragua); *Las mujeres en el MINT* (1987, D, V, made in Nicaragua).

5. Velasco, María Elena, "La India María." In the early 1970s, actress Velasco created the comic character "La India María" for television and has since starred in, produced, and sometimes directed films featuring this character. These include: *Pobre pero honrada* (1972, directed by Fernando Cortés), *La madrecita* (1973, directed by Fernando Cortés); *La presidenta municipal* (1974, directed by Cortés); *Sor Tequila* (1977, directed by Rogelio A. González); *El coyote emplumado* (1983, directed by Velasco); *Ni Chana ni Juana* (1984, directed by Velasco); *Ni de aquí ni de allá* (1988, directed by Velasco); *Se equivocó la cigüeña* (1993, directed by Velasco); *Las delicias de poder* (1997, directed by Iván Lipkies). She also has appeared on stage in her own productions, such as the post-election comedy revue *México canta y aguanta* (Teatro Blanquita, 1994).

6. Weiss, Pola. Pioneering video artist who presented the first thesis on video at UNAM in 1975. She later cofounded the Televisa program *Videocosmos* and made promotional spots for Carlos Salinas's presidential campaign in 1988. According to Vega, her total videography included more than 150 works ("Video Works by Women" 55). These include: *Videodanza a dos tiempos, La venusina renace y reforma, OM, Acto de amor, Flor cósmica, Mi corazón* (dates unknown); *Ciudad-mujer-ciudad* (1978); *Sol o águila* (1980); *Se extrapola se interpola Weiss* (1982); *Videorigen de Weiss* (1984); *Videoart of a Tragedy* (1986); *Mi cor-a-zón* (1986, about the 1985 earthquake); *Merlín* (1987). Weiss died in 1990 at age 42.

1981–1990

In the 1980s, the number of women film students increased, as did the number of graduates working professionally in film and television production. At the end of the decade, strong first features by Marisa Sistach, Busi Cortés, and María Novaro signaled both the recuperation of Mexico's "quality" film sector and the emergence of a "women's cinema."

Centro Universitario de Estudios Cinematográficos

The number of women studying at CUEC continued to increase in the 1980s. In 1985, Marcela Fernández Violante became the school's director. The decade's students and their films included:

1. Aguilar Fernández, Sandra Luz. *La intrusa* (1986, S); *Años más tarde* (1987, S); *Carmen Vampira* (1988, S); *La envidia* (1989, S). Later worked in print journalism and television.

2. Becerril, Rebeca. *La luz por una rendija* (1982, S, super8); *Amor del bueno* (1983, S); *Dime algo por última vez* (1986, S); *A destiempo* (1987, M). Later moved to Germany.

3. BUSTILLO MOYA, ALEJANDRA. *La mujer atorada* (1985, S); *Buky* (1986, S); *Final feliz* (1986, M); later directed *Ponchada* (IMCINE 1994, S) and worked as a producer for the BBC in Mexico.

4. CAMUS, MARIE-CHRISTINE (MARÍA CRISTINA). *J.M.* (1982, S); *Conmigo la pasarás muy bien* (1982, S, codirected by María Novaro); *Olvídalo, no tiene importancia* (1983, S); *Tercera llamada* (1985, S); *Feliz viaje* (1987, S). Camus was part of the editing team "las Ninfas" with María Novaro and Silvia Otero; she later worked in film, TV and video production.

5. CARRASCO QUEIJEIRO, ROSSANA. *El lugar del corazón* (1986, S); *Murallas* (1987, S); *Soliloquio* (1988, S); *No quiero decir nada* (1989, S). Before entering CUEC, directed several Super8 films: *Football, Quesadillera,* and *Rumbo a Ajusco* (all c.1982). Later worked for Televisa, UTEC, and TV-UNAM.

6. CARVAJAL JUÁREZ, TERESA. *Una vida por la libertad* (1988, S, D about documentary filmmaker Luis Frank and the Spanish Civil War). Later worked at UNAM in various departments.

7. CHAVARRÍA DECANINI, URANIA. *Hacia el fin de la noche* (1988, S, story involving the guerrilla of the 1970s); *Angeles de octubre* (1989, S, story reflecting on the 1968 Tlatelolco massacre); *Cantos de amor divino* (1991, S). Later worked as screenwriter for educational television.

8. COUTURIER BAÑUELOS, MARCELA. *Los buzos diamantistas* (1988, S); *De la cabeza al cielo* (1990, M). Later worked for state TV and in private video production.

9. DE ALBA DEL CASTILLO DE NEGRETE, TERESA. *Thanatos* (1985, S). Later produced and directed documentary films and videos for the company Comunicación Activa.

10. DÍAZ CORIA AGUILAR, SILVIA. *La otra cara de la luna* (1989, S); *Fuera de lugar* (1990, S). Later worked as screenwriter in film and television.

11. DOMÍNGUEZ, JOSEFINA. *Frontón* (1982, S, codirected by Rogelio Herrera, Ricardo Moreno Soto, Gerardo Lara); *Vampiro* (1982, S, codirected by Rogelio Herrera); *Reo, S. A.* (1985, S, D about a 1960s political prisoner). Formed the production company Videos Educativos y Culturales in 1989.

12. ESCAMILLA LUJÁN, KARINA AMELIA. *Revistas* (1989, S, D); *Domicilio conocido* (1990, S); *Amigas* (1991, S). Also produced videos for the private company B.E.P.S.A.

13. ESPINOZA CABRERA, GABRIELA. *Cosas de la vida* (1984, S, codirected by Laura Iñigo); *El cliente es primero* (1985, S); *Para muestra basta un botón* (1986, S, D about garment workers and the 1985 earthquake, codirected by Sergio Franco López). Later worked as sound technician for public television and as assistant director to Juan Mora Catlett on *Retorno a Aztlán* (1990).

14. GODÍNEZ PINTOR, ANGÉLICA. *Adriana* (1989, S).

15. GÓMEZ MORAGAS, MARÍA CRISTINA. *Intramuros* (1983, S based on a story by Julio Cortázar); *El huésped* (1985, S); *Poker de ases* (1986, S). Later returned to her native Argentina.

16. HOLGUÍN MAYORA, LUCÍA. *Papalote azul* (1989, S); *Portal de sotavento* (CUEC/IMCINE 1990, S, D about the port of Veracruz). Costume designer on Novaro's *Lola*.

17. IÑIGO DEHUD, LAURA. *Cosas de la vida* (1984, S, codirected by Gabriela Espinoza); *Gráfica* (1984, S, D about Mexican popular graphic art); *Animación #2* (1986, S, A); *Jorobita* (1986, S, A); *Un cuento de ciudad* (1987, S, A). Later did postgraduate work at the Film Institute of Moscow and founded the company Púrpura Comunicación Gráfica.

18. IRANZO, GISELA. *El aventón* (1982, S, codirected by Gregorio Rocha); *Episodios* (1982, S); *La espera* (1982, S); *Alta noche* (1983, S); *Laberintitis* (1985, S, D/Fic. about artist José María Iranzo); *El dedo en la llaga* (1985, S based on a text by Roland Barthes). Later returned to her native Puerto Rico.

19. LIGUORI, ANA LUISA. *Amores difíciles* (1983, S); *El conde se esconde* (1985, S); *Jesu S.A.* (1986, S, D about actress/theater director Jesusa Rodríguez, codirected by Eduardo Sepúlveda). Also on the editorial board of *Debate feminista*.

20. MÉNDEZ GARCÍA, ROSA MARÍA. *Barco de papel* (1982, S); *Película para niños* (1982, S); *Para qué se entrega* (1985, S); *Milagro* (1987, S). Worked for the CCC and later for UTEC and UAM.

21. MÉNDEZ SILVA, ALBA MORA. *Ejercicio colectivo no. 1 sin título* (1983, S, codirected by José Peguero, José Luis Pérez, Dolores Payas); *Avril... y después* (1984, S); *No me arrepiento* (1985, S, collective project); *Había una vez* (1985, S); *Tiempos de sombras* (1986, S). Originally from Bolivia, Méndez worked in Mexico making documentaries and promotional pieces for government institutions.

22. MINTER, SARAH. *541-69-96* (1982, S, codirected by Gregorio Rocha); *San Frenesí* (1983, S, codirected by Gregorio Rocha); later directed independent films and videos including *Nadie es inocente* (1986, M, V); *Mex-metro* (c.1989, S, V); *Dear Diary* (1992, S, A); *Video Road* (c.1994); and others.

23. MONTES DE OCA VEGA, ANA LUISA. *Pedro Gringoire* (1988, S); *La voluntad melancólica* (1989, S); *La bella y la bestia* (1990, M).

24. MORGAN, PATRICIA. *Nuevos horizontes* (1989, S, D about cancer); *Video congelado* (1990, S); *La cantante calva* (1991, S); *Abarrotes "La Chabela"* (c.1994).

25. OLVERA SAN MIGUEL, MARÍA GUADALUPE. *Claridad* (1990, S).

26. OTERO MÁRQUEZ, SILVIA. *Luego platicamos* (1982, S); *El curso habitual* (1983, S); *Game Over* (1985, S); *Eliza* (1986, S). Part of the editing team "las Ninfas" with

María Novaro and Marie-Christine Camus; later worked on the UTEC series *De la vida de las mujeres,* on Novaro's *Danzón,* and with the company Macondo Cine-Video.

27. PAYAS, DOLORES. *Ejercicio colectivo no. 1 sin título* (1983, S, codirected by José Peguero, José Luis Pérez, Alba Mora Méndez); *Levanta más la pierna* (1983, S); *Totus tuus* (1985, S, satire about the Pope in Mexico); *Salome, virgen y mártir* (1985, S). Catalan; later returned to Spain.

28. PECANINS, MARÍA LUISA. *La Maga* (1984, S); *Rumbótica* (1987, M). Later worked as an art director, including on Novaro's *Lola* and *Danzón* and on Francisco Athié's *Lolo* (1991).

29. PREVIDI ARÍAS, TERESA. *Voy por todas* (1986, S, codirected by Amparo Romero); *Enredando sombras* (1987, S); *Los ángeles se han fatigado* (1988, S). Later moved to Puerto Rico.

30. REYES CANCHOLA, DHARMA ESTHER. *Tambien la muerte puede morir* (1990, S). A producer at TV-UNAM in the mid-1980s, Reyes later worked for the filmworkers union (STPC).

31. RIQUER, SONIA ZAMUDIO. *Desalojo* (1985, S); *Entreaguas* (1987, S). Riquer worked for Radio Educación from 1978 on, and in the early 1990s, worked making AIDS prevention videos.

32. ROMERO, AMPARO. *Voy por todas* (1986, S, codirected by Teresa Previdi); *Fuera de lugar* (1987, S); *Una noche fuera* (1989, S). Later worked freelance and as an assistant director in Teresa de Alba's production company, Comunicación Activa.

33. VENTURA RAMÍREZ, NANCY. *Umbrales* (1989, S); *Jesús Contreras* (1990, S, D about sculptor); *Pueblo Viejo* (n.d., exhibited in 1994–1995).

34. VIOLANTE LÓPEZ, ALICIA. *Reencuentros* (1989, S); *El almohadón* (1990, M).

Centro de Capacitación Cinematográfica

The number of women at the CCC continued to grow in the 1980s; more women than men were admitted in 1987, and the school's first feature was directed in 1988 by a woman (Cortés's *El secreto de Romelia*). Students included:

1. DIEZ DÍAZ, ANA. *Elvira Luz Cruz: Pena máxima* (1985, M, D, codirected by Dana Rotberg). Later returned to her native Spain and directed the feature *Andea Eta Yul* in the Basque Country in 1988.

2. GENTILE, ANDREA. *La neta . . . no hay futuro* (1988, S, D about marginalized youth of Ciudad Nezahualcóyotl). Later worked at the CCC and for television.

3. HEIBLUM, LAILA. *Espacios* (1984, S); *Entre la presencia y el olvido* (1988, S, D about the town of Real de Catorce, codirected by Claudia Rocha). Heiblum, who began working in video in 1970, became an assistant director with the production company Cine Testimonio in 1991.

4. LÓPEZ SÁNCHEZ, EVA. *No se asombre sargento* (1989, S); *La venganza* (1989, S); *Recuerdo de domingo* (1990, S, V); *Yapo Galeana* (1990, S, D about a native of the coast of Guerrero); *Objectos perdidos* (1992, S, 35mm). Debut feature: *Dama de noche* (CCC 1992, screenplay López Sánchez based on the novel by David Martín de Campo, cinematography Rodrigo Prieto, performed by Rafael Sánchez Navarro, Cecilia Toussaint, Miguel Córcega, Regina Orozco, distributed by IMCINE).

5. MAGLI, CLAUDIA. *Coyoacán* (1983, M). Italian-born ethnographer who entered the CCC in 1978. She later wrote scripts for feature documentaries, worked for Estudios Churubusco, and directed *Templo Mayor* (1985, M, D about Mexico City).

6. MARTÍNEZ DE VELASCO VÉLEZ, PATRICIA. *El sótano* (1988, S); *Acopilco* (CCC/UNESCO 1990, S, D about ecological problems of a zone in the Federal District); *Matilde Landeta* (CCC/IMCINE 1992, S, D). Author of *Directoras de cine: Proyección de un mundo obscuro,* Martínez de Velasco also made films at the Universidad Iberoamericana (1983–1985), where she worked on Cortés's *El secreto de Romelia* before entering the CCC in 1986.

7. MÉNDEZ, ELSIE. *El Rutas* (1987, M). Later produced educational television programs.

8. MENDICUTI, TERESA. *A la misma hora* (1987, M).

9. RODRÍGUEZ, MARÍA. *La divina providencia* (1987, S). Taught at CCC after graduation and attended the Escuela de Cine y TV in Cuba in 1988. Worked as director and screenwriter for the Televisa series *La hora marcada* (1988–1989), then as assistant director in a commercial production company.

10. SÁNCHEZ, ANGELES. *Nina* (1990, S, D about rock singer Nina Galindo); *A propósito del humo, la contaminación y esas cosas . . .* (CCC/Universidad Iberoamericana 1992, S, D codirected by Claudio Valdez Kuri).

Other Schools

In 1987, the CIEC was established at the Universidad de Guadalajara. Among its first graduates was Marta Vidrio, director of the 1989 short *La novia perfecta.* This school also sponsored research on and restoration of the films of Adela Sequeyro. At the Mexico state campus of the Instituto Tecnológico y de Estudios Superiores de Monterrey (ITESM), Susana Jiménez Colchado directed her thesis film *Continuidad* in 1990. At the Universidad Iberoamericana, Romelia Alvarez Sánchez made the short film *Tempagua* in 1988, and Iberoamericana graduate Ana Revuelas directed *Confidencias de un cineasta: Alejandro Galindo* (Filmoteca de la UNAM/STPC 1990).

Individual Directors

1. BARCO, JULIA. Born in Colombia, Barco studied at Massachusetts Institute of Technology before coming to Mexico. In the early 1980s, she made films for the Uni-

versity of Oaxaca's Institute of Social Research, then became director of the audiovisual department at the Universidad Autónoma Benito Juárez de Oaxaca (UABJO). Her documentaries, covering various aspects of life in Oaxaca's indigenous communities, are collaborative and feminist in nature; she has also played an important role in the international feminist media movement as an organizer of the first Cocina de Imagenes festival in 1987, a founder of Telemanita, and a participant in festivals, seminars, and conferences all over the Americas (Saalfield 29–30). Her films include: *Totoperas* (1980, Super8, D about Isthmus of Tehuantepec women); *Mero ikootsa—verdaderos nosotros* (UABJO 1982); *Agarro camino* (UABJO 1984); *Vela: Tradición y cambio en Juchitán* (UABJO 1985); *Preñadas de sueños* (1988, D about the fourth Encuentro Feminista Latinoamericano y del Caribe); *El parto siempre ha sido natural* (1989, D about midwives from the Isthmus of Tehuantepec).

2. DEUK, SOFÍA. *Contaminación* (1982, D, V); *Equinosis* (1982, S, super8); *Entre la vida y la muerte* (1983, S, super8); *El hijo* (1985, S). Duek's work is listed in Toledo; no further information is available.

3. GARCÍA, FRANCIS. Founder in 1982 of Redes Cine-Video, the predecessor of alternative video collective Canal 6 de Julio, whose name comes from the date of the 1988 elections that they documented in *Crónica de un fraude* (directed by Carlos Mendoza, 1988, produced by García). In addition to making videos herself, García and her company often provided technical assistance and equipment to communities and social organizations (Vega, "Video Works by Women" 55). García's own videos include *Somos cientos, miles, y millones* (1984, S, D about Guatemalan women, V); *No al monstruo de la Laguna Verde* (1987, D denouncing a nuclear power project); and *Por la paz, por la vida, por la tierra* (1992, S, D about a gathering of indigenous Ñahñu people held to commemorate the 500 years of resistance).

4. GRUNER, SILVIA. Experimental media artist. *Pecado original/reproducción* (1986, S, Super8 transferred to V); *El vuelo* (1989, Super8 and Hi8 V transferred to 3/4″ V).

5. PALAFOX, TEÓFILA. Through workshops sponsored by INI, indigenous men and women in different parts of the country received training in video production. One of these was Oaxacan artisan Palafox, who (under the guidance of Luis Lupone) made *La vida de una familia Ikoods* about her community in 1987 (shown at the Toronto Film Festival in 1991), and directed *Las ollas de San Marcos* (1992), a short documentary about Zapotec women potters.

6. PIÑÓ SANDOVAL, ANA. Anthropologist Piñó Sandoval has worked as a researcher and writer on documentaries made by UTEC and CONACULTA. In 1986, she codirected with Juan Francisco Urrusti *Piowachowe (La vieja que arde)*, a documentary about the Cerro de Chichonal coproduced by INI and IMCINE.

7. SPATARO, FRANCESCA. A producer and director at TV-UNAM and director of the production company OKIO, Spataro directed several short films in 1989, most of which criticized mass media and consumer culture: *Sueño en el 842, Tentación Cheese, El medio es el mensaje, Manual para cambiar la personalidad,* and *Bad Breath.* In the 1990s, she directed such videos as *It Makes Me Wonder* and *Sueño marca Acme.*

8. VEGA, ISELA. *Una gallina muy ponedora* (1981, F, codirected by Rafael Portillo); *Las amantes del Señor de la Noche* (1984, F, Vega directed, wrote, produced, and starred; co-stars Irma Serrano). Actress in film, theater, and television and one of few women to direct commercial films. Varied career includes video distribution and production in Los Angeles, California.

9. OTHERS. Carmen Garza (*De hierbas y caracoles* 1986, D), Mónica González (*Soneros* 1982, D), and Lourdes Grobet (*Lotería* 1981, A) are cited by Toledo; no further information is available.

The 1990s

In spite of the economic crisis and other obstacles, the number of women filmmakers continued to grow in the 1990s. Today, the proliferation of films and videos directed by women makes a comprehensive filmography nearly impossible and quickly obsolete. With the increasing number of women film students, independent videomakers, social activists producing media through their own channels, and other mediamakers working outside of traditional channels of production, gender alone as an organizing principle for categorization becomes increasingly unwieldy—which, from a feminist perspective, is cause for celebration. This concluding section, therefore, is no more than a modest attempt at mapping the various territories of film production which women traversed during the past decade.

Commercial Film Production

Perhaps as a result of women directors' success in the state-supported film sector, the barriers keeping women out of industrial film production seemed to break down somewhat by the mid-1990s. In 1994, writer Sabina Berman and TV producer Isabelle Tardán, after directing only one short film (*El arbol de la música,* 1994) for IMCINE, codirected a film version of Berman's popular play *Entre Villa y una mujer desnuda* for Televicine; in 1996, CCC graduate Leticia Venzor directed *El amor de tu vida S.A.* for the same company. In 1995, singer Beatriz Adriana was reported to be producing, writing, starring in and directing *Yo y mi banda,* combining her own concert footage with a fictional narrative ("Beatriz Adriana"). The hiring of Marisa Sistach to direct *Cilantro y perejil* (Rafael Montero, 1996) and the Televisa *telenovela La jaula de oro* was another indication of the industry's acceptance of women directors, even though

Sistach ultimately abandoned both projects. The surplus of experienced professional directors during a period of limited public funding for cinema will probably mean that more women will work for Televisa and other commercial television and film companies, with arguably less creative control but far greater potential exposure.

Documentary Production

In the 1990s, oppositional currents and social movements proved to be fertile terrain for the use of increasingly accessible video technology not only by professional filmmakers but also by participants documenting their own struggles. From 1994 on, the ongoing conflict in Chiapas, including the crucial role of women in defining and articulating the Zapatista position, was the catalyst for such documentaries as Carmen Ortiz and José Luis Contreras's *Aguascalientes: La patria vive* (1994, M, V, D about the Convención Nacional Democrática held in Chiapas in August 1994), *El EZLN y las mujeres, las siempre olvidadas* by the Colectivo Las Brujas, and *Las compañeras tienen grado* by CCC students Guadalupe Miranda and María Inés Roqué, the latter two videos exhibited in the festival Ninón '98. One of the best productions of the decade was Gloria Ribé's 1995 *El efecto tequila* (see CCC above), which analyzed Mexican politics through the ironic use of clips from classic films and through other parodic appropriations.

The feminist media production, training, and distribution center Telemanita facilitated the production of a number of video documentaries: *Gritos poéticos de la urbe* (1995) and *Angeles de la ciudad obscura* (1997) by Susana Quiroz and Inés Morales; *Hoy las mujeres mayas* (1997), produced by the Organización de Mujeres Madre Tierra, directed by Ana María Rodríguez and Blanca Anzurez, with a script by Telemanita's Alejandra Novoa; *Danza por la comunidad* filmed by Novoa in October 1996; and beginning in 1997, the *Enlace lésbico* series, which included episodes about an International Women's Day event in downtown Mexico City, a book presentation by lesbian authors, the 1997 Lesbian and Gay Pride March, and the lesbian Day of the Dead commemorations held outside the Museo de las Bellas Artes in 1997 and 1998.

Traditional documentaries sponsored by public and private institutions continued to be produced as well, and although film students produced fewer documentaries than in previous epochs, many filmmakers trained in the 1970s and 1980s, including Alejandra Islas, Maricarmen de Lara, and María Eugenia Tamés, continued to make the documentary a crucial arena of feminist production.

Student Filmmaking

The film schools continued to produce diverse work despite the economic crisis, with video replacing 16mm as the dominant instructional medium. Students at the CCC included: Marcela Arteaga (*Un sandwich*, 1990; *Al otro lado del mar*, 1994); Silvana Zuanetti (*Lagartos*, 1990; *Nadie es inocente*, 1990; *Sandra*, 1991, 35mm; *Giovanni e morto*, 1992); Carolina Amador (*Cómo se filmó "La mujer de Benjamín"*, 1991); Leticia Venzor Castañeda (*El viudo José*, 1992, 35mm); Jimena Perzábal (*Resurrección*, 1992; *Pez muerto no nada*, 1996, 35mm); Laura Gardos Velo (*Antes de la música* and *Estar a tiempo*, 1995, 35mm); Patricia Zubieta (*Puro corazón*, 1990; *Efectos especiales*, 1991; *Las inútiles fantasías de Tania*, 1993); Guadalupe Miranda and María Inés Roqué (*Las compañeras tienen grado*, 1995); Christine Burkhard (*Simultánea*, 1997); Adele Schmidt (*El viaje de Juana*, 1997); Tatiana Ixquic Huezo Sánchez (*Tiempo caústico*, 1997); Paula Astorga Riestra (*Guantánamo*, 1997); Lucrecia Gutiérrez (*Marea de sueño*, 1997); Irene Banchilk (*En tránsito*, 1997); Eva Bodenstedt (*Ciudad de puertas*, 1997); Celia Barona (*La venganza de Desdémona*, 1998); and Lourdes Rébora (*El jardín botánico*, 1998).

CUEC filmmakers of the 1990s included: Conchita Perales (*La pareja ideal* and *Nicolás*); Laura Rojas (*Murallas de silencio*, 1994, about a lesbian couple dealing with rape); and Valentina Leduc (*Un volcán con lava de hielo*, 1994). At the University of Guadalajara, Kenya Márquez directed *Cruz*, a short comedy made in 35mm with support from Aeroméxico, Resonancia, and the local government of Guadalajara.

Experimental /Alternative Video

The high costs of film production, the advent of Hi8 and the commercial legitimacy of the short music video or "videoclip" made video an increasingly attractive alternative for filmmakers of the 1990s. Women's experimental video (and some film) appeared in many festivals throughout the decade, beginning with Mexico 90: Primera Bienal de Video. This large video showcase featured many works by women, including Sarah Minter and Andrea di Castro's *Mex-metro;* Ana María Ortega's *Cama de sueños;* Cecilia Navarro's *Cerraduras;* María Morfín and Gustavo Domínguez's *Reflexión;* Pamala Safari's *Si él pudiera volver . . . y es que Angel murió;* Francesca Spataro's *It Makes Me Wonder;* Leticia Salas's *El mole prieto;* Rosa María Méndez García's *Tú decides sobre el sida,* produced by the Banco Nacional de México; Karin Esperanza Amador's *Aldea de pescadores,* produced by Radio-Televisión Oaxaca; María Victoria Llamas's *La muerte viva;* and María R. Pasilla's *Fiesta en la meseta purépecha,* produced by the Universidad de Aguascalientes. Subsequent Bienal programs continued to feature work by women; in 1999, the Bienal was renamed Vide@rte and included multimedia works as well as video.

In October 1994, a showcase of short experimental videos by women at Mexico City's Museo del Chopo included Sarah Minter's *Video Road;* Angélica Rodríguez's *Metro y medio* (1993); Marina García Gamés's *Que no se marchite* (1992) and *Nos iremos borrando;* Cecilia Sánchez's *Grabados;* Lydia Neri's *Thelema* and *Dolor de muñecas;* Leticia Venzor's *En tinta* (1991); Francesca Spataro's *It Makes Me Wonder* and *Sueño marca*

Acme; María Aimée de Laborde's *Casa de la sal;* Patricia Zubieta's *Las inútiles fantasías de Tania;* Lisi Monserrat's *En las nubes;* Teresa de Alba's *El sueño* and *Reyes, el Mono y el Tragabalas;* Pilar Rodríguez's *La idea que habitamos;* Pilar Sánchez Souza's *Presagio;* Laura Martínez Díaz's *Gotas de mercurio, Víboras I, II, y III,* and *Videojuegos;* Araceli Zúñiga's *Ser.Nacer;* Ximena Cuevas's *Corazón sangrante* (1993); and others.

The Telemanita-sponsored ExplorAcción festival in 1996 included Lisi Montserrat and Guadalupe Ortega's *Viernes de luna llena* (1996) and *Virgen y mala madre* (1996), Montserrat and Pilar Sánchez's *Venidas y salidas* (1995), Cuevas's *Corazón sangrante* and *Medias mentiras,* and Lillian Haugen's *Mis otros . . . rostros* (1992). In 1998, the experimental showcase of the festival Ninón '98 included videos by Ximena Cuevas and others, and the Mexperimental Cinema project, curated by Rita González and Jesse Lerner and exhibited in the United States and Mexico, included works by Cuevas, Pola Weiss, and Silvia Gruner.

Ximena Cuevas was easily the most widely recognized and successful artist in this field. Born in 1963, she began her career restoring films for the Cineteca Nacional and has worked in various capacities (from script clerk to editor) on such feature films as *Rojo amanecer,* Fernández Violante's *Nocturno amor que te vas* and *Golpe de suerte,* Ripstein's *El evangelio de las maravillas* (1998), and many others. Showing no interest in directing mainstream cinema herself, she has instead worked in video and Super8 since the late 1970s. Her work includes: *Noche de paz* (1989, S, V, episode of Televisa program *Hora marcada,* written by Paz Alicia Garciadiego); *Profanando al Ambrosio* (1990, M, V); *Corazón sangrante* (1993, S, V, music video with Astrid Hadad); *Medias mentiras* (1994, S, Hi8 V); *Bocetos al natural* (1994); *Víctimas del pecado neoliberal* (1995, V, collaboration with Jesusa Rodríguez); *Cuerpos de papel* (1997, V); *El diablo en la piel* (1998, V); *Lo que el viento se llevó* (1998, 16mm); *La cama* (1999, V).

Sources

Where possible I used the films and videos themselves as the sources of information; where this was not possible, I relied on the efforts of the many writers, programmers, and catalogue compilers who had previously attempted all or part of the difficult task of data collection and organization. All of my sources, including catalogues and exhibition programs, are included in the list of works cited; however, special mention must be made of Octavio Moreno Ochoa, who researched more than one hundred directors (speaking personally with many of them) while preparing his 1992 thesis *Catálogo de directoras de cine en México;* he is thus the only source on the professional careers of many film school graduates. Teresa Toledo's *Realizadoras Latinoamericanas/Latin*

American Women Filmmakers: Cronología/Chronology (1917–1987) is another important source; although not as detailed, it lists the works of many independent film- and videomakers not mentioned elsewhere. Finally, the Internet-accessible electronic databases at the Filmoteca de la UNAM and IMCINE are convenient references, especially for scholars outside of Mexico.

Notes

Introduction

1. "Mi intención y mi defensa para hacer cine, era hacer 'el otro cine.' Hacer el otro mundo. Las mujeres somos la mitad de la humanidad, pero casi todo está explorado y explicado a través del hombre. La mujer explicada a través del hombre. Entonces pensé que el cine que hiciera, y todavía lo pienso hasta la fecha, que el cine que haga es del punto de vista de la mujer. No de la mujer romántica y sometida, sino al contrario, de la mujer pensante" (Landeta, in Martínez de Velasco, *Directoras de cine: Proyección de un mundo obscuro* 64).

Translations are mine except where source materials already have been translated for publication or, in the case of films, subtitled.

2. Dates for Mexican films normally indicate when filming began; release dates are often two or more years later. In September 1989, *El secreto de Romelia* became the first of this group of films to be released.

3. Much U.S.-based scholarship on Mexican cinema has focused on questions of gender. Charles Ramírez Berg's *Cinema of Solitude: A Critical Study of Mexican Film, 1967–1983,* for instance, devotes two chapters to the changing use of female archetypes; Ana López's articles on Golden Age melodrama perform a feminist analysis of that narrative mode in Latin America; Hershfield also looks at classical cinema's construct of Woman in *Mexican Cinema/Mexican Woman: 1940–1950.* Franco's two film analyses in *Plotting Women: Gender and Representation in Mexico* examine constructs of Woman as figures of mediation and exchange in works by Emilio Fernández and Luis Buñuel; while for the contemporary period, scholars such as Román-Odio and Wu have debated the gender politics of Alfonso Arau's 1991 film *Como agua para chocolate.* Other examples include Mahieu, "Feminine Types and Stereotypes in Mexican and Latin American Cinema"; Mora, *Mexican Cinema: Reflections of a Society, 1896–1988* and "Feminine Images in Mexican Cinema: The Family Melodrama; Sara García, 'The Mother of México'; and the Prostitute"; Ramírez Berg, "Cracks in the 'Macho' Monolith: 'Machismo', Man, and Mexico in Recent Mexican Cinema" and "The Image of Women in Recent Mexican Cinema"; and Rich, "An/ Other View of New Latin American Cinema."

Gender issues also have become an important part of film scholarship in Mexico, as demonstrated by Julia Tuñón's 1997 book, *Mujeres de luz y sombra en el cine mexicano: La construcción de una imagen (1939–1952),* the work of researchers Torres, Iglesias, Martínez de Velasco, Millán, and others, the film criticism of Ayala Blanco, and an impressive number of academic theses. As most of the latter have been carried out within the social sciences, Mexican scholarship in this area has been notably more empirically based than its U.S. equivalent.

4. Franco's book was originally published in 1967 as *The Modern Culture of Latin America: Society and the Artist;* the later Mexican edition contains the additional chapters cited here.

5. Figures are from *Statistical Abstract of Latin America.*

6. Anne T. Doremos pointed out the ideological differences between film and literary texts in her conference paper "Articulations of the Revolutionary in Mexican Literature and Film, 1929–1935."

7. See also Torrents, "Mexican Cinema Comes Alive," 224–225.

8. Ironically, two of the Mexican businessmen who ended up acquiring part of the COTSA properties, Gabriel Alarcón and Manuel Espinosa Yglesias, were exhibitors forced out of the business by nationalization decades earlier (Alberto Aguilar in *El Financiero*).

9. These figures were reported by Jorge Elizondo in *Pantalla,* Patrícia Davalos in *El Sol de México,* and Ricardo Camargo in *El Nacional.*

10. This special issue of *Nexos* was titled "Entre las sábanas: El México sexual de los noventas" and included reports on prostitution, pornography, table dance and other sexual entertainments, AIDS, and male homosexuality, as well as first-person narratives.

11. Feminist intellectuals have become increasingly vocal about challenging anti-abortion restrictions. Among those who have publicly supported decriminalization are theater director Jesusa Rodríguez, singer Eugenia León, and writer Carmen Boullosa, as well as feminist publishers and activists Marta Lamas and Esperanza Brito (Judith Calderón Gómez, in *La Jornada*).

12. Hernández Carballido specifically criticized Cecilia Soto, the presidential candidate for the small but highly visible Partido del Trabajo. In the same issue of *fem,* Hernández Carballido praised two PRD congressional candidates, Hilda Aguirre and María Victoria Llamas, for their commitment to women.

13. This essay was based on a research project coordinated by García Canclini and described in detail in *Los nuevos espectadores: Cine, televisión y video en México.*

Chapter One

1. "¿Cómo lograron introducir su contrabando en fronteras tan celosamente vigiladas? Pero sobre todo ¿qué fue lo que las impulsó de modo tan irresistible a arriesgarse a ser contrabandistas? Porque lo cierto es que la mayor parte de las mujeres están muy tranquilas en sus casas y en sus límites sin organizar bandas para burlar la ley. Aceptan la ley, la acatan, la respetan. La consideran adecuada" (Castellanos, "Sobre cultura femenina" 19).

2. On Beltrán see de la Vega, "Fichero de cineastas nacionales" 18–19 and Martínez de Velasco 38; on La Duquesa Olga see Martínez de Velasco 40; on Rahon see Deffebach 181–183.

3. Landeta told *Cine* in 1980, "Pero eran pocos antecedentes; para qué decirle en América Latina, no había nada" (in García Diego, "Matilde Landeta: Entrevista" 3).

4. Whereas Mora refers to Derba mainly as an actress, Torres considers her *La tigresa* to be the starting point for the history of women's filmmaking in Mexico ("Las primeras realizadoras" 2). King emphasizes the patriotic intent of Derba's films: "their main device was to film the country-side in all its aspects, equating nationalism with the variety and 'difference' of the land" (19). Al-though he considers her technique a throwback to still photography, a similar equation of land-scape and nation can be seen in the more sophisticated cinematography of the Golden Age, especially that of Gabriel Figueroa and Emilio Fernández. On the other hand, Aurelio de los Reyes points out that in practice, Derba's costume melodramas were based on stories of European royalty and had little to do with Mexican experience (quoted in Torres, "Las primeras realiza-doras" 4).

5. Matilde Landeta worked on this film as well, as script clerk.

6. In addition to the 1997 monograph *Adela Sequeyro*, Torres has published articles on Se-queyro in the United States and Mexico. These include "Adela Sequeyro, Mexican Film Pioneer" and "Redescubriendo a una rara avis del cine sonoro mexicano," as well as the works already cited. Torres and de la Vega received a grant from the Mexico-U.S. Fund for Culture to support the restoration of Sequeyro's films.

7. On Adolfo Best Maugard see Garmendia, "*La mancha de sangre:* Un clásico recuperado"; on *estridentismo* see List Arzubide, *El movimiento estridentista*, and Schneider, *El estridentismo: Antología.*

8. This film was directed by Alfonso Corona Blake and titled *Camino de la vida;* it won several Arieles in 1957, including one for Landeta's script.

9. See Ramos Escandón et al. for an exemplary collection of feminist historiography.

10. On *Trotacalles* see Chapter 6.

11. For a general account of this period see de la Vega, "Origins, Development and Crisis of the Sound Cinema (1929–1964)." For an interesting discussion of the political economy of the in-dustrial cinema see Tello, "Notas sobre la política económica del 'viejo' cine mexicano" 21–32.

Chapter Two

1. Fernández Violante, in Burton, "Inside the Mexican Film Industry" (199).

2. "Nosotras somos parte de las corrientes de pensamiento que buscan darle voz a los que luchan por una vida mejor, por la dignidad y el respeto. Por la solidaridad humana" (Navarro, "Una reflexión sobre el papel de la mujer" 152).

3. Isabel later appeared in Novaro's *Danzón*, Fernández Violante's *Golpe de suerte*, and Roberto Sneider's *Dos crímenes* (1994), among others.

4. As reported in *Excélsior* on 15 March 1992 ("Se estrenará"), the film was shown in March at the Latino Theater as an homage to Manzano, with multiple sponsors, but not in the Hoy cycle. In September 1992, the film's impending commercial opening was announced in a note in *Cine Mundial;* yet Ayala Blanco reviewed the film for *El Financiero* in February 1993, and the *Dicine* reviews appeared in October 1994, when the film was shown for a week at the Cineteca Nacional. In an interview published in the Cineteca program, Fernández Violante said *Golpe de suerte* opened during the World Cup (July 1994) and for that reason was ignored by the public and withdrawn from theaters after a week. Although she was invited to show the film abroad, she had no money for the print or subtitling. As of this writing, the film has received no further attention.

Chapter Three

1. Note: The original spelling of Sistach's first name, Marysa, appears in the credits of her early films; she later adopted the standardized spelling used here.

"Creo que a las mujeres les toca inventar en nuestro terreno de trabajo un nuevo lenguaje que se alimente en las experiencias comunes de nuestras historias individuales. Esta palabra de mujer debe inscribirse en nuestra cultura. Destruir el falso espejo de la mujer que es, por lo general, el cine. . . . Se trata de reapropriarnos de nuestra imagen y buscar así nuestra identidad" (Sistach, in Martín and Pérez Grovas, "Encuesta a las estudiantes de cine" 35).

2. In reviews of the film, the same question discussed in Chapter 6 in relation to *Danzón* regarding whether the film was "feminine" or "feminist" inevitably arose, with most writers calling *Los pasos de Ana* "feminine." For Ayala Blanco, it represented the painful aftermath of a no longer viable feminist dream: "Después de la borrachera militante, viene la cruda moral" [After the militant binge comes the moral hangover] (*La disolvencia* 512).

3. The participation of her children has been a constant feature of Sistach's films. In *Conozco a las tres,* Valdiri played Ana's son, while Sistach, pregnant with Pía, claims that she only stopped filming to give birth (Vega, "Entrevista" 4). In *El cometa,* both children have minor roles.

4. *Cartas a Clementina Otero,* Owen's letters from the 1920s, was published by the Universidad Autónoma Metropolitana in 1988.

5. Bovenschen's essay "Is There a Feminine Aesthetic?" was published in *Aesthetick und Kommunikation* in 1976 and in *New German Critique* the following year.

Chapter Four

1. "Como mujer cineasta me interesa ofrecer la visión, el ser, sentir y actuar de la mujer de mi época . . ." (Cortés, in Gallegos, "Deseo mostrar").

2. Citations are from "The Widower Román," the Ruth Peacock translation included in *A Rosario Castellanos Reader.*

3. The Lecumberri prison, where the student leaders were held, and its horrendous conditions became the subject of José Revueltas's novel *El apando;* the prison's name is strangely (or perhaps appropriately?) translated in the English subtitles of the UCLA Mexican Film Project print as "law school."

4. It is interesting to note that the original script contained several references to Dolores's support for the oppositional campaign led by Cuauhtémoc Cárdenas in 1988. Although at first these were ignored by the government authorities who partially funded the film, when Cortés showed them the rough cut, she was accused of producing *cardenista* propaganda. Because she herself felt that the allusions detracted from the film's main dramatic conflict, she agreed to what she called her *autocensura,* or self-censorship (Fernández Escareño 130).

5. As Omar Chanona explained at the Encuentros de Comunicación Social conference in August 1990, increasing the involvement of states and the private sector in film production, distribution, and exhibition was one of IMCINE's major goals during the Salinas administration (83–86).

Chapter Five

1. Schyfter, in Presner, "Insights from an Outsider" (12).

Chapter Six

1. "Me encanta jugar con los clichés. Sin embargo, tienes que asumirlos, romperlos, darles la vuelta, regodearte en ellos. En *Danzón* están casi todos los clichés del cine mexicano: la música, las rumberas, el romanticismo, el melodrama, la cursilería, en fin, están todos jugados" (Novaro, in Michel).

2. The Spanish expression for the fairy-tale notion of Prince Charming is *príncipe azul,* literally "blue prince"; Novaro's short film *Azul celeste* also evokes this association. In *Una isla rodeada de agua,* the protagonist's blue eyes enable her to "see reality in different colors than everyone else sees" (Novaro, in Fernández Escareño 138).

3. Among others, they remade the classic melodrama *La mujer del puerto* (1990) and inverted the family melodrama in *Principio y fin* (1993), the *cabaretera* genre in *Reina de la noche* (1994), and the road movie in *Profundo carmesí* (1995).

4. "Intimist" is an awkward rendering of the term *intimista* that was commonly used to describe the personal, emotional narratives made by directors in the 1990s, especially women.

5. Novaro wrote the script for *Lola* at the Escuela Internacional de Cine in Cuba and at the Sun-

dance Institute, whose Latin American program was headed by García Márquez. Her cinematographer, Rodrigo García, is García Márquez's son.

6. These events are documented in Poniatowska's book *Nada, nadie: Las voces del temblor*.

Chapter Seven

1. Rotberg, in Rufinelli and Tanner, "Angel of Fire" 14.

2. Pérez Turrent's references are to the "achievements" of the Salinas era: Aspe was finance minister and chief architect of neoliberal reform, Solidaridad (PRONASOL) was a social welfare program notable for its paternalism and use as a tool of self-promotion for the Salinas regime, and the Torre de Cristal was Mexico City's new Stock Exchange building, about which a leftist French magazine had proposed an article.

3. Ironically, Rotberg cast ten-year-old Noé Alberto Montealegre for this role after viewing him in a commercial for Solidaridad (Quiroz Arroyo, "Trabajar en *Angel de fuego*").

4. Joderowsky was mentioned in reviews of *Angel de fuego* in *El Economista, El Día, El Nacional, Uno Más Uno* (twice), and *La Jornada Semanal*. Mauricio Peña in *El Heraldo* and an anonymous writer for *Cine Mundial* both compared *Angel de fuego* to *Los olvidados*.

5. The notion of the "dirty screen" is taken principally from the Brazilian filmmakers mentioned; see Stam, "On the Margins: Brazilian Avant Garde Cinema" 312.

6. Victoria Reifler Bricker's *Ritual Humor in Highland Chiapas* remains a useful study of Mayan practices; similar rituals have been found to exist throughout the Americas.

7. On Maldita Vecindad see Rubén Martínez, 150–165. For related commentary on urban youth culture see Monsiváis, "Los rituales del caos" 120–124.

Conclusion

1. "El cine mexicano hace un rato que murió. . . . La gente no tiene pa' comer ¿cómo va a tener para ir al cine?" (Medina, in Soto Viterbo, "Las nuevas reinas del cine mexicano").

2. "Quiero que todas las mujeres se despierten y siembren en su corazón la necesidad de organizarse. Con los brazos cruzados no se puede construir el México libre y justo que todos soñamos" *(Comunicado del Ejército Zapatista de Liberación Nacional en voz de la Comandante Ramona)*.

3. On the relationships between personal and sociopolitical themes in Latin American women's writing see Fernández Olmos and Paravisini-Gebert 26–32 and Basnett 2–7.

4. See for instance: Miller, *Latin American Women and the Search for Social Justice;* Nash and Safa, *Women and Change in Latin America;* Fisher, *Out of the Shadows: Women, Resistance and Politics in South America;* and Küpper, *Compañeras: Voices from the Latin American Women's Movement*.

5. In *Los nuevos espectadores,* García Canclini offers further examples of the idiosyncratic nature of Mexican film criticism and the wide divergence between critics and spectators vis-à-vis such films as *Como agua para chocolate.*

6. The study was later repeated with groups in Tijuana and Ciudad Juárez that were divided according to sexual orientation as well as to age and sex. See Iglesias's article in Burton-Carvajal et al. for a description of the later study.

7. English translations of his work addressing this topic have been published in King, López, and Alvarado 140–146, Paranaguá 145–151, and in the Monsiváis collection *Mexican Postcards.*

8. The party representatives offered the explanation during a Global Exchange delegation visit to PAN and PRI headquarters in Chilpancingo on 18 August 1994.

9. At this point, the Zapatista army itself was not deemed criminal and was in fact engaged in negotiations with the government. See Rashkin.

10. In a talk given in Los Angeles in April 1997 and broadcast on the cable access program *Todos Somos Marcos,* Benavides discussed her experiences in Chiapas and, importantly, made explicit the connection between the Mexican guerrilla of the 1970s (of which she was a part) and that of Chiapas in the 1990s. Obviously the case of the accused Zapatistas in 1995 was only partly about alternative media production; the persistence of the struggles of the 1960s and 1970s in the present moment (in the cinema as well as other arenas) is certainly an overlooked subject worthy of further attention.

11. Words of Comandante Ramona to the National Indigenous Congress, Mexico City, October 1996.

12. See Snow.

13. As this book went to press, Trevi and her partner and manager, Sergio Andrade, were in prison awaiting judgment on charges of child corruption, kidnapping, and other offenses involving young women who had been part of Trevi's performances and recordings. Following Trevi's arrest, coverage of the case portrayed the singer as having herself been manipulated and victimized by the domineering impresario Andrade. While the sensational scandal dominated television and tabloid headlines for months, the facts are far from clear, and the outcome remains uncertain.

Works Cited

Books, Journals, Magazines, and Conferences

Aguilar Camín, Héctor, and Lorenzo Meyer. *In the Shadow of the Mexican Revolution: Contemporary Mexican History, 1910–1989.* Translated by Luis Alberto Fierro. Austin: University of Texas Press, 1993.

Alberro, Solange. "Herejes, brujas y beatas: Mujeres ante el tribunal del Santo Oficio de la Inquisición en la Nueva España." In *Presencia y transparencia: la mujer en la historia de México,* Carmen Ramos Escandón et al., 79–94. Mexico City: El Colegio de México, 1987.

Amado, Ana María. "Entrevista al Colectivo Cine-Mujer." *Imagenes* 8 (July 1980): 12–19.

Anderson, Benedict. *Imagined Communities: Reflections on the Origin and Spread of Nationalism.* Rev. ed. New York: Verso, 1991.

Anzaldúa, Gloria. *Borderlands/La Frontera: The New Mestiza.* San Francisco: Aunt Lute, 1987.

Arredondo, Isabel. "La ola de las escuelas: El aceso a la dirección a través de las escuelas de cine." Paper presented at the meeting of the Latin American Studies Association, Guadalajara, Mexico. 18 April 1997.

Ayala Blanco, Jorge. "El movimiento estudiantil." In *Hojas de cine: Testimonios y documentos del nuevo cine latinoamericano,* vol. 2, 57–67. Mexico City: SEP/UAM/Fundación Mexicana de Cineastas, 1988. First published in *La búsqueda del cine mexicano* (Mexico City: Universidad Autónoma de México, 1974).

———. "El parto de los montes feministas." In *Intolerancia* 2 (March–April 1986): 3–20.

———. *La condición del cine mexicano (1973–1985).* Mexico City: Posada, 1986.

———. *La disolvencia del cine mexicano: Entre lo popular y lo exquisito.* Mexico City: Grijalbo, 1991.

Azuela, Mariano. *Los de abajo: novela de la Revolución mexicana.* 1915. Reprint, Mexico City: Fondo de Cultura Economica, 1960. Published in English as *The Underdogs: A Novel of the Mexican Revolution,* translated by E. Munguía (New York: Signet, 1963).

Basnett, Susan, ed. *Knives and Angels: Women Writers in Latin America.* London: Zed, 1990.

Benavides, Elisa. Speech. *Todos Somos Marcos.* Episode 24. MediaOne Channel 26, Carson, Calif. August 1997. Videotape.

Bhabha, Homi. *The Location of Culture.* London and New York: Routledge, 1994.

Bigsby, C. W. E. *Dada and Surrealism.* London: Methuen, 1972.

Bonfil Batalla, Guillermo. *México profundo: Una civilización negada.* Mexico City: Grijalbo, 1987, 1990. Published in English as *México Profundo: Reclaiming a Civilization,* translated by Philip A. Dennis (Austin: University of Texas Press, 1996).

Bovenschen, Silvia. "Is There a Feminine Aesthetic?" Translated by Beth Weckmueller. *New German Critique* 10 (winter 1977). First published in *Aesthetik und Kommunikation* 25 (September 1976).

Bracho, Diana. "El cine mexicano: ¿Y en el papel de la mujer . . . Quién?" *Mexican Studies* 1.2 (summer 1985): 413–423.

Bricker, Victoria Reifler. *Ritual Humor in Highland Chiapas.* Austin: University of Texas Press, 1973.

Burton, Julianne. "Inside the Mexican Film Industry: A Woman's Perspective." *Cinema and Social Change in Latin America: Conversations with Filmmakers.* Austin: University of Texas Press, 1986.

Burton-Carvajal, Julianne, Patricia Torres, and Angel Miguel, eds. *Horizontes del segundo siglo: Investigación y pedagogía del cine mexicano, latinoamericano y chicano.* Guadalajara and Mexico City: Universidad de Guadalajara and IMCINE, 1998.

Bustos, Victor. "María Novaro: De *Lola* a *Danzón.*" *Dicine* 40 (July 1991): 10–11.

———. "Matilde Landeta: 40 años después." *Dicine* 50 (March 1993): 30–31.

Caletti Kaplan, Rubén Sergio. "Communication Policies in Mexico: An Historical Paradox of Words and Actions." In *Media and Politics in Latin America: The Struggle for Democracy,* edited by Elizabeth Fox, 67–81. London: Sage, 1988.

Camp, Roderic A. *Intellectuals and the State in Twentieth Century Mexico.* Austin: University of Texas Press, 1985.

"Carmen Toscano de Moreno Sánchez." *Cuadernos de la Cineteca Nacional* 9 (1979): 51–52.

Carro, Nelson. "Cine mexicano de los ochenta: Ante el cadáver de un difunto." *Dicine* 33 (March 1990): 2–5.

———. Introduction to *Angel de fuego,* by Dana Rotberg and Omar A. Rodrigo. Mexico City: Ediciones El Milagro, 1993.

Castellanos, Rosario. *A Rosario Castellanos Reader.* Edited by Maureen Ahern. Austin: University of Texas Press, 1988.

———. "Sobre cultura femenina." Master's thesis, Universidad Autónoma de México. Mexico City: Ediciones de América, *Revista Antológica,* 1950.

Cato, Susana. "*Danzón* dedicado a . . ." Review of *Danzón. Proceso,* 24 June 1991.

CEPROPIE (Centro de Producción de Programas Informativos y Especiales). *Memoria 1988–1994.* Mexico City: CEPROPIE, 1994.

Chanona, Omar. "Cine: Descentralización y promoción." In *Encuentros de comunicación social,*

83–86. Reynosa, Tamaulipas, Mexico: Dirección General de Radio, TV y Cinematografía, 1990.

Colectivo Alejandro Galindo. "El cine mexicano y sus crisis." Part 1. *Dicine* 19 (May–June 1987): 12–13.

———. "El cine mexicano y sus crisis." Part 2. *Dicine* 20 (July–August 1987): 15–16.

———. "El cine mexicano y sus crisis." Part 3. *Dicine* 21 (September–October 1987): 16–18.

Coronado, Juan. Introduction to *De la poesía a la prosa en el mismo viaje*, by Gilberto Owen, 11–17. Mexico City: Consejo Nacional para la Cultura y las Artes, 1990.

Cox, Alex. "Roads to the South: In Praise of Mexican Cinema." *Film Comment* November–December 1995: 26–35.

Cross, John. "Formalizing the Informal Economy: The Case of Street Vendors in Mexico City." Paper presented at the American Sociological Association, Washington, D.C., 21 August 1995. *Papers in Mexican Politics*. Online at http://daisy.uwaterloo.ca/~alopez-o/politics/.

Davis, Diane E. *Urban Leviathan: Mexico City in the Twentieth Century*. Philadelphia: Temple University Press, 1994.

de la Vega Alfaro, Eduardo. "El cine independiente mexicano 1942–1965." In *Hojas de cine: Testimonios y documentos del nuevo cine latinoamericano*, vol. 2, 69–82. Mexico City: SEP/UAM/ Fundación Mexicana de Cineastas, 1988. First published in *Filmoteca* 1.1 (November 1978).

———. "Fichero de cineastas nacionales." *Dicine* 38 (March 1991): 18–19.

———. "Origins, Development, and Crisis of the Sound Cinema (1929–1964)." In *Mexican Cinema*, edited by Paulo Antonio Paranaguá and translated by Ana M. López, 79–93. London: BFI, 1995.

———. "Tercera Muestra de Cine Mexicano en Guadalajara." Part 2. *Dicine* 25 (May–June 1988): 14.

de Lauretis, Teresa. "Aesthetic and Feminist Theory: Rethinking Women's Cinema." In *Female Spectators: Looking at Film and Television*, edited by E. Deidre Pribram, 174–195. London and New York: Verso, 1988.

———. *Technologies of Gender*. Bloomington and Indianapolis: University of Indiana Press, 1987.

de Orellana, Margarita. "The Circular Look: The Incursion of North American Fictional Cinema 1911–1917 into the Mexican Revolution." In *Mediating Two Worlds: Cinematic Encounters in the Americas*, edited by John King, Ana M. López, and Manuel Alvarado, 3–14. London: BFI, 1993.

Deffebach, Nancy. "Alice Rahon: Poems of Light and Shadow, Painting in Free Verse." *On the Bus* 8/9 (1991): 176–187.

del Diestro, Lucía. Review of *Golpe de Suerte*. *Dicine* 58 (October 1994): 35.

Doremos, Anne T. "Articulations of the Revolutionary in Mexican Literature and Film, 1929–1935." Paper presented at Cine-Lit III, Portland, Ore., 19 February 1997.

Elizondo, Jorge. "La exhibición cinematográfica: Retrospectiva y futuro." *Pantalla* 15 (winter 1991): 1–36.

Elizondo, Salvador. "El cine mexicano y la crisis." In *Hojas de cine: Testimonios y documentos del nuevo cine latinoamericano,* vol. 2, 37–46. Mexico City: SEP/UAM/Fundación Mexicana de Cineastas, 1988. First published in *Nuevo Cine* 2.7 (August 1962).

Equipo de Ciencias Sociales, Centro Antonio de Montesinos (CAM). "Los niños de la calle." MEX-PAZ *Analisis/Pulso* 80: 11 July 1996. Online. Available by e-mail: ANALISIS@uibero.uia.mx.

Escárcega, Ignacio. Review of *Danzón. Dicine* 41 (September 1991): 21.

Espinasa, José María. "El cine de Dana Rotberg." *La Jornada Semanal,* 13 September 1992: 8–9.

———. "Los pasos de una película." *Nitrato de Plata* 5 (May–June 1991): 3.

Esteinou Madrid, Javier. *La comunicación y la cultura nacionales en los tiempos del libre comercio.* Mexico City: Fundación Manuel Buendía, 1993.

Fanon, Franz. *The Wretched of the Earth.* New York: Grove, 1963.

Fernández Escareño, Itzia Gabriela. "Diez estudios de caso de directoras de largometrajes de ficción, dentro de los canones industriales, en la historia del cine mexicano (1935–1992)." Bachelor's thesis, Universidad Autónoma Metropolitana at Azcapotzalco, 1996.

Fernández Olmos, Margarite, and Lizbeth Paravisini-Gebert, eds. *Pleasure in the Word: Erotic Writing by Latin American Women.* Fredonia, N.Y.: White Pine Press, 1993.

Fernández Violante, Marcela. "El cine universitario." In *Hojas de cine: Testimonios y documentos del nuevo cine latinoamericano,* vol. 2, 83–87. Mexico City: SEP/UAM/Fundación Mexicana de Cineastas, 1988.

———. "Las directoras de la industria cinematográfica nacional." In *La mujer en los medios audiovisuales: Memorias del VIII Festival Internacional del Nuevo Cine Latinoamericano.* Cuadernos de Cine 32, 139–147. Mexico City: Universidad Nacional Autónoma de México, Coordinación de Difusión Cultural, 1987.

———. "Objetivos y funciones del Centro." In *La docencia y el fenómeno fílmico: Memoria de los XXV años del CUEC, 1963–1988,* edited by Marcela Fernández Violante. Mexico City: Dirección de Literatura, Coordinación de Difusión Cultural, Universidad Nacional Autónoma de México, 1988.

Fisher, Jo. *Out of the Shadows: Women, Resistance, and Politics in South America.* London: Latin American Bureau, 1993.

Franco, Jean. *La cultura moderna en América Latina.* Translated by Sergio Pitol. Mexico City: Grijalbo, 1985. First published as *The Modern Culture of Latin America: Society and the Artist* (New York: Praeger, 1967).

———. *Plotting Women: Gender and Representation in Mexico.* New York: Columbia University Press, 1989.

———. "What's Left of the Intelligentsia? The Uncertain Future of the Printed Word." NACLA *Report on the Americas* 28.2 (September–October 1994): 16–21.

Galeano, Eduardo. *The Book of Embraces.* Translated by Cedric Belfrage with Mark Schafer. New York and London: W. W. Norton, 1989.

García, Amalia. Interview. "Mujeres sin amor." *60 Minutos.* Telemundo, 22 January 1995.

García, Gustavo. "Retrato del cineasta adolescente." *Intolerancia* 4 (1987): 2–10.

García Canclini, Néstor. *Culturas híbridas: Estrategias para entrar y salir de la modernidad.* Mexico City: Grijalbo, 1990. Published in English as *Hybrid Cultures: Strategies for Entering and Leaving Modernity,* translated by Silvia L. López (Minneapolis: University of Minnesota Press, 1995).

———. "¿Habrá cine latinoamericano en el año 2000?: La cultura visual en la época del postnacionalismo." *La Jornada Semanal,* 21 February 1993, 27–33.

García Canclini, Néstor, coordinator. *Los nuevos espectadores: Cine, televisión y video en México.* Mexico City: Consejo Nacional para la Cultura y las Artes/IMCINE, 1994.

García Diego, Elío, ed. *Seis mujeres cineastas mexicanas.* Mexico City: Instituto Nacional de Bellas Artes (c.1986).

García Riera, Emilio. "Cuando el cine mexicano se hizo industria." In *Hojas de cine: Testimonios y documentos del nuevo cine latinoamericano,* vol. 2, 11–20. Mexico City: SEP/UAM/Fundación Mexicana de Cineastas, 1988. First published in *Revista de la Universidad de México,* 26.10 (June 1972).

———. "Perlita: Los comienzos de Adela Sequeyro." *Dicine* 47 (September 1992): 18–19.

Garmendia, Arturo. "*La mancha de sangre:* Un clásico recuperado." *Dicine* 63 (July–August 1995): 13–16.

Gaxiola, Fernando. "Entrevista con Matilde Landeta." *Otrocine* 3 (July-September 1975): 12–17.

Gayoso, María del Carmen. "Hay que seguir apostando por la paz." *La Jornada del Campo,* 13 December 1994: 14–16.

Glantz, Jacobo (Ya'akov Glants). *Kristobal Kolon.* Tel Aviv: Farlag Y. L. Perets, 1980.

Glantz, Margo. "Danzón: Los pies de las mexicanas." *Nitrato de Plata* 17 (1994): 18–21.

———. *Las genealogías.* Mexico City: M. Casillas, 1981.

González Rubio, Javier. Review of *El secreto de Romelia. Dicine* 31 (November 1989): 18.

Hart, John M. "Agrarian Reform." In *Twentieth Century Mexico,* edited by W. Dirk Raat and William H. Beezley, 6–16. Lincoln: University of Nebraska Press, 1986.

Henning, Edward B. *The Spirit of Surrealism.* Cleveland: Cleveland Museum of Art, 1979.

Hernández Carballido, Elvira. "Cecilia Soto: De mujeres . . . nada." *fem* (July 1994): 27.

———. "Gloria Trevi: Cuerpo, mente y alma." *fem* (July 1995): 11–14.

Hershfield, Joanne. *Mexican Cinema/Mexican Woman: 1940–1950.* Tucson: University of Arizona Press, 1996.

Hojas de cine: Testimonios y documentos del nuevo cine latinoamericano. Vol. 2. Mexico City: SEP/UAM/Fundación Mexicana de Cineastas, 1988.

Honey, Marta. "El aborto clandestino en México: Un secreto a voces." *Nexos* (November 1994): 35–39.

Horton, Andrew. "'We Are Losing Our Identity': An Interview with Mexican Director Marcela Fernández Violante." *Film/Literature Quarterly* 15.1 (1987): 2–7.

Huaco-Nuzum, Carmen. "Ni de aquí, ni de allá: Indigenous Female Representation in the Films of Maria Elena Velasco." In *Chicanos and Film: Essays on Chicano Representation and Resistance,* edited by Chon Noriega. New York and London: Garland, 1992.

Iglesias, Norma. "Danzón y su recepción por genero." Paper presented at Cine-Siglo: A Working Conference on Women's Creative Agency and Changing Paradigms of Gender in Latin American and Latino Film, University of California at Santa Cruz, 26 June 1995.

Johnston, Claire. "Dorothy Arzner: Critical Strategies." In *Feminism and Film Theory,* edited by Constance Penley. London and New York: Routledge, 1988.

Kandell, Jonathan. *La Capital: The Biography of Mexico City.* New York: Henry Holt, 1988.

Kaplan, E. Ann. *Women and Film: Both Sides of the Camera.* New York and London: Methuen, 1983.

King, John. *Magical Reels: A History of Cinema in Latin America.* London: Verso, 1990.

King, John, Ana M. López, and Manuel Alvarado, eds. *Mediating Two Worlds: Cinematic Encounters in the Americas.* London: BFI, 1993.

Küpper, Gaby, ed. *Compañeras: Voices from the Latin American Women's Movement.* London: Latin American Bureau, 1994.

La mujer en los medios audiovisuales: Memorias del VIII Festival Internacional del Nuevo Cine Latinoamericano. Cuadernos de Cine Series, 32. Mexico City: Universidad Nacional Autónoma de México, Coordinación de Difusión Cultural, 1987.

Leñero Franco, Estela. "Entrevista con María Rojo." *Nitrato de Plata* 12 (1992): 3–5.

Lerner, Ira T. *Mexican Jewry in the Land of the Aztecs, a Guide.* Mexico City: B. Costa-Amic, 1973.

List Arzubide, Germán. *El movimiento estridentista.* Mexico City: Secretaría de Educación Pública, 1967.

López, Ana M. "Celluloid Tears: Melodrama in the 'Old' Mexican Cinema." *Iris* 13 (summer 1991): 29–52.

———. "Tears and Desire: Women and Melodrama in the 'Old' Mexican Cinema." In *Mediating Two Worlds: Cinematic Encounters in the Americas,* edited by John King, Ana M. López, and Manuel Alvarado, 147–163. London: BFI, 1993.

López Aranda, Susana. "Dana Rotberg: Entre la realidad y la imaginación." *Dicine* 46 (July 1992): 8–9.

———. "VII Muestra de Cine Mexicano en Guadalajara." *Dicine* 46 (July 1992): 2–4.

———. "X Muestra de Guadalajara: El fin del ciclo." *Dicine* 63 (July–August 1995): 9–12.

Maciel, David. "El Imperio de La Fortuna: Mexico's Contemporary Cinema, 1985–1992." In *The*

Mexican Cinema Project, edited by Chon Noriega and Steven Ricci, 33–44. Los Angeles: UCLA Film and Television Archive, 1994.

Mahieu, José Agustín. "Feminine Types and Stereotypes in Mexican and Latin American Cinema." *Cultures/UNESCO* 8.3 (1982): 83–92.

Maldita Vecindad y los Hijos del Quinto Patio. *El Circo.* Bertelsmann de México, 1991.

Maldonado, Veronica. Review of *El jardín del Edén. Dicine* 65 (January–February 1996): 26–27.

"Manifiesto del Frente Nacional de Cinematografistas." In *Hojas de cine: Testimonios y documentos del nuevo cine latinoamericano,* vol. 2, 129–131. Mexico City: SEP/UAM/Fundación Mexicana de Cineastas, 1988. First published in *Otrocine* 1.3 (July–September 1975).

"Manifiesto del Grupo Nuevo Cine." In *Hojas de cine: Testimonios y documentos del nuevo cine latinoamericano,* vol. 2, 33–35. Mexico City: SEP/UAM/Fundación Mexicana de Cineastas, 1988. First published in *Nuevo Cine* 1.1 (April 1961).

Martín, Lucrecia and Cecilia Pérez Grovas. "Encuesta a las estudiantes de cine." *Cine* 22 (January–February 1980): 31–35.

Martín Barbero, Jesús. "Communication from Culture: The Crisis of the National and the Emergence of the Popular." Translated by Philip Schlesinger. *Media, Culture and Society* 10 (1988): 447–465.

———. "Modernity, Nationalism, and Communication in Latin America." In *Beyond National Sovereignty: International Communication in the 1990s,* edited by Kaarle Nordenstreng and Herbert I. Schiller, 132–147. Norwood, N.J.: Ablex, 1993.

Martínez, Rubén. "Corazón del Rocanrol." In *The Other Side: Notes from the New L.A., Mexico City, and Beyond,* 150–165. London: Verso, 1992.

Martínez de Velasco Vélez, Patricia. *Directoras de cine: Proyección de un mundo obscuro.* Mexico City: IMCINE and CONEICC, 1991.

Mathews, Steve. "An Interview with Jean Franco." *Iowa Journal of Cultural Studies* 12 (1993): 156–169.

"Matilde Landeta: Entrevista." In *Seis mujeres cineastas mexicanas,* edited by Elío García Diego, 3–16. Mexico City: Instituto Nacional de Bellas Artes (c.1986). First published in *Cine* 22 (January–February 1980).

Medina de la Serna, Rafael. "1987: Poco público, menos cine." *Dicine* 24 (March–April 1988): 6–9.

Mendoza, Carlos. "Canal 6 de Julio: Documental y contrainformación." *Estudios cinematográficos* 3.9 (July–September 1997): 54–60.

Meyer, Jean. "Revolution and Reconstruction in the 1920s." In *Mexico since Independence,* edited by Leslie Bethell, 201–240. Cambridge: Cambridge University Press, 1991.

Michel, Daniela. "Entrevista con María Novaro." *Milenio,* 24 May 1992.

Millán, Márgara. "El placer de la cámera femenina: Construcción de la imagen en el cine de Busi

Cortés, María Novaro y Marisa Sistach." Paper presented at meeting of the Latin American Studies Association, Guadalajara, Mexico, 17–19 April 1997.

Miller, Francesca. *Latin American Women and the Search for Social Justice.* Hanover, N.H.: University Press of New England, 1991.

Monsiváis, Carlos. "All the People Came and Did Not Fit on the Screen: Notes on the Cinema Audience in Mexico." In *Mexican Cinema,* edited by Paulo Antonio Paranaguá and translated by Ana M. López, 145–151. London: BFI, 1995.

———. "Mexican Cinema: Of Myths and Demystifications." In *Mediating Two Worlds: Cinematic Encounters in the Americas,* edited by John King, Ana M. López, and Manuel Alvarado, 140–146. London: BFI, 1993.

———. *Mexican Postcards.* Translated by John Kraniauskas. London and New York: Verso, 1997.

———. *Los rituales del caos.* Mexico City: Ediciones Era, 1995.

Mora, Carl J. "Feminine Images in Mexican Cinema: The Family Melodrama; Sara García, 'The Mother of México'; and the Prostitute." *Studies in Latin American Popular Culture* 4 (1985).

———. *Mexican Cinema: Reflections of a Society, 1896–1988.* Berkeley and Los Angeles: University of California Press, 1989.

Morris, Meaghan. "The Pirate's Fiancée: Feminists and Philosophers, or Maybe Tonight It'll Happen." In *Feminism and Foucault: Reflections on Resistance,* edited by Irene Diamond and Lee Quinby, 21–42. Boston: Northeastern University Press, 1988.

Mosier, John, and Alexis Gonzales. "Marcela Fernández Violante: A Filmmaker Apart." *Américas,* January–February 1983, 14–19.

Mujica, Barbara. "Angeles Mastretta: Women of Will in Love and War." *Américas,* August 1997, 36–43.

Muñoz, Braulio. *Sons of the Wind: The Search for Identity in Spanish American Indian Literature.* New Brunswick, N.J.: Rutgers University Press, 1982.

Nash, June, and Helen Safa, eds. *Women and Change in Latin America.* South Hadley, Mass.: Bergin and Garvey, 1985.

Navarro, Berta. "Una reflexión sobre el papel de la mujer, su compromiso y responsabilidad dentro de los medios audiovisuales y de la comunicación de masas." *La mujer en los medios audiovisuales: Memorias del VIII Festival Internacional del Nuevo Cine Latinoamericano.* Cuadernos de Cine Series 32, 149–155. Mexico City: Universidad Nacional Autónoma de México, Coordinación de Difusión Cultural, 1987.

Nayeli, Claudia. "Danzón dedicado a los niños indígenas." *Tiempo Libre,* 22 September 1994: 21.

Necoechea, Angeles. "Una experiencia de trabajo." *La mujer en los medios audiovisuales: Memorias del VIII Festival Internacional del Nuevo Cine Latinoamericano.* Cuadernos de Cine Series 32, 157–161. Mexico City: Universidad Nacional Autónoma de México, Coordinación de Difusión Cultural, 1987.

Nissán, Rosa. *Novia que te vea*. Mexico City: Planeta, 1992.

Noriega, Chon, and Steven Ricci, eds. *The Mexican Cinema Project*. Los Angeles: UCLA Film and Television Archive, 1994.

Novoa, Alejandra. Personal interview. 9 October 1998.

Oroz, Silvia. "Melodrama: El cine de lágrimas de América Latina." *Pantalla* 16 (spring 1992): 32–36.

Owen, Gilberto. *Cartas a Clementina Otero*. Mexico City: Universidad Autónoma Metropolitana, 1988.

———. *De la poesía a la prosa en el mismo viaje*. Mexico City: Consejo Nacional para la Cultura y las Artes, 1990.

Palma Cruz, Enrique C. "El cine mexicano de los 80: Agudización de su crisis." Bachelor's thesis, Universidad Nacional Autónoma de México, 1990.

Paranaguá, Paulo Antonio, ed. *Mexican Cinema*. Translated by Ana M. López. London: BFI, 1995.

Paz, Octavio. *The Labyrinth of Solitude*. Translated by Lysander Kemp. New York: Grove, 1961.

Pérez Turrent, Tomás. "*Angel de fuego* y otros asuntos." *Dicine* 46 (July 1992): 5–7.

———. "Crises and Renovations (1965–1991)." In *Mexican Cinema*, edited by Paulo Antonio Paranaguá and translated by Ana M. López, 94–115. London: BFI, 1995.

Pinal, Silvia. "Experiencias personales." In *La mujer*, Margarita Michelena, Margarita García Flores, Ana María Guzmán de Vásquez Colmenores, and Silvia Pinal, 49–63. Mexico City: Fondo de Cultura Económica, 1975.

Poniatowska, Elena. *Hasta no verte Jesús mío*. Mexico City: Ediciones Era, 1969.

———. *Massacre in Mexico*. Translated by Helen R. Lane. New York: Viking Press, 1975. Originally published as *La noche de Tlatelolco: testimonios de historia oral* (Mexico City: Era, 1971).

———. *Nada, nadie: Las voces del temblor*. Mexico City: Era, 1988. Published in English as *Nothing, Nobody: The Voices of the Mexico City Earthquake*, translated by Aurora Camacho de Schmidt (Philadelphia: Temple University Press, 1995).

———. "Report from Mexico." *Harper's Bazaar*, August 1994, 74+.

———. "Women, Mexico, and Chiapas." In *First World, Ha Ha Ha!: The Zapatista Challenge*, edited by Elaine Katzenberger. San Francisco: City Lights, 1995.

Presner, Kathryn. "Guita Schyfter: Insights from an Outsider." *Angles* 2.3 (1994): 12–13.

Rama, Angel. *The Lettered City*. Translated and edited by John Charles Chasteen. Durham and London: Duke University Press, 1996.

Ramírez, Gabriel. *Crónica del cine mudo mexicano*. Mexico City: Cineteca Nacional, 1989.

Ramírez Berg, Charles. *Cinema of Solitude: A Critical Study of Mexican Film, 1967–1983*. Austin: University of Texas Press, 1992.

———. "Cracks in the 'Macho' Monolith: 'Machismo', Man, and Mexico in Recent Mexican Cinema." *New Orleans Review* 16.1 (spring 1989).

————. "The Image of Women in Recent Mexican Cinema." *Journal of Latin American Popular Culture* 8 (1989).

Ramos Escandón, Carmen, et al. *Presencia y transparencia: la mujer en la historia de México.* Mexico City: El Colegio de México, 1987.

Rashkin, Elissa. "Jailing the Messenger." *Toward Freedom,* August–September 1996, 8–9.

Rich, B. Ruby. "An/Other View of New Latin American Cinema." *Iris* 13 (summer 1991): 5–28.

Rivera, Héctor. "Murió Pola Weiss, y con ella lo mejor del videoarte en México." *Proceso,* 28 May 1990.

Robles, Xavier. "Matilde Landeta, la Mujer Cine." *Nuevo Siglo* 9 (August 1992): 32–34.

Rocha, Glauber. "An Esthetic of Hunger." In *Brazilian Cinema,* edited by Randal Johnson and Robert Stam, 68–71. Austin: University of Texas Press, 1982. Originally published in *Revista Civilização Brasileira* (July 1965).

Rojas González, Francisco. *La negra Angustias.* 1944. Reprint, Mexico City: Fondo de Cultura Económica, 1984.

Román-Odio, Clara. "From Writer to Producer: Conflicting Voices in *Like Water for Chocolate.*" Paper presented at Cine-Lit III, Portland, Ore., 19 February 1997.

Rossbach, Alma, and Leticia Canel. "Los años 60: El Grupo Nuevo Cine y los dos concursos experimentales." In *Hojas de cine: Testimonios y documentos del nuevo cine latinoamericano,* vol. 2, 47–56. Mexico City: SEP/UAM/Fundación Mexicana de Cineastas, 1988.

Rotberg, Dana, and Omar A. Rodrigo. *Angel de fuego.* Script. Mexico City: Ediciones El Milagro, 1993.

Rufinelli, Jorge, and Lauri Tanner. "Dana Rotberg: Angel of Fire." *Angles* 2.3 (1994): 14–15.

Russell, Philip L. *Mexico under Salinas.* Austin: Mexico Resource Center, 1994.

Saalfield, Catherine. "Pregnant with Dreams: Julia Barco's Feminist Visions from Latin America." *The Independent,* December 1991: 29–30.

Salcedo Romero, Gerardo. "*Golpe de suerte:* Habla Marcela Fernández Violante." *Cineteca Nacional Programa Mensual* (October 1994): 42–43.

Sánchez, Alberto Ruy. *Mitología de un cine en crisis.* Mexico City: La Red de Jonás/Premia Editora, 1981.

Sarabia, Carlos Fabián. "*El jardín del Edén.*" *Nitrato de Plata* 17 (1994): 22–26.

Saragoza, Alex M., with Graciela Berkovich. "Intimate Connections: Cinematic Allegories of Gender, the State and National Identity." In *The Mexican Cinema Project,* edited by Chon Noriega and Steven Ricci, 25–32. Los Angeles: UCLA Film and Television Archive, 1994.

Schneider, Luis Mario, ed. *El estridentismo: Antología.* Mexico City: Universidad Nacional Autónoma de México, 1983.

Serrano, Irma, and Elisa Robledo. *A calzón amarrado.* Mexico City: Selector, 1978, 1983.

Sganzerla, Rogério. "Everybody's Woman." In *Brazilian Cinema,* edited by Randal Johnson and Robert Stam, 84–85. Austin: University of Texas Press, 1982.

Silva Martínez, Marco A. "Por un cine con humor y contexto político: entrevista con Guita Schyfter." *Nitrato de Plata* 22 (1996): 24–28.

Smith, Peter H. "Mexico since 1946: Dynamics of an Authoritarian Regime." In *Mexico since Independence,* edited by Leslie Bethell. Cambridge: Cambridge University Press, 1991.

Snow, K. Mitchell. "New Mayan Scribes." *Américas,* June 1997, 22–29.

Solís, Teresa. "Cineastas mexicanas." *Pantalla* 12 (November 1990): 24–27.

Soto, Moira. "Mexico's Feminist Pioneer." *World Press Review* (September 1990): 72.

Soto Viterbo, Felipe. "Las nuevas reinas del cine mexicano," *Somos* 16, August 1995, 39–53.

Stam, Robert. "On the Margins: Brazilian Avant-Garde Cinema." In *Brazilian Cinema,* edited by Randal Johnson and Robert Stam, 306–327. Austin: University of Texas Press, 1982.

———. *Subversive Pleasures: Bakhtin, Cultural Criticism, and Film.* Baltimore and London: Johns Hopkins University Press, 1989.

Statistical Abstract of Latin America. Los Angeles: University of California at Los Angeles, Latin American Center, 1970 and 1994.

Stavans, Ilan. *Imagining Columbus: The Literary Voyage.* New York: Twayne, 1993.

———. "Lost in Translation." *The Massachusetts Review* 34 (winter 1993/1994): 489–502.

Stavans, Ilan, ed. *Tropical Synagogues: Short Stories by Jewish-Latin American Writers.* New York and London: Holmes and Meier, 1994.

Steele, Cynthia. *Politics, Gender, and the Mexican Novel, 1968–1988: Beyond the Pyramid.* Austin: University of Texas Press, 1992.

Steiger, Janet. *Interpreting Films: Studies in the Historical Reception of American Cinema.* Princeton: Princeton University Press, 1992.

Tello, Jaime. "Notas sobre la política económica del 'nuevo cine' mexicano." In *Hojas de cine: Testimonios y documentos del nuevo cine latinoamericano,* vol. 2, 113–127. Mexico City: SEP/UAM/Fundación Mexicana de Cineastas, 1988. First published in *Octubre 7* (July 1980).

———. "Notas sobre la política económica del 'viejo' cine mexicano." In *Hojas de cine: Testimonios y documentos del nuevo cine latinoamericano,* vol. 2, 21–32. Mexico City: SEP/UAM/Fundación Mexicana de Cineastas, 1988. First published in *Octubre 6* (September 1979).

Torrents, Nissa. "Mexican Cinema Comes Alive." In *Mediating Two Worlds: Cinematic Encounters in the Americas,* edited by John King, Ana M. López, and Manuel Alvarado, 222–229. London: BFI, 1993.

Torres San Martín, Patricia. "Adela Sequeyro, Mexican Film Pioneer." *Journal of Film and Video* 44.3/4 (fall 1992/winter 1993): 27–32.

———. "Adela Sequeyro, primera mujer que dirige cine sonoro." *Armario: La cultura en occidente,* 12 March 1995, 4–5.

———. "Entrevista con Guita Schyfter." *Dicine* 55 (1994): 24–26.

———. "La investigación sobre el cine de mujeres en México." In *Horizontes del segundo siglo:*

Investigación y pedagogía del cine mexicano, latinoamericano y chicano, edited by Julianne Burton-Carvajal, Patricia Torres, and Angel Miguel. Guadalajara and Mexico City: Universidad de Guadalajara and IMCINE, 1998.

———. "Las primeras realizadoras en México." Paper presented at Cine-Siglo: A Working Conference on Women's Creative Agency and Changing Paradigms of Gender in Latin American and Latino Film, University of California at Santa Cruz, 28 June 1995.

———. "Matilde Landeta." *Pantalla* 16 (spring 1992): 26–31.

———. "Redescubriendo a una rara avis del cine sonoro mexicano." *Armario: El Sol de Morelia en la Cultura,* 24 December 1995, 5.

Torres San Martín, Patricia, and Eduardo de la Vega Alfaro. *Adela Sequeyro.* Guadalajara: Universidad de Guadalajara, 1997.

Townsen, John H. *Clowns.* New York: Hawthorn, 1976.

Toussaint, Florence. "México 90: Primera Bienal de Video." *Dicine* 37 (November 1990): 8–10.

Trejo, Angel. *¡Hey, Familia, Danzón Dedicado a. . . !* Mexico City: Plaza y Valdes, 1992.

"Tres mujeres conversan." *Nexos* 203 (November 1994): 64–71.

Tuñón, Enriqueta. "La lucha política de la mujer mexicana por el derecho al sufragio y sus repercusiones." In *Presencia y transparencia: la mujer en la historia de México,* Carmen Ramos Escandón et al., 181–189. Mexico City: El Colegio de México, 1987.

Tuñón, Esperanza. *Mujeres en escena: de la tramoya al protagonismo (1982–1994).* Mexico City: Coordinación de Humanidades, Programa Universitario de Estudios de Género, Universidad Autónoma de México, 1997.

Tuñón, Julia. *Mujeres de luz y sombra en el cine mexicano: la construcción de una imagen (1939–1952).* Mexico City: El Colegio de México/IMCINE, 1998.

Ugalde, Víctor. "Laberinto cinematográfico: O cómo filmar en México." *Estudios Cinematográficos* 2.6 (June–August 1996): 56–62.

Vega, Patricia. "Entrevista con Marisa Sistach." *Nitrato de Plata* 5 (May–June 1991): 3–6.

———. "Krauze: Incluso Clinton pagaría un 'costo altísimo' si hay fraude aquí." *La Jornada,* 28 June 1997.

———. "La disolvencia del cine mexicano." *La Jornada,* 4 January 1992.

———. "Video Works by Women." In *Latin American Visions,* edited by Patricia Aufderheide, 54–56. Philadelphia: The Neighborhood Film/Video Project of International House, 1989.

Vélez-Ibañez, Carlos G. *Rituals of Marginality: Politics, Process and Culture Change in Central Urban Mexico, 1969–1974.* Berkeley and Los Angeles: University of California Press, 1983.

Viñas, Moisés. "*Angel de fuego:* Un drama de la conciencia que tiene que ver con las grandes abstracciones." *El Universal,* 28 February 1993.

———. Review of *Los pasos de Ana. Dicine* 52 (July 1993): 36.

———. "Treinta Años de Nuevo Cine." *Dicine* 42 (November 1991): 14–17.

Williams, Linda. "'Something Else Besides a Mother': Stella Dallas and the Maternal Melodrama." In *Home Is Where the Heart Is: Studies in Melodrama and the Woman's Film,* edited by Christine Gledhill, 299–325. London: BFI, 1987.

Wolf, Eric. *Sons of the Shaking Earth.* Chicago: University of Chicago Press, 1959.

Wu, Harmony. "Eating the Nation: Selling *Like Water for Chocolate* in the USA." Paper presented at the meeting of the Latin American Studies Association, Guadalajara, Mexico, 18 April 1997.

Newspapers

Aguilar, Alberto. "Nombres, nombres y . . . nombres." *El Financiero,* 21 January 1992.

Aviles Duarte, Abel. "Se revitalizará el ámbito cinematográfico, con la incorporación de más mujeres, Dana Rotberg." *Excélsior,* 11 March 1990.

Azuela, Rodrigo. "El cine en video." *El Universal,* 29 October 1994.

"Beatriz Adriana, cineasta." *La Opinión,* 1 February 1995.

Calderón Gómez, Judith. "Artistas y escritoras proponen despenalizar el aborto en México." *La Jornada,* 29 September 1994.

Camacho, Patricia. "Matilde Landeta: Mujer que no se desmorona." *La Jornada,* 6 April 1992.

Camarena, Amelia. "Dana Rotberg: 'La mujer se ganó a pulso su espacio como cineasta.'" *Esto,* 21 January 1992.

Camargo, Ricardo. "Cierra COTSA 26 salas en el DF; indemniza a 246 trabajadores." *El Nacional,* 1 July 1992.

Carrera, Mauricio. "*Danzón,* himno a la cachondería." *El Nacional,* 5 January 1992.

Davalos, Patricia. "Dana Rotberg prefiere no maquillar la realidad y cuenta una historia." *El Sol de México,* 12 April 1992.

———. "En efecto, Azcárraga quiere comprar COTSA; no cerrarán más salas fílmicas." *El Sol de México,* 4 July 1992.

Espinosa, Tomás. "Con T de Teatro." *Ovaciones,* 19 March 1992.

"El estado financió 57 filmes en 6 años." *Esto,* 29 September 1994.

Feliciano, Enrique. "No exhibir, es atentar contra los creadores y los productores." *Esto,* 7 February 1992.

Gallegos, José Luis. "Afirma Busi Cortés: El circuito cultural de exhibición de películas mexicanas, en todo el país, es una buena opción." *Excélsior,* 14 July 1992.

———. "Cambiaría todos los homenajes por media película: Matilde Landeta." *Excélsior,* 14 September 1990.

———. "Debe haber continuidad en la producción de buenas películas, manifiesta Busi Cortés." *Excélsior,* 8 October 1992.

———. "Deseo mostrar en el cine el ser y sentir de la mujer, afirma Busi Cortés." *Excélsior,* 25 April 1992.

————. "Guita Schyfter filma la película *Novia que te vea.*" *Ultimas Noticias,* 17 June 1992.

————. "Ha ganado la mujer importantes espacios en los medios de comunicación, afirma Busi Cortés." *Excélsior,* 20 May 1990.

————. "Matilde Landeta: Tenemos la esperanza de que la mujer tenga más continuidad en la dirección de filmes." *Excélsior,* 4 January 1992.

García, Guadalupe. "El cine, aquí: *Angel de Fuego.*" *El Sol de México,* 9 July 1992.

García Cruz, Rubén. "Las realizadoras ganamos terreno en la cinematografía mexicana." *El Nacional,* 9 September 1990.

García-Torres de Novoa, María. "Sensibilidad femenina." *Uno Más Uno,* 27 April 1992.

Gómez, Juan Manuel, and Rodrigo Molina. "Clausuran las autoridades mexicanas estación de radio ciudadana (Radio Pirata)." 23 April 1995. Online. Mexico 94. Available by e-mail: MEX-ICO94@profmexis.dgsca.unam.mx.

González Mello, Flavio. "*Angel de fuego:* circo y fanaticismo en la pantalla." *El Economista,* 2 June 1992.

Gracida, Ysabel. "Cine mexicano: tres presencias en 1991." *El Universal,* 4 February 1992.

Gutiérrez Oropeza, Manuel. "El cine quiere un 'Golpe de suerte.'" *Esto,* 2 February 1992.

"Ilespañol Interactivo." *Israel en Español,* September 1996. Online at http://www.ilespnl.com.

Jaimes, Candelaria. "Busi Cortés: 'Hay que apoyar a los guionistas para frenar su desinterés.'" *El Heraldo,* 22 March 1992.

Lazcano, Hugo. "Abren camino: Mujeres tras la camera." *Reforma,* 10 June 1996.

Leal, Alejandro. "María Novaro es descarada feminista y antimachista." *El Universal,* 4 October 1992.

Leyva, Eduardo. "Cine al día." Review of *Angel de fuego. El Día,* 31 May 1992.

"María Novaro, becada por la Fundación Rockefeller." *El Nacional,* 29 March 1992.

"María Rojo llegó hasta la cumbre de su gran carrera." *Cine Mundial,* 1 June 1992.

Melche, Julia Elena. Review of *Angel de fuego. La Jornada,* 31 May 1992.

Moheno, Gustavo. Review of *Serpientes y Escaleras. El Sol de México,* 25 March 1992.

Nájar, Alberto. "Varios artistas acuerdan crear el Barzón de las Estrellas." *La Jornada,* 27 September 1996.

Ortega Mendoza, Jesús. Review of *Angel de fuego. El Universal,* 24 February 1993.

Peguero, Raquel. "El cine mexicano renacerá hasta que el público vuelva a creer en él: Busi Cortés." *La Jornada,* 14 January 1992.

"La prensa de N.Y. se interroga por la mujer de *Danzón:* Su creadora Novaro responde." *El Heraldo,* 19 October 1992.

Preston, Julia. "Mexican TV Star Alters Script, and Plot Thickens." *New York Times,* 2 December 1996. Online at http://www.nytimes.com.

Quiroz Arroyo, Macarena. "Existe censura en la actual administración ya que no se autoriza la exhibición del video *Crónica de un fraude.*" *Excélsior* 15 October 1992.

———. "Marcela Fernández Violante: La censura en el cine no sólo se ejerce al quitar cuadros a una película sino también al darle una pésima distribución y exhibición." *Excélsior,* 4 June 1992.

———. "Me gustaría que México tuviera una televisión sin censura: María Rojo." *Excélsior,* 3 July 1992.

———. "No estoy dispuesta a seguir con la burocracia del Imcine y perder mi dinero: Ofelia Medina." *Excélsior,* 17 March 1993.

———. "Trabajar en *Angel de Fuego,* la máxima experiencia para Noé Alberto Montealegre." *Excélsior,* 11 May 1992.

Rascón, Marco. "CIRT, Televisa y el gobierno contra Tele Verdad," *La Jornada,* 11 October 1994.

Reyes Morales, Felipe, et al. Letter. *La Jornada,* 3 October 1994.

Rodríguez, Juan. "Cine: Una apetecible aventura amorosa." *La Opinión,* 26 February 1993.

"Se estrenará el próximo martes en el Cine Latino la película *Golpe de suerte,* última cinta en la que actuó Miguel Manzano." *Excélsior,* 15 March 1992.

"Solicita la familia de Miguel Manzano a Víctor Flores Olea que se estrene en el Latino la película *Golpe de suerte,*" *Excélsior,* 3 February 1992.

Suárez Ojeda, Gustavo. "*Angel de Fuego,* historia citadina con enorme contenido crítico-social." *Cine Mundial,* 21 February 1993.

Szclar, Elba. "Afrontemos el reto." *Kesher,* 15 April 1997.

Torralba, Daniel. "Los críticos son injustos con el cine mexicano: Busi Cortés." *El Sol de México,* 27 December 1992.

Vásquez, Juan Antonio. "Update from Radio Huaya." 26 April 1995. Online. Chiapas-l. Available by e-mail at CHIAPAS-L@profmexis.dgsca.unam.mx.

Velásquez, Carolina. "La idea de la película *Lola* es mostrar los lados oscuros de la maternidad, indica su directora María Novaro." *El Financiero,* 24 November 1989.

Zuñiga, Juan Antonio, and Herman Bellinghausen. "Me hice zapatista para mejorar nuestras comunidades: Trinidad." *La Jornada,* 14 May 1995.

Catalogues, Programs, Filmographies, and Databases

Centro de Capacitación Cinematográfica. *Catálogo 1975–1994.* Mexico City: Consejo Nacional para la Cultura y las Artes/IMCINE/CCC, 1994.

Centro Universitario de Estudios Cinematográficos. *Catálogo de Ejercicios Fílmicos Escolares, 1963–1988/9.* Mexico City: Universidad Nacional Autónoma de México Coordinación de Difusión Cultural/CUEC, 1989.

Cocina de Imágenes: Primera Muestra de Cine y Video Realizados por Mujeres Latinas y Caribeñas. Exhibition program. 1–11 October 1987.

El Cine en México. Instituto Mexicano de Cinematografía. 1 February 1999. Online at http:// www.imcine.gob.mx.

ExplorAcción: Tercera Muestra de Videos Hechos por Mujeres. Exhibition program. Cineteca Nacional, Mexico City. 9–13 July 1996. Organized by Telemanita A. C.

Festival of Festivals: 16th Toronto International Film Festival. Exhibition program. 5–14 September 1991.

Filmografía Mexicana. Filmoteca de la Universidad Nacional Autónoma de México. 9 February 1999. Online at http://www.unam.mx//filmoteca/.

Latin American Video Archives catalogue. New York: International Media Resource Exchange, 1996.

Moreno Ochoa, Octavio. "Catálogo de directoras de cine en México." Bachelor's thesis, Universidad Nacional Autónoma de México, 1992.

Mujeres Cineastas Mexicanas. Exhibition program. Museo de los Constituyentes, Mexico City (c.1983).

Nobody's Women: A Series of Films Directed by Mexican Women, 1935–Present. Exhibition program. Tulane University, New Orleans. 8–13 October 1995.

Toledo, Teresa. *Realizadoras Latinoamericanas/Latin American Women Filmmakers: Cronología/ Chronology (1917–1987).* New York: Círculo de Cultura Cubana, 1987.

Zafra catalogue. Mexico City: Zafra, 1986.

Index

Entries are in the language in which they appear in the text. Spanish entries are alphabetized according to the first word after the article, as in English. Italic page numbers indicate illustrations.

18 lustros de la vida en México en este siglo (television series), 68, 134

abortion, 18–19, 24; campaign for legalization, 73, 237, 266n11; in *Cosas de mujeres,* 69, 71–72; as feminist issue, 68, 70, 85, 237
Aguilar Camín, Héctor, 54, 65
Akerman, Chantal, 93, 96, 97, 100, 111
Alarcón, Norma, 119
Alazraki, Benito, 58
Alcoriza, Luis, 58, 90
Alemán, Miguel, 175
Allá en el Rancho Grande, 40–41, 43, 223
Amado, Ana María, 72
Amantes del Señor de la Noche, Las, 75, 259
Amnesty International, 23, 229
Angel de fuego, 2, 192–213, 215, 221, 222; alienation in, 198, 200, 207, 211; circus in, 192–193, 195, 197, 206, 207; credits, 246; incest in, 197, 207, 208; Jewish influence on, 199–200; marginality in, 195, 196, 211; as personal film, 193, 216; reception of, 202–204; religious themes in, 195, 199, 200; urban landscape in, 192, 195, 205; women in, 201–202, 212
Angeles de la ciudad obscura, 236, 260
Anoche soñé contigo, 113, 114–115, 216; credits, 243
Anzaldúa, Gloria, 119, 190
Arau, Alfonso, 22, 228. *See also Como agua para chocolate*

Arau, Sergio, 219
Argos (production company), 227, 230–231
Armendáriz, Pedro, 54, 96
Arredondo, Isabel, 104, 219, 238
Arzner, Dorothy, 39, 47
Aventurera, 90, 175, 184
Avila Camacho, Manuel, 131
Ayala Blanco, Jorge, 265n3; on *Las amantes del Señor de la Noche,* 75; on *Conozco a las tres,* 95, 102; on feminist films, 69–70, 72; on *El grito,* 64; on India María, 76; on Matilde Landeta, 47; on *Los pasos de Ana,* 268n2
Azuela, Mariano, 4
Azul, 78, 241
Azul celeste, 269n2 (ch.6), 189, 245

Bakhtin, Mikhail, 206
Banco Cinematográfico, 47, 60, 65; privatized, 82
Barbachano Ponce, Manuel, 58
Bartra, Roger, 219
Barzón, El, 227, 232
Belkin, Arnold, 149
Beltrán, Candida, 31, 32, 246
Benavides, María Gloria (Elisa), 231, 271n9
Berkovich, Graciela, 138, 186
Berman, Sabina, 153, 216, 259
Best Maugard, Adolfo, 43
Bhabha, Homi, 9
Bichir, Demián, 227

289

cinema, 174, 224; and *México de mis amores*, 74; on urban culture, 210, 211, 270n7

Mora, Carl, 40, 267n4

Moraga, Cherríe, 119

Morales, Esther, 64, 68, 247–248

Morales, Inés, 236, 260

Morris, Meaghan, 16

Motivos de Luz, Los, 13

Muestra de Cine Mexicano en Guadalajara, 82, 113, 227, 229

Muestra Internacional de Cine (Mexico City), 82

Mujer de Benjamín, La, 167

Mujer de nadie, La, 41–43, 44, 45, 240

Mulvey, Laura, 58, 95

Muñoz, Braulio, 51

Nada personal (telenovela), 227

National Democratic Convention (CND), 224

National Indigenous Congress (CNI), 234, 271n11

National Indigenous Institute (INI), 51, 132

Navarro, Berta, 59, 74, 84, 252

Nazarín, 201, 202

Necoechea, Angeles, 68, 70, 73, 250–251

Negra Angustias, La, 46, 48, 52–54, 56, 118; credits, 241; rape in, 175

neoliberalism, 6, 21, 24, 85, 194, 230; and Salinas film policy, 13, 14, 21, 22

New Latin American Cinema, 10, 61, 62, 72, 193, 202

New Latin American Cinema Foundation, 74

"new Mexican cinema" (1990s), 24, 117, 167, 194, 215, 228

New World Order, 23, 184

Ni de aquí, ni de allá, 12, 76, 253

Niño raramuri, El, 81; credits, 242

Nissán, Rosa, 143, 153, 155; and *Novia que te vea* (novel), 142, 153, 154, 161

Nocturno amor que te vas, 82; credits, 242

Nocturno a Rosario, 2, 46, 47, 56; credits, 241

No es por gusto, 69, 70, 72, 250, 251

No les pedimos un viaje a la luna, 187, 250, 252

North American Free Trade Agreement (NAFTA), 20, 23, 224, 225, 226

Novaro, Beatriz, 180

Novaro, María, 1, 2, 168, 216, 217, 233, 237, 245; and Cine-Mujer, 72, 73; on *Danzón*, 167, 179, 188; on feminism, 73–74, 180; film style of, 170, 173, 174; and intellectual sector, 190; politics of, 185; use of water imagery, 189. *See also under film titles*

Novia que te vea, 1, 142, 143–163, 164, 199; activism in, 145–146; advertising of, 161–162; anti-Semitism in, 151, 152; Aztec references in, 150, 153; credits, 244; differences from novel, 155; documentary influence on, 144; gender ideology in, 145, 155–158, 222; "gran familia mexicana" in, 149, 151, 153; *indigenismo* in, 150–151; and melodrama, 159–161; painting in, 149; reception of by Jews, 153; religious ambivalence in, 144–145. *See also* Jews in Mexico

Novoa, Alejandra, 236, 260

Nube de Magallanes, La, 74, 248

Nuevo Cine (magazine), 61

Nuevo Cine group. *See* Grupo Nuevo Cine

Obregón, Alvaro, 38

Olvidados, Los, 165, 193, 201–202

Organización de Mujeres Madre Tierra, 236, 260

Orozco, José Clemente, 147, 148, 149, 152

Otero, Clementina, 107, 110; as character in *Los pasos de Ana*, 107, 108, 109, 111, 112

"other cinema." *See otro cine*

otro cine, 2, 27, 58, 68, 220, 232; and Comandante Ramona, 233; and Busi Cortés, 118; and Matilde Landeta, 1, 47. *See also* feminist cinema; women's cinema

Owen, Gilberto, 107, 110–112